ENERGY IN THE AMERICAS

ENERGY HISTORIES, CULTURES, AND POLITICS

SERIES EDITOR:
Petra Dolata, Associate Professor, Department of History, University of Calgary

ISSN 2562-3486 (Print) ISSN 2562-3494 (Online)

This series features original research at the intersection of energy and society. It welcomes works that contribute to international discussions on the history, culture, and politics of energy and speaks to the energy humanities and energy social sciences. The series has a strong interest in, but is not limited to, North American issues.

No. 1   *Imperial Standard: Imperial Oil, Exxon, and the Canadian Oil Industry from 1880*
        Graham D. Taylor

No. 2   *Energy in the Americas: Critical Reflections on Energy and History*
        Edited by Amelia M. Kiddle

ENERGY IN THE AMERICAS
Critical Reflections on Energy and History

EDITED BY
Amelia M. Kiddle

Energy Histories, Cultures, and Politics Series
ISSN 2562-3486 (Print) ISSN 2562-3494 (Online)

© 2021 Amelia M. Kiddle

University of Calgary Press
2500 University Drive NW
Calgary, Alberta
Canada T2N 1N4
press.ucalgary.ca

All rights reserved.

No part of this book may be reproduced in any format whatsoever without prior written permission from the publisher, except for brief excerpts quoted in scholarship or review.

This book is available in a digital format which is licensed under a Creative Commons license. The publisher should be contacted for any commercial use which falls outside the terms of that license.

Library and Archives Canada Cataloguing in Publication

Title: Energy in the Americas : critical reflections on energy and history / edited by Amelia M. Kiddle.
Names: Kiddle, Amelia M. (Amelia Marie), editor. | Energy in the Americas: Critical Reflections on Energy and History (Conference) (2014 : University of Calgary)
Series: Energy histories, cultures, and politics ; no. 2.
Description: Series statement: Energy histories, cultures, and politics, 2562-3486 ; no. 2 | Based on a conference held at the University of Calgary in 2014 titled "Energy in the Americas: Critical Reflections on Energy and History." | Includes bibliographical references and index.
Identifiers: Canadiana (print) 20210218134 | Canadiana (ebook) 20210218304 | ISBN 9781552389393 (softcover) | ISBN 9781552389409 (Open Access PDF) | ISBN 9781552389416 (PDF) | ISBN 9781552389423 (EPUB)
Subjects: LCSH: Petroleum industry and trade—North America—History. | LCSH: Petroleum industry and trade—South America—History.
Classification: LCC HD9578.N67 E54 2021 | DDC 338.2/728097—dc23

  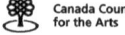

Copyediting by Ryan Perks
Cover image: Coloubox 21385256, 11974906, and 24653463
Cover design, page design, and typesetting by Melina Cusano

Table of Contents

List of Tables — VII
List of Figures — IX
Acknowledgements — XI

Introduction. "When Will We See the Pendulum Effect?" — 1
    Critical Reflections on Energy and History in the Americas
        Amelia M. Kiddle

1   Unpacking Latin American Oil and Gas Policies: Views on — 17
    Energy as a Market, Common, and Political Good
        Pablo Heidrich

2   Primary Energy Consumption and Economic Growth in — 43
    Chile, 1844–2010
        César Yáñez Gallardo

3   The Commercial and Political Dynamics of the Crude — 67
    Oil Industry: The Case of the Royal Dutch/Shell Group in
    Venezuela, 1913–1924
        Brian S. McBeth

4   Exxon and the Rise of Producer Power in Venezuela — 99
        Joseph A. Pratt

5   Current Concerns: Canadian–United States Energy — 123
    Relations and the St. Lawrence and Niagara Megaprojects
        Daniel Macfarlane

6   Tellico Dam, Dickey Dam, and Endangered Species Law in — 151
    the United States during the 1970s
        Michael Camp

7	Seismic Innovations: The Digital Revolution in the Search for Oil and Gas	179
	Tyler Priest	
8	Optimism, Fear, and Free Trade: Canada's Winding Path to a Globalized Petroleum Industry, 1930–2005	211
	Paul Chastko	
9	The New Political Economy of Petroleum in Brazil: Back to the Future?	243
	Gail D. Triner	
10	The Expropriation of YPF in Historical Perspective. Limits of State Power Intervention in Argentina, 1989–2015	273
	Esteban Serrani	
11	Coming Full Circle: Mexican Oil, 1917–2018	295
	Linda B. Hall	
12	The Neoliberal Transformation of Colombia's Energy Sector and Some Implications for Democratization in the Post-conflict Period	323
	Dermot O'Connor and Juan Pablo Bohórquez Montoya	

List of Contributors	347
Bibliography	351
Index	381

List of Tables

TABLE 1.1	A Theoretical Scheme for Resource Nationalism	20
TABLE 1.2	Sample Characteristics of Energy as a Market Good	26
TABLE 1.3	Sample Characteristics of Energy as a Common Good	27
TABLE 1.4	Sample Characteristics of Energy as a Political Good	29
TABLE 1.5	Energy Policies in Selected Latin American Countries, 1990–2015	31
TABLE 2.1	Energy Consumption and Economic Growth	46
TABLE 2.2	GDP per Capita at PPP and Annual Growth Rates, 1800–1913	50
TABLE 2.3	GDP per Capita at PPP and Annual Growth Rates, 1913–2010	54
TABLE 3.1	Average Cost of Delivered Crude Oil to the Atlantic Seaboard: Comparison between US, Venezuela, and Rest of World (Including Venezuela), 1927–1930 ($/barrel)	70
TABLE 9.1	Global Petroleum Reserves (Year-End 2009; Billions Barrels of Oil Equivalent)	249
TABLE 9.2	Petroleum Royalties	257

List of Figures

FIGURE 2.1A	Changes in Energy Intensity of Chile Compared to Brazil (TOE per Unit of GDP PPP)	48
FIGURE 2.1B	Changes in Energy Intensity of Chile Compared to Argentina (TOE per Unit of GDP PPP)	48
FIGURE 2.1C	Changes in Energy Intensity of Chile Compared to UK and Wales (TOE per Unit of GDP PPP)	49
FIGURE 2.1D	Changes in Energy Intensity of Chile Compared to US (TOE per Unit of GDP PPP)	49
FIGURE 2.2A	Apparent Consumption of Coal, 1844–1880	52
FIGURE 2.2B	Apparent Consumption of Coal, 1881–1913	52
FIGURE 2.3	Evolution of the Chilean Energy Matrix, 1944–2010	56
FIGURE 2.4	Energy Consumption per Capita and Energy Transition	57
FIGURE 2.5	Hydroelectric Production and Percentages of Total Modern Energy	59
FIGURE 2.6	Generation of Hydro and Thermoelectricity in Chile, 1960–2010 (GWh)	60
FIGURE 3.1	Shell Production: Total, Venezuela, Mexico, and US, 1923–1930 (BOPD and %)	72
FIGURE 3.2	Shell: Venezuelan Crude Oil Production by Subsidiaries, 1917–1935 (BOPD)	72
FIGURE 3.3	VOC and BCO: Net Profits and Return on Equity (ROE), 1920–1931 ($)	73
FIGURE 5.1	Hydroelectric Landscape of Niagara Falls	135
FIGURE 5.2	Beck Stations and Moses Station	136

Figure 5.3	Lake St. Lawrence	138
Figure 5.4	Moses-Saunders Powerhouse	138
Figure 7.1	Offshore Reflection Seismic Survey Diagram	184
Figure 7.2	Shell Oil Bright Spot Seismic, Posey Prospect, Eugene Island 330 Field	194
Figure 7.3	GSI's 3D Seismic Pioneers	198
Figure 7.4	3D Seismic Image with Salt Domes in Deep Blue	199
Figure 8.1	Average Price Alberta Oil versus World Prices ($/bbl), 1947–1961	222
Figure 8.2	US Imports of Canadian Crude, 1987–2000 (bbl)	235
Figure 9.1	Crude Petroleum Imports (Value) % of Total, 1960–2011	247
Figure 9.2	World Petroleum Prices, 1960-2010 Real (2005)	247
Figure 9.3	Oil Production and Reserves, % from Offshore, 1970–2010	248
Figure 9.4	Offshore and Pre-salt Petroleum Reserves in Brazil	248
Figure 9.5a	Ordinary Shares Distributed by Ownership (%)	261
Figure 9.5b	Total Shares (Ordinary + Preferred) Distributed by Ownership	262

Acknowledgements

I am deeply grateful to the many people who contributed to this project from its inception to its completion. It has been a long journey from meeting in 2014 to engage in this dialogue to the publication of this volume, so I sincerely hope I don't forget anyone!

Upon arriving in Treaty 7 territory at the University of Calgary in 2012, and given my own research interests in the Mexican oil expropriation of 1938, I began to conceive of a conference that would bring together energy scholars from the Americas to discuss histories of energy and society in ways that were more reflective than the uncritical boosterism that pervaded the oil industry boom going on here at that time. I received tremendous support and encouragement from the the Department of History, Faculty of Arts, the Office of the Vice President for Research, University of Calgary International, and especially the Latin American Research Centre (LARC) at the University of Calgary, which enabled me to secure a SSHRC Connection Grant for the organization of the conference. LARC program coordinator Monique Greenwood, and several student assistants, provided invaluable logistical support. Colleagues from History, Latin American Studies, Political Science, and Anthropology all stepped up to participate in the three-day event, and I am grateful to Hendrik Kraay, Saulesh Yessenova, Denise Brown, Stephen Randall, Heather Devine, Pablo Policzer, and Sarah Jordaan, as well as Annette Hester, then of the Inter-American Development Bank, for chairing panels and facilitating our discussions. Harrie Vredenburg gave a stimulating keynote, and Peter Fortna, Hereward Longley, and Tara Joly of Willow Springs Strategic Solutions and Bori Arrobo, representing the Fort McKay First Nation, presented the film *Moose Lake: Home and Refuge* and led a discussion of Indigenous perspectives on Alberta oil sands development.

We welcomed an amazing group of scholars from all over the world, including my colleagues Paul Chastko, Petra Dolata, and Dominique Perron, as well as senior and emerging scholars who presented exciting research from throughout the hemisphere: Juan Pablo Bohórquez Montoya, Michael Camp, Gustav Cederlof, Elvin Delgado, Joseph García, Martín Garrido Lepe, Eric Gettig, Linda Hall, Chris Hebdon, Pablo Heidrich, Don Kingsbury, Robert Lifset, Daniel Macfarlane, Jeffrey Manuel, Brian McBeth, Patricia McCormack, Dermot O'Connor, Joseph Pratt, Tyler Priest, João Rodrigues Neto, Isabelle Rousseau, Mar Rubio, Esteban Serrani, Mark Sholdice, Gail Triner, Richard Unger, and César Yáñez. The depth and quality of our discussions in Calgary and Banff were a testament to the excellent research this wonderful group of scholars presented.

Because we were fortunate to be so numerous at the conference, the fact that not all of the presenters' works are represented in this volume should definitely not be taken as a reflection of the quality of their contributions to the literature; it is, rather, simply a matter of logistics. Several of the participants joined in a discussion with the students of my undergraduate integrative seminar in Latin American Studies (LAST 401), and I am grateful for the quality of these students' engagement in the conference and their wonderful work on the topic of energy over the course of the semester. Allan Abbasi, Sarah Arnett, Mike Baker, Mayda Borbely, Alem Cherinet, Anita Demeter, Camilo Gil González, Dominik Maslanka, Rayna Oryniak, and Lina Pulido: I'm sure I learned as much from you as I did from the conference itself!

The journey from conference proceedings to published book has taken seven long years and has included more than the usual number of delays that edited volumes seem always to occasion, and I am deeply grateful for the continued patience of my collaborators and of Brian Scrivener and Helen Hajnoczky at the University of Calgary Press. My colleagues Hendrik Kraay and Petra Dolata, editors, respectively, of the Latin America and Caribbean Studies and the Energy Histories, Cultures, and Politics series at the University of Calgary Press, both provided constant encouragement, and Petra in particular generously gave significant feedback on my introduction to this volume. Graduate students Davíd Barrios, Andrés Lalama Vargas, and Andrew Wiley each provided invaluable assistance. I am also grateful to the anonymous reviewers who helped to make the volume better in so many ways, by pushing us all to sharpen our focus and increase the dialogue between and among the contributors' chapters. Copy editor Ryan Perks similarly pushed us to tighten up our prose. The entire team at the press has been excellent to work with and I appreciate their professionalism. I would also never have been able to complete this project if not for the support of my husband, research facilitator extraordinaire Jonathan Jucker, and not only because he did the index.

By the time this book was ready to go to press, the University of Calgary and the Province of Alberta had entered a period of austerity due to the real challenges presented by the falling international price of oil as well as the manufactured crisis provoked by the provincial government's policy choices, making the heady days of 2014 seem like a distant memory. I am forever grateful to Brian Scrivener for finding enough spare change between the couch cushions in the face of significant budget cuts to get this volume published. The conference—which brought together an outstanding interdisciplinary cast of participants and resulted in student engagement and community participation—and this volume, which presents evidence-based, peer-reviewed research in an open-access format, both speak to the importance of strong public investment in higher education. I am glad to have been able to have finally brought this project to fruition, and I appreciate the contributions of everyone who helped along the way.

Thank you! Merci! Obrigada! Gracias! Nitsiniiyi'taki.

Calgary, Alberta
March 2021

INTRODUCTION

"When Will We See the Pendulum Effect?" Critical Reflections on Energy and History in the Americas

Amelia M. Kiddle

One of the most notable features of any survey of the history of energy regimes in the Americas over the past century is the "pendulum effect." Anecdotal though the observation may be, it is clear that despite the broad and incremental transformational changes that have occurred in the global energy landscape over time, individual countries have undergone wild swings in the way they have met these changes. Like the workings of a grandfather clock in the front hall of some stately home, there is a seeming inevitability to these alternations between market orientation and a more interventionist approach, and while time advances hour by hour in a forward motion, this momentum is always underpinned by the movement of the pendulum.

In her chapter in this volume on the Mexican oil industry, Linda B. Hall quotes one opponent of the country's 2014 energy reform, who asked in *La Jornada*, "When will we see the pendulum effect? How can we go back?" This individual might have been surprised to learn that in four years' time one of the principal opponents of the project, Andrés Manuel López Obrador, would be elected president. The pendulum has swung again in Mexico, just as it has done throughout Latin America over the decades, as successive governments have oscillated between market-based energy policies and state control. By contrast, the energy policies of the United States and Canada have appeared relatively consistent over time. And yet, as the contributors to this volume show, these policies have also varied greatly depending on the energy source and the region in which it is produced. Analysts who focus on Latin America alone tend to naturalize market-based energy regimes and blame the "resource curse" for Latin America's seemingly mercurial policies.[1] However, critical reflection shows this to be an incomplete picture.

This volume adds to an emerging body of literature on the role of energy and extractive industries in various societies by bringing the diverse energy histories of American nations into conversation with each other.[2] It emerged from a conference held at the University of Calgary in 2014 titled "Energy in the Americas: Critical Reflections on Energy and History." The majority of the participants (and therefore most of the contributors to this volume) were historians, people whose stock in trade is change over time. Allied social sciences can provide tools, as they do here, with which we can bolster the analytical precision of our accounts, but one of our chief concerns as historians is the dynamics of social change. By comparing energy histories from both North and South America, this volume seeks to better understand both the history of energy and the history of the Americas. Although not all countries were represented at the conference, or in this volume, it is our contention that it is analytically useful to examine the energy history of the Americas as a whole. Despite the apparent differences between countries, including them in the same analytical frame allows us to break down many of the assumptions that implicitly underlie most studies that examine the North or the South in isolation.

When we met in Calgary in October of 2014, we had little inkling that the bottom was about to drop out of the global price of oil. We spoke of the shale revolution, the Alberta oil sands, and deep-water drilling as certainties propelled by technological advances and the lure of profits and royalties. Although we discussed the significance of climate change and Indigenous rights to free prior and informed consent, the pace of development at the time was such that neither seemed likely to hinder continued production. Venezuela's Hugo Chávez had recently died, but the political project he began, underpinned by high oil prices, seemed destined to continue under his successor, Nicolás Maduro. The Alberta

Progressive Conservative Party had been in power for forty-four years, rivalling Mexico's Partido Revolucionario Institucional (PRI)—which had also been buoyed by oil rents—for North America's longest unbroken electoral run. Returned to the presidency in 2012, the PRI under Enrique Peña Nieto was confident that international investment would pour into Mexico following changes to the Constitution. Optimism of a different kind also reigned in Argentina, where YPF (Yacimientos Petrolíferos Fiscales) had been renationalized in 2012, and where little thought was being given to the environmental effects of shale production in the Vaca Muerta. And although Operation Car Wash had begun to delve into Brazil's culture of political corruption in 2014, Petrobras's development of ultra-deepwater reserves in the pre-salt basin seemed assured.

The landscape has since changed considerably. Although prices have recovered slightly, the political fallout from the drop in global oil prices has been far-reaching throughout the Americas. In Brazil, President Dilma Rousseff was impeached, her predecessor Luiz Inácio Lula da Silva was imprisoned, and the ultra-right Jair Bolsonaro was elected president. Bolsonaro's ideological cousin, Donald J. Trump, became president of the United States—although the fact that he did not win re-election in 2020 suggests that the US electorate became disenchanted with this particular form of bravado. Several of the governments that favoured resource nationalism in 2014, as part of the so-called Pink Tide in Latin America, have fallen apart or tempered their radicalism. Ecuadorean president Lenín Moreno withdrew his country from ALBA (Alianza Bolivariana para los Pueblos de Nuestra América, or Bolivarian Alliance for the Peoples of Our America), the regional organization founded by Venezuela, which no longer has the wherewithal to lead it since its economic collapse under Maduro. Likewise, several market-oriented regimes are undergoing change, including Peru, which during the short-lived presidency of Martín Vizcarra (who took up the presidency after the resignation of Pedro Pablo Kuczynski only to be overthrown two years later) introduced South America's first climate change law. Under the leadership of the New Democratic Party, the Canadian province of Alberta introduced a far-reaching Climate Leadership Plan—while also supporting the construction of pipelines to carry Alberta's oil to market—but in yet another swing of the pendulum, the subsequently elected United Conservative

Party was determined to reverse course. Some countries have maintained a steady trajectory: since the introduction of association contracts in 1974, Colombia has been perhaps the strongest proponent of market-based policies in Latin America, and the government of Iván Duque Márquez has doubled down on oil exploration and foreign investment. But in most cases, the pendulum has swung.

The remarkable changes of the last few years have cast the contributions to this volume in a new light. In the middle decades of the twentieth century, an extraordinary degree of consensus reigned in the Americas, and around the world, which held that governments had a role to play in providing consumers with access to energy products that provided them with a better quality of life. To this end, many countries created national energy companies; some, like Petro-Canada, were relatively short-lived, while others, such as Uruguay's ANCAP (Administración Nacional de Combustibles, Alcoholes y Portland, or National Administration of Combustibles, Alcohols and Portland), founded in 1931, have endured. In countries where energy products were produced in abundance, these industries were organized so as to enable citizens to benefit from the country's resources, according to the economic thinking prevalent in each country. However, with the rise of neoliberalism, governments throughout the region have struggled to determine the appropriate role of the state. Although the broad trend has been toward market orientation, fundamental ideological disagreement has led to an astounding level of vacillation in energy policies, as it has in social and economic policies. This is because of what is perceived to be at stake. The links between energy production and consumption, and between modernization and national identity, have been particularly fraught in the history of the Americas. The questions raised by energy regimes and energy transitions within any country go to the very core of the conception of the rights and obligations of the state and its citizens. Rather than E. A. Wrigley's typology of organic and mineral energy regimes, I refer here to the political and economic structures that frame policy decisions, investment, and environmental regulations, and the incentives and disincentives that businesses and consumers face in making decisions about their energy use.[3] The construction of the rights and obligations that govern energy use is an inherently political process, and this is particularly true given that these conceptions are shaped by unequal power relations between and among peoples and countries in this hemisphere, which for much of the twentieth century has been home to the world's largest superpower. The chapters in this volume demonstrate that these issues are still very much up for debate in most of the Americas.

In their comprehensive analysis of energy policies and their relationship to populism in Latin America, Rubén Berríos, Andrae Marak, and Scott Morgenstern conclude that resource nationalism—the idea that resource wealth should be used for the benefit of the nation—cannot be solely attributed to populist ideology, as is commonly assumed.[4] Individual cases, such as Bolivia, suggest a much more complex relationship between domestic politics, international constraints, and energy policy.[5] The nationalization of the Bolivian oil industry in 1937 was followed by the opening of the hydrocarbon sector to private investment *after* the Bolivian Revolution of 1952, and its renationalization by a nationalist military regime in 1969. President Evo Morales's use of natural gas royalties to underwrite Bolivian development (and prolong his political career—that is, before the 2019 election that saw his removal from office) might seem to confirm the association between resource nationalism and populism, but such an interpretation would ignore a century of struggle over Bolivia's hydrocarbon regime and the appropriate role of energy in society.[6] Berríos, Marak, and Morgenstern suggest that political leaders, regardless of ideology, have a strong preference for maintaining the status quo, and while that is certainly true in the large number of cases they analyze, neither the pendulum effect, nor incremental change over time, are explained by this observation.[7]

In his analysis of the technological imperative that has driven Petrobras's advances in offshore exploration, Tyler Priest suggests that one important consideration is the context surrounding the formation of national oil companies. Mexico's and Venezuela's state oil companies emerged during domestic oil booms that commenced under international oil companies, which were subsequently nationalized. In contrast, Argentina's and Brazil's energy giants emerged in a situation of scarcity that propelled the search for energy resources.[8] Both Petrobras and YPF were founded by governments intent on finding oil and using it to propel their development, both in terms of industrialization and social welfare.[9] Canada's high-modernist hydroelectricity projects follow these examples.[10] Priest relates this to the role of business and technological innovation, but the observation nevertheless suggests a compelling historical explanation for the divergence of state energy policies and the changes they have undergone over time. Does the starting point—the historical construction of energy's place in each society—and not merely the status quo ante, shape the array of energy policies adopted in each country?[11]

A second historical explanation, which Paul Chastko outlines in this volume in his chapter on Alberta's oil industry, is the extent of economic diversification in a given economy. Whereas the economic engine of Canadian development throughout the twentieth century was the manufacturing sector in Ontario—which relied upon hydroelectric power—Alberta's oil boom was only ever secondary to the creation of the levels of economic growth that could provide federal governments with the resources to create the kind of society that they envisioned. Although oil became central to regional identity in the Prairie West, hydro played a more important role in the construction of Central Canadian identity, as Daniel Macfarlane shows in his chapter in this volume. Given Central Canada's political and economic dominance, this meant that it was generally unnecessary to exercise tight state control over the oil industry.[12]

By contrast, when oil is virtually the only game in town, as it is in Ecuador, the stakes are higher. The lack of economic diversification means that the amount of revenue from hydrocarbons can determine whether a government can afford to pursue economic and social development. As a growing body of literature shows, it also determines the extent to which resident populations and their traditional territories are socially constructed as expendable, with their interests, health, and ways of life sacrificed to an economic project that is deemed to be for the greater societal good.[13] The struggle of the Cofán people of the Ecuadorian Amazon to defend their right to cultural reproduction, and to collect punitive damages for the harm inflicted upon them by the multinational interests of Texaco (now Chevron), has drawn support from academics and activists worldwide.[14] The "slow violence" of extractivism that Michael Cepek identifies as having structured the Cofán people's "life in oil" continues to be inflicted upon the lands and bodies of peoples deemed marginal in other international, national, and regional contexts.[15] This slow violence is central to the stories of the Hunkpapa Lakota, Sihasapa Lakota, and

Yanktonai Dakota of Standing Rock, North Dakota, where the grassroots protests against the Dakota Access Pipeline emerged; the Dene, Cree, and Métis community of Alberta's Fort McKay First Nation, surrounded by open pit oil sands mines;[16] and the marginalized fishing communities who suffer the environmental degradation of Venezuela's Lake Maracaibo.[17] Ostensibly progressive governments, such as those of Barack Obama or Evo Morales, treated Indigenous rights to free, prior, and informed consent as enshrined in the International Labour Organization Convention 169 with ambivalence. If a leftist government in Brazil enabled Petrobras to move deeper into the Amazon, failing to consult Indigenous Peoples in the area,[18] how will the same groups fare under Bolsonaro, who transferred responsibility for Indigenous land rights to the Ministry of Agriculture by executive order immediately after his inauguration? Some outlets accused him of planning a "genocide" of Indigenous Peoples in Brazil.[19] And while this may seem alarmist to some, successive inquiries into the treatment of Indigenous Peoples in Canada have used the same term.[20] In Canada, as in Brazil, the dispossession of Indigenous Peoples is directly connected to resource production.[21]

The unequal conflict between industry and government, on the one hand, and Indigenous Peoples and cultures, on the other, is central to critical analysis of energy history in North and South America. Not only do Indigenous Peoples reside upon or have rights to so much of the land where the extraction and production of energy resources occurs, but the historical construction of national identity has been associated with modernity and progress. A vast literature that spans the continent demonstrates how Indigenous Peoples have served as a foil in many national histories for the construction of a modern nation-state by the predominately European-descended settlers of the Americas.[22] The exploitation of Indigenous Peoples and lands was overdetermined because energy production and consumption have also served as markers of modernity in these national narratives. Traditional energy sources such as firewood and charcoal are deemed backward, whereas more modern forms of energy, such as fuel oil and hydroelectricity, are seen in both popular thought and in much of the literature on energy history as being measurable evidence of economic and social development.[23] The most prolific proponent of this perspective is Vaclav Smil, whose influential work on energy transitions has added much to our understanding of the world economy and the place of energy in society.[24] By employing this approach, César Yáñez in this volume demonstrates how Chile's continued reliance on coal was associated with its comparatively poor industrial progress in the twentieth century, and suggests that relative lack of hydroelectric power represented a concomitant lack of modernization. Macfarlane, taking a page from Timothy Mitchell, argues in this volume that the development of hydro in Ontario led to the emergence of "hydro democracy," a state in which the citizenry accepted the validity of government intervention in the economy and its management of natural resources, including energy.[25] The contributors to a recent volume on the petroleum industry in Alberta, by contrast, suggest, in a manner that is reminiscent of the resource curse narrative, that the oil industry has had deleterious effects on the quality of democracy not only in Alberta, but in Canada at large.[26]

The idea that the predominant type of energy resource employed in a given country affects the quality and form of its government, its citizens' quality of life, and the development of its economy—either positively or negatively—clearly holds broad sway. Fernando Coronil, in his *Magical State*, provided a masterful demonstration of this effect in the Venezuelan context,[27] and as Matthew T. Huber shows, the connection between oil and development shaped not only the scholarly literature but also popular thought.[28] In the US, this led voters steeped in postwar consumer culture to demand cheap gasoline, and in turn prompted successive governments to pursue policies that have delivered it through aggressive capitalist expansion—much of it, not coincidentally, in Latin America. By contrast, in Brazil, the oil-development nexus has given popular meaning to the refrain "o petróleo é nosso" (petroleum is ours) (which has its equivalents in other parts of the Americas: Quebec's "nous sommes tous Hydro-Québécois,"[29] and Mexico's "el petróleo es nuestro"[30]). This widely held belief sustained the idea that, once found, petroleum wealth should propel Brazil's import substitution industrialization in the postwar era, and its ascent as one of the so-called BRICS emerging economies (comprised of Brazil, Russia, India, China, and South Africa) at the beginning of the twenty-first century.[31] Although Brazilian voters also value cheap gasoline, they believe even more strongly in the role of Petrobras, or at least they did until Operation Car Wash.

One of the keys to understanding the diversity of energy histories in the region, as well as the pendulum effect that is evident in the energy policies of various national governments, is found through the analysis of the mechanisms by which workers and the expanding middle classes were incorporated into the political process in countries throughout the Americas over the course of the twentieth century. In Michael Camp's contribution to this volume, he describes how the fate of Maine's Dickey Dam, which was derailed by environmental objections, differed from that of the Tennessee Valley Authority (TVA), one of the showpieces of the New Deal under Franklin Delano Roosevelt.[32] Although the United States is generally considered the bastion of private capitalism, the political and technological feats of the hydroelectric engineers of the TVA were an example to the world of the advantages of state intervention in the energy market, while also speeding the incorporation of poor southerners into the US body politic. The TVA was based on lessons learned from the earlier nationalization of hydro power in the Niagara region through the Hydro-Electric Power Commission of Ontario, established in 1906, as well the engineers' understanding of the revolutionary land reform and irrigation projects underway in "Mexico's New Deal" under President Lázaro Cárdenas. During the Cold War, Latin American politicians and engineers (and their global counterparts in Asia and Africa) who visited the TVA took away both technological and political lessons, which helped their respective governments think through how to respond to their own challenges.[33] The goals of these projects were as political as they were environmental, and they ranged from providing irrigable land for marginal rural workers who had newly obtained the franchise, to stopping the spread of international communism during the Alliance for Progress. Decades later, the proponents of the Dickey Dam, like those of Chile's controversial HidroAysén project (cancelled in 2014),[34] faced very different political and economic terrain than had FDR's New Dealers.

Conceptions of the state's role in providing a stable source of energy, protecting the environment, and providing basic social welfare, have varied not only according to country, but also across time and space. At the beginning of the twentieth century, during the era of export-led growth throughout the Americas, the dominant mode of thinking was that private companies possessed the expertise and capital to propel economic growth, and governments therefore allowed and generally encouraged private companies to pursue resource development through concessions. To attract investors, governments pursued policies that would lure investors, such as repressive social control, low wages, and liberal tax regimes.[35] The United States and Canada should not be excluded from this characterization, given the internal colonialism that investment firms and their contemporary multinational successors continue to engage in. This arrangement was cut short in Mexico in the wake of the 1910 revolution and the oil expropriation of 1938,[36] but throughout the entire region, the rise of mass politics brought significant social dislocation. As governments throughout the hemisphere scrambled to mitigate the effects of the Great Depression, many necessarily experimented with early forms of import substitution industrialization as export markets dried up and imports became unavailable.[37] The growth that most countries experienced after the Second World War, during the era of massive government intervention in the economy, enabled fragile democracies in the region to begin to improve the standard of living for workers and reduce poverty rates, earning loyal voters in the process. But Latin American economies, with their vast natural resources and commodity endowments, remained export-oriented, and the fundamental disagreement over whether the government's role was to provide a social welfare state or a favourable environment for investment (which it was assumed would eventually benefit the populace through economic growth) was never resolved. The pace and timing of swings are produced by the complex energy histories of each country in North and South America, in tandem with increasingly interdependent international energy markets; but in its international, regional, and local dimensions, it is this basic disagreement that provides the pendulum's kinetic energy.

The chapters included in this volume represent some of the best emerging research on the national cases they describe. Although energy resources are among the most globalized commodities, these are national stories, with a few exceptions where technology and corporate actors take the stage. And although the volume focuses on the role of governments and politics in the creation of energy regimes, rather than the role of the workers who sustain energy industries, people are still at the heart of the discussion, because energy policies affect consumers, workers, and indeed all of the members of society whose lives are affected by the existence or absence of the social welfare state.[38] In his chapter, Pablo Heidrich proposes that the conception of energy as either a market good, a common good, or a political good can help to break through the ideological paradigms that colour analyses of energy policies. The often unconscious ideas we hold about the role of energy in society shape our investigations in this area as much as they influence the decisions of CEOs and governments, as the chapters in this volume—many of which employ Heidrich's schema—show. In Linda Hall's chapter, which is written from the perspective of a scholar who has written extensively on the triumphant construction of the Mexican oil monopoly, its undoing seems nonsensical. In the NAFTA (now CUSMA) era of free trade that firmly posits energy as a market good, however, this about-face seems to have been foretold in changing ideas about the place of government regulation of the economy. Just as Gail Triner points out in her chapter that economic theory predicted that the opening of Brazil's economy in the 1990s should have eliminated rent-seeking behaviour and improved the performance of Petrobras, academics (the contributors to this volume included) make a whole host of assumptions regarding economic behaviour and capitalism, and these of course shape our conclusions. Ernesto Serrani's chapter on the (re)nationalization of the Argentine energy industry may appear to be at odds with the Brazilian example outlined by Triner, but in both cases the management of energy transitions (in Brazil from conventional onshore to deepwater drilling in the pre-salt basin, and in Argentina with the emergence of a potentially lucrative shale gas industry) contributed significantly to the political changes that they accompanied. And as Paul Chastko suggests in his analysis of the Canadian experience in the Alberta oil sands, the whims of the market can precipitate energy transitions in even the most politically unlikely places. Heidrich's exhortation that we analyze energy as either a market good, a common good, or a political good, rather than resorting to the knee-jerk truisms that have guided so much of the conversation thus far, is another way that we can integrate histories of energy in the Americas. However, Dermot O'Connor and Juan Pablo Bohórquez Montoya, in their chapter on contemporary energy production in Colombia, remind us that treating energy as a common good holds its perils, because although it breaks down the naturalization of market-based energy policies, the common good is also a historically constructed idea that continues to sacrifice the interests of marginal groups to those of the majority.

In his chapter in this volume, which examines the experience of Exxon in Venezuela, Joseph Pratt identifies three periods in the oil giant's activities, that of unabashed exploitation, the assertion of national control (or abashed exploitation), and accommodation. This broad periodization can guide our understanding of energy experiences throughout the hemisphere. Brian McBeth's chapter on the early years of oil exploration and development in Venezuela demonstrates that even at the dawn of the period of unabashed exploitation, energy firms were constrained by local realities and personalities that hindered their freedom of action. As O'Connor and Bohórquez Montoya show, these constraints continue, such that international companies must pay careful attention to local conditions and involve local populations in decisions over their own futures. The social constraints faced by energy companies and governments alike are joined by environmental and technological constraints and opportunities. Daniel Macfarlane shows how environmental, as well as political and ideological, differences in the nationalist sensibilities of the United States and Canada during the mid-twentieth century played a role in the sometimes tense negotiations over the construction of the Niagara and St. Lawrence hydro projects. And as Camp shows, environmentalism intertwined with politics to create a very different outcome in the case of the Dickey Dam, which was never constructed. César Yáñez's long-run consumption analysis of Chile shows that, despite the ebb and flow of public policies, changes in energy production—and energy transitions in particular—tend to happen at a much slower pace. Whereas each country's transition from one energy regime to another can help explain its developmental outcomes, Tyler Priest's chapter shows that these transitions also occur within an international context that reflects the prevailing thinking on technology and science; these attitudes drive change in energy industries and the regulatory regimes adopted by governments, which in turn influence ideas about the state's role in society.

Taken together, these chapters demonstrate that we have much to learn from a comparative examination of energy histories in the Americas. Such an approach enables us to re-evaluate many of the accepted truths that have held sway, influencing policy-making and research production alike. The contributors to this volume are at the forefront of a new wave of scholarship on the history of energy production and regulation. By bringing them into dialogue, this volume broadens the conversation by de-emphasizing the traditional focus on national peculiarities in favour of a more integrated understanding of the role of energy in society.

NOTES

1   See, for example, Michael L. Ross, *The Oil Curse: How Petroleum Wealth Shapes the Development of Nations* (Princeton, NJ: Princeton University Press, 2012). For a contrasting perspective, see Pauline Jones Luong and Erika Weinthal, *Oil Is Not a Curse: Ownership Structure and Institutions in Soviet Successor States* (New York: Cambridge University Press, 2010).

2   Recent edited volumes on Latin America from the perspective of anthropology and political ecology and geographical economy have brought much theoretical precision to the study of energy regimes in Latin America. Together with the special issues of the *Journal of American History* (vol. 99, no. 1 [June 2012]) and the *Canadian Journal of History* (vol. 53, no. 3 [Winter 2018]), which include chapters on Canada and the United States as well as Mexico, these volumes constitute an emerging field of comparative research. In particular, see Anthony Bebbington and Jeffrey Bury, eds., *Subterranean Struggles: New Dynamics of Mining, Oil, and Gas in Latin America* (Austin: University of Texas Press, 2013); Anthony Bebbington, ed., *Social Conflict, Economic Development and the Extractive Industry: Evidence from South America* (London: Routledge, 2012); Håvad Haarstad, ed., *New Political Spaces in Latin American Natural Resource Governance* (Basingstoke, UK: Palgrave Macmillan, 2012); Kalowatie Deonandan and Michael L. Dougherty, eds., *Mining in Latin America: Critical Approaches to the New Extraction* (London: Routledge, 2016); Andrea Behrends, Stephen P. Reyna, and Günther Schlee, eds., *Crude Domination: An Anthropology of Oil* (New York: Berghahn Books, 2011); and John-Andrew McNeish, Axel Borchgrevnik, and Owen Logan, eds., *Contested Powers: The Politics of Energy and Development in Latin America* (London: Zed Books, 2015).

3   E. A. Wrigley, *Continuity, Chance and Change: The Character of the Industrial Revolution in England* (New York: Cambridge University Press, 1988).

4   Rubén Berríos, Andrae Marak, and Scott Morgenstern, "Explaining Hydrocarbon Nationalization in Latin America: Economics and Political Ideology," *Review of International Political Economy* 18, no. 5 (December 2011): 673–97.

5   See Kevin A. Young, "From Open Door to Nationalization: Oil and Development Visions in Bolivia, 1952–1969," *Hispanic American Historical Review* 97, no. 1 (2017): 95–129; Kevin A. Young, *Blood of the Earth: Resource Nationalism, Revolution, and Empire in Bolivia* (Austin: University of Texas Press, 2017); Stephen C. Cote, *Oil and Nation: A History of Bolivia's Petroleum Sector* (Morgantown: West Virginia University Press, 2016).

6   Derrick Hindery, *From Enron to Evo: Pipeline Politics, Global Environmentalism, and Indigenous Rights in Bolivia* (Tucson: University of Arizona Press, 2013).

7   Berríos, Marak, and Morgenstern, "Explaining Hydrocarbon Nationalization in Latin America."

8   Carl E. Solberg, *Oil and Nationalism in Argentina* (Stanford, CA: Stanford University Press, 1979). See also Elana Shever, *Resources for Reform: Oil and Neoliberalism in Argentina* (Stanford, CA: Stanford University Press, 2012).

9   The contrasting case of Cuba, which was intent upon finding oil reserves that never materialized, is analyzed in Erig T. Gettig, "Oil and Revolution in Cuba: Development, Nationalism, and the U.S. Energy Empire, 1902–1961," (PhD diss., Georgetown University, 2017).

10 Tina Loo, "High Modernism, Conflict, and the Nature of Change in Canada," *Canadian Historical Review* 97, no. 1 (Spring 2016): 34–58; James L. Kenny and Andrew G. Secord, "Engineering Modernity: Hydroelectric Development in New Brunswick, 1945–1970," *Acadiensis* 39, no. 1 (Winter/Spring 2010): 3–26; Daniel Macfarlane, *Negotiating a River: Canada, the US and the Creation of the St. Lawrence Seaway* (Vancouver: UBC Press, 2014).

11 Tyler Priest, "Petrobras in the History of Offshore Oil," in *New Order and Progress: Development and Democracy in Brazil*, ed. Ben Ross Schneider, 53–77 (New York: Oxford University Press, 2016).

12 Also see these authors' monographs: Paul Chastko, *Developing Alberta's Oil Sands: From Karl Clark to Kyoto* (Calgary: University of Calgary Press, 2004); Macfarlane, *Negotiating a River*; Daniel Macfarlane, *Fixing Niagara Falls: Environment, Energy, and Engineers at the World's Most Famous Waterfall* (Vancouver: UBC Press, 2020).

13 For one example, see Sherry Smith and Brian Frehner, eds., *Indians and Energy: Exploitation and Opportunity in the American Southwest* (Santa Fe, NM: School for Advanced Research Press, 2010).

14 Suzana Sawyer, *Crude Chronicles: Indigenous Politics, Multinational Oil, and Neoliberalism in Ecuador* (Durham, NC: Duke University Press, 2004); Marc Becker, *Indians and Leftists in the Making of Ecuador's Modern Indigenous Movements* (Durham, NC: Duke University Press, 2008).

15 Cepek uses Rob Nixon's term "slow violence" to describe the experience of the Cofán in *Life in Oil: Cofán Survival in the Petroleum Fields of Amazonia* (Austin: University of Texas Press, 2018).

16 A documentary on the Moose Lake reserve near Fort McKay, *Moose Lake: Home and Refuge*, presented by Bori Addobo, who represented the Fort McKay First Nation, and Peter Fortna, Tara Joly, and Hereward Longley of Willowsprings Strategic Solutions, provided the opportunity for discussion of corporate social responsibility frameworks at the "Energy in the Americas" conference. See Fort McKay First Nation, *Moose Lake: Home and Refuge*, online documentary, 20:49, 20 August 2013, https://vimeo.com/72715280.

17 Elvin Delgado, "Spaces of Socio-ecological Distress: Fossil Fuels, Solar Salt, and Fishing Communities in Lake Maracaibo, Venezuela," (PhD diss., Syracuse University, 2012).

18 Adriana Huber, "The Dark Side of Brazil: Oil Giant Petrobras Moves into 'Deepest Amazon,'" *Survival International*, 27 March 2014, https://www.survivalinternational.org/news/10088.

19 Sara Burrows, "Brazil's New President Openly Threatens Genocide of Indigenous Amazonians," *Returntonow.net*, 6 November 2018, https://returntonow.net/2018/11/06/brazils-new-president-openly-threatens-genocide-of-Indigenous-amazonians.

20 See Truth and Reconciliation Commission of Canada, *Honouring the Truth, Reconciling for the Future: Summary of the Final Report of the Truth and Reconciliation Commission of Canada* (Winnipeg: Truth and Reconciliation Commission of Canada, 2015), http://www.trc.ca/assets/pdf/Honouring_the_Truth_Reconciling_for_the_Future_July_23_2015.pdf; National Inquiry into Missing and Murdered Indigenous Women and Girls, *Reclaiming Power and Place: The Final Report of the National Inquiry into Missing and Murdered Indigenous Women and Girls* (Ottawa: National Inquiry into Missing and Murdered Indigenous Women and Girls, 2019), https://www.mmiwg-ffada.ca/final-report; National Inquiry into Missing and Murdered Indigenous Women and Girls, *A Legal Analysis of Genocide: Supplementary Report of the National Inquiry into Missing and Murdered Indigenous Women and Girls* (Ottawa: National Inquiry into Missing and Murdered Indigenous Women and Girls, 2019), https://www.mmiwg-ffada.ca/wp-content/uploads/2019/06/Supplementary-Report_Genocide.pdf.

21 See, for example, Brittany Luby, "From Milk-Medicine to Public (Re)Education Programs: An Examination of Anishinabek Mothers' Responses to Hydroelectric Flooding in the Treaty #3 District, 1900–1975," *Canadian Bulletin of Medical History* 32, no. 2 (2015): 363–89.

22 See Rebecca Earle, *Return of the Native: Indians and Myth-Making in Spanish America, 1810–1930* (Durham, NC: Duke University Press, 2007); Richard White, *The Middle Ground: Indians, Empires, and Republics in the Great Lakes Region, 1650–1815*, anniversary ed. (New York: Cambridge University Press, 2010); Paige Raibmon, *Authentic Indians: Episodes of Encounter from the Late-Nineteenth-Century Northwest Coast* (Durham, NC: Duke University Press, 2005).

23 For examples of the environmental consequences of fuelwood's longevity in Canada, and the shift from biomass to cooking oil in Mexico City, see, Joshua MacFadyen, "Hewers of Wood: A History of Wood Energy in Canada," in *Powering Up Canada: A History of Power, Fuel, and Energy from 1600*, ed. R. W. Sandwell (Montreal: McGill-Queen's University Press, 2016), 129–61; Matthew Vitz, " 'To Save the Forests': Power, Narrative, and Environment in Mexico City's Cooking Fuel Transition," *Mexican Studies/Estudios Mexicanos* 31, no. 1 (Winter 2015): 125–55.

24 Vaclav Smil, *Energy Transitions: Global and National Perspectives*, 2nd ed. (Santa Barbara, CA: Praeger, 2017).

25 Timothy Mitchell, *Carbon Democracy: Political Power in the Age of Oil* (London: Verso, 2011).

26 Meenal Shrivastava and Lorna Stefanick, eds., *Alberta Oil and the Decline of Democracy in Canada* (Edmonton: Athabasca University Press, 2015).

27 Fernando Coronil, *The Magical State: Nature, Money, and Modernity in Venezuela* (Chicago: University of Chicago Press, 1997). See also Miguel Tinker Salas, *The Enduring Legacy: Oil, Culture, and Society in Venezuela* (Durham, NC: Duke University Press, 2009).

28 Matthew T. Huber, *Lifeblood: Oil, Freedom, and the Forces of Capital* (Minneapolis: University of Minnesota Press, 2013).

29 Dominique Perron, " 'On est Hydro-Québecois': Consommateur, producteur ou citoyen? Analyse de la nationalisation symbolique d'Hydro-Québec," *Globe: Revue internationale d'études québécoises* 6, no. 2 (2003): 73–97.

30 This slogan has served diverse projects, from the energy reform of Enrique Peña Nieto to a popular podcast, intended as a primer on the energy landscape in Mexico for US audiences. For the former, see Presidencia Enrique Peña Nieto, "Reforma energética—el petróleo es nuestro," YouTube video, 0:29, 12 August 2013, https://www.youtube.com/watch?v=UhSGfplcAs0; for the latter, see *El Petroleo es Nuestro: A History of Oil in Mexico*, hosted by Brandon Seale, https://podcasts.apple.com/ca/podcast/el-petroleo-es-nuestro-a-history-of-oil-in-mexico/id1078689026.

31 Peter Seaborn Smith, *Oil and Politics in Modern Brazil* (Toronto: MacMillan, 1976); Jeffrey D. Wilson, "Resource Powers? Minerals, Energy and the Rise of the BRICS," *Third World Quarterly* 36, no. 2 (2015): 223–39.

32 Also see Camp's monograph, *Unnatural Resources: Energy and Environmental Politics in Appalachia after the 1973 Oil Embargo* (Pittsburgh: University of Pittsburgh Press, 2019).

33 Tore C. Olsson, *Agrarian Crossings: Reformers and the Remaking of the US and Mexican Countryside* (Princeton, NJ: Princeton University Press, 2017).

34 Claudio Broitman and Pablo Kreimer, "Knowledge Production, Mobilization and Standardization in Chile's HidroAysén Case," *Minerva* 56, no. 2 (2018): 209–29.

35 Victor Bulmer-Thomas, *The Economic History of Latin America since Independence*, 3rd ed. (New York: Cambridge University Press, 2014).

36 Linda B. Hall, *Oil, Banks, and Politics: The United States and Postrevolutionary Mexico, 1917–1924* (Austin: University of Texas Press, 1995); Joel Álvarez de la Borda, *Los orígenes de la industria petrolera en México, 1900–1925* (Mexico City: Archivo Histórico de Petróleos Mexicanos, 2005). The environmental and labour dimensions of the change are analyzed in Jamie C. Christy, "*Somos Petroleros*: Mexican Petroleum Workers' Challenge to the El Águila Oil Company, 1900–1938" (PhD diss., University of Houston, 2011), and Myrna I. Santiago, *The Ecology of Oil: Environment, Labor, and the Mexican Revolution, 1900–1938* (New York: Cambridge University Press, 2006).

37 Paulo Drinot and Alan Knight, eds., *The Great Depression in Latin America* (Durham, NC: Duke University Press, 2014).

38 For an excellent volume focusing on petroleum labourers, see Elisabetta Bini Atabaki and Kaveh Ehsani, eds., *Working for Oil: Comparative Social Histories of Labour in the Global Oil Industry* (New York: Palgrave Macmillan, 2018).

Unpacking Latin American Oil and Gas Policies: Views on Energy as a Market, Common, and Political Good

Pablo Heidrich

Since the early twenty-first century, North American and European debates on Latin American oil and gas issues have consistently shown concerns about a resurgent "resource nationalism." This is particularly the case when it comes to the policy changes made in several countries in the region, from Chavez's Venezuela and Morales's Bolivia, to Brazil, Argentina, or even Ecuador.[1] A couple of decades earlier, when most Latin American countries and others in the developing world were enacting pro-market reforms in their energy sectors during the 1980s, a similar analysis helped observers imagine that such changes would increase production, income, and economic development for these countries, bringing along wide support from local populations for market rules in the energy sector.[2] We now know, however, that these developments did not come to pass. In fact, popular resistance and electoral backlash against those pro-market reforms in energy policies were fundamental to changes in government in several countries, namely, Bolivia, Brazil, Ecuador, Peru, and Venezuela, and they contributed significantly to protests in several others, such as Argentina, Chile, and Mexico.[3]

This chapter argues that the concept of resource nationalism (RN), used systematically since the 1970s to assess energy policies in developing countries, needs to be further specified to interpret policy evolutions in the oil and gas industry in Latin America, and most likely in other parts of the world as well. As theories of interpretation go, current versions of RN lack the capacity to explain policy choices because they are based on a fundamentally external view of what are in fact internal decisions, and as such, they suffer from an excessive sector-specific bias that impedes an understanding of the crucially embedded nature of energy policy-making in the pursuit of economic development. In other words, analyses employing RN as a guiding concept need to move beyond viewing energy policy as a field where nationalism is simply invoked against foreign or international energy firms and their direct or indirect domestic supporters, and instead fully incorporate the wider development goals governments have when enacting them.

To this end, this chapter develops a different set of concepts to interpret the resurgence of RN in Latin American energy policies. Grounded on more widely used precepts of political economy, as already employed in other areas of public policy, energy policy is defined here by taking its subject matter—energy—as either a market, common, or political good. This perspective has several advantages over externally driven views or energy-sector-specific theories such as resource nationalism. Firstly, it standardizes and integrates energy with other subjects and goals of public economic policy-making—the goal being to facilitate a less industry-specific analysis that can then better link energy policy-making with other aspects of government policy, such as infrastructure, industry, income inequality, poverty reduction, or international trade. Secondly, this alternative is a priori neutral to the outcomes of energy policy in terms of states' and markets' relative spheres of governance, giving theoretical equanimity to perspectives that are either more market-oriented or state-driven.

This work proceeds by first comparing the frames used by RN with those proposed here—energy as a marketable, common, or political good—to study the political economy of energy in Latin America. Detailed examples from two countries, Argentina and Brazil, help to illustrate in detail the proposed frame. The chapter concludes with recommendations for future research on this subject.

The Baseline for Resource Nationalism

Resource nationalism is usually defined as the effort by resource-rich nations to shift political and economic control of their energy and mining sectors from foreign and private interests to domestic and state-controlled companies.[4] This approach treats natural resources, such as energy or mineral commodities, as part of a country's "national patrimony," which is to be used for the benefit of national development.[5] However, "development" is often left under-specified in these definitions, which either describe it as the provision of common goods for the general public or, more frequently, as substantial benefits for specific constituencies.[6]

Instead, the focus of RN remains natural resources policy, with energy policy at its crucial centre, and operates with an implicit understanding of what the government's role should be as a regulator of economic activities, which, in turn, are to be chiefly driven by market forces.[7] RN assesses the extent of government intervention in an industry that is a priori considered to be run globally and for the most part by market forces and private firms. For example, a government is judged on how it regulates the extraction, processing, and, if a national market exists, the distribution of natural resources such as energy goods by either completely or partially setting prices, quantities, or timing for these activities.[8] In other words, energy policies viewed through a standard RN lens are seen as exercises in regulation that ought to have as goals the expansion of the industry and the prosperity of the private firms operating in it.[9] The implicit notion is therefore that minimal regulation would result in the optimal performance of market forces.

Current understandings of RN recognize the finite quality of natural resources such as oil and gas, and therefore accept that governments obtain compensatory rents from energy goods—for example, by setting up rates for royalties and other specific taxes or levies applied to the sector.[10] In the RN context, this is perhaps the single most important way of assessing the quality of energy policies. It confirms the analytical bias toward the "natural role" states and markets should occupy vis-à-vis one another, meaning that governments should not seek to appropriate a bigger share than private investors, or more generally, what market forces consider acceptable profit margins.[11] Given this tendency, there is unsurprisingly

Table 1.1 A Theoretical Scheme for Resource Nationalism

Energy Policy	Market-Driven	←==================→		State-Driven
Ownership	Private	Private w/ restrictions	State w/private partners	State monopoly
Taxation and rents	As low as needed to bring in local or foreign investment		As high as possible to maximize current rents	
Operational mode	Privately owned concessions	Production-sharing deals	Operational contracts	State company as sole operator
Prices and subsidies	Supply/demand driven	Monopoly moderating regulations	Prices with producer-paid subsidies for local economy	
Solutions to market failures	Publicly or privately funded?		Government funded	
State energy company	None	Yes, but with profit-oriented management	Yes, with private participation	Sole operator

no mention of state-provided promotional regulations such as tax exemptions or holidays to import needed capital goods or to recover exploration expenses often given to the energy industry. The same applies to the credit guarantees governments provide for energy companies to build the necessary infrastructure projects for their exports, such as pipelines and seaport terminals.

Given the genealogy of RN, which originated from the literature on bargaining between multinational firms and states of the 1970s[12] and '80s,[13] it is not surprising that many of its current formulations still follow a one-dimensional line stretching from minimum to maximum regulation of market forces in the energy industry. This thinking is applied to its many specific dimensions, such as operations, actors, prices, and tax regimes. RN is not, however, a theory for understanding the role of energy policy in wider national development strategies, whether formulated explicitly or implicitly, by state actors. For that perspective, one must necessarily start from the development strategies being applied to a national economy and deduce from that standpoint what the role assigned to the energy sector is. The result would be a development-centred understanding of energy policies and not an energy policy–centred assessment of development strategies.

The following two examples can clearly illustrate this problem as it relates to the use of the standard RN analytical prism. Firstly, if energy policy is analyzed in a political or historical vacuum resulting from the under-specification of the larger development priorities of the country in question, no clear insight into the sources of those policies can be obtained except by locating them outside the country—for example, in higher international commodity prices—or from long-standing (ex-temporal) characteristics such as weak institutional development. This is problematic, as countries react differently to similar external stimuli and government institutions can only be assessed accurately by observing more than one policy case across different industries.

A more plausible explanation for the need of RN to resort to external or institutional factors is that the implicit logic of the theory as it relates to the roles of states and markets is overly normative, and decisions (regarding economic policies, including energy policies) tend not to be the result of their political circumstances. In other words, RN-based analysis might consider markets as central to economic activity, but decision-makers in developing regions such as Latin America might envision markets as just one of several means to advance their respective nation's economic development, which is their larger (and perhaps only real) goal.

Secondly, RN consequently lacks the capacity to deduce what is likely to happen with energy policy in the countries studied. Since RN considers decision-making in other aspects of public policy as exogenous to energy policy-making, policy changes in other sectors, such as agriculture, industry, or even trade and financial policies, are supposedly irrelevant. Even more implausibly, macroeconomic policy choices, such as those related to fiscal or monetary policy, are also considered analytically exogenous or, in the case of oil-driven export economies, a function of energy policy. Therefore, when changes in energy policy happen, they are always, and almost by definition in the framework of RN, a surprise. In fact, such breaks are interpreted that way because there is an unfortunate blindness to what energy policy means in the greater context of all other sectoral and national macroeconomic policies. In other words, there is a lack of insight regarding what energy policies mean for the development strategies of the countries in question.

Energy Policy in Economic Development: A Market, Common, or Political Good?

In the previous section, I identified three spaces for improvement in the RN literature: the under-specification of the developmental goals of energy-rich countries, the dependence on an implicit notion of what roles states and markets should have in this industry, and an excessive focus on the progress of the energy sector to the exclusion of wider, national understandings of national economies in developing countries. In order to advance the theory of RN, as applied to energy policy, this chapter proposes an alternative framework that explicitly includes wider economic development concerns, as articulated by each country, and that incorporates market-state relations in a non-normative manner.

Developing countries, such as those in Latin America, have engaged in a succession of economic policy experiments in order to advance their development, framed as higher per capita income levels. From the original post-colonial consensus in the nineteenth and early twentieth centuries regarding economic liberalism and laissez-faire regulation of markets, trade, and investment, the mid-twentieth century saw a series of experiments in import substitution industrialization.[14] That process, which in the 1930s was originally confined to the larger and more economically diversified countries, such as Brazil, Mexico, and Argentina, gradually extended to most of the region by the early 1960s. Once the debt crisis began in the 1980s, an extended process of economic deregulation and liberalization began, expanding rapidly in the 1990s and stalling again in the mid-2000s in most countries, while it was partially reversed in others.[15]

Consistently throughout the decades, blueprints for economic development have been applied across sectors either in form (e.g., enforcing import substitution, enforcing liberalization, enforcing reregulation, etc.) or, most importantly, in order to complement or support larger goals established for national development.[16] For example, export agriculture was heavily taxed in Argentina and Brazil during the import substitution period because these states wanted to extract profits from agricultural exporters to invest in industrialization projects, not because there was a general tendency to tax all economic activities more than before. There was no other reason for such bias against export agriculture except a utilitarian one, even though arguments against large landowners were used to legitimize such policies.[17]

The same type of bias was later applied to industry in the 1990s across much of South America and in Mexico when neoliberal policies of trade liberalization, deregulation, and currency overvaluation were used to bring in foreign direct investment and short-term financial capital flows to restart economic growth. There was "nothing personal" against industry (and its margins of protection) except that it stood in the way of a pragmatic expectation that foreign private capital could rescue Latin American economies from the 1980s doldrums of debt and recessions.[18] In fact, deregulation and liberalization were quite unevenly applied depending on how much they supported that larger goal, in spite of the apparently overarching discourse on the merits of minimal state involvement.[19]

Therefore, it seems more appropriate to look at sectoral policies such as energy programs initiated by governments from the point of view of what they want to get from the sector and where they place it in their real hierarchy of goals implicit in their own views for economic development. A good a priori indicator of whether a sectoral policy is in fact central or rather more subsidiary to that overarching development vision could be the actual relative size of the sector in the national economy, as well as its short to mid-term potential for growth (relative to that of other sectors) that could contribute to the country's overall wealth. For example, the energy policy of Uruguay or Chile is more likely to be a function of the policies already being applied to the more relevant sectors of those economies, such as agriculture in the first case and mining in the second. It is quite different in other countries with great energy resources, such as Bolivia or Venezuela, where, logically, energy policies would be of fundamental importance to whatever is possible to do in any other sector, such as industry or agriculture.

Ideological discourses are traditionally given great importance in studies on energy policies in Latin America. Intrinsic characteristics of the sector, such as high optimal firm concentration, its attractiveness to multinational capital, the possibility of extraordinary profits, and apparent possibilities for backward and forward linkages supporting industrialization, all seem to invite tinkering in search of great political and economic payoffs. Moreover, standard formulations of the RN literature give central importance to this aspect of ideology, referred to as *developmentalism*, often to the exclusion of other more practical preoccupations that policy-makers also have in regards to the rest of a national economy, such as competitiveness and growth.

Another significant linkage between ideology and the place that energy policy might have in overall development plans is the urgency attached to policies of social welfare and income distribution. In energy-exporting nations, where extraordinary profits can be obtained from the production and sale of this good to international markets given the enormous difference between production costs and global prices in recent years, the application of this surplus to deal with social and economic inequality is obvious. The ideological mediation takes place not only in terms of how those profits are extracted, as a sector-centric RN analysis would do, but in the estimation of the social issues that are going to be addressed. In other words, it is in the ideological (used as a neutral term) assessment of social and economic inequality that ideology primarily matters, and this will determine the size of the surplus extracted from the energy sector.

As such, energy policy can then be "essentialized" in terms of policies regarding that type of good in an economy. The categorization proposed here is structured into three parts, articulated along a continuum that deems energy policy subsidiary to wider developmental goals and cognizant of the relative importance of the sector in the overall economy. We can take, then, energy as a marketable good, where energy is seen as any other market-produced and -traded good; energy as a common good, where energy is observed as a distinct type of good whose production and commercialization needs to be regulated for the maximization of the common good; and energy as a political good, where energy is taken as the basis for the construction of an alternative polity and society to the one currently in existence. The following paragraphs describe each category in further detail; in a subsequent section, I illustrate each with current examples.

Policies for Energy as a Market Good

When governments take energy as a market good (hereafter EMG), they regulate its production and commercialization as they would any other good or service in that economy. For most recent and current Latin American governments, this denotes a market-supportive approach to regulation that can nonetheless account for the non-renewable nature of oil and gas—for example, by levying specific taxes or royalties on extractive firms.

The character of regulation in EMG is, however, promotional in the sense that it fosters the arrival of foreign direct investment, as well as local investors in all aspects of the energy business, from exploration, production, refining, and distribution to commercialization. This perspective on energy is grounded in the notion that demand will be met by supply, which will bring the optimal social and economic result for the country, regardless of the process and actors involved in production. Taxation and energy prices in EMG are again set according to the levels that will secure as much (private) investment in the sector as possible, which, for example, precludes using below-market prices as subsidies for other industries.

Public investments are often needed in this industry, however, as there are areas of partial or total market failure, including in production research, geological prospection, storage, pipelines across borders, docks, inspections to maintain security and environmental standards, just as there are in other industries. In the most common EMG approach, state participation in these aspects is kept at the lowest level possible, deferring to private initiatives, self-regulation, and private credit procurement. In the strictest EMG versions, state involvement tends to be limited to providing state guarantees for private loans and diplomatic support to open new markets for exports or securing stable sources for imports. The net result of maintaining that preference for assigning the driving seat to market forces in the form of private firms, while keeping practices of state promotion for the sector, amounts to a subsidy to the sector that is paid for by the rest of the economy, either through higher prices or taxes or a combination of both.

Table 1.2 Sample Characteristics of Energy as a Market Good

Aspects of Energy Policy	General Characteristics
Ownership	Mostly or fully private, with a state importer for price stabilization purposes
Regulation	Self-regulation, minimum state involvement in safety, environment, financial, or labour practices
Taxation and rents	Optimized to maximize and promote investment in the sector, royalties set considering non-renewable character of reserves
Operational mode	Foreign or privately owned operators, generous exploration rights, marginal or legacy state operator
Market failures	State subsidies for exploration, loan guarantees for extraction and export/import infrastructure, consumer-subsidized distribution investments

Energy as a Common Good

In contrast to the above, governments that take energy as a common good (ECG) focus most closely on the national character of the assets and the actual production process involved in making those energy goods available to the rest of the national economy. In that sense, energy is conceptualized as a qualitatively different type of good than others, and thus merits a specific regulatory framework. The regulatory framework will contain market elements, as in other production sectors, but will also have specific regulations that will overwhelmingly reflect the public-patrimony character of energy as an input for the rest of the economy and a demander of goods and services from the rest of the economy.[20] As in EMG, the non-renewable aspect of energy goods is also considered in taxation, but here it is subordinated to the needs of the economy in its current state, and not set by investment-promotional parameters or income-smoothing notions.

The character of regulation in ECG is therefore subsidiary to the needs of the rest of the economy, with the main balance point allocated between demanders of energy goods, such as industry and consumers, and providers of inputs for the local production and distribution of energy goods, such as specialized oil and gas engineering companies, and manufacturers

Table 1.3 Sample Characteristics of Energy as a Common Good

Aspects of Energy Policy	General Characteristics
Ownership	Can be partially private, but with a dominant state company to set sector policies. Can also be a state monopoly.
Regulation and prices	Comprehensive in all operational aspects to enhance or maximize local transfer and use of technologies, services, and labour. Active control of financial flows and subsidized prices.
Taxation and rents	Slightly favourable or neutral measures to attract investment in operations, exploration, or both. High royalties and special taxes.
Operational mode	Foreign or privately owned operators allowed, best areas given to state operator. Joint ventures with local private or state firms are common.
Market failures	State subsidies for exploration, state-directed distribution, and production investments.

of other specialized goods needed for this sector (pipelines, drills, ships, storage facilities, etc.). A fundamental aspect to facilitate this process is the ownership of the firm or firms in charge of the production of energy. If it were of state or domestic capital, problems in administering the special status of the sector in ECG are substantially reduced, since incentives can be easily aligned among the bureaucracies running the energy firms, with the government running the sectoral policy and its political masters being accountable for its results.

The public to which this last group is accountable is the electorate, the members of which are also the recipients of either energy subsidies in terms of below-global-levels domestic prices and/or energy sourcing or provisioning to areas of the country that market forces (i.e., private energy firms) would not otherwise exploit or provide. Besides these wider constituencies, there are specific ones for ECG, such as intensive users of energy goods like metal smelters, and petrochemical plants typical of countries with intermediate levels of industrialization, as well as domestic firms that specialize in the provision of energy industry goods and services.

Therefore, the elements one can encounter in ECG are those already present as sector-specific subsidies in EMG plus a framework that holds firms accountable for how they invest in terms of domestic versus foreign-sourced inputs, where they invest, how much they allocate to exploration, extraction, and commercialization, and the prices they charge for their final output. Given the relevance of other sectors of the economy in energy policy-making, domestic price subsidies in ECG might easily mean export controls or prohibitions to make the former possible.

The crucial distinction here between ECG and the previous EMG is the subsidiary character of the energy sector to the rest of the national economy in the former versus the latter. That subordinated conceptualization of energy to the greater whole, identified here as the "common good," is what paves the way for systematic regulation in ECG in favour of the interests of other groups over those of the energy industry itself. One must note, however, that the apparently intermediate approach of EMG often covers up economy-wide subsidies for the energy industry through state guarantees or direct financing of sector-specific inputs and facilities.

Energy as a Political Good

While EMG and ECG entail an implicit acceptance of the wider political status quo in terms of government regime, national institutional framework, and the overall relationship between state and markets, governments undertaking uses of energy as a political good (EPG) employ energy policy as the driver to alter all of the above through the strategic use of the sector's surplus, contracts, prices, and pace of production. Furthermore, EPG has fundamental foreign policy implications because of the need to secure a safety perimeter within which the revolutionary domestic changes can happen.

In order to achieve their domestic and foreign policy goals, governments undertaking EPG would therefore seek to maximize operational control to make the clearest statement of resource ownership, at least on a symbolic level. From that point of departure, EPG would prefer contracts in which private local or foreign investors are exclusively operators paid an extraction fee, or paid through share contracts, then taxed as much as possible. That revenue flow from either royalties or taxes—or most likely a

Table 1.4 Sample Characteristics of Energy as a Political Good

Aspects of Energy Policy	General Characteristics
Ownership	State monopoly. Private operators might be allowed in joint ventures.
Regulation and prices	Extensive in operational aspects to maintain control of private operators and, especially, of the state enterprise itself. Most attention given to the control of financial flows and maximization of subsidized prices.
Taxation and rents	Highest possible royalties and special taxes, even if they diminish investments.
Operational mode	Foreign or privately owned operators allowed, with best areas given to state operator. Joint ventures with local private or state firms.
Market failures	State-directed exploration, production, and distribution investments.

combination of both—seeks to maximize the flow of funds to the state to finance the goal of social and economic change. Beyond the flow of funds to the state, the largest and widest possible provision of energy subsidies is another cornerstone of EPG, as that creates another source of popular support for this model, especially from those who benefit less from social programs (i.e., the wealthy and the urban middle classes). These subsidies are by conception different than those sometimes present in ECG, which are designed to help industrial development and not necessarily to increase popular support. Moreover, in contrast to ECG, there is little consideration of directly linking energy sector policies with the development of the local economy through industrial linkages and contracts.[21]

While both types of governments—those that undertake ECG (energy as a common good) and those that undertake EPG (energy as a political good)—intervene heavily in the sector, their aims, and therefore direction, are very different. While ECG seeks a medium- to long-term goal in the type of economy a country has via industrial upgrading and technology transfer, EPG leverages its energy sector in order to change social and economic relations in its domestic society in the short term via state investments in social policy, nationalizations, and consumer subsidies.

Energy as a Market, Common, or Political Good in Latin America

Adapting this analytical framework to improve upon the visions of RN in Latin America requires acceptance that reality across the region is indeed very complex, impeding neat characterizations for each country in one of these three categories. Table 1.5 attempts, however, to fit each country into one of these frames, understanding them as best if still insufficient descriptors of energy policies in each nation.

The following paragraphs provided a short description of the policies applied in each country in the 1990–2015 period to explain their location in this categorization.

Energy as a market good (EMG) was more popular in Latin America during the 1990s than it is today, as most of the region embarked on a series of neoliberal reforms that liberalized trade and investment and privatized state assets, including those of state energy firms. In the case of Argentina (described in detail below), the whole of the industry was privatized and the regulatory framework modified to maximize opportunities for investors vis-à-vis consumers and industry, while in other cases, such as Chile, Bolivia, and Peru, privatization was partial and a state energy company with regulatory capacity was preserved as a marginal producer.[22] Pricing was only controlled to avoid monopoly rents but subsidies were eliminated, while state-guaranteed loans were simultaneously provided to energy producers and distributors to improve infrastructure for import (Chile) and even for export (Bolivia, Peru, and Argentina).[23] Colombia, a late entrant into EMG, reduced taxes and royalties for the sector in the early 2000s in an attempt to bring in new investors and develop new production from existing reserves, while simultaneously partially privatizing its state energy firm and subsidizing the construction of export infrastructure such as pipelines and port terminals.[24]

Energy as a common good (ECG) has traditionally been the preferred mode for energy policies in Latin America since the mid-twentieth century. Those countries that managed to maintain such policies under the pressures of neoliberalism in the 1990s did so by mixing market forces and private investment into what had previously been a more rigidly controlled sector. Brazil (described in detail below), Venezuela, Ecuador, and

Table 1.5 Energy Policies in Selected Latin American Countries, 1990–2015

	1990	1995	2000	2005	2010	2015
Argentina		Market			Common	
Bolivia		Market			Political	
Brazil		Common				
Chile		Market				
Colombia		Common			Market	
Ecuador		Common			Political	
Mexico		Political			Common	
Peru		Market			Common	
Venezuela		Common			Political	

Colombia (up to the early 2000s) engaged private investors in exploration and distribution while seeking to keep production and refining in state hands.[25] That inclusion of private—mostly foreign—investors required, in turn, reductions in royalties and liberalization of the operational regulatory framework to allow foreign contracting of expertise and the import of new technologies. Ironically, as this flexibilization of ECG was bearing fruit, several of the adopting countries, such as Venezuela and Ecuador, changed their model altogether to one that privileges the maximization of rent over developmental spillovers.[26] In other cases, such as Brazil, the change has been more gradual, seeking to balance the former with the latter.[27]

Finally, energy as a political good (EPG) has been the ascendant tendency in the region, expanding from the original model in Mexico to Bolivia, Ecuador, and Venezuela since the early 2000s. Perhaps that trend has given impetus to the more simplistic interpretations of resource nationalism. Nonetheless, EPG has existed in Latin America since the 1930s—namely, in Mexico, where it assumed evolving forms that initially gave more emphasis to industrialization goals, only to later become an almost exclusive instrument to minimize taxation in the local economy, particularly on local capitalists.[28] The version appearing nowadays in the region, with the leading examples of Venezuela, Bolivia, and Ecuador, focuses instead on state ownership of all reserves and joint ventures between state and foreign capital in extraction and refining. This model prioritizes current rent extraction above all else, be that industrialization spillovers or the search for future reserves.[29] In a sense, it is similar to EMG as it considers the energy sector exclusively from the perspective of the financial surplus it generates, without giving it any distinct value of its own. But in the praxis of EPG, the heavy-handed intervention of state actors, or the leading roles assigned to them over private investors, makes it more similar to ECG.

Illustrative Cases

The following two cases illustrate in more detail the different types of energy policies identified in this chapter. The first deals with Argentine economic policy from the 1990s to the present, as it changed from an EMG framework to one best characterized as ECG. In the second case, Brazil demonstrates the policy movements inside ECG, as it includes elements from a more market-oriented perspective along with another, more political approach. The goal of this section is to show that, beyond any typology, what matters when it comes to more accurately analyzing energy policies is their overall national political and economic context.

Argentina's Energy Path from Marketable to Common Good

Energy policy in Argentina has been part and parcel of that country's overall policy changes since the 1990s. After more than half a century of import substitution industrialization, the Carlos Menem administration, which came into office in 1989, embarked on a series of radical pro-market reforms that comprehensively deregulated and liberalized the economy, and it brought in massive amounts of foreign direct investment (FDI). To this end, a monetary policy that effectively tied the Argentine peso at an overvalued rate to the US dollar was used to eliminate high inflation and overvalued state assets were sold in order to reduce government debt. By the end of the 1990s, Argentina, which now ranked as one of the most deregulated economies in the western hemisphere, had signed multiple free trade agreements and reduced import barriers to attract over US$80 billion in FDI, mostly through the sale of state companies.

In terms of energy policy, this turn to neoliberal policies resulted in the sale between 1990 and 1994 of almost all state properties, including the national oil company, Yacimientos Petrolíferos Fiscales (YPF), the national gas company (Gas del Estado), all regional gas distribution networks, and the totality of the pipeline network, as well as associated facilities in seaports.[30] In all, more than US$40 billion was collected by the Argentine government, mostly from European (above all, Spanish) and US investors. Simultaneous with this privatization drive, regulatory changes along the lines of those described above as EMG were made to enforce market mechanisms in the setting of rates among producers, transporters, and distributors of energy goods, and prices were set by government in terms that would be most likely to bring in further investment. In fact, Argentina went from having subsidized energy prices for consumers and industries in the 1980s to having some of the most expensive energy rates in the Americas, adjusted by US (and not Argentine) inflation, and explicitly dollarized.[31]

The combination of ample reserves, excellent energy transportation infrastructure, and a consumer-subsidizing home market allowed the new owners of Argentine energy assets to embark on extensive plans to export surplus gas and oil to neighbouring countries, especially to Chile. The Argentine government facilitated the signing of an energy treaty with its neighbour and provided the credit guarantees to build seven pipelines that by the end of the decade were exporting billions of dollars in gas.[32]

At the end of the 1998–2002 economic crisis, the new government of Eduardo Duhalde froze and "pesofied" energy rates to shield consumers and local industry from the costs of the devaluation made in 2002. This measure passed on to the energy sector the cost of shielding the home market from international energy prices in the context of an unprecedented economic depression. Given the fiscal deficit at the time, Duhalde also imposed a 10 per cent export tariff on all commodities, which targeted mostly agricultural goods such as soybeans, but also affected oil and gas exports.

In 2003, the newly elected administration of Néstor Kirchner reaffirmed that change in policy and started building up a regulatory framework to maintain it over the long term. To further entrap and redirect the private-owned energy sector along his preferred policy lines, the Kirchner administration capped the price oil and fuel exporters could receive for their foreign sales at a fraction of international prices, reducing their incentives to sell abroad instead of on the low-priced domestic market, and for gas exporters, it directly banned exports until producers could guarantee total provisioning of the local market.[33]

The electricity market, the main consumer of gas, was reorganized with a clearing centre that provided subsidies to distributors, transporters, and producers according to their operational costs and not international prices, along the lines of a clear ECG framework. Any profits were to be reinvested in "energy bonds," which were to be used by the government to construct more electricity-generation plants to keep up with the explosive growth of consumption, itself a by-product of economic recovery and subsidized consumer and industrial rates. The ECG framework also applied here as the government basically appropriated any profits from the private sector and then assigned them to firms chosen to construct new power plants. A nuclear power plant, a huge hydroelectric dam (Yacyretá), and a series of gas-powered plants were thus finished in the first decade of the 2000s. In all cases, Argentine engineering and construction firms were assigned the most important contracts, in clear contrast to the power-generation plants built in the 1990s by foreign investors, who usually brought firms from their own countries.

This ECG strategy of imprisoning foreign investors from the previous EMG stage suffered from a significant weakness. YPF, the main oil and gas producer, now in the hands of Spain's Repsol, could not be legally forced to increase exploration to maintain or increase production levels. Other smaller producers followed suit, speculating that the government would have to accept price increases in order to bring its investment strike to an end. However, the Néstor Kirchner and Cristina Fernández administrations preferred to create a state entity, ENARSA, which since 2007 has imported sizeable quantities of gas and other fuels needed to feed the ever-growing demand for energy in the local economy.[34] By 2010, the government had locked itself into its combination of growth-accelerating policies such as energy subsidies to create an environment of accelerating inflation. In that context, subsidies could not be undone without a further acceleration of expected inflation, which in turn weakened more fiscal accounts and made the import of energy to maintain the scheme more expensive.

Just as the tug-of-war between energy producers and the government seemed to be moving in favour of the former, the Fernández government took ECG to a different level, expropriating control of YPF from Repsol in 2012 and bringing in a new set of foreign investors from China and Chevron in the United States to develop shale gas and oil reserves recently discovered (but not exploited) by YPF. The newly nationalized firm would allocate all profits to reinvestment to bring energy production up to self-sufficiency, while embarking on systematic policies of import substitution of inputs and services for the energy industry. Meanwhile, the government continues to subsidize consumer and industrial rates and to import energy goods to cover the deficit to the tune of US$10 billion in 2014.[35]

Brazil's Experimentation with Energy as a Common Good

Energy production and distribution in Brazil have long been considered matters of national security. Since its founding in the 1950s until the 1970s, Petrobras, or Petróleo Brasileiro, was led by generals from the armed forces, and its strategy for development was closely aligned with national defence and territorial control.[36] The procurement of energy inputs for the economy was seen as an issue of national security, articulated by plans to purchase imported energy goods from diversified but diplomatically allied sources such as the United States and Middle Eastern and North African countries.[37] The surplus obtained from the sale of this imported energy in the domestic market was then reinvested in highly ambitious and systematic exploration schemes in the Amazon and on the Atlantic coast, targets also chosen for national security considerations. Such efforts met success starting in the 1970s, when the Campos fields close to Rio de Janeiro started to bring in significant production.[38]

Until the late 1980s, major emphasis along the lines of ECG was put into developing local providers for the energy industry, and into a downstream industrial complex to process imported and locally produced outputs in refineries and petrochemical plants. In order to create a geographically diversified development matrix, hydroelectric dams were built across the country, from the Northeast to the Amazon, an effort undertaken in coordination with Paraguay in order to expand Brazil's area of diplomatic influence in the Southern Cone. Energy policy thus took on a tripartite goal of promoting local industrial linkages, seeking autonomy from international markets, and developing regional assertiveness, as was the case with other areas of public policy, such as general industrial development and the territorial expansion of export agriculture.

During the 1990s, as a wave of neoliberal perspectives on development gained greater currency in Brazil, the Fernando Collor, Itamar Franco, and Fernando Cardoso administrations proceeded to partially undo this ECG model by privatizing most of the electricity-generating plants and urban distribution networks. Given the massive protests against this policy, Petrobras was exempted and only two-thirds of its shares turned over to the market, while the government kept more than 50 per cent of voting rights.[39] Further deregulation facilitated the entry into the market of private firms, including foreign ones, in exploration, production, and commercialization of both oil and electricity. Meanwhile, gas-powered generation was included in the energy mix with imported gas from Bolivia, a process spearheaded by Petrobras and taking as an example the similar venture undertaken with Paraguay in the 1970s with the Itaipu Dam.

In terms of regulation, the Cardoso administration moved slowly but decisively to bring market forces, foreign investors, and market prices into energy policy-making, just as it was simultaneously doing the same with other parts of the economy, such as telecommunications, infrastructure, and other natural resource industries such as mining.[40] A separate set of regulatory agencies, independent from the federal government, were set up to regulate electricity markets and the allocation of exploration rights, which effectively created firewalls to protect energy policy from political pressures in the allocation of contracts and the setting of consumer or industrial prices.[41] The results of this opening were a very significant flow of FDI and Brazilian private investment in the energy sector, either through the purchase of privatized facilities or the acquisition of stocks and bonds from the partially privatized Petrobras.

With the arrival of the Lula Da Silva administration in 2003, Brazil moved the pendulum back toward a more conventional ECG plan that added successive layers of local content clauses to new auctions for exploration blocks for oil and gas, and set demands for local contracting in the construction of new hydroelectric dams and power plants. The independent regulatory agencies originally established by the Cardoso administration were gradually starved of funds and policy capacity, while the Brazilian executive, especially the Office of the Chief of the Civil Service, has taken control of energy policy, including rates charged to consumers, industry, and energy wholesalers or distributors. Together with the Ministry of Mines and Energy (MME), this office has reasserted regulatory control over the energy sector, particularly after it came under the leadership of Dilma Rousseff, who had previously served as minister in charge of the MME.[42]

In addition to centralization and an increased emphasis on realigning the provision of energy with the market needs of Brazilian domestic industry and construction companies, the Da Silva administration ordered the Brazilian National Bank for Economic and Social Development to take the lead when it comes to financing energy and infrastructure projects.[43] This decision has made this institution central to the development of energy policy, once again strengthening government control over markets in regards to strategy and investment allocation.[44]

Once sizeable new oil and gas reserves were discovered by Petrobras in the Santos Basin (Tupi fields) in 2007, the government's position on energy changed again, still further in the direction of ECG. These new resources, which analysts estimate are four times bigger than pre-existing national reserves, will be regulated by another entirely new framework that gives central control to Petrobras and relegates foreign firms to the position of production operators.[45] Significantly, this scheme allows for the participation of a new set of entrants, state-owned firms from China, with which several years' worth of export agreements have already been pre-arranged. The sum total of these changes moves energy policy in Brazil, at least as it relates to oil and gas, to where it was before the big changes of the 1990s, except that now, privileged foreign partners are other state-owned firms instead of private Western multinationals.

Conclusions and Further Research Directions

This chapter has undertaken a critical revision of the commonly used framework of resource nationalism, as applied to contemporary Latin America, and suggested two crucial aspects for improving its analysis of energy policies in the region: the inclusion of wider national development goals in the construction of energy policies, and exclusion of the normative understanding of the roles that states and markets ought to play in this industry. This results in a more realistic understanding of the role and characteristics of energy policies in Latin America's long economic development path, and a better theory in terms of its predictive power to assess when and how countries would change their policies in regards to this crucial industry.

In order to guide these theoretical changes, the proposed framework characterized energy policies in Latin America according to how, in general terms, they view energy as an actual good—in this case, either as a market, common, or political good. If taken as a market good (EMG), energy policies are to support the interaction of supply-and-demand market forces, just as they would do in other industrial sectors, with the state in a supportive role for suppliers or producers. However, if energy is taken as a distinct and common good (ECG), energy policies instead take the role of supporting affordable access and the development of industrial and service linkages with the rest of the economy, effectively subordinating the energy sector to the wider goals set by states for their national economies. And if energy is taken as a political good (EPG), then energy policies seek the expansion of government rents to either finance the state, instead of other tax income, or to provide additional state funding to overhaul social and economic relations in the whole country. In other words, such policies aim to leverage energy resources in order to undertake a social reform or revolution.

While this chapter provides comprehensive examples from most South American countries and Mexico, not all of Latin America is represented here. Most of the countries not mentioned—such as those in Central America, or Uruguay and Paraguay—are exclusively importers of energy and, as such, have fewer alternatives when it comes to developing energy policies. Nonetheless, this characterization of energy policies inside wider national development frameworks would benefit from the inclusion of other Latin American cases, as well as from much more detailed analysis of the nations mentioned.

Additionally, this work has only addressed the oil and gas part of energy policies; it has included neither electricity generation nor new, alternative sources being developed in the region, such as biofuels, solar, or wind. Given the technical and policy differences between oil and gas, on the one side, and alternative energy sources, on the other, the theoretical comparative framework used here would definitely gain in both precision and relevance once these other aspects are included.

In conclusion, the current diversity of experiences regarding energy policy in Latin America provides a panoramic view of how energy policies are being used in the different visions of economic development. A perspective that incorporates that wider view and sidelines normative concerns over the roles played by states and markets in the energy sector will facilitate our comprehension of the meanings of energy policy in the region.

NOTES

1 David Mares, *Resource Nationalism and Energy Security in Latin America* (Houston: Baker Institute for Public Policy, Rice University, 2010); Rubén Berríos, Andrae Marak, and Scott Morgenstern, "Explaining Hydrocarbon Nationalization in Latin America," *Review of International Political Economy* 18, no. 5 (2010): 673–97; Eric Farnsworth, *Energy Security Opportunities in Latin America and the Caribbean* (Washington, DC: Council of the Americas, 2013).

2 Eleodoro Mayorga-Alba, "Revisiting Energy Policies in Latin America and Africa: A Redefinition of the Private and Public Sector Roles," *Energy Policy* 20, no. 10 (1992): 995–1004; Sidney Weintraub, ed., *Energy Cooperation in the Western Hemisphere: Benefits and Impediments* (Washington, DC: Center for Strategic and International Studies, 2007).

3 Anthony Bebbington and Jeffrey Bury, eds., *Subterranean Struggles: New Dynamics of Mining, Oil, and Gas in Latin America* (Austin: University of Texas Press, 2013): Francisco J. Monaldi, *Is Resource Nationalism Fading in Latin America? The Case of the Oil Industry* (Houston: Baker Institute for Public Policy, Rice University 2014); Joaquín Melgarejo Moreno, Mª Immaculada López Ortiz, and Borja Montaño Sanz, "From Privatisation to Nationalisation: Repsol-YPF, 1999–2012," *Utilities Policy* 26 (2013): 45–55.

4 Ian Bremmer and Robert Johnston, "The Rise and Fall of Resource Nationalism," *Survival: Global Politics and Strategy* 51, no. 2 (2009): 149–58.

5 Paul Stevens and Evelyn Dietsche, "Resource Curse: An Analysis of Causes, Experiences and Possible Ways Forward," *Energy Policy* 36, no. 1 (2008): 56–65.

6 Mares, *Resource Nationalism and Energy Security in Latin America*; Paul Stevens, "National Oil Companies and International Oil Companies in the Middle East: Under

the Shadow of Government and the Resource Nationalism Cycle," *Journal of World Energy Law and Business* 1, no. 1 (2008): 5–30.

7   Halina Ward, *Resource Nationalism and Sustainable Development: A Primer and Key Issues* (working paper, International Institute for Environment and Development, London, 2009); Jeffrey Wilson, "Understanding Resource Nationalism: Economic Dynamics and Political Institutions," *Contemporary Politics* 21, no. 4 (2015): 399–416.

8   Richard Tissot, *Latin America's Energy Future* (Discussion Paper IDB-DP-252, Inter-American Development Bank, Washington, DC, 2012).

9   Weintraub, *Energy Cooperation in the Western Hemisphere*.

10 Monaldi, *Is Resource Nationalism Fading in Latin America?*

11 Stevens, "National Oil Companies and International Oil Companies in the Middle East."

12 Raymond Vernon, *Sovereignty at Bay: The Multinational Spread of U.S. Enterprises* (New York: Basic Books, 1971); Stephen Kobrin, "Foreign Enterprise and Forced Divestment in LDCs," *International Organization* 34, no. 1 (1980): 65–88.

13 Theodore Moran, *Multinational Corporations: The Political Economy of Foreign Direct Investment* (New York: Lexington Books, 1985); Paul Evans, *Dependent Development: The Alliance of Multinational, State, and Local Capital in Brazil* (Princeton, NJ: Princeton University Press, 1979).

14 Victor Bulmer-Thomas, *The Economic History of Latin America since Independence*, 3rd ed. (New York: Cambridge University Press, 2014).

15 Patrice Franko, *The Puzzle of Latin American Economic Development* (Lanham, MD: Rowman & Littlefield, 2007).

16 Rosemary Thorp, *Progress, Poverty and Exclusion: An Economic History of Latin America* (Washington, DC: Inter-American Development Bank, 1998).

17 John Coatsworth, "Structures, Endowments, and Institutions in the Economic History of Latin America," *Latin American Research Review* 40, no. 3 (2005): 126–44.

18 Kurt Weyland, "Neopopulism and Neoliberalism in Latin America: Unexpected Affinities," *Studies in Comparative International Development* 31, no. 3 (1996): 3–31.

19 Eduardo Lora, *Structural Reforms in Latin America: What Has Been Reformed and How to Measure It* (Working Paper No. 466, Inter-American Development Bank, Washington, DC, 2001).

20 A similar argument is made in Christopher Simon, "Is Energy a Public Good?," *Renewable Energy World*, 2 July 2007, http://www.renewableenergyworld.com/articles/2007/07/is-energy-a-public-good-49201.html.

21 Discourses along those lines do exist in certain EPG cases, such as Bolivia and Ecuador, but the policies implemented by those countries have not yet resulted in any significant development of energy-related clusters. In other countries with EPG, such as Venezuela and Mexico, the emphasis on revenue maximization has actually reduced the clusters that did exist before, as state companies drastically lowered their purchases and investments. For examples of these policies, see David Mares, *Oil Policy Reform in*

Resource Nationalist States: Lessons from Mexico (Houston: Baker Institute for Public Policy, Rice University, 2011).

22 Lora, *Structural Reforms in Latin America.*

23 Fabio García and Pablo Garcés, *La industrialización del petróleo en América Latina y el Caribe* (Quito: Organización Latinoamericana de Energía, 2013).

24 Robin Sickles et al., *Convergence, Regulatory Distortions, Deregulatory Dynamics and Growth Experiences of the Latin American and Brazilian Economies* (Houston: Baker Institute for Public Policy, Rice University, 2004).

25 Ariela Ruiz Caro, *La seguridad energética de América Latina y el Caribe en el contexto mundial* (Santiago: CEPAL, 2007).

26 Tissot, *Latin America's Energy Future.*

27 María José Paz Antolín and Juan Manuel Ramírez Cendrero, "How Important Are National Companies for Oil and Gas Sector Performance? Lessons from the Bolivia and Brazil Case Studies," *Energy Policy*, no. 61 (2013): 707–16.

28 Isidro Morales, *The Twilight of Mexico's State Oil Monopolism: Policy, Economic, and Political Trends in Mexico's Natural Gas Industry* (Houston: Baker Institute for Public Policy, Rice University, 2013).

29 Bianca Sarbu, *Ownership and Control of Oil: Explaining Policy Choices across Producing Countries* (London: Routledge, 2014).

30 Roberto Kozulj, *The Quest for Energy Security in Argentina* (Winnipeg: International Institute for Sustainable Development, 2010).

31 James Haselip and Clive Potter, "Post-neoliberal Electricity Market 'Re-reforms' in Argentina: Diverging from Market Prescriptions?," *Energy Policy* 38, no. 2 (2010): 1168–76.

32 David Mares, "Sector energético latinoamericano: Integración a todo gas," *Contrapunto* (Mexico City) (April–June 2006): 90–6.

33 David Mares, *The Geopolitics of Natural Gas: Political Economy of Shale Gas in Argentina* (Houston: Baker Institute for Public Policy, Rice University, 2013).

34 Melgarejo Moreno, López Ortiz, and Montaño Sanz, "From Privatisation to Nationalisation," 45–55.

35 Gabriel Di Bella et al., *Energy Subsidies in Latin America and the Caribbean: Stocktaking and Policy Challenges* (IMF Working Paper WP/15/30, International Monetary Fund, Washington DC, 2015).

36 Alberto Cisneros-Lavaller, "Latin American Geopolitics vs. Energy Patterns: Ideology, Energy Production Sustainability, and U.S. Security," *Journal of Energy and Development* 32, no. 1 (2007): 23–44.

37 José Paz, "Oil and Development in Brazil: Between an Extractive and an Industrialization Strategy," *Energy Policy*, no. 73 (2014): 501–11.

38 Adilson de Oliveira, *Energy Security in South America: The Role of Brazil* (Winnipeg: International Institute for Sustainable Development, 2010).

39 Chris Ellsworth and Eric Gibbs, *Brazil's Natural Gas Industry: Missed Opportunities on the Road to Liberalizing Markets* (Houston: Baker Institute for Public Policy, Rice University, 2004).

40 Hirdan Katarina de Medeiros Costa and Edmilson dos Santos, "Institutional Analysis and the 'Resource Curse' in Developing Countries," *Energy Policy*, no. 63 (2013): 788–95.

41 Jewellord Tolentino Nem Singh, "Towards Post-neoliberal Resource Politics? The International Political Economy of Oil and Copper in Brazil and Chile," *New Political Economy* 19, no. 3 (2014): 329–58.

42 Singh, "Towards Post-neoliberal Resource Politics?"

43 De Oliveira, *Energy Security in South America*.

44 Michael Zisuh Ngoasong, "How International Oil and Gas Companies Respond to Local Content Policies in Petroleum-Producing Developing Countries: A Narrative Enquiry," *Energy Policy*, no. 73 (2014): 471–9.

45 Luciana Braga and Alexandre S. Szklo, "The Recent Regulatory Changes in Brazilian Petroleum Exploration and Exploitation Activities," *Journal of World Energy Law and Business* 7, no. 2 (2014): 120–39.

Primary Energy Consumption and Economic Growth in Chile, 1844-2010

César Yáñez Gallardo

This chapter presents a reflection on the path of the Chilean economy throughout the nineteenth and twentieth centuries, using the consumption of modern primary energy (coal, oil, hydroelectricity, and natural gas) as the main indicator. This is the result of the collective work of a large team of Chilean and Spanish researchers who systematically gathered series of apparent consumption of modern energy sources for all Latin America countries.[1] The results presented here correspond only to the Chilean case between 1844 and 2000.[2] The main ideas underlying this work is that the primary consumption of fossil energy marks the transition toward economic modernity, and that the history such consumption helps to explain long-term economic trends. These ideas were first championed in 1994 by Vaclav Smil in his pioneering work *Energy in World History*.[3] In that book, Smil asserts that, thanks to the contribution of fossil fuels, and coal specifically, it was possible to overcome centuries of declining economic growth and initiate an era of steady increases in the productivity scale. The English Industrial Revolution of the mid-eighteenth century was based on this distinctive feature (increasing productivity based on the technical potential of machinery driven by steam coal), which laid the foundations for an economic system capable of generating surpluses well above subsistence levels—which in turn explains the inequality of later periods.[4] In any case, it is important to note the complexity of the relationship between economic growth and energy consumption. Historical evidence indicates that there is a close relationship between the two variables. Throughout the twentieth century, both increased sixteen-fold worldwide. However, the amount of energy per product (energy intensity) and the path of energy efficiency are not similar in all countries, not even among countries with the same level of economic development. Specific features of technological development, economic policies, the endowment of natural energy resources, and energy dependency help explain differences in national paths.

The aim of this chapter, then, is to review how the Chilean economy set off on the path to modernization. The evidence on modern energy consumption suggests that Chile was "blessed" with coal deposits in the areas of Arauco and Concepción, which were exploited from the 1840s on—relatively early in the Latin American and international context.[5] The increasing introduction of coal into the Chilean financial system since the mid-nineteenth century was behind the modernization of the systems of production, as reflected in improvements in productivity. By the late nineteenth century, Chile faced the dilemma of overcoming what I call the "middle income trap." Alejandro Foxley posited in 2012 that Chile and other Latin American countries with incomes between US$9,000 and US$22,000 at PPP (purchasing power parity) were "halfway to becoming advanced economies."[6] The present chapter argues that Chile had faced this situation a century earlier and that the cause was the introduction of coal in production and transportation activities, an important component of which was national fuel. However, in the 1914–90 period, the country's economy was challenged by significant restrictions to the fuel supply, which had a negative impact on economic modernization. The high external dependence on oil led to a difficult transition between fossil fuels, making the transition from steam engines to the use of oil and combustion engines a difficult one. A very rigid energy matrix was also behind delays to the process of electrification in Chile, adversely affecting the process of industrialization, which required modern energy sources.

Energy consumption and economic growth in Chile

The relationship between modern energy consumption and Chile's long-term economic growth broadly concurs with Smil's assertions, which also highlight the particularities of the Chilean case (see table 2.1). In the first place, throughout the twentieth century, the expansion of energy consumption and GDP (at PPP) developed as smoothly as it had in the international context. Energy and GDP grew 29.5 times between 1900 and 2005. In any case, the global average, as Smil suggested, only multiplied by sixteen in both indicators, a figure that Chile reached in the mid-1990s. The strong economic growth of the late-twentieth and early twenty-first centuries explains the difference between Chile and the world average. Beyond any historical specificity, as it was demonstrated, the Chilean economy required proportional amounts of energy to sustain its economic growth. The Chilean economy also followed the international trend regarding energy intensity (units of energy per unit of GDP). In 1900, Chile required 126 units of energy per unit of production, the same number as in 2005. Yet, in contrast to the experiences of countries where Smil observed a steady decline in energy intensity, Chile's stages of contraction and expansion after 1930 were rather erratic.

Empirical evidence suggests that the processes of economic development underwent an initial phase in which more and more energy was consumed per unit of production, and that this later switched to the opposite trend. Technical change was crucial in this regard. More efficient energy converters enabled those countries that accelerated the increase in productivity to do so by means of energy-saving machinery. Yet the specific paths were very different, influenced by specific historical elements.

The specific evolution of energy intensity in the Chilean economy shows steady growth from the mid-1800s until 1917. This is the period when coal and steam engines took centre stage. The entry of oil-based fuels during the First World War, which saw the introduction of combustion engines and turbines, led to an abrupt change in the trend until 1930. Thereafter, the behaviour of energy intensity set a trend toward stability, with relatively few intense, short-term variations.

The comparison with the United Kingdom and Wales, and especially with the United States, highlights the differences in the levels of modern

Table 2.1 Energy Consumption and Economic Growth

Year	Energy per Ton of Coal					Product and Energy	
	Total	Coal	Oil	Natural Gas	Hydroelectricity	GDP	Energy Intensity
1850	25	25				1,313	19
1900	816	800	16			6,492	126
1930	2,047	889	981		117	12,195	168
1950	2,835	1,848	1,169		182	22,352	127
1970	7,290	1,225	4,455	1,130	480	49,011	149
2005	24,151	2,758	11,300	7,831	2,262	191,954	126

energy use between advanced countries and relatively underdeveloped countries like Chile. In the nineteenth century, both the United Kingdom and the United States had abundant coal reserves in the subsoil that were used extensively to support their industrialization. The availability of fossil fuels in their territories allowed them to sustain economic development and incorporate equipment into their production processes. In any case, there is no rule that directly relates energy intensity to the levels of development achieved. The United Kingdom came to consume ten times more energy per product than Chile, while the United States was ten times more intense, energetically speaking, than the United Kingdom. The structural characteristics of the sectors in which economic modernization was based were (and still are) factors determining the level of energy consumed per product. This appears to be confirmed by comparing Chile with two countries within its economic environment, Argentina and Brazil: the levels are much closer and have clear periods of convergence.

It is valuable when comparing the paths of long-term energy intensities to consider the trends. England, which had reached industrial maturity in the mid-nineteenth century, began to reduce energy intensity as soon as it ceased to grow extensively based on fossil resources while seeking greater energy efficiency. The United States, meanwhile, reached industrial maturity before the First World War. From that moment, it turned toward greater energy efficiency, reducing the amount of energy per unit of production. In both cases, the reduction in energy intensity is a historical trend that is projected to the present. Chile, by contrast, had only five years of sharp decline between 1917 and 1922, followed by a long period of erratic behaviour, with a pronounced tendency to stagnate in energy intensity. This trend contrasts clearly with Argentina and Brazil, which increased the energy per unit of product.[7]

The cause of the stagnation is likely to be found in the nature of the energy transition between fossil fuels (the move from coal to oil) and the scant importance of hydroelectric power within the Chilean energy matrix. In 1970, hydropower accounted for only 6.5 per cent of primary energy consumption in Chile, and in 2005, less than 10 percent. The probable effect has been an economy with increasing energy dependence and increasing restrictions on energy consumption, especially at a time when industry required a fluid and cheap electricity supply.

Coal, the Key to the Prosperity of Nineteenth-Century Chile

One hundred years before Alejandro Foxley drew attention to the trap of middle-income countries, Chile confronted a similar situation. Even from the late nineteenth century, the Chilean economy (as in Argentina and Uruguay) showed a dynamism that resulted in a per capita GDP similar to a middle-income country—slightly ahead of Italy, Spain, and Sweden, though far from the United Kingdom (see table 2.2). Historians have argued that institutional reasons can explain Chilean prosperity in the nineteenth century,[8] forgetting to analyze changes in the production structure that are associated with the introduction of fossil energy sources in the production system. To what extent can we explain Chile's economic prosperity during the nineteenth century and until 1913 by the elite consensus regarding the need to impose the oligarchic social order? Luis Ortega has suggested a different explanation, but he has not yet clarified how important it was that Chile joined other economies with an inorganic energy base in the mid-1840s.[9]

The precedents of the coal era are little known. Chile's energy history is only starting to be written. One estimate of the number of inhabitants and their distribution over the territory allows us to state that in 1843, 15 billion tons of firewood were produced and consumed, an equivalent of

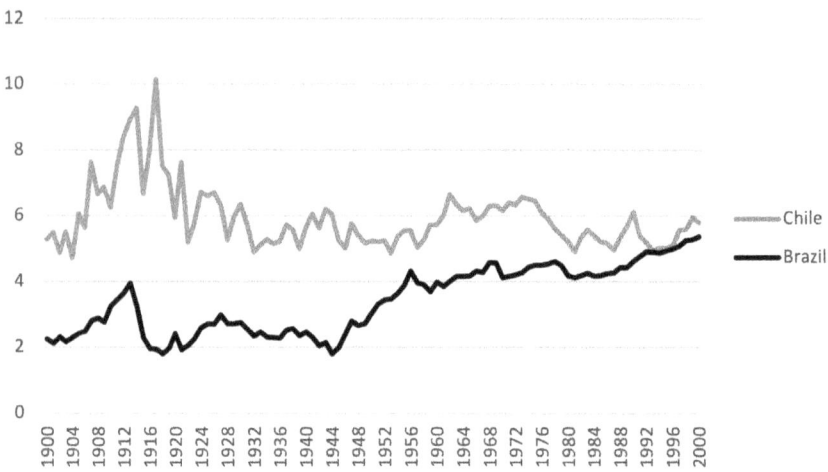

Figure 2.1a Changes in Energy Intensity of Chile Compared to Brazil (TOE per Unit of GDP PPP)

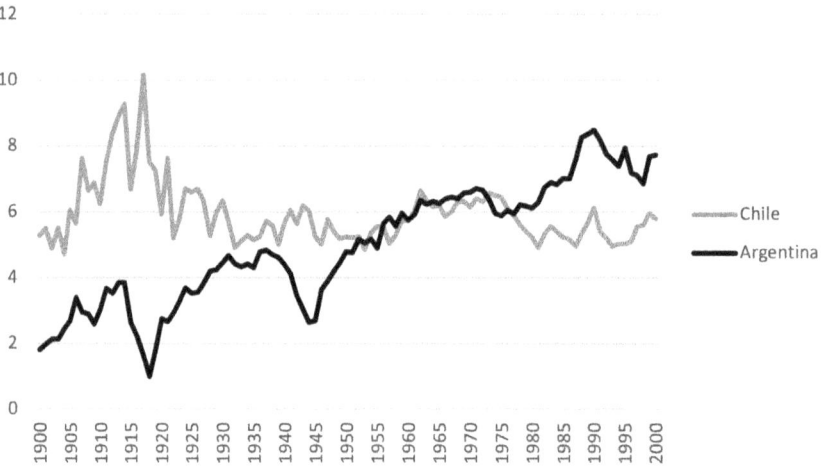

Figure 2.1b Changes in Energy Intensity of Chile Compared to Argentina (TOE per Unit of GDP PPP)

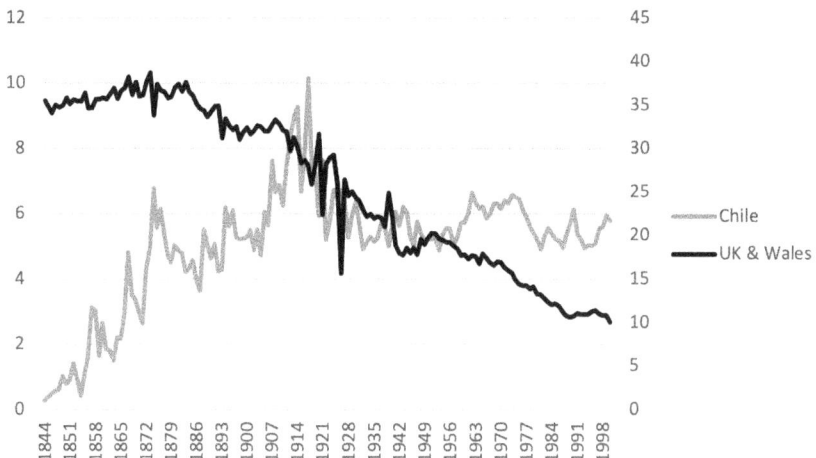

Figure 2.1c Changes in Energy Intensity of Chile Compared to UK and Wales (TOE per Unit of GDP PPP)

Figure 2.1d Changes in Energy Intensity of Chile Compared to US (TOE per Unit of GDP PPP)

Table 2.2 GDP per Capita at PPP and Annual Growth Rates, 1800–1913

Year	Chile	Argentina	Uruguay	Latin America	Spain	Italy	Sweden	United Kingdom
GDP per Capita at PPP US$ of 1990 (Maddison Project)								
1800	626	931	1,036		916	1,363	857	2,097
1820	605	998	1,165	639		1,511	888	2,074
1850	910	1,251	1,468		1,079	1,481	1,076	2,330
1870	1,290	1,468	2,181	794	1,207	1,542	1,345	3,190
1890	1,966	2,416	2,174	1,052	1,624	1,690	1,635	4,009
1900	2,194	2,875	2,219	1,181	1,786	1,855	2,083	4,492
1913	2,988	3,797	3,310	1,586	2,056	2,305	2,874	4,921
Growth Rate (%) GDP per Capita								
1800–20	-0.17	0.35	0.59			0.52	0.18	-0.06
1820–50	1.37	0.76	0.77			-0.07	0.64	0.39
1850–70	1.76	0.80	2.00		0.56	0.20	1.12	1.58
1870–90	2.13	2.52	-0.02	1.42	1.49	0.46	0.98	1.15
1890–1900	1.10	1.75	0.21	1.16	0.96	0.94	2.45	1.14
1900–13	2.40	2.16	3.12	2.29	1.09	1.68	2.51	0.70

Source: Maddison Project.

542 tons of oil equivalent (TOE). Of these, 70 per cent were in the central zone of the country, between the Aconcagua and Maule Rivers, where most of the population lives. Moreover, the northern region known as the "Norte Chico" had little vegetation suitable for use as fuel, and the southern zone, rich in forests, was scarcely populated.

The main fuel in the country was firewood, a readily available resource used mainly for processing food in the domestic domain and for the heating of homes. A fraction of the firewood (the exact amount remains difficult to identify) was used in metal foundries. Mauricio Folchi has documented with qualitative sources the deforestation of the Norte Chico as a result of the intensive use of firewood in copper foundries.[10] Prior to this, in the eighteenth century, the gold-mining boom gave rise to the use of a variety of techniques for grinding the mineral—known as the "Chilean mill"—that adapted to hydraulic energy while at the same time employing ancient Inca techniques using human and animal energy.[11]

Until the arrival of coal as a fuel, the growth rate of the economy was sluggish—typical of organic economies. It was only from the 1840s that Chile entered the economic modernity of rapid growth thanks to the arrival of steam engines on the scene (see table 2.2 and figures 2.2 and 2.3).

Chile's economic growth accelerated in the first half of the nineteenth century (see growth rates in table 2.2), which is explained mainly by the introduction of coal to its economic activities. The Chilean "path toward capitalism" is full of coal—to paraphrase Ortega. The only means of escape from the Malthusian trap of decreasing returns and constant 1.73 per cent compound annual growth rates throughout the nineteenth century (note that in the twentieth century, the compound annual growth rate was only 1.6 per cent) was to stop relying solely on organic energy sources. The fact that Chile started exploiting coal deposits in the area of Concepción in the 1840s, and that this was on the route of English steamboats connecting to the Pacific Ocean, explains Chile's advantages—similar only to those of Cuba—compared to other Latin American countries.[12] Between 1844 and 1913, Chile consumed 33,804,440 tons of coal (as measured in TOE), starting with 6,314 TOE up to 1,731,145 TOE. The progression can be seen in figure 2.2. Chile produced coal during this entire period, exporting a small fraction into neighbouring countries (especially Bolivia), and complementing the requirements of its economy with imports coming mainly from the United Kingdom, the United States, Germany, France, Belgium, and occasionally from Australia. However, the period is not homogeneous because there is a major change from 1880. Prior to 1851, when the steepest climb started, almost all coal consumption was domestic, meeting the needs of metal smelting, processing refractory bricks, milling, food manufacturing, and railways.[13] The compound annual growth rate of coal consumption for this period was 12 per cent. After 1880, the period known in Chile as the "Nitrate Cycle" (*Ciclo Salitrero*), the demand for coal continued to expand, increasing more than three times but at a

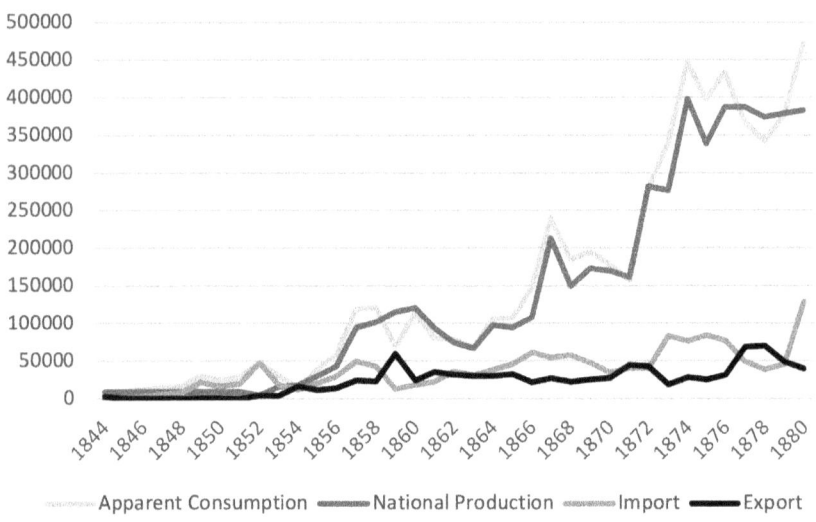

Figure 2.2a Apparent Consumption of Coal, 1844–1880

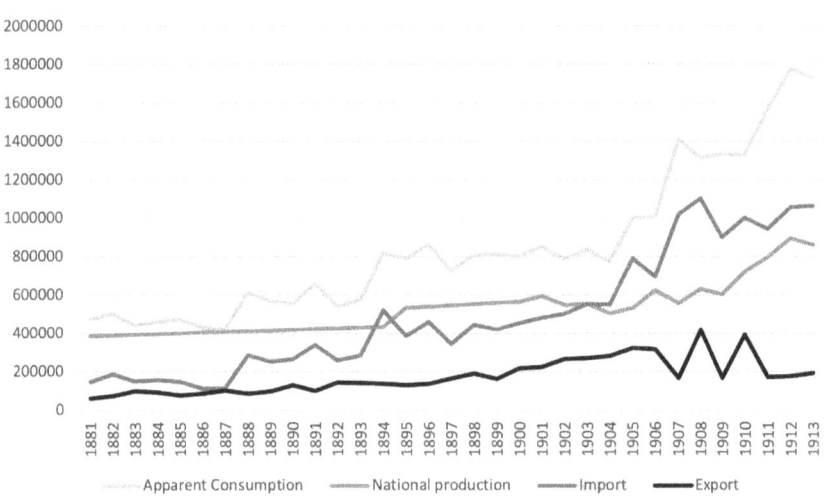

Figure 2.2b Apparent Consumption of Coal, 1881–1913

more moderate cumulative annual growth rate of 4 per cent (7.5 per cent between 1903 and 1913), and with a growing supply of imported coal. At the start of the First World War, Chile was consuming more foreign than domestic coal. The nitrate export economy invigorated the whole economy. Mining, industry, and transport were gradually modernized technologically alongside the use of coal and steam engines.

The introduction of fossil fuels into the Chilean economy allowed a portion of productive activities to avoid the structural risk of recurring cycles of decreasing returns. From the 1850s on, therefore, sustained economic growth relied on those sectors with the capacity to incorporate technology associated with the use of coal as an energy source. By 1860, there were 132 steam engines in Chile, 38 (29 per cent) of which were locomotives for railways, 16 (12 per cent) for coal mining (exploitation and driving), and 44 (33 per cent) for processing industries.[14] Most of these machines, according to the 1860 Statistical Yearbook, still used firewood as an energy source. But in the following decades, coal occupied all the niches of opportunity provided by the Chilean economy. The Statistical Yearbook reports that in 1910–11, 40 per cent of fossil fuels were consumed by mining (34.5 per cent of nitrate), 24 per cent by railways, and the remaining third by industry and other services such as gas and electricity. The Chilean economy not only grew but was also transformed. The US$600 per PPP of the early nineteenth century is an expression of a subsistence economy caught in the Malthusian trap. The US$2,988 PPP in 1913 shows an economy characterized by capitalism and following the modernizing currents of the time. Fossil fuels generated a modern segment in the Chilean economy leading the economic growth.

Economic growth in the sixty years before 1913 correlates perfectly with coal consumption in Chile. However, it would be a mistake to think that this means firewood consumption was not relevant. My own estimates highlight that firewood production in Chile continued for a long time, without experiencing a sudden drop in absolute terms. Figure 2.3, which shows the Chilean energy matrix, is most telling here: although firewood production fell proportionally, it was not until 1907 that it ceded its hegemony to fossil fuels. Despite this, clear signs of firewood's diminishing importance only emerged again in the 1930s.

Table 2.3 GDP per Capita at PPP and Annual Growth Rates, 1913-2010

Year	Chile	Argentina	Uruguay	Latin America	Spain	Italy	Sweden	United States
GDP per Capita at PPP US$ of 1990 (Maddison Project)								
1913	2,988	3,797	3,310	1,586	2,056	2,305	2,874	5,301
1929	3,455	4,367	3,847	2,053	2,739	2,778	4,063	6,899
1950	3,677	4,987	4,659	2,696	2,189	3,172	6,739	9,561
1973	5,034	7,962	4,974	4,878	7,661	10,414	13,494	16,689
1985	5,030	6,835	5,560	5,461	9,722	14,010	16,189	20,717
2010	13,883	10,256	11,526	7,770	16,797	18,520	25,306	30,491
Growth Rate (%) GDP per Capita								
1913-29	0.56	0.54	0.58	1.00	1.11	0.72	1.34	1.02
1929-50	0.30	0.63	0.92	1.31	-1.06	0.63	2.44	1.57
1950-73	1.38	2.05	0.28	2.61	5.60	5.30	3.06	2.45
1973-85	-0.01	-1.26	0.93	0.95	2.01	2.50	1.53	1.82
1990-2010	4.14	1.64	2.96	1.42	2.21	1.12	1.80	1.56

Source: Maddison Project.

In the Chilean economy, firewood has doggedly refused to disappear—in the first place, because it is an abundant resource, and secondly, because modernizing forces have not reached the furthest corners of the country. The excruciating inequality that has characterized Chile's economic history has gradually left behind those economic activities dependent on traditional energies throughout the nineteenth century, and indeed for most of the twentieth century, up to the present.[15]

Society also changed during this period. New business conglomerates of national and foreign origin, new segments of the working class, and new economic relations gave rise to political and labour conflicts.[16] The state acquired new capacities, starting with increased spending on infrastructure and intervention in social issues.[17] But modernization did not reach all socio-economic strata. Extensive rural and urban areas remained on the periphery of modernity, their inhabitants surviving on incomes that bordered on subsistence levels.[18]

Economic Crises and Energy Transitions in the Last Hundred Years

The last century of Chilean economic history is characterized by two contractionary and two expansive cycles. The interwar period of 1913–50, including the Great Depression, and the period between 1973 and 1985, covering much of the military dictatorship and the foreign debt crisis, saw very low growth. In contrast, the years of strong public intervention in the economy, as in the 1950–73 period (affected by an unprecedented population growth), and the turn of the twenty-first century—both characterized by a strong expansion within an ultra-liberal policy framework—were periods of moderate growth (see table 2.3).

This hundred-year period also saw the complication of the energy matrix (see figure 2.3) and a transition between fossil fuels (from coal to oil and natural gas) coupled with the insufficient expansion of hydro power. These economic crises have affected the country's energy modernization by halting investments that would have allowed the transformation of the energy matrix, which has in turn resulted in continuous energy bottlenecks that eventually weigh on economic growth. Unlike the nineteenth century, during which the country had its own energy resources (coal), in the aftermath of 1913, Chile has become increasingly dependent on fossil fuel energy, delaying its commitment to hydro power and other alternative energy sources that might have satisfied demand with less tension on prices.

The economic crisis that began with the First World War represented a drastic contraction in the consumption of modern energy.[19] In 1913, Chile consumed a total of 2,227,000 TOE (0.60 tons per capita); in 1915, this figure had dropped to 1,386,000 (0.36 tons per capita)—a 40 per cent decrease in energy use in just two years. With ups and downs, the twenties saw a worse decline. But the Great Depression caused a further drop in energy consumption, 1,055,000 TOE (0.22 tons per capita). The recovery of the 1930s and '40s (including the Second World War) was very slow. Only

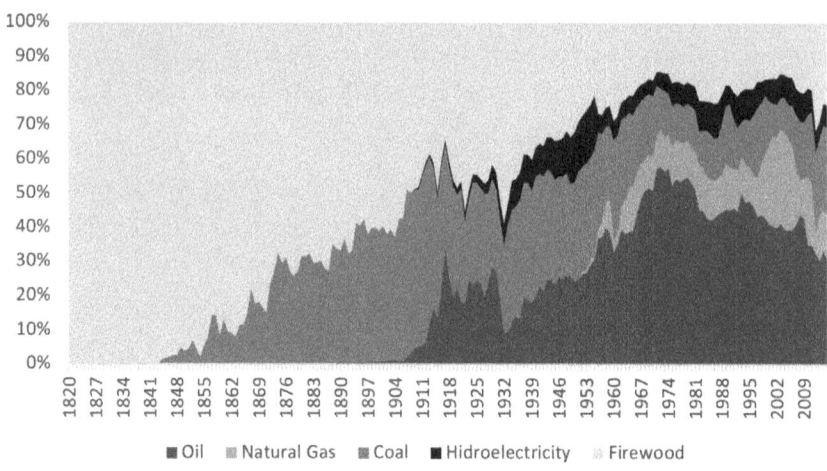

Figure 2.3 Evolution of the Chilean Energy Matrix, 1944–2010

in 1961 were the per-capita consumption levels of the pre–First World War period recovered. Half a century of stagnation in modern energy consumption was induced by the contraction of the economic activity. How to explain what happened?

Everything points to the energy transition depicted in figure 2.4. During the First World War and for the following twenty-five years, the substitution of coal by oil was interrupted. With the collapse of exports of natural resources (mainly salt), activities considered technically archaic—represented in this case by the oldest steam machines, which were also the least energy efficient—were abandoned. Hence, energy intensity dropped sharply until just before the Great Depression, as we saw in figure 2.1. Chile also lost purchasing power abroad during this period, preventing the importation of part of the coal purchased in foreign markets. It also had to contain the expansion of oil consumption, which was entirely imported; this affected the expansion of the most modern and efficient energy activities. Energy intensity stopped declining and tended toward recovery in the 1930s. For the Chilean economy, the effects of this double crisis of export and energy consumption were doubly negative. On the one hand, it

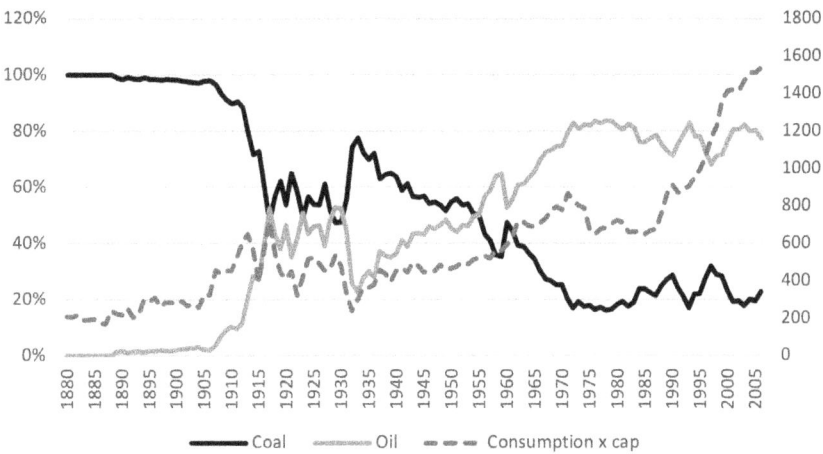

Figure 2.4 Energy Consumption per Capita and Energy Transition

destroyed economic activity, probably of lower productivity, lower energy efficiency, and greater labour intensiveness. On the other hand, the crisis prevented these sectors from being replaced by more modern, productive, and energy-efficient activities because there were no resources to import modern energy (oil), which was indispensable. The concurrence of lower energy consumption with lower oil consumption between 1932 and 1935 confirms this idea.

The economic recovery that started in 1933-4 was gradual and slow. Per capita GDP grew at a rate of 0.30 per cent between 1929 and 1950. External factors related to the shifting international and domestic situation, to which the change in economic policy is relevant, are behind this poor performance.[20] Contributing factors include the recovery of the energy supply, which was slower than the economic recovery, and which in turn slowed down the transition from coal to oil by almost three decades.

During the Great Depression, the country was forced to return to its original sources of coal, boosting mining in all its coal basins. The reluctance to switch from coal to oil was in part a response to the external conditions faced by the Chilean economy, which was unable to import fuel (on account of its inability to access foreign currency and the dwindling world supply of fuel), and also to the government's decision to promote domestic production to meet local demand.[21] The effort was enormous and the results unsatisfactory. The decline of the Chilean coal industry from the 1930s to the 1970s was unstoppable. In addition, oil was still difficult to import and the supply of energy, mainly for industry, remained an obstacle for decades. Reports from the engineers of the Corporación de Fomento de la Producción (CORFO) are conclusive in this regard.[22] The industrial electricity supply cannot be ensured without a constant supply of fossil fuels for thermoelectric power production. The 1939 Immediate Action Plan emphasised that an additional 100,000 tons of coal were needed. Twenty years later, in 1960, CORFO engineers reported that the electricity industry could not meet domestic demand and that constant power outages prevented an increase in industrial output. If the electricity supply remained dependent on fossil fuels, they said, and the coal industry continued to decline (as actually happened), the external power supply would put the country in position of external dependence, thereby jeopardizing plans for a successful process of industrialization. The alternative was to invest in the production of hydroelectric power.

Again, in a repeat of the drama over coal production, the effort was huge but ineffectual. Figure 2.5 reveals clearly that, although new hydroelectric power plants were opened, their place in the country's energy matrix remained insufficient. Despite the efforts made between 1945 and the late 1960s, electricity produced from water sources failed to overcome the barrier of 7 per cent of the Chilean energy matrix. The problem was not resolved, and domestic industry continued to suffer.

The economic crisis that began in 1973—and which corresponded at the international level with the first oil crisis—left its mark once more on total primary energy consumption. Once again, per capita consumption fell, this time reaching levels lower than those of 1913. At the same time, energy intensity also fell, suggesting that production units (especially factories) that used more antiquated and inefficient energy sources were closing. Chile responded to the increase in oil prices with the two options it had at hand, coal and hydroelectricity. The possibilities represented by the former were limited: the coal basins were unable to offer a solution like they had in the thirties.[23] Nevertheless, there was a new opportunity

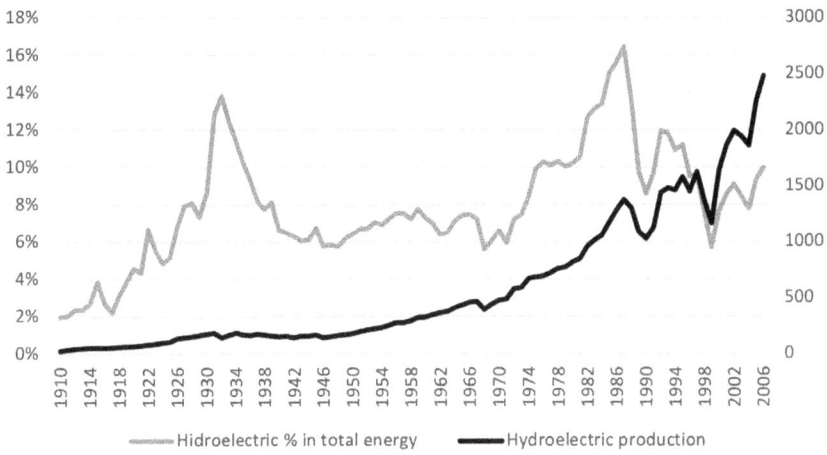

Figure 2.5 Hydroelectric Production and Percentages of Total Modern Energy

for the coal sector, which recovered a small share of the energy matrix (see figure 2.3). But these bad years for the economy were in the end a boon for hydroelectricity, the production of which increased: it henceforth came to represent 16 per cent of total primary energy consumption. The investments of the previous decades bore fruit, highlighting that in this sector of energy, long-term projection is a decisive factor.

Economic prosperity at the turn of the twenty-first century has boosted the consumption of modern energy above 1 ton (TOE) per capita for the first time in Chile's history (see figure 2.4). The barrier of 1 ton per person is significant because the countries that previously followed the path to economic development did so with similar levels of primary energy consumption. This final thought allows us to recall Foxley's analysis about the pitfalls of middle-income economies and the challenges Chile has faced on its way to development. From the point of view of the relationship between energy and the economy, this last phase of expansion continues generating risks. The main risk is that the economy will suffer energy restrictions again, though this time adjusted through prices and

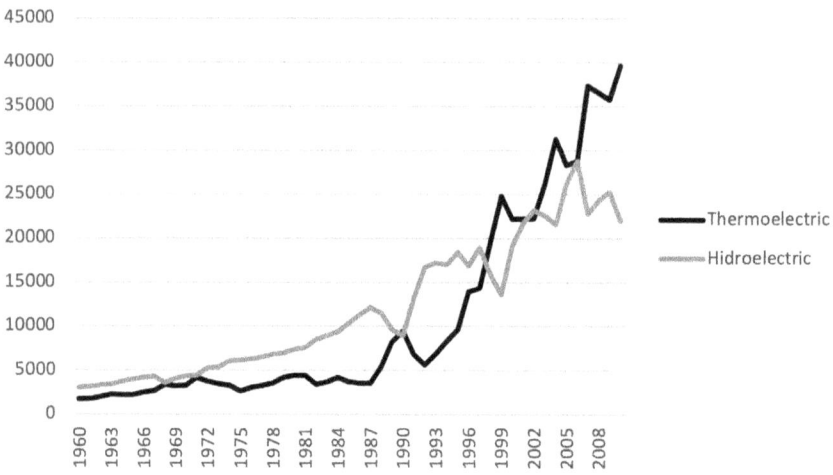

Figure 2.6 Generation of Hydro and Thermoelectricity in Chile, 1960–2010 (GWh)

not via outages, but with similar effects in terms of reducing the future growth potential of the economy.

During these years of prosperity and greater energy consumption, short-term solutions have been implemented to meet local demand—specifically, the importation of natural gas from Argentina (see figure 2.3). Imported natural gas found its opportunity in the face of the collapse of the national coal basins, the oil price pressures caused by the wars in the Middle East, and the hydroelectricity that failed to win a share in the energy matrix (figures 2.3 and 2.5), thus increasing energy dependency. This dependency is aggravated by its link to neighbouring countries with which Chile does not have robust and stable economic relations. In 2004, for example, when the Argentine government decided to limit gas sales to Chile, the consequences were felt immediately with an electricity crisis and rising prices, with the attendant effects on potential economic growth.[24]

The bid for thermal electricity is reflected in figure 2.6. Above all, it is worth noting that since 1992 the generation of thermoelectricity has increased at ten times the rate of hydroelectricity. Whereas the former expanded at an annual rate of 11.5 per cent, the latter did so at only 1.5 per cent. The most notable economic effect of this energy policy, together with the external dependency mentioned above, was high electricity prices. In 2008, Chilean electricity prices were the highest in Latin America, and in 2010 they were nearly double the average among OECD countries.[25]

Some Lessons from Energy History

We know that there is a close relationship between energy consumption and economic growth, and that this relationship is not simple. We cannot fail to recognize that each national experience has left a record of the unique opportunities and challenges connecting energy to economic growth. In the case of nineteenth-century Chile, an abundant supply of energy (with a high component of domestic coal) contributed to economic growth. The two economic crises of the twentieth century adversely affected the country's energy supply because of the difficulty it had accessing international markets and the delay it faced in securing investments needed to increase domestic energy production. The harmful effect of not acting against energy dependence is also clear, which in the Chilean case over the last hundred years resulted from the country not having made a clear commitment to hydropower. Finally, energy solutions have to be undertaken over the long term, and they require advance planning that cannot be left in the hands of those economic actors who favour the short-term view.

The nineteenth century—which from the perspective of Chile's energy history, with its majority consumption of traditional fuels (especially firewood), extends to 1907—was the period in which coal drove the modernization of the economy. The railways were central to modernization, and they were powered entirely by steam engines. The mining industry in its different sectors (mainly copper and coal) was complemented by the railways, generating a technological critical mass that spilled over into manufacturing. But it was not strong enough to defeat the atavistic tendencies of those sectors that were stuck in the tradition of organic energies. The clearly marked trends of the nineteenth century, characterized by the rise of coal and the relative demotion of firewood, were not repeated in the following fifty years. The energy transition in Chile was long and complex. Until the 1950s, oil did not clearly dominate coal and firewood. The interwar period, with the Great Depression as its nadir, were marked by economic stagnation (see table 2.3), which in turn made it difficult to translate technological innovation into improved productivity. As a result, the period is associated with an energy intensity that neither improved nor worsened (figure 2.1). Only in the 1960s was the energy transition resolved, at which point a new matrix of primary energies began emerging (figure 2.3). A combination of the old and the new continued until 2010. Firewood stabilized at a magnitude of close to 20 per cent and coal at 10 per cent. Meanwhile, oil and natural gas became consolidated as the country's most important primary energy sources. As both were imported—unlike firewood and coal—this accentuated Chile's energy dependency. Hydroelectricity, which had aroused such high hopes at the beginning of Chilean electrification, occupied a marginal place: an average of 7 per cent between 1960 and 2010.

The electricity sector, which has been so decisive in promoting economic development in past decades, has deepened Chile's energy dependency. The country's bid for thermoelectricity, especially after 1990, meant that electricity generation came to depend heavily on oil and natural gas prices. Furthermore, because generation has been handed almost entirely to private enterprises, which are very sensitive to market signals, the projection of demand has not always coincided with the expansion plans of the electricity sector, which is more sensitive to short-term price fluctuations.

NOTES

This chapter was translated by David Barrios Giraldo with the assistance of Andrew Wiley.

1   These are the results of the Spanish Ministry of Technology research projects *Importaciones y modernización económica en América Latina, 1890–1960* (BEC2003-00412) and *Energía y economía en América Latina y el Caribe, entre mediados del siglo XIX y mediados del siglo XX* (SEJ2007-60445/ECON), led by Albert Carreras at the Universitat Pompeu Fabra from 2003 to 2010. The most recent contributions to this work were made with the support of Fondecyt (Chile) Project 1161425, "Historia de las transiciones energéticas y el cambio estructural en la economía chilena (siglo XIX a XXI)," of which César Yáñez is the principal investigator.

2   The main publications that resulted from the projects mentioned above are María del Mar Rubio, César Yáñez, Mauricio Folchi, and Albert Carreras, "Energy as an Indicator of Modernization in Latin America, 1890–1925" *Economic History Review* 63, no. 3 (2010): 769–804; César Yáñez and Albert Carreras, eds., *The Economies of Latin America: New Cliometric Data* (London: Pickering and Chatto, 2012); César Yáñez, María del Mar Rubio, José Jofré, and Albert Carreras, "El consumo aparente de carbón mineral en América Latina, 1841–2000. Una historia de progreso y frustración," *Revista de Historia Industrial* 53, no. 21 (2013): 25–77. The only publication on the Chilean case is César Yáñez and José Jofré, "Modernización económica y consumo energético en Chile, 1844–1930," *Historia 396* 1, no. 1 (2011): 127–56.

3   Vaclav Smil, *Energy in World History* (Boulder, CO: Westview Press, 1994). See also the following by Vaclav Smil, *Energías. Una guía ilustrada de la biósfera y la civilización*, trans. Ignacio Zúñiga (Barcelona: Crítica, 2001); *Energy at the Crossroads: Global Perspectives and Uncertainties* (Cambridge, MA: MIT Press, 2003); *Creating the Twentieth Century: Technical Innovations of 1876–1914 and their Lasting Impact* (New York: Oxford University Press, 2005); and *Energy in Nature and Society: General Energetics of Complex Systems* (Cambridge, MA: MIT Press, 2008). My co-authors and I have defended this argument in our publications of 2010, 2011, and 2012, cited in the previous note.

4   Two traditions of economic history converge here with the history of energy proposed by Vaclav Smil. The first is that proposed by Edward A. Wrigley in *Energy and the English Industrial Revolution* (Cambridge: Cambridge University Press, 2010) and by Robert Allen in *The British Industrial Revolution in Global Perspective* (Cambridge: Cambridge University Press, 2009), both of which focus on the English Industrial Revolution. The second is the history of the great global economic trends, represented by the seminal work of Kenneth Pomeranz, *The Great Divergence: Europe, China, and the Making of the Modern World Economy* (Princeton, NJ: Princeton University Press, 2000).

5   The reference to Chile being "blessed" refers to the discussion prompted by Sachs and Warner's work about the "curse" or "blessing" of the natural resources to economic growth in developing countries. See Jeffrey D. Sachs and Andrew M. Warner, "Natural Resource Abundance and Economic Growth" (NBER Working Paper No. 5398, National Bureau of Economic Research, Cambridge, MA, December 1995).

6   Alejandro Foxley, *La trampa del ingreso medio. El desafío de esta década para América Latina* (Santiago: Cieplan, 2012).

7   Nicholas Craft, Stephen Leybourn, and Terence Mills, "The Climacteric in Late Victorian Britain and France: A Reappraisal of the Evidence," *Journal of Applied Econometrics* 4, no. 2 (1989): 103–17.

8   A modern version of these interpretations from the perspective of political history can be found in Ana María Stuven, *La seducción de un orden. Las élites y la construcción de Chile en las polémicas culturales y políticas del siglo XIX* (Santiago: Ediciones de la Universidad Católica de Chile, 2000). A nuanced vision of institutional approaches, arising from the economic history, can be seen in César Yáñez, "Economic Modernization in Adverse Institutional Environments: The Cases of Cuba and Chile," in *The Economies of Latin America: New Cliometric Data*, ed. César Yáñez and Albert Carreras (London: Pickering and Chatto, 2012), 105–17. See also Luis Bértola, "Bolivia (Estado Plurinacional de), Chile y Perú desde la Independencia: Una historia de conflictos, transformaciones, inercias y desigualdad," in *Institucionalidad y Desarrollo en América Latina*, ed. Luis Bértola and Pablo Gerchunoff (Santiago: CEPAL, 2011), 227–85.

9   Luis Ortega Martínez, *Chile en ruta al capitalismo. Cambio, euforia y depresión 1850–1880* (Santiago: DIBAM-LOM-Centro de Investigaciones Diego Barros Arana, 2006).

10 Mauricio Folchi Donoso, "La insustentabilidad de la industria del cobre en Chile. Los hornos y los bosques durante el siglo XIX," *Revista Mapocho* no. 49 (2001): 149–75.

11 Inés Herrera Canales, "Trabajadores y técnicas mineras andinas en las fiebres del oro del mundo en el siglo XIX," *Nuevo Mundo/Mundos Nuevos* (online), 10 March 2015, https://doi.org/10.4000/nuevomundo.67746. Herrera says that "it was in the 18th century that gold production in Chile expanded in the same regions as the panning sites of previous centuries with the resulting subterranean seams and veins. Along with this, there was a growth in the use of mining crushers and stamp mills, powered by water. . . . Small owners continued to use *marayes* [small pre-Hispanic mineral mills of Inca origin], artisanal mills powered by draught animals or human power or they took their minerals to big mills" (my translation).

12 Yáñez, "Economic Modernization in Adverse Institutional Environments"; Yáñez and Jofré, "Modernización económica y consumo energético"; and Yáñez et al., "El consumo aparente de carbón mineral."

13 Yáñez and Jofré, "Modernización económica y consumo energético."

14 Yáñez and Jofré, "Modernización económica y consumo energético."

15 Javier Rodríguez Weber, *Desarrollo y desigualdad en Chile (1850–2009). Historia de su economía política* (Santiago: Centro de Investigaciones Barros Arana/DIBAM, 2017).

16 For an excellent example of the changes generated by capitalism in the Chilean economy, see Mario Matus, *Crecimiento sin desarrollo. Precios y salarios reales durante el Ciclo Salitrero en Chile (1880–1930)* (Santiago: Editorial Universitaria, 2012).

17 For more on economic infrastructure spending, see Hernán Cerda Toro, "Inversión Pública, infraestructuras y crecimiento económico chileno, 1853–2010" (PhD diss.,

Universidad de Barcelona, 2013). A summary of this scholar's investigation can be found in the papers presented at the Second Chilean Congress of Economic History; see Hernán Cerda Toro, "Evolución de la inversión pública en infraestructuras productivas, 1853–2010," in *Chile y América en su historia económica*, ed. César Yáñez (Valparaíso: Asociación Chilena de Historia Económica, Universidad de Valparaíso, 2013), 179–94. On the role of the government in the new social and labour conflicts of the early twentieth century, see Juan Carlos Yáñez, *La intervención social en Chile, 1907–1932* (Santiago: RIL Editores, 2008).

18 Income inequality has been studied in detail by Javier Rodríguez Weber, "La economía política de la desigualdad del ingreso en Chile, 1850–2009" (PhD diss., Universidad de la República [Uruguay], 2014). For a summary of the Gini index of income inequality, consult Javier Rodríguez Weber, "De Manuel Montt a Michelle Bachelet. 160 años de distribución del ingreso en Chile," in *Chile y América en su historia económica*, ed. César Yáñez (Valparaíso: Asociación Chilena de Historia Económica, Universidad de Valparaíso, 2013), 455–73.

19 In Chile this period represents an inflection point for exports of saltpetre, ending a growth cycle that began with the War of the Pacific (1879–81), when the country obtained by force natural resources belonging to Peru and Bolivia.

20 Patricio Meller, *Un siglo de economía política chilena (1890–1990)* (Santiago: Editorial Andrés Bello, 1996); Ricardo French-Davis, Óscar Muñoz Gomá, José Miguel Benavente, and Gustavo Crespi, "La industrialización chilena durante el proteccionismo (1940–1982)," in *Industrialización y Estado en la América Latina. La leyenda negra de la posguerra*, ed. Enrique Cárdenas, José Antonio Ocampo, and Rosemary Thorp (Mexico City: El Trimestre Económico/Fondo de Cultura Económica, 2003), 159–209.

21 Martín Garrido Lepe, "El consumo de carbón en Chile, 1933 a 1960," in *Chile y América en su historia económica*, ed. César Yáñez (Valparaíso: Asociación Chilena de Historia Económica, Universidad de Valparaíso, 2013), 329–52; César Yáñez and Martín Garrido Lepe, "El consumo de carbón en Chile entre 1933–1960. Transición energética y cambio estructural," *Revista Uruguaya de Historia Económica* 5, no. 8 (2015): 76–95.

22 Chile. Corporación de Fomento de la Producción, *Fomento de la Producción de Energía Eléctrica* (Santiago: Editorial Nascimento, 1939); Corporación de Fomento de la Producción, *Geografía Económica de Chile*, vol. 3 (Santiago: Talleres Gráficos La Nación, 1962).

23 César Yáñez and Martín Garrido Lepe, "El tercer ciclo del carbón en Chile de 1973 a 2013: del climaterio al rejuvenecimiento," *América Latina en la historia económica* 24, no. 3 (September–December 2017): 224–58.

24 Vittorio Corbo, ed., *Growth Opportunities for Chile* (Santiago: Editorial Universitaria, 2014).

25 Chile. Biblioteca del Congreso Nacional de Chile, "Informe: Comparación de precios de electricidad en Chile y países de la OCDE y América Latina," 6 November 2017, http://bcn.cl/13vae.

The Commercial and Political Dynamics of the Crude Oil Industry: The Case of the Royal Dutch/Shell Group in Venezuela, 1913–1924

Brian S. McBeth

The development of the oil industry in Venezuela took place during the dictatorship of General Juan Vicente Gómez, who came to power in a bloodless coup on 19 December 1908 and died in his sleep on 17 December 1935. In order to secure peace and stability at the beginning of his rule, Gómez maintained a delicate neutrality between the various political factions that were claiming him as their true leader. Venezuela in 1908 was little known to the outside world, but by the time of Gómez's death almost three decades later, the country was the second-largest crude oil producer in the world and of vital strategic importance to the British Empire, as well as a significant supplier of crude oil to the Atlantic Seaboard of the United States.

Venezuelan historiography tends to treat as predetermined the fact that the country would by 1928 be the world's second-largest crude oil producer after the United States. There is also the widespread assumption that the Royal Dutch/Shell Group (henceforth Shell) was protected by the Gómez government. However, as we shall see, Shell's experience during the early phase of the industry's development was far from easy. Between

1913 and 1924, most of its oil concessions were disputed by the Venezuelan government, American oil companies, and foreign and Venezuelan nationals, in particular close members of Gómez's family.[1] As a way of illustrating the non-operational problems faced by a foreign oil company developing a nascent oil industry, this chapter, after a brief look at Gómez's economic plans and the international oil industry, examines Shell's initial entry into Venezuela and the legal difficulties encountered by its various operating subsidiaries.

Background

The political and economic problems that Gómez faced at the beginning of his rule in December 1908 were considerable. Gómez's initial economic plans were ambitious, given the backwardness of the country's economic infrastructure and Venezuela's bad reputation in the major international money markets. Gómez was well aware of the economic constraints operating in the country and the adverse influence that German trading houses exerted on its economy. It was therefore necessary to stimulate the development of an independent source of revenue free from traditional political influence. Consequently, from the outset of his rule, Gómez encouraged the establishment of a healthy and thriving mining industry.[2] There was nothing new in this idea, as past rulers had also pinned their hopes on large mining revenues. What was novel in Gómez's case was that he achieved his objective through exploitation of the country's crude oil reserves during the 1920s. As a result, Venezuela was one of the few countries in Latin America to survive intact the Great Depression of the 1930s, largely due to increasing government revenues from the crude oil industry. When Gómez came to power in 1908, the foreign debt stood at $43.3 million and the internal debt at $13.9 million. In the ensuing years after 1908, the debt was gradually paid off every year until 1930, when a budget surplus of $20.6 million allowed Gómez to celebrate the December 17 centenary of Simón Bolívar's death by cancelling the country's large foreign debt.[3] Similarly, the domestic public debt, which stood at $13.9 million in 1908, was almost completely paid off by the time of the dictator's death in December 1935.[4]

The relationship between oil companies and governments is one of continuous adjustment to the changes in the international oil markets and the local economic and political situation, with the host government being in a fundamentally weaker position than the companies. At the beginning of the twentieth century, especially after the invention of the diesel engine, world oil consumption increased rapidly.[5] The First World War demonstrated the importance of oil as a cheap source of energy, as well as the dependence of the industrial world on this new motive power. At the time, the two main oil-producing countries in the world were the United States and Russia, with the former accounting for 68 per cent of total world oil production in 1918. Western Europe did not possess large reserves of crude oil, with countries having to source their crude oil supply from outside the region. The British government, for example, in order to guarantee crude oil supplies to its navy in 1914, acquired a 51 per cent stake in the Anglo-Persian Oil Company, which held a large oil concession in Persia (Iran).[6] Prior to the First World War, the United States produced enough crude oil to supply itself and its foreign markets, but after the cessation of hostilities in 1918 it became alarmed at the possibility that it would no longer be able to supply its domestic market. With the decline of production from its continental oil fields, it was predicted that the US would soon be importing large volumes of foreign crude oil to satisfy its growing demand for petroleum products in the transport and industrial sectors.[7] As a result, after the First World War American crude oil companies started to explore "how and where [they] can secure a sufficiency of crude to enable it to meet both the domestic and foreign demand for refined products."[8] In 1919, the State Department sent a circular to all US ambassadors and ministers urging them to assist American capital in its search for oil concessions.[9] This allowed Shell, and later Exxon and Gulf Oil, to supply their foreign markets with cheap Venezuelan oil at relatively high US prices through the "Gulf +" pricing structure then in use for international crude oil trades.[10]

The rapid development of the Venezuelan oil industry was directly linked with the exploitation of the crude oil concessions held by Shell. In the 1920s, Venezuela offered Shell an alternative source of oil that was more attractive than a politically unstable Mexico, which was 5,000 miles away from Britain, compared to Venezuela's 3,700 miles.[11] The decade also

Table 3.1 Average Cost of Delivered Crude Oil to the Atlantic Seaboard: Comparison between US, Venezuela, and Rest of World (Including Venezuela), 1927–1930 ($/barrel)

Area of Activity	US Domestic	Venezuela	Rest of the World
Cost of production	1.09	0.62	0.87
Selling costs	0.04	0.0	0.0
Pipeline costs	0.49	0.0	0.0
Tanker charges	0.27	0.25	0.28
Total	**1.89**	**0.87**	**1.15**

Source: US House of Representatives, 1932, House Document No. 195, Adapted, Table 25, 49.

saw increasing doubt about the sustainability of Mexican crude oil production, with many oil companies looking for a secure alternative source of crude oil to supplement US domestic oil production. Venezuelan crude oil first entered the United States in large quantities in 1926, when 12.5 million barrels were imported; this rose to 50.7 million barrels in 1929, while Mexico's share of total oil imported into the United States declined from 99 per cent in 1920 to 14 per cent in 1936. Venezuela's share of US crude oil imports increased from 2 per cent in 1925 to 70 per cent in 1936.[12] Venezuela also became the largest crude oil supplier to Britain, delivering 40 per cent of the country's total demand on the eve of the Second World War.[13] Venezuela's large increase in oil production was accompanied by a huge rise in foreign capital investment in the country's oil industry. US investments in the country grew from $8 million in 1914 to $247.2 million in 1930, compared with British investments of $125 million in 1930.[14]

The Royal Dutch/Shell Group

In 1913, Shell secured large crude oil concessions in Venezuela by purchasing two General Asphalt Company (GAC) subsidiaries, the US-registered Caribbean Petroleum Company (CPC), which held the Rafael Maximiliano Valladares concession of 2 January 1912,[15] and the British-registered Colon Development Company Ltd. (CDC), which held the

Andrés Jorge Vigas concession of 31 January 1907.[16] Sir Henri Deterding, managing director of Shell, later acknowledged that this was the group's "most colossal deal."[17] In addition, in 1915 Shell further added to its acreage by acquiring the British-registered Venezuelan Oil Concessions Ltd. (VOC), which held the Antonio Aranguren concession of 28 February 1907.[18]

Shell first found crude oil in commercial quantities on 31 July 1914, when CPC drilled and completed the Zumaque No. 1 well that discovered the large Mene Grande oil field. Eight years later, on 14 December 1922, VOC drilled the Los Barrosos-2 well, which initially produced 87,600 barrels of oil per day (BOPD) and discovered the La Rosa oil field.[19] These discoveries meant that Shell would play an important role in developing Venezuela's oil industry, and it soon became the country's largest oil producer. Shell produced 166,005 BOPD in 1933, equivalent to 51.2 per cent of the country's total production, followed by Exxon, with 30.5 per cent of the total.[20] Shell's crude oil production in Venezuela increased so rapidly that in 1925 it overtook the company's production in Mexico, and by 1929 it surpassed its domestic US production (see figure 3.1).

In 1925, as figure 3.2 shows, VOC overtook CPC to become Shell's largest oil-producing subsidiary in Venezuela.

Shell's activities in the country yielded spectacular financial results, with VOC reporting net profits averaging $10.6 million between 1927 and 1929 and a return on equity above 80 per cent in 1928–9.[21] As we can see in figure 3.3 below, Shell's performance is even more outstanding when compared with the financial results of the Canadian-registered British Controlled Oilfields Ltd. (BCO).

With Shell's entry into Venezuela in the 1910s, there was optimism in government circles that an oil bonanza was about to start, especially after the company constructed in 1912 a small 1,200-BOPD refinery at San Lorenzo, Zulia State.[22] In spite of this optimism, the various Shell subsidiaries faced a number of major operational drawbacks, the most important being the country's lack of adequate infrastructure. In addition, the initial progress made by VOC was hampered by unhealthy working conditions and the impossibility of preventing workers from getting malaria. In the case of CDC, its geological prospecting team also had to contend with attacks by the Indigenous Motilone people.[23] As a result, most of Shell's

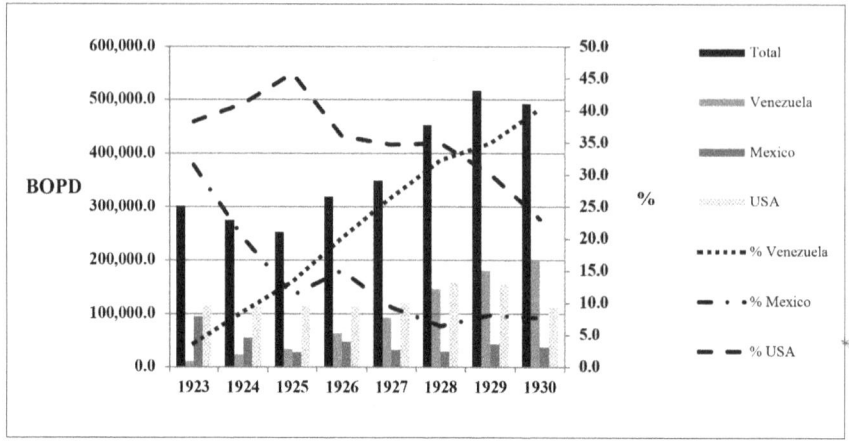

Figure 3.1 Shell Production: Total, Venezuela, Mexico, and US, 1923–1930 (BOPD and %)

Source: Adapted from Royal Dutch Company, *Annual Reports*, 1923-1930.

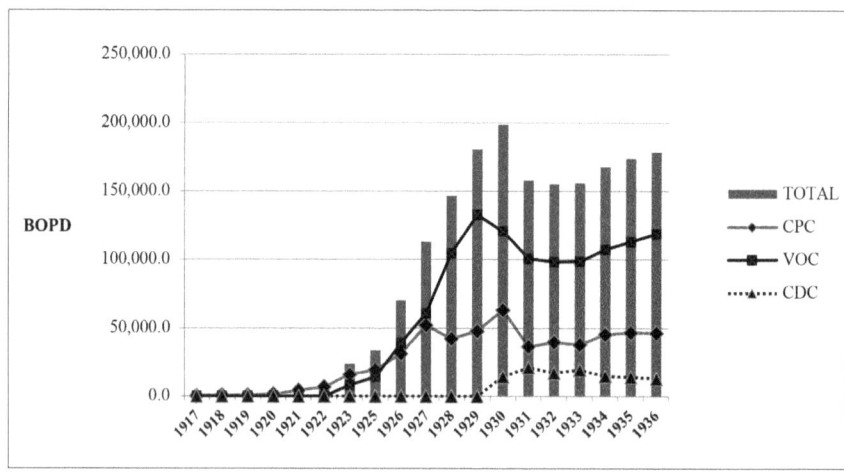

Figure 3.2 Shell: Venezuelan Crude Oil Production by Subsidiaries, 1917–1935 (BOPD)

Source: Adapted from Royal Dutch Company, *Annual Reports*, 1917-1935.

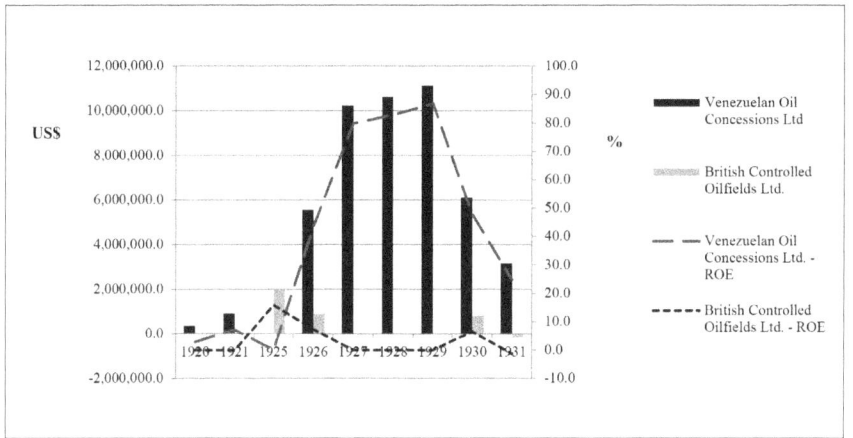

Figure 3.3 VOC and BCO: Net Profits and Return on Equity (ROE), 1920–1931 ($). To simplify matters, the net profits of VOC and its parent company, OCHCL, were added together.

Source: Calculated from *Oil News*, *Petroleum Times*, and *South American Journal*, 1920–1931.

acreage remained unexploited, and government revenues from the nascent oil industry remained low. This caused friction between the government and Shell, as the former threatened to cancel the company's concessions if large-scale exploitation of its acreage did not start soon. Furthermore, a number of American oil companies that entered Venezuela after the First World War were prepared to acquire Shell's oil assets if the government rescinded the company's concessions. Other vested interests that wanted to acquire Shell's assets included close members of Gómez's family, in particular the dictator's brother, General Juan Crisóstomo Gómez (Juancho Gómez), who since 4 August 1913 had served as president of the Federal District.[24] Juancho Gómez was one of the main instigators—with the backing, in some cases, of certain American oil companies—who sought to challenge the legality of Shell's concessions. Hence, the biggest problem that Shell faced at this early stage was not operational but, rather, the struggle to retain its large concessions. The legal challenges to Shell's concessions, examined in more detail below, can be grouped into three broad categories: (1) threats from private interests; (2) the slow development of its concessions; and (3) overlapping claims over the same acreage.

Threats from Private Interests

THE MERCADO-ARANGUREN DISPUTE

On 4 March 1907, Aranguren sold half his concession to Lorenzo Mercado and Manuel Revenga for Bs. 15,000.[25] A year later, in March 1908, Aranguren bought back Revenga's share and sold a further 5 per cent stake to Mercado, who transferred it to Eduardo Brasch and David Bickart.[26] When the Mining Law of 29 June 1910 was enacted, the Aranguren concession was rescinded because it was awarded under the previous Mining Law of 14 August 1905 and its regulations of 23 February 1906. However, on 28 June 1912, Aranguren adapted his concession to the new 1910 Mining Law.[27] Mercado, however, did not adapt his 25 per cent share of the concession to the 1910 Mining Law, allowing Aranguren to inadvertently retain the sole right to the whole concession.

On 29 May 1913, Aranguren transferred his concession to VOC. Two years later, in early 1915, the company ran into financial difficulties and was taken over by Shell.[28] On 28 June 1915, with VOC now a Shell subsidiary, Mercado initiated at the Juzgado de Primera Instancia en lo Civil in Caracas a suit against Aranguren and the company in which he claimed that 25 per cent of the concession, valued at "*two million* bolívars," still belonged to him.[29] Aranguren and VOC countered that Mercado's claim was null and void because he failed to adapt his share of the concession to the 1910 Mining Law. Moreover, article 7 of the 1905 Mining Law and article 132 of the attached regulations prohibited the transfer of a contract to a foreigner without the previous consent of the Development Ministry, something that Mercado, a Spanish citizen, had failed to obtain. Finally, when Mercado was expelled as *persona non-grata* by the Cipriano Castro government on 11 July 1908, he lost his concession because the 1905 Mining Law automatically rescinded any concessions held by a foreigner when they left the country.[30] As a result, the court dismissed Mercado's suit on 14 December 1915.[31]

Mercado appealed to the Superior Court of the Federal District to get the decision revoked, arguing, *inter alia*, that the concession's transfer to VOC was null and void because no price was stipulated in the contract.[32] VOC and Aranguren opposed the action, using the same arguments they had brought before the lower court. Mercado now sought to obtain a favourable decision in his appeal by using his influence in government circles. Dr. Antonio María Delgado Briceño, secretary general of the Federal District—described by Preston McGoodwin, US minister, as "unscrupulous and brutal in the extreme"[33]—met with Justices Juan Pablo Colmenares, Juvenal Anzola, and Carlos Jesús Rojas Fernández to inform them that Juancho Gómez required a court sentence "favourable to Mercado."[34] A few days later, Delgado Briceño handed Rojas Fernández, the chancellor of the court, a letter from Alejandro Urbaneja, Mercado's attorney, containing the text of the decision the court should render and reinforcing Juancho Gómez's desire that the court should follow Urbaneja's instructions in deciding the case.[35] Rojas Fernández took the matter directly to Juancho Gómez, who declared that neither he nor his brother had interfered in the legal case, as they "wanted the absolute independence of the Judiciary and the strict adherence of the law."[36] Following this clarification, which was later strengthened by orders received directly from Gómez on the judiciary's independence, Rojas Fernández concluded that Delgado Briceño and Urbaneja were influencing the court's proceedings for personal gain, with the court deciding on 28 June 1916 in favour of Aranguren and VOC.[37] In spite of the Superior Court's sentence, Mercado on 18 January 1917 appealed the decision at the Federal and Cassation Court (CFC in Spanish).[38]

In London, the rumours that VOC was about to lose its concession because of its dispute with Mercado had an adverse impact on the company's financial standing.[39] As a result, Duncan Elliott Alves, VOC's chairman, appealed to Gómez in October 1918 to resolve the quarrel; it was, he explained, causing "great dissatisfaction" among VOC's shareholders to the detriment of Venezuela's creditworthiness.[40] Alves stressed that the development of the oil industry would be hindered unless the court decided in VOC's favour.[41] He also explained his fears to Pedro César Domínici, Venezuelan minister at London, who informed Gómez that any delay in resolving the case would only increase the hostile sentiment against

Venezuela—again, to the detriment of the country's ability to access British money markets—because "these English merchants are only interested in making money."[42] Gómez replied to Alves assuring him and his shareholders that a quick solution would be reached in the dispute by persuading VOC and Mercado to negotiate an out-of-court settlement.[43]

THE ERCON WALD WOLSTAM HODGE CLAIM

Under the Código de Hacienda (Treasury Regulations) of the time, any oil concessions that were subsequently found to have been granted under illegal terms reverted to the state, with the government granting 40 per cent of the property to the denouncer of the illegal contract. On 16 February 1917, Ercon Wald Wolstan Hodge, a Trinidadian, entered a petition at the CFC against the Ministries of Finance and Development claiming that "the Valladares concession (held by CPC) was illegal and unconstitutional."[44] A week later, on 23 February 1917,[45] Hodge sold his legal case for Bs. 10,000 to the Paria Transport Corporation (PTC),[46] an American company that would acquire 40 per cent of the Valladares concession if the claim was upheld.[47]

Urbaneja, now attorney general, needed to consider a number of issues before allowing the court to adjudicate on the case, including the government's ability to decide under the Treasury Act whether the property was indeed denounceable, whether the property in question belonged to the government, and whether there was sufficient proof on which to base a claim.[48] In the end, Urbaneja did not need to consider these issues as the law provided a convenient escape clause by allowing the government to determine whether a valid claim was in the best interests of the country.[49] In assessing whether the claim was beneficial to Venezuela, the government considered a possible US reaction to CPC, an American-registered company, losing its concession to a company owned by "undisputed American capital."[50] Bernardino Mosquera, foreign affairs minister, concluded after seeing McGoodwin on March 13 that the American government would probably press for compensation for CPC.[51] PTC did not want the State Department's help because it felt that the government would cancel the concession to appease an American government that was intensely irritated with Venezuela's avowed neutrality during the First World War.[52] The State Department, however, showed no interest in the case because its only concern was to help bona fide American interests that had been "manifestly denied justice."[53] The cabinet, after debating the Hodge claim, concluded on 17 March 1917 that the Valladares concession was null and void from a legal point of view.[54] However, after consulting with Gómez,[55] the cabinet decided that cancellation of the Valladares concession was not in the national interest, and so declared the Hodge claim "inappropriate."[56]

The Slow Development of Oil Concessions

CPC

The slow development of CPC's large concession, with production increasing from 0.25 BOPD in 1912 to a paltry 87.8 BOPD five years later in 1917, brought it into conflict with the Development Ministry. On 7 February 1918, Development Minister Gumersindo Torres informed the company that it was not fulfilling its legal requirement to develop its concession.[57] Lewis J. Proctor, CPC's managing director, believing that the company was being harassed by the government because of a misunderstanding,[58] replied to Torres on 12 April 1918 that CPC was not only at the forefront of the country's nascent oil industry—it was also the largest company exploiting Venezuela's natural resources, with total capital investments of Bs. 20,782,842,[59] second only to the Callao Gold Mining Company, which started exploiting its gold reserves in 1870, with total investments in 1918 of Bs. 20,000,000.[60] Moreover, Proctor argued that CPC's operating concession was stricter than other mining companies, as it had to drill on each of its selected exploration blocks, whereas other concessions only required work on one site for the government to declare the concession in production. Additionally, CPC's tax bill in 1917–18 of Bs. 1,495,960 was higher than any other oil/mining company in the country.[61] However, CPC's taxes on crude oil production amounted to a trifling Bs. 56,960, equivalent to 3.8 per cent of the total paid, while the prorogation of titles and stamp duty accounted for 61 per cent of total taxes.[62]

In May 1918, Torres decided that the best way forward was for the cabinet to discuss the issue. It ultimately concluded that CPC could retain its concession provided it paid the minimum production tax of Bs. 1,000 for each of its 185 production blocks, even though almost all of them were not in production, and that its remaining 235 exploration blocks should also pay the minimum production tax per block and be in production within three years, something the company accepted.[63]

CDC

The government was also unhappy with CDC's slow development of its Vigas concession, which in 1915 only had three blocks in production covering 800 hectares out of its total of 1.98 million hectares.[64] The problem was that Shell had no intention of developing CDC's concession until it had resolved the problem of the Vigas "B" minority shares in the company held by the American-owned Carib Syndicate Ltd. (CS). The shares gave CS the automatic right to a 25 per cent participation in any future funding without having to pay for the additional equity issue.[65] CDC decided to ignore the government's enquiry, but after waiting for eighteen months for a reply, Torres, who felt that this was "too long for an answer,"[66] informed the company in October 1919 that it "could not claim exclusive right to all the petroleum deposits in the district," and that its concession would be declared lapsed.[67] Cecil Dormer, British minister, felt that Torres had been "got at by some Americans acting through Julio Felipe Méndez, Gómez's son-in-law"[68] because "the threat was such a monstrous one and so in direct contradiction to the terms of the contract that it seemed to be a clumsy attempt to induce the company to give up a part of the concession out of fear."[69]

In spite of Torres's impending legal action, CDC still refused to address the minister's concerns. Consequently, on 5 January 1920 the government notified the company that it was taking it to court,[70] an action that CDC protested vigorously. Further notes followed in which both parties reiterated their divergent views. However, in early March 1920, Torres appeared to have changed his mind, as he informed Major Stephen H. Foot, CDC's representative in Caracas, that he was ready "to discuss the matter in a friendly way."[71] Dormer immediately met with Esteban Gil Borges, foreign relations minister, to seek an explanation for Torres's attitude, explaining that he was "at a loss to understand it after the repeated assurances of General Gómez and Dr. Victorino Márquez Bustillos, the Provisional President of the country, that foreign capital was safe in this country."[72] Dormer further warned Gil Borges of the consequences if

CDC's concession was rescinded, but the minister denied that such action was contemplated and promised to speak to Torres. After the meeting, Dormer reported to the Foreign Office in London that Gil Borges was so "emphatic that I no longer felt any misgivings."[73]

However, at the next cabinet meeting Attorney General Guillermo Tell Villegas Pulido was instructed to start legal action at the CFC against CDC to get the company to either reduce its concession to its current 800 hectares or pay the surface tax of Bs. 2 per hectare over its entire concession.[74] Dormer immediately sought Gil Borges's explanation for this unexpected turn of events, with the foreign affairs minister expressing "the greatest concern" about the problem and assuring the British minister that "the matter had never come before the Cabinet."[75] This was a blatant distortion of the facts by Gil Borges, probably designed to keep Dormer at bay because he later confessed privately to the British minister that he was unable to do anything for "fear of being accused of having a personal interest" in the case.[76] Dormer felt that the issue was "more than a departmental matter," because there were a number of concession hunters in the country, including Exxon, who were backing the government's position, and he advised London that he wanted to give the government "a friendly warning that, if the courts decided against the company, His Majesty's Government would not look with indifference on the setting aside of a contract."[77]

In spite of its posturing, the Venezuelan government was looking for an early settlement, with Dormer encouraging Foot to arrange with Villegas Pulido a postponement of the litigation, which was achieved on March 15, the very day that CDC needed to respond to the charges the government had introduced at the CFC.[78] Torres interpreted CDC's move as a moral victory for the administration, proof that the company was ready to accept the government's terms. Gómez also felt the same way, expressing to McGoodwin in early April that the concession was too large for CDC and that he intended to press it to "show cause why concession should not be annulled for non-compliance with terms."[79] However, as there was no further progress with CDC, on 7 April 1920 Gómez took matters into his own hands and initiated legal proceedings to get "Shell to pay annual taxes of Bs. 3,800,000 (retroactive from 1915) or renounce its concession."[80]

The government, encouraged at this juncture by Exxon, "who may be making determined efforts to turn out the British companies,"[81] was also considering challenging the concessions held by VOC and BCO. Dormer reported that "American secret support of [the] government's attitude is more patent than concealed,"[82] a view that was later confirmed by David W. Murray, head of the Latin American Division at the State Department, in a memorandum to Sumner Welles, assistant secretary of state, that indicated that the American government's main aim was to get CDC's concession cancelled[83] and that it therefore refused to assist any companies that were "either British controlled or closely affiliated with British control companies,"[84] including, *inter alia*, CDC, GAC, and CS. On 16 April 1920, the American Addison H. McKay,[85] who was closely connected with Méndez and Juancho Gómez,[86] offered on behalf of the Sun Oil Company and Exxon to pay $1,350,000 each to the government and Gómez for the privilege of exploring for one year the concessions held by CDC, VOC, and BCO.[87]

In London on 11 May 1920, Foreign Office representatives and the directors of CDC, VOC, and BCO held urgent talks with Domínici, who afterwards telegraphed Gómez to say that the intended legal action against the British oil companies had caused "deep concern in financial circles interested in oil development."[88] In a lengthy report to Gómez the next day, Domínici explained that forcing the companies to pay the production tax of Bs. 2 per hectare on their entire concessions would mean BCO would have to pay an additional annual tax of Bs. 1 million, with the other companies paying slightly less, leading to the "abandonment of production" and "panic among thousands of shareholders in those companies."[89] Moreover, the dispute would significantly delay the development of the Venezuelan oil industry "because nobody in England would invest a penny before knowing the outcome of the legal case." According to Domínici, that was bound to "cause us abroad more harm than good," with a loss of confidence that "will take a long time to regain."[90]

CS also viewed developments in Caracas with "great alarm," because if the Vigas concession was annulled it would lose its investment in CDC, which was valued at $10,000,000.[91] GAC was also concerned about its stake in CDC, with a series of meetings between CS, GAC, and State Department officials in Washington that culminated on 18 May 1920 when Carl Kendrick MacFadden, CS managing director, requested US assistance in the company's legal fight.[92] However, the American government refused to help a British-controlled company resolve its problems in Venezuela.[93] In London, the Foreign Office was also concerned, instructing Dormer that he should take "all possible action to prevent any reduction in areas for which concessions have been obtained."[94]

The Venezuelan government did not want to rescind the concession, but instead was trying to reach a compromise solution, agreeing on three consecutive occasions to postpone its legal action against CDC up to a final deadline of June 10.[95] However, as there was no adequate response from CDC, the cabinet at a meeting in early June decided unanimously to annul the Vigas concession because the company had been given ample time to reach a settlement.

Dormer believed that Gómez did not want to alienate British capital and was sure the debacle would end once he was fully aware of the unintended consequences that such action would entail. Consequently, on June 10, Dormer sent such a strong diplomatic note to Gil Borges that it left the latter no option but to forward it to Gómez. In it, Dormer stressed that the British government did not "support a reduction in the area of concessions acquired by legal contract between the government of Venezuela and the British Companies if said reduction is not freely agreed between both parties."[96] Two days after forwarding Dormer's note to Gómez, Gil Borges sent a copy to Torres, who was extremely angry because it was in stark contrast to the "moral obligation given by Mr. Dormer and signed by Mr Foot" to seek an amicable solution with the Development Ministry that had granted three extensions to CDC to facilitate a settlement.[97] Torres concluded that CDC's lack of any serious proposals showed that the company was reluctant to engage in legal battle, and that it was instead aspiring to "make it a diplomatic issue" as this was the only way it could win the dispute.[98]

The government's ineffective actions to get itself out of the imbroglio worsened further when Gómez received Domínici's and Alves's correspondence. Although Gil Borges had informed Dormer on June 7 that he had not received any information from Domínici on the impending court action against the British oil companies, it is clear that the foreign affairs minister had reviewed the correspondence, as he commented to Torres that the Venezuelan minister in London "seems to act more as an employee of the Colon than as an official representative of Venezuela."[99]

On June 12, Villegas Pulido requested the CFC to either force CDC to pay the full taxes demanded by the government or annul the Vigas concession, leaving the company with its three producing blocks. Similar legal action would follow against VOC, BCO,[100] and the North Venezuelan Petroleum Company (NVPC), a small British company that held the Francisco Jiménez Arraiz concession.[101] If the court's decision favoured the government, then the long-term effects on Shell and other British oil companies would be devastating.[102] While the future of a number of British oil companies was in play, six of the largest American oil companies were in Venezuela looking to acquire concessions. McGoodwin reported on June 11 that the companies were "confident of the ability to secure contracts covering" the concessions held by CDC, VOC, BCO, and NVPC prior to the "adjournment of Congress" on 27 June 1920.[103] By this point, CDC appeared to be in a hopeless position, as it was only a matter of days before the court's decision to rescind its concession appeared in the *Official Gazette*, thereby rendering it official. However, no announcement was published because according to McGoodwin a number of "legal complications had arisen."[104]

The pernicious influence of Juancho Gómez was again in evidence, with the British minister reporting that the government was acting on the orders "of General Gomez's [sic] brother."[105] Dormer felt that the situation was so serious that it warranted diplomatic intervention in spite of the signs that the government was "looking for a way out of the crisis,"[106] and that Gómez did not "realise the importance of the matter, because no one dares to incur his brother's hostility by telling him the facts."[107]

Gil Borges's evasiveness with Dormer in early June was intended to gain time to negotiate an agreement where the government did not lose face. Domínici's and Alves's reasoning convinced the government that an amicable solution was needed because the loss of confidence among the international bankers and capitalists of London willing to invest in the country would not only mean that an important source of credit dried up, but also that Venezuela would be wholly dependent on American capital. Such a situation would lead to the country's oil industry being mostly developed by American oil companies, something Gómez wanted to avoid as this could lead in the future to possible US intervention. Torres remained hopeful that an agreement would be reached even though there were "probably strong influences at work" getting the concession rescinded.[108] Nevertheless, in order to prevent a miscarriage of justice, Torres requested from his legal advisers Juan Mendoza and Pedro Itriago Chacín (a justice at the CFC) an opinion on CDC's legal position with its concession. Torres's advisers concluded that the Vigas concession, together with the other oil concessions awarded in 1907, were badly drafted and ambiguous, with the result that CDC could retain its 1.9-million-hectare concession unexploited as long as it paid the minimum surface and production taxes.[109] While this was occurring in Caracas, the State Department modified its policy toward the Vigas "B" minority rights that belonged to CS, which would acquire "all the rights of the original holder of the concession" if the government was persuaded to respect these rights.[110] Such an argument convinced Secretary of State Bainbridge Colby to instruct McGoodwin on 24 June 1920 that CS's equitable rights in CDC should be "recognised and protected"[111] by the Gómez administration.[112]

It was clear that CDC had the legal right to retain its concession but it would either have to fully develop it or pay back taxes of Bs. 19,000,000, which was the total minimum annual tax of Bs. 3,800,000 over the previous five years. CDC could not pay such a heavy tax bill on an unproductive property, and it proposed instead in August 1920 to pay Bs. 40,000 annually as a minimum production tax.[113] Torres rejected the proposal and the dispute dragged on for several more months. During this period, the appetite of the American oil companies in the country for acquiring CDC's concession waned, with Dormer reporting in October 1920 that there was "no great danger at present of our oil interests in Venezuela being injured."[114] The prospects of an amicable arrangement between CDC and the government improved and a settlement was agreed on 15 March 1921 that allowed CDC to retain its full concession for a further ten years in order to explore its acreage.[115] At the end of the first five-year period, CDC would pay an additional annual surface tax of Bs. 0.20 per hectare on its selected acreage. A second five-year exploration period would follow, allowing CDC to determine the tracts it wanted to exploit. Any acreage not selected by CDC at the end of the period reverted to the government.

The surface and production taxes remained at Bs. 2 per hectare per year and Bs. 2 per ton, respectively.

Soon afterwards, on 4 April 1921, the government brought a similar suit at the CFC against VOC arguing that its production was inadequate for the size of its concession. This time it only took three weeks for the company to reach an agreement on 25 April 1921 on the same terms as CDC.[116] According to Villegas Pulido and Henry Hammond Dawson Beaumont, Dormer's replacement as British minister, the settlement was directly attributable to Gómez's intervention.[117]

Overlapping Claims

THE VALBUENA-ESPINA-BOHÓRQUEZ (VEB) DISPUTE

The threat to CPC's concession continued in 1921 when it was involved in a particularly nasty private litigation action. On 16 May 1904, Andrés Valbuena, Andrés Espina, and Federico Bohórquez (VEB) obtained the titles to the asphalt mines of San Juan, Rosario, Monteverde, and Santa Efigencia in Zulia State, with a surface area of 1,200 hectares.[118]

Soon after registering their asphalt titles on 12 July 1915 under the 1910 Mining Law, VEB demanded that CPC vacate its oil blocks of Zigualzamara, Zamarises, Zamaro, Zampalo, and Zambo, which partly covered their asphalt mines.[119] CPC ignored this request, believing that VEB's "titles had been annulled" when it acquired the Valladares concession. VEB then sued CPC at the Juzgado de Primera Instancia en lo Civil for the annulment of its concession.[120] It was clear at this early stage that VEB had powerful backers in the government, with Juancho Gómez holding a 25 per cent stake in their titles.[121] On 15 April 1916, the court, "in spite of orders from certain government officials that a decision should be given against the Company," decided in favour of CPC because the plaintiffs' concession was awarded under the 23 January 1904 Mining Code, which only referred to asphalt deposits and not to crude oil reserves.[122]

VEB appealed to the Corte Suprema Accidental del Distrito Federal con Asociados to reverse the lower court's decision, which on 8 July 1916 confirmed VEB's sole right to all the minerals found on its four blocks. Once again, Delgado Briceño was the "evil influence at work . . . trying to subvert the course of Justice" on behalf of Juancho Gómez.[123] CPC felt that the court's decision was flawed because VEB's original contract under the 1904 Mining Code allowed various parties to exploit different resources on the same acreage. However, the procedural irregularities and the attempts to influence the judges against CPC were the main reasons for the company appealing to the superior court. VEB employed the same dirty tactics as before, trying to get three justices removed and succeeding in replacing two judges "closely connected to one of the people having an interest in the suit."[124] The other justices were irritated when they received instructions from Juancho Gómez on the outcome of the dispute and appealed to Gómez for fair treatment, who counselled that "under no circumstances were they to be influenced by anyone and that all cases in the Court should be decided on their merits."[125] Nevertheless, on 29 September 1917 the CFC confirmed the lower court's decision, ordering CPC to pay the plaintiffs' costs of Bs. 75,000.[126]

Though CPC then appealed to the CFC, it felt that it would never get a fair hearing because of the influence exercised by Juancho Gómez. Proctor suggested to McGoodwin that he should discuss the case with Foreign Affairs Minister Mosquera, in order for him to persuade Gómez to prevail on the presiding justice of the court to "consider the case *en banc*, instead of permitting the decision to be prepared by one of the Associate Justices."[127] The outcome of the meeting was that Delgado Briceño was dismissed as secretary general to Juancho Gómez and warned not to influence or issue instructions on how the court should proceed.[128]

At this juncture, CPC was confident of winning the legal case because the Supreme Court of the Federal District could only apply the principles outlined by the CFC. However, further delays and complications followed as none of the justices that had previously presided over the case were eligible to hear it again. Finally, on 11 June 1920, "much to the surprise of nearly everybody,"[129] the CFC rendered its decision in favour of VEB and ordered CPC to transfer its blocks to the plaintiffs. CPC immediately requested that the court freeze any further action by VEB while it appealed the decision. A favourable outcome for CPC was vital because under Venezuelan law costs and damages could be a maximum of 50 per cent of the value of the assets under litigation, which was approximately Bs. 5,200,000.[130] Moreover, if CPC did not settle immediately, VEB could freeze its other assets, such as its refinery at San Lorenzo and its oil-producing wells.

In early 1921, William Tecumseh Sherman Doyle, who up to 1913 was chief of the Division of Latin American Affairs at the State Department, replaced Proctor as CPC's managing director. Doyle felt that it was almost certain that CPC would lose the case because VEB controlled the majority of the court's panel considering the case, and the plaintiffs intended to influence Rojas Fernández, the presiding justice at the CFC. Doyle approached McGoodwin for help because he had been instrumental in resolving CDC's dispute with the government.[131] On 14 March 1921, Doyle requested that the American minister take up CPC's case with Gil Borges, and if necessary with Gómez. Later that day, McGoodwin saw Gil Borges and "impressed him with the importance of taking prompt action."[132] The foreign affairs minister left the following morning for Maracay to confer with Gómez. On his return to Caracas the next day, Gil Borges informed McGoodwin that within four days Gómez would instruct Rojas Fernández to have the case heard *en banc*. This did not happen, and a week later Rojas Fernández ruled against CPC, which meant that once the decision appeared in the *Official Gazette*, the company would have to pay VEB's legal costs and damages of approximately Bs. 2.6 million.[133] Gil Borges, however, delayed the publication of the ruling in the *Official Gazette* until after his departure to the United States on an official visit. Pedro Itriago Chacín, deputy foreign affairs minister, replaced Gil Borges in his absence and was reluctantly persuaded by McGoodwin to confer with Gómez to receive new instructions. Afterwards, on April 3, Itriago Chacín informed McGoodwin at a "rather formal social call" that the case would be heard *en banc*, and that there was "every indication that justice would be given" because Gómez had instructed the three members of the court and the presiding judge to remain impartial.[134]

However, in April 1921 the State Department withdrew its support of CPC when it became aware that it was an American-registered company that was 75 per cent owned by Shell, with the remaining 25 per cent equity held by GAC.[135] Shell then requested British diplomatic assistance in the hope that "the American Minister may be disposed to co-operate."[136] It was also becoming clear to CPC and to both the American and British legations in Caracas that VEB's litigation was financed by speculators, "the exact identity of whom has not been disclosed."[137] R. S. Fuerth, a naturalized American of German origin,[138] was the most likely candidate as he was closely associated with General Francisco Antonio Colmenares Pacheco, Gómez's brother-in-law.[139] Fuerth claimed to have purchased VEB's property on 15 September 1920 for $2,000,000,[140] but Willis C. Cook, the new American minister, felt that what he acquired from VEB was a spurious option to purchase the property and that he would be "paid a commission" for his services in the event that the suit succeeded.[141]

The connivance between VEB and Fuerth provided GAC with a good reason to renew its representation for US assistance. On 8 June 1922, Frank Seamans, vice-president of GAC, met with State Department officials to request that the Venezuelan government be "informally advised that the State Department is interested in seeing justice being done in this case, and justice will not be done unless the litigation shall be speedily and justly concluded."[142] A week later, on June 14, GAC made a formal request for US help,[143] but the State Department declined initially because it was being extremely cautious on account of the CDC affair and did not want to be "misinterpreted in any quarter."[144] Seamans countered that the State Department's previous involvement in CDC's case was precisely the reason why American intervention was needed, because the Venezuelan government would interpret such a refusal as a loss of interest by the US government in the outcome of the litigation. Seamans reasoned that if the British and Dutch interests assumed a similar position, no corporation would invest in Latin America for fear of being inadequately protected by their respective governments.[145] After the meeting, the State Department began to modify its view on the dispute, with Fred Kenelm Nielsen of the department's Office of the Solicitor advising that the reason for "non-interference is a narrow one,"[146] while his boss, Richard W. Flournoy, the solicitor at the State Department, also felt that the US government could, "without violating international laws, extend protection to the Caribbean Petroleum Co. because it was incorporated in the U.S., although only 25 percent of its stock is held by American citizens."[147]

In Caracas, while CPC renewed its request for British help,[148] the Foreign Office declined primarily because of the anti-Shell feeling in the United States[149] at the time, but also because British shareholders held only 30 per cent of the company's equity, compared with 45 per cent for

Dutch shareholders and GAC the remaining 25 per cent, so that "the British connection of the company would appear to be hardly sufficient" to justify British involvement.[150] All was not lost, however, as Horace James Seymour, head of the South American Department at the Foreign Office, felt that Willem George Emile d'Artillac Brill, the Dutch minister at Caracas, could assist CPC. Beaumont was then instructed to support any representations made by D'Artillac Brill on behalf of CPC to ensure that British interests were "not adversely affected."[151] In Washington, the State Department concluded after further debate that both sides had sufficient legal grounds under various Venezuelan laws to stick to their original position, and that it would be "exceedingly difficult to reach a decision based strictly on Venezuelan law."[152] Consequently, Secretary of State Charles Evans Hughes instructed Cook to join his British and Dutch counterparts in preventing any "further unreasonable delay in reaching a fair settlement."[153]

The VEB court case was to drag on further as it was always difficult to find justices to preside at the court. When a complete panel was assembled, Beaumont reported that the same associates of Juancho Gómez exercised their influence and a decision against the company was prepared, which was only avoided by the resignation of one of the presiding justices.[154] On 6 April 1923, Beaumont, Cook, and D'Artillac Brill held an urgent meeting about the case with Itriago Chacín.[155] Beaumont stressed that a "decision against the company or even further prolonged delay in issuing a final judgement, would react very unfavourably on the importation of foreign capital indispensable for the development of the growing oil industry to the importance of which the President is fully alive."[156] Gómez, after being briefed by Itriago Chacín on the meeting, took an "interest in the matter in order to prevent a miscarriage of justice" by ensuring that no further attempts were made by the plaintiffs to influence the court's decision.[157]

The fortunes of CPC took an unexpected turn on 23 June 1923 when Juancho Gómez was murdered in Miraflores Palace, the president's official residence in Caracas.[158] The loss of VEB's most influential supporter meant that a compromise agreement was reached with CPC, whereby VEB's asphalt mines together with CPC's petroleum blocks were sold as one unit and the proceeds divided equally between the parties after deducting operational and legal costs.[159] On 21 December 1923, the VEB heirs finally agreed to the wording of the settlement, which on 2 February 1924 was approved by the CFC.[160] On 12 September 1927, the property was sold for Bs. 3,380,000 to the Rio Palmar Oilfields Exploration Corporation, an Exxon subsidiary, which struck oil on 23 December 1927.[161]

Conclusion

Shell's entry into Venezuela in the 1910s, while it assured the development of the country's oil resources, also redounded to the company's own advantage. Deterding's decision to take Shell into Venezuela was a bold step at the time and served the group well because the advantages associated with being first, such as securing the best oil-bearing lands and favourable taxation, gave it a considerable edge over its rivals. While Venezuelan historiography tends to treat the oil industry's development as a *fait accompli*, Shell's experience at this early stage indicates the contrary, and the widespread assumption that the group faced little opposition from the Gómez government is not proven by the events detailed in this chapter. Shell's experience during this early phase of development was far from easy; the company's activities produced a great deal of resentment, with most of its oil titles disputed between 1913 and 1924 by the Venezuelan government, American oil companies, and both Venezuelan and foreign nationals.

During these early days, the government initiated legal action to get Shell's subsidiaries and others to increase crude oil production as revenues from this source did not live up to expectations. Such a situation drove the British and American oil companies to enlist the support of their respective governments when their oil concessions were threatened. The Venezuelan government's intention was not to drive Shell away from Venezuela because such action would only limit the development of the country's oil resources to one predominant group or, worse still, entail the complete withdrawal of all the oil companies. Gómez instead wanted to benefit from the rising tax revenues that an increase in oil production would bring, and failing such an outcome wanted the companies to pay surface taxes over all their large concessions.

The case of the Valladares concession held by CPC, which came under a long and determined attack during the 1910s that took almost ten years to resolve, illustrates the difficulty of establishing an oil company in a country without an existing hydrocarbon industry. It is clear that without the intervention of the British government, CPC would have lost its valuable concession to an American oil company. The legal dispute between VEB and CPC also illustrates some of the problems Shell faced in its attempts to develop the new industry. The Foreign Office's superior local knowledge allowed it to outmanoeuvre the State Department, with McGoodwin defending the interests of Shell to the detriment of American oil interests. Gómez used such rivalry in another dispute to encourage CDC to develop its concession at a faster rate. In the end, a compromise was reached whereby the government withdrew its suit to rescind the concession and the company agreed to develop its acreage according to a fixed timetable.

Shell also had to deal with the malicious influence of the Gómez family. Juancho Gómez, in particular, interfered with the judiciary for his own pecuniary benefit, and was one of the most influential persons within the Gómez entourage when it came to finding loopholes in some of the concessions, to secure them for himself and his backers in order to transfer them to the highest bidders, especially the American crude oil companies that were entering the country at the time. It is clear that Gómez was fully aware of the involvement of certain close family members with the oil industry, and it is more than likely that he gave them his tacit encouragement to pursue some of these legal claims.[162] Gómez did not have a completely free hand, though, as he had to weigh the short-term pecuniary benefits to his family against the long-term gains that a thriving oil industry would bring not only to close family members and friends but to the country as a whole. Hence, when it was clear that Juancho Gómez and company had abused the judiciary by openly subverting the legal system, Gómez allowed the courts to resolve these issues according to the rule of law. In the end, Gómez's concern for the impartial administration of the country's mining laws, under which the crude oil concessions were issued during this period, helped to harmonize relations with the international powers involved, as well as prevent the development of major political crises within the country, while at the same time laying the foundation for the remarkable stability and growth of the country's oil industry, which increased its production from 331.5 BOPD in 1917 to 425,000 BOPD in 1936.[163] In spite of the various legal threats to Shell, it weathered this storm, albeit with help from the Foreign Office and the State Department, and by the early 1920s, the group, with its three operating companies, was poised for a large increase in oil production that would propel Venezuela to the forefront of the world's major oil producers.

NOTES

1   In Venezuela, the ownership of the subsoil mineral rights, including hydrocarbons, is vested in the government under what is called the dominial system. Under this system, the government sets the rules and is responsible for vetting the applicants that apply for a licence to explore and exploit the natural resource under what is known as a concession system.

2   At the time, the exploitation of the country's hydrocarbon reserves was treated as a mining activity.

3   All dollar figures given in this chapter refer to US currency.

4   In Gómez's view, this secured the country's economic independence, just as Bolívar's independence movement had secured the country's political independence in the nineteenth century. According to Gómez, "I thought to myself that if they achieved political independence, then I must complete the work by gaining economic independence, establishing peace and organizing public finances to ensure that the country's credit worthiness is stronger than its previous parlous state when I started." Archivo Histórico del Palacio de Miraflores, Copiadores (AHMCOP), 284, Juan Vicente Gómez to Juan Bautista Pérez, 22 May 1930.

5   See Miriam Jack, "The Purchase of the British Government's Shares in the British Petroleum Company 1912–1914," *Past & Present*, no. 39 (1968) 139–69; Gerald D. Nash, *United States Oil Policy, 1890–1964: Business and Government in Twentieth-Century America* (Pittsburgh: University of Pittsburgh Press, 1968); Chester Lloyd-Jones, "Oil in the Caribbean and Elsewhere," *North American Review* 202, no. 719 (1915): 536–43; Brian S. McBeth, *Juan Vicente Gómez and the Oil Companies in Venezuela, 1908–1935* (Cambridge: Cambridge University Press, 1983).

6   United Kingdom, Parliamentary Papers, 1914, "Agreement with Anglo-Persian Oil Company, with an Explanatory Memorandum and the Report of the Commission of Experts on their Local Investigation," Command, 7419, 54, 505–16.

7   United Kingdom, National Archives, Foreign Office, Political, Series 371 (FO 371)/4585 Despatch No. 989, Sir A. Geddes to Earl Curzon, Washington, 20 July 1920.

8   FO 371/4585 HM Embassy, Trade Dept., Washington, "A Statistical Survey of the Petroleum Situation in the United States of America," undated.

9   FO 371/5641 US State Department, "Circular to US Consuls," Washington, 16 August 1919.

10 The Gulf+ pricing structure was based on *Platt's Oilgram Price Service*, and it tended to prevent price wars because it meant that production was determined by the requirements of the large US and European markets. Under normal competitive conditions, foreign oil suppliers had a greater advantage because of lower costs and more favourable locations vis-à-vis their counterparts in the United States, and they inevitably secured a greater share of the world oil market.

11 The "Shell" Transport and Trading Co. Ltd., "Annual Report, 1917," reprinted in *The Times* (London), 13 July 1917.

12 William Diebold Jr., "Oil Import Quotas and 'Equal Treatment,'" *American Economic Review* 30, no. 3 (1940): 569–73.

13 United Kingdom, National Archives, Ministry of Power (POWE) 33/572 "Imports of Crude Petroleum and Refined Products into the United Kingdom during the Year 1938."

14 *Latin American World*, no. 14 (January 1933): 5.

15 Venezuela, Ministerio de Fomento (MinFo), *Memoria* (1911): 118.

16 Venezuela, *Gaceta Oficial*, 31 January 1907.

17 Sir Henri Deterding, *An International Oilman* (London: Ivor Nicholson and Watson Ltd., 1934), 97.

18 MinFo, *Memoria* (1906), 1:392–5.

19 MinFo, *Memoria*, (1922): 81–7.

20 See United Kingdom, National Archives, Foreign Office, Political, Series 371, FO 371/12063 "Memorandum on Oil Production in Venezuela," 19 August 1927, and *Oil News*, 1 February 1935.

21 This includes VOC's parent company, the Venezuelan Oil Concessions Holding Company Ltd.

22 MinFo, *Memoria* (1911): vii. For more background on Venezuela's oil industry, see Joe Pratt's chapter in this volume, "Exxon and the Rise of Producer Power in Venezuela." For further historical information on the development of the Argentine oil industry, see Esteban Serrani's chapter, "The Expropriation of YPF in Historical Perspective: Limits of State Power Intervention in Argentina, 1989–2015." Gail D. Triner's chapter, "The New Political Economy of Petroleum in Brazil: Back to the Future?," also has historical information on the Brazilian oil industry. Finally, Linda B. Hall, in her chapter on Mexico, "Coming Full Circle: Mexican Oil, 1917–2018," adds an invaluable historical perspective on that country's crude oil industry.

23 FO 371/4254 HM Petroleum Executive, "Report on Venezuelan Oilfields," 27 May 1919.

24 Venezuela, Vol. 36 of *Recopilación de leyes y decretos de Venezuela* (RLDV) (Caracas: Imprenta Bolívar, 1913), Doc. 11,435.

25 MinFo, *Memoria*, (1906), 1:392.

26 See Venezuela, Distrito Federal, Juzgado de la Primera Instancia en lo Civil, *Juicio seguido por Lorenzo Mercado contra Antonio Aranguren y la Compañía Venezuelan Oil*

Concessions Limited. Informes de los Doctores L. Herrera Mendoza y F. Arroyo Parejo en Primera y Segundas Instancias (Caracas: Empresa El Cojo, 1916).

27 José Santiago Rodríguez, *Informes ante el Tribunal de Primera Instancia en lo Civil del Distrito Federal en representación de la compañía inglesa "The Venezuelan Oil Concessions Limited" en el juicio promovido contra ella y contra el señor Antonio Aranguren por el señor Lorenzo Mercado y sentencia recaída en el asunto* (Caracas: Lit. y Tip. del Comercio, 1916), 9.

28 "Venezuelan Oil Concessions (Ltd.). Agreement with the 'Shell' Group. Terms of the Contract," *Daily Telegraph* (London), 15 December 1915.

29 Rodríguez, *Informes leídos ante la Corte Superior*, 47.

30 Venezuela, Ministerio de Relaciones Exteriores (MinRelExt), *Memoria* (1908): 458.

31 Rodríguez, *Informes leídos ante la Corte Superior*, 96.

32 Rodríguez, *Informes leídos ante la Corte Superior*, 46.

33 Records of the Department of State (DS) relating to the Internal Affairs of Venezuela, DS 831.6375/C23/7 Preston McGoodwin to Robert Lansing, 29 October 1918.

34 Venezuela, Archivo Histórico de Miraflores, Correspondencia Presidencial (AHMCP), Enero 16–31, 1917, Carlos Jesús Rojas to Gómez, 18 January 1917.

35 AHMCP Enero 16–31, 1917, Carlos Jesús Rojas to Gómez, 18 January 1917.

36 AHMCP Enero 16–31, 1917, Carlos Jesús Rojas to Gómez, 18 January 1917.

37 Rodríguez, *Informes leídos ante la Corte Superior*, 56.

38 Venezuela, Corte Federal y de Casación (CFC), *Memoria* (1917): 3.

39 AHMCP Oct 1–31 1919 [sic], Duncan Elliott Alves to Gómez, 14 October 1918.

40 AHMCP Abril 1–30 1919, Pedro César Domínici to Gómez, 15 April 1919.

41 AHMCP Oct 1–31 1919 [sic], Alves to Gómez, 14 October 1918.

42 AHMCP Abril 1–30,1919, Domínici to Gómez, 3 April 1919.

43 AHMCP Mayo 1–30,1920, Domínici to Gómez, 12 May 1920.

44 Julio César Silva to Ministro de Hacienda, and E. W. Hodge to Ministro de Hacienda, in Venezuela, Ministerio de Hacienda (MinHa), *Memoria* (16 February 1917): 47 and 48, respectively.

45 MinHa, *Memoria* (1917): 50.

46 AHMCP Marzo 1–15, 1917, McGoodwin to Gómez, 25 March 1917.

47 MinHa, *Memoria* (1917): "Exposición," x and 49–50.

48 In mining terms, to denounce a mine means to serve legal notice to the government that owns the mining rights of one's intention to exploit the natural resources found within a declared area.

49 AHMCP Febrero 1–28, 1917, Alejandro Urbaneja to Gumersindo Torres, 27 February 1917.

50 DS 831.6375/C23/2 McGoodwin to Lansing, 15 March 1917.

51 DS 831.6375/C23/6 E. P. Greene "Memorandum," 24 April 1917.

52 See Brian S. McBeth, *Dictatorship & Politics: Intrigue, Betrayal, and Survival in Venezuela, 1908–1935* (Notre Dame, IN: University of Notre Dame Press, 2008), 91–129.

53 DS 831.6375/C23/4 William Phillips to Messrs. Douglas, Obear & Douglas, 17 April 1917.

54 Venezuela, Archivo Histórico de Miraflores, Varios (AHMV) 1917–1920, "Informe sobre la situación jurídica de the Caribbean Petroleum Company," 24 February 1917.

55 AHMCP Marzo 1–15,1917, Victorino Márquez Bustillos to Gómez, 17 March 1917.

56 MinFo, *Memoria* (1917), 1:iv; MinHa, *Memoria* (1917): 51–2.

57 Torres to Rafael Max, Valladares, 7 February 1918, in MinFo, *Memoria* (1918): 200.

58 AHMV, 1917–1920, Lewis J. Proctor, "Memorándum que presenta the Caribbean Petroleum Company sobre haber cumplido la obligación de explotar sus concesiones y sobre la negativa de los Guardaminas a expedirle las planillas para el pago de impuestos y certificados de comienzo de explotación," 12 April 1918.

59 Venezuela, Archivo del Ministerio de Fomento (AMF), Proctor to Torres, 21 May 1919.

60 AMF, Telegram Charles Couchet to Torres, 16 May 1919.

61 AHMV, 1917–1920, Proctor, "Memorandum," 1918.

62 AHMV, 1917–1920, Proctor, "Memorandum," 1918.

63 Torres to Proctor, 2 May 1918, in MinFo, *Memoria* (1918): 220.

64 DS 831.6363 McGoodwin to Bainbridge Colby, 11 June 1920.

65 DS 831.6363/473 "Statement of facts with respect to the Vigas Concession, its transfer to the Colon Development Co. Ltd. and the interests of the Carib Syndicate Limited therein" (New York: Evening Post Job Printing Office, 1929), 66.

66 AHMCP Julio 1–30, 1920, Torres, "Memorándum," 10 July 1920.

67 FO 371/4622 Cecil Dormer to Lord Curzon, 16 March 1920.

68 UK National Archives, Foreign Office, Venezuela, Embassy and Consular Archives, Series 199, FO 199/181 Dormer to Henry Hammond Dawson Beaumont, 20 November 1919.

69 FO 371/4622 Dormer to Lord Curzon, 16 March 1920.

70 Torres to CDC, 5 January 1920, in MinFo, *Memoria* (1919), 3:327.

71 FO 371/4622 Dormer to Lord Curzon, 16 March 1920.

72 FO 371/4622 Dormer to Lord Curzon, 16 March 1920.

73 FO 371/4622 Dormer to Lord Curzon, 16 March 1920.

74 Torres to Guillermo Tell Villegas Pulido, 7 February 1920, in MinFo, *Memoria* (1919): 329; also in CFC, *Memoria* (1920): 167.

75 FO 371/4622 Dormer to Lord Curzon, 16 March 1920.
76 FO 371/4622 Dormer to Lord Curzon, 16 March 1920.
77 FO 371/4622 Dormer to Lord Curzon, 16 March 1920.
78 Archivo Particular del Dr. Gumersindo Torres, Copiador (AGTCop) 5, Gumersindo Torres to Gómez, 25 March 1920.
79 DS 831.6363 McGoodwin to Colby, 7 April 1920.
80 Edwin Lieuwen, *Petroleum in Venezuela: A History* (Berkeley: University of California Press, 1954), 51–2.
81 FO 371/4623 J. C. Clarke to Lord Curzon, London, 12 May 1920.
82 FO 371/4623 Dormer to Lord Curzon, 23 July 1920.
83 DS 831.6363/93 David W Murray to Sumner Welles, 27 April 1920.
84 DS 831.6363/33 F. M. Dearing to McGoodwin, 6 May 1920.
85 McKay was a concessionaires' agent acquiring and transferring many crude oil concessions to American oil companies; see AHMCP Dic. 16–22, 1924, Addison H. McKay to Gómez, 17 November 1924.
86 Venezuela, Archivo Histórico de Miraflores, Correspondencia del Secretario General (AHMCS) Abril 1920, Felipe S Toledo to Enrique Urdaneta Maya, 19 January 1920.
87 DS 831.6363/26 McGoodwin to Colby, 26 April 1920, and DS 831.6363/58 McGoodwin to Colby 5, May 1921.
88 AHMCP Mayo 1–30, 1920 Domínici to Gómez, 12 May 1920.
89 AHMCP Mayo 1–30, 1920 Domínici to Gómez, 12 May 1920.
90 AHMCP Mayo 1–30, 1920 Domínici to Gómez, 12 May 1920. Alves also warned Gómez of the impending disaster for Venezuela; see AHMCP Junio 15–30 1920 [sic] Alves to Gómez, 17 May 1920.
91 DS 831.6363/26 C. K. MacFadden to Colby, 3 May 1920.
92 DS 831.6363/29 MacFadden to Colby, 18 May 1920.
93 DS 831.6363/27 Alvey A. Adee to MacFadden, 29 May 1920.
94 FO 371/4623 Lord Curzon to Dormer, 18 May 1920.
95 AGTCop 6, Torres to Esteban Gil Borges, 26 June 1920.
96 AHMCP Julio 1–30, 1920, Dormer to Gil Borges, 10 June 1920.
97 AGTCop 6, Torres to Gil Borges, 26 June 1920.
98 AGTCop 6, Torres to Gil Borges, 26 June 1920.
99 AHMCP Julio 1–30 1920, Torres to Gómez, 14 July 1920.
100 DS 831.6363/33 McGoodwin to Colby, 11 June 1920.
101 Walter R. Skinner, *The Oil and Petroleum Manual* (1920): 123.
102 Lieuwen, *Petroleum in Venezuela*, 52.

103 DS 831.6363/33 McGoodwin to Colby, 11 June 1920.
104 DS 831.6363/58 McGoodwin to Colby, 4 May 1921.
105 FO 371/4623 Dormer to Lord Curzon, 17 June 1920.
106 FO 371/4623 Dormer to Lord Curzon, 17 June 1920.
107 FO 371/4623 Dormer to Lord Curzon, 4 June 1920.
108 FO 371/4623 Dormer to Lord Curzon, 4 June 1920.
109 AHMCS Feb 1923 [sic] Juan J Mendoza to Torres, 10 August 1920.
110 DS 831.6363/33 Dearing to McGoodwin, 6 May 1921. Repeats MacFadden to Colby, New York, 16 June 1920.
111 DS 831.6363/33 Colby to McGoodwin, 24 June 1920.
112 DS 831.6363/63 McGoodwin to Charles Evans Hughes, 14 June 1921.
113 AGTCop 6 Torres to Gómez, 11 August 1920.
114 FO 371/4623 Dormer to Lord Curzon, 9 October 1920.
115 MinFo, *Memoria* (1921), 1:10–11.
116 MinFo, *Memoria* (1921), 1:12–13.
117 AHMCP Feb. 1–28 1921 [sic] Villegas Pulido to Gómez, 15 February 1920, and FO 371/5722 Beaumont to Lord Curzon, 19 February 1921.
118 Venezuela, Distrito Federal, Juzgado de la Primera Instancia en lo Civil, *Juicio seguido por Lorenzo Mercado contra Antonio Aranguren*.
119 RLDV (1915): Vol. 38, Doc. 11,788, 106–7.
120 FO 199/229 and DS 831.6385/C23/18, "Extract from Report of Caracas Counsel," 28 January 1921.
121 AHMCP 1–14 September 1923 Julio F. (Méndez) to Gómez, 13 September 1923.
122 DS 831.6375/C23/7 Lewis J Proctor, "Memorandum on the Espina, Bohórquez vs The Caribbean Petroleum Company Suit," undated, enclosed in McGoodwin to Lansing, 29 October 1918.
123 DS 831.6375/C23/7 McGoodwin to Lansing, 29 October 1918.
124 DS 831.6375/C23/7 Proctor "Memorandum on the Espina."
125 DS 831.6375/C23/7 Proctor "Memorandum on the Espina."
126 CFC, *Memoria* (1919): 253.
127 DS 831.6376/C23/15 McGoodwin to Hughes, 12 April 1921.
128 DS 831.6376/C23/15 McGoodwin to Hughes, 12 April 1921.
129 FO 199/229 and DS 831.6375/C23/18, "Extract from Report of Caracas Office of Counsel," 28 January 1921.
130 DS 831.6375/C23/15 McGoodwin to Hughes, 12 April 1921.

131 DS 831.6363/53 McGoodwin to Hughes, 25 May 1921.

132 DS 831.6375/C23/15 McGoodwin to Hughes, 12 April 1921.

133 DS 831.6375/C23/15 McGoodwin to Hughes, 12 April 1921.

134 DS 831.6375/C23/15 McGoodwin to Hughes, 12 April 1921.

135 DS 831.6375/C23/15 Hughes to McGoodwin, 3 May 1921.

136 FO 371/7325 Clarke to Lord Curzon, 23 June 1922.

137 DS 831.6375/023/15 McGoodwin to Hughes, 12 April 1921.

138 Commercial Bank of Spanish America (CBSA) Archive, Letter Box 8, CBSA to R. S. Fuerth, 13 October 1913.

139 S. Pearson & Sons Ltd. Archive, W. G. Beavan, "Mission to Venezuela, Report No.5," 4–7 August 1923; and AHMCP 1–14 Oct. 1923, F. A. Colmenares Pacheco to Gómez, 31 October 1923.

140 DS 831.6375/C23/20 Willis C. Cook to Hughes, 24 April 1922.

141 FO 199/229 Clarke "Memorandum on Venezuelan Litigation," 23 August 1922.

142 DS 831.6375/C23/22 Frank Seamans to Hughes, 9 June 1922.

143 DS 831.6375/C23/23 Seamans to Hughes, 14 June 1922. A letter followed on the same date.

144 DS 831.6375/C23/24 Leland Harrison to Seamans, 30 June 1922.

145 DS 831.6375/C23/26 Seamans to Hughes, 5 August 1922.

146 DS 831.6375/C23/32 FKN[ielsen] to R. W. Flournoy, 17 July 1922.

147 DS 831.6375/C23/32 RWF[lournoy] to Nielsen, 18 July 1922.

148 FO 371/7325 H. Seymour to Beaumont, 6 July 1922.

149 See Brian S. McBeth, *British Oil Policy, 1919–1939* (London: Frank Cass & Co., 1985).

150 FO 371/7325 H. Seymour to Beaumont, 6 July 1922.

151 FO 371/7325 H. Seymour to Beaumont, 6 July 1922.

152 DS 831.6375/C23/34 WFM, "Memorandum for Mr White on Suit in Venezuela against Caribbean Petroleum Company," 2 September 1922.

153 DS 831.6375/C23/29 Hughes to Cook, 21 September 1922.

154 FO 199/229 Beaumont to Lord Curzon, 10 April 1923.

155 AHMCS Mayo 1923, Pedro Itriago Chacín to Urdaneta Maya, 7 April 1923.

156 FO 199/229 Beaumont to Lord Curzon, 10 April 1923.

157 DS 831.6575/C23/37 and FO 199/229 Roy W. Merritt, "Memorandum," 4 February 1924.

158 McBeth, *Dictatorship & Politics*, 188–9.

159 DS 831.6575/C23/37 and FO 199/229, Roy W. Merritt, "Memorandum," 4 February 1924.

160 CFC, *Memoria* (1924): 339.

161 DS 831.6363/391 Alexander K. Sloan, "Facts and rumours from the Maracaibo Oilfields," 21 June 1928.

162 McBeth, *Juan Vicente Gómez*, 70–108.

163 Venezuela, Ministerio de Minas e Hidrocarburos, *Petróleo y otros datos estadísticos, 1964* (Caracas: Central de Evaluaciones, 1964), 139.

Exxon and the Rise of Producer Power in Venezuela

Joseph A. Pratt

Venezuela is one of the oldest and largest producers of crude oil for export in the Americas. Texas-based Exxon is one of the oldest, most profitable, and most criticized of the large international oil companies.[1] Swings from co-operation to confrontation have marked the century-long relationship between the two. During this time, Venezuela evolved from an oil colony in the early twentieth century, to a leader in the move toward producer power in the mid-twentieth century, to a symbol of resource nationalism in the early twenty-first century.[2] Throughout this process, Exxon has played a major role in the development of oil in Venezuela. This case study examines the nation's halting journey toward control of its own oil, as well as Exxon's efforts to adapt its operations to the rise of producer power in Venezuela.

The often tense relationship between the nation and the company is key to understanding the evolution of the oil industry in the Americas, which long provided the basic energy source for much of the region. Venezuela has numerous claims to leadership in the South American petroleum industry. The sheer size of its reserves shaped the total production and exportation of petroleum on the continent as a whole throughout much of the twentieth century.

In addition, its location proved ideal for exports to the United States, the largest market for oil exports in the Americas. Until the 1970s, tankers from the major oil companies active in the United States provided transportation to this market, along with access to these companies' large, technologically advanced refineries on the Texas-Louisiana Gulf Coast to process Venezuela's crude oil into refined products. Venezuela's oil thus came to hold a special place in the operations of the US- and British-based international oil companies (IOCs), and even in the foreign-policy calculations of their respective governments. As they sought to retain access to Venezuela's traditional oil reserves in the mid-twentieth century, the IOCs looked forward to the future development of technology capable of bringing to market both the vast heavy oil reserves in the Orinoco Basin and the extensive natural gas reserves in Venezuela.

The timing of Venezuela's entry into the oil industry gave it a head start toward becoming and remaining the leading oil exporter in the Americas. When Mexico's brief dominance of oil exports to the United States and Europe waned in the 1920s and '30s, Venezuela stood ready to take its place. Both before and after the expropriations of 1938, the major foreign companies active in Mexico responded by aggressively moving people, facilities, and investment dollars to the much more permissive political environment in Venezuela in the years between the two world wars. Early ties between the IOCs and the Venezuelan government helped forge a special relationship that shaped their interactions for much of the century.

Its massive reserves skewed the focus of the Venezuelan economy in the direction of oil-led development, with the long-term goal of using oil revenues to hasten the growth of a more diversified economy. But this approach never quite succeeded. Instead, the nation's reliance on foreign markets, technology, and capital in an oil-dominated economy produced the most extreme case of what is sometimes referred to as the oil curse in the Americas, with the distribution of both the benefits and the costs of oil-led development creating political and social tensions within Venezuela. The nation remains a model—or at least a cautionary tale—for other oil producers in the Americas concerned about the long-term impacts of an overreliance on oil.

As it grappled with problems raised by oil-led development, Venezuela gained an international prominence not shared by any other South

American oil-producing nation until the rapid growth of Petrobras, Brazil's national oil company, in the late twentieth century. Venezuela gained standing in the international industry in the 1940s, when it pushed through a 50/50 profit-sharing agreement with the IOCs that controlled the operations of its oil industry. This agreement quickly became the norm for major IOCs and large producing nations. After the Second World War, Creole (Exxon's subsidiary) granted concessions to Venezuelan oil workers that also became a model for numerous major oil companies. The nation's crucial role in creating the Organization of Petroleum Exporting Countries (OPEC) in 1960 cemented its claim to leadership in the industry, particularly in South America.

One final difference between Venezuela and its regional competitors was its long, tortuous journey toward some form of democratic capitalism capable of asserting control of the country's oil. The resulting political uncertainties proved costly to Exxon and other IOCs as they sought to survive and prosper amid the stops and starts of the nation's ever-changing oil policies. Exxon, for example, entered and exited several times as the nation moved from dictatorship to near democracy, from nationalization to the return of foreign companies, from the more radical policies of Hugo Chávez to an era of chaotic instability. Because of the continuing importance of Venezuelan oil exports, the world took note of the regular and chaos-producing tensions in the nation's politics. In many ways, Venezuela and PDVSA (its national oil company after the early 1970s) became the international symbol of both the prospects and the perils of oil development in the Americas.[3]

Exxon's Strengths and Weaknesses in South America

Although Exxon could not turn back the tide of producer power, it used its considerable strengths to adapt to changing conditions in Venezuela. Its access to global markets, capital, and political decision-makers provided distinct advantages when it came to dealing with less developed nations. Its vertically integrated management structure allowed it to coordinate activities across national boundaries. Its ace in the hole was state-of-the-art technology, which often was not readily available in producing nations. These strengths had been established before the company entered Venezuela, as had been the focus on financial discipline, engineering efficiency, and competitive zeal that made Exxon one of the most successful companies in the world.[4]

Long-term success embedded in Exxon's corporate culture a strong commitment to business values learned in the days of John D. Rockefeller in the late nineteenth century. Thus, when the company entered Venezuela in the early twentieth century, it favoured markets unfettered by government, survival of the fittest in the marketplace, tight control of corporations over labour and other internal operations, and the sanctity of contracts. It also brought to Venezuela simple operating assumptions—namely, that the nation needed the company more than Exxon needed Venezuela's oil, and that the company's experts should set the terms of access, which should be written into contracts that were binding and not open to renegotiations. In the long term, producing nations would benefit if they gave companies such as Exxon near autonomy in developing their oil. The company brought with it skepticism of government, disdain for politicians, and a sense of racial and technical superiority. It also displayed a confidence in its abilities to find and produce oil that bordered on arrogance.[5] It would be challenged over the next century to adjust its attitudes and its operations as the government gradually asserted control over Venezuela's oil.

The Era of Unabashed Exploitation: Historical Baseline for Change through Time

Venezuela has been an important part of Exxon's operations since the company entered the nation in search of oil in the 1920s. In its early years in Venezuela, it profited from its close relationship with Juan Vicente Gómez, a military dictator. According to sources within Exxon, he ruled the nation "like a feudal baron" from 1908 to 1935. During its fifteen years of operations under the Gómez regime, the company grew through acquisitions and internal expansion into the largest of four major IOCs active in Venezuela.[6] Gómez ceded to these companies considerable control over the development of the nation's oil; Exxon's lawyers even helped draft the nation's landmark petroleum law in 1922. The IOCs reaped most of the benefits from oil; the low taxes and royalties paid to the government enriched Gómez and his family and friends but had little impact on the nation as a whole.[7]

Exxon's exploitation of Gómez's Venezuela was unabashed. The company took full advantage of the imbalance of power between itself and the government in the formative years of Venezuelan oil. It was as if the Martians had landed, bringing advanced technology and expertise to a nation with vast oil resources but few tools with which to develop them. When it entered Venezuela, Exxon found a world in which "graft, traditional and universal as it had become, was not condemned, provided that the gratuities were adequate, generously dispensed, and given to the right people." The nation had quite limited infrastructure for transportation or communication, and in many of the remote locations where Exxon discovered oil, it built company towns marked by extreme paternalism. Finding few skilled Venezuelan workers, the company brought in technicians and supervisors from Texas. These expatriates were men of their time, and they generally held assumptions about the inferiority of Venezuelan workers; they found them to be unaccustomed to industrial labour and complained that they had "no loyalty to the company or to good work." Gómez opposed workers' organizations and brutally repressed any attempts at organization. Had Exxon wanted to improve the conditions of labour, it would have been opposed by the man who held control over its access to Venezuelan oil. Drawing from Exxon's internal records and interviews with employees, the authors of Exxon's corporate history found it ironic that the company prospered in the "strict civil order" created by an "iron-handed military dictator." They noted, however, that Gómez had one attribute much valued by the company: "The oil men soon learned that Gómez respected contracts."[8] In practice, the company operated comfortably and successfully in the strict civil order that Gómez had created, and it firmly established itself as an important factor in the development of Venezuelan oil.

The mass of Venezuelan citizens gained little from oil development in these early years. They watched foreign companies dominate their nation's largest industry to the exclusive benefit of a corrupt, oppressive dictator and his closest associates. They saw Venezuelan workers relegated to common labour while foreigners held technical and managerial positions and lived in the best housing in work camps segregated according to nationality. The historical memory of the conditions in these early years played an important role in the public's reaction to the power of the foreign oil companies. Although conditions of labour gradually improved over the decades, memories of the behaviour and tone of foreign oil companies in the formative years of the Venezuelan oil industry left an anger and sense of injustice that lingered long after 1935, the year in which Gómez died. In public memory, these oil companies remained symbols of Gómez's harsh rule.

The dictator's demise brought a new era in the relations between Venezuela and the IOCs. His replacement as president, General Eleazar López Contreras, supported increasing the taxes paid by the oil companies, improving the treatment of workers, and revising aspects of the contracts signed during Gómez's dictatorship. A generation of young reformers long excluded by Gómez entered the political process and pushed for much stronger measures. Faced with growing demands for greater control over the power and behaviour of the oil companies, Exxon and the other IOCs had a clear choice: resist or accommodate.

Initially, the company's leaders stood firmly against change, especially on issues involving the principle of the inviolability of contracts. A contract was a contract; it should be honoured even if it had been made with a corrupt dictator with little regard for the national interest. Political pressure for change in existing contracts intensified with the emergence of the Democratic Action Party (Acción Democrática, or AD), which was determined to use new laws to extract concessions from the oil companies. Reformers in the party sought much higher oil revenues that could be used to encourage economic development, a process they called "sowing the petroleum" (*sembrar el petróleo*).[9]

The opening of politics to broader input from citizens after Gómez's death required Exxon to reconsider its stance toward reforms, and the ensuing debate within the company about how to respond to these new demands became heated. Executives with first-hand experience of their company's futile efforts to create lasting outposts of production in Bolivia, Argentina, and Mexico challenged the traditional hardline approach. In these years of reform (1935–48), a new consensus gradually took hold within Exxon. New attitudes emerged, especially on the key issues of taxes and the conditions of labour. One younger executive stressed the "need for practicality" and criticized as inequitable and unsustainable the old way of unabashed exploitation. He argued that existing contracts in Venezuela were "defective and in jeopardy" because they were the work of an unrepresentative dictator in a corrupt bargaining process. Such contracts were unfair to the mass of the Venezuelan people, and, thus, indefensible in the court of public opinion. A colleague with long experience in Latin America took this argument one step further by noting the dangers of too rigid an opposition to potential changes in laws and contracts, since laws were only as strong as "the opinions and attitudes behind them."[10] Change was in the air.

Never far below the surface in these internal debates was the shared experience of the Mexican expropriation of 1938, which called into question the effectiveness of the hardline stance of opposing all manner of government oil policies. Chastened by its loses in Mexico, the company became more flexible in its dealings with Venezuela's government and its oil workers. Of utmost importance was Exxon's acceptance of large increases in taxes and royalties. Under Gómez, the IOCs had enjoyed very large concessions and very low royalties of 7.5 to 11 per cent of the value of oil produced. From 1943 to 1948, the AD, under the leadership of Rómulo Betancourt, put growing pressure on the IOCs to accept large increases in taxes and royalties. The leaders of Exxon and its major subsidiary in Venezuela, Creole, finally bent to the inevitable and accepted the so-called 50/50 agreement. This epoch-defining agreement raised total oil revenues to approximately half of the IOCs' net earnings—as measured largely by the IOCs themselves. It quickly became the global norm, introducing a new era of much higher oil revenues for major exporting nations.[11]

New labour laws also encouraged Exxon to pick up the tempo of its efforts to improve conditions of labour. Under pressure from the Venezuelan government, Creole put in place a program of welfare capitalism similar to programs Exxon had established in the United States in the 1920s. This included worker pensions, paid vacations, recognition of worker organization short of independent unions, higher wages and benefits, and technical training for increasing numbers of local workers. To this basic framework the Venezuelan government added labour boards with powers to mediate disputes between the companies and their employees. Exxon's top management, both at its corporate headquarters in New York and on the ground in Venezuela, initially resisted these labour boards, which they thought were an unwarranted intrusion into management's traditional authority. But they soon recognized the wisdom of accommodating demands for government involvement in labour disputes. Their acquiescence reflected in part the memory that labour disputes had pushed the Mexican president to nationalize the properties of foreign oil companies. Longer-term views also dictated compromise on labour issues. One prominent Exxon executive argued that "good employee relations might be the decisive factor" in the company's future success. Especially during and after the demands for increased outputs during the Second World War, Creole's leaders asserted that they had made "every effort to build an understanding and loyal workforce."[12] Venezuelans pushing for greater control over their oil industry could certainly have presented Creole's management a long list of additional changes needed in the treatment of labour, but even they could agree that significant change had been made since the days of Gómez.

The willingness of Exxon's top management to listen to new voices from within Creole and adapt to changed political realities in Venezuela proved essential to the company's economic health in the post–Second World War oil boom. From the war until the 1970s, Venezuela was the company's largest source of crude oil and profits, making it abundantly clear that better treatment of the producing nations was both necessary and good for the bottom line. Henrietta Larson, who wrote the volume of the company's history that covered these years, concluded that "the importance of the amicable settlement of the Venezuelan issues can hardly be overstated."[13]

The Road to Nationalization: Venezuela Asserts Control

As events unfolded in the 1940s, Exxon accepted a demanding new truth: the oil-exporting nations inevitably would control their own oil. Looking back with the insight of years at the highest levels of the oil business, Jack Clarke, long-time Exxon attorney and adviser to the company's CEOs, gave a simple summary of this reality: "If Venezuela were running the oil business in Texas, how long do you think we would like them to do that? . . .

It's only natural for people to want to take it over."[14] Long-term profitability required Exxon to retain access to crude oil by satisfying the producers' demands for increased oil revenues and improved working conditions. The IOCs' strategy was to manage the process by accommodation in an attempt to retain as much control as possible for as long as possible over the price of oil and the quantity produced.

Accommodation was both a short-term necessity and a long-term strategy. At one level, it was simply a way to buy off discontent; at another, it was a symbol that company and country were partners of a sort as they pursued their own self-interests, which at times nonetheless overlapped. Political pressure from reformers accelerated the pace of change, at times overriding Exxon's concerns that government policies were "infringing too much on essential managerial prerogatives."[15] Even after the overthrow of the elected government and the ascension of a new military dictator in 1948, the reforms of the previous decade remained in place, becoming the foundation for a new era of oil policy in Venezuela.

Exxon prospered in this new order. In the 1950s and '60s, Creole became the linchpin of Exxon's global production. The company's output in Venezuela soared from about 400,000 barrels a day (B/D) in 1945, to 660,000 B/D in 1950, to almost 1.5 million B/D in 1974. In the postwar era, Creole accounted for as much as 40 per cent of Exxon's global profits. Despite the higher taxes won by Venezuela, Creole remained a pillar of strength within Exxon. It had moved from seeking to exert control over its workforce in order to safeguard its corporate interests to a search for programs that recognized the mutual interests of company and labour. The rapid growth of its workforce after the Second World War encouraged improvements in the recruitment, training, and retention of good employees. Indeed, Exxon voiced great pride in its employee relations in Venezuela, calling its operations an "industrial showcase in Latin America, if not the world."[16]

Yet forces in Venezuela and the oil industry as a whole worked to limit the duration of this golden era for Exxon. Oil was, after all, key to the future growth of both the Venezuelan economy and Exxon's global operations. But the self-interests of the country and the company were not necessarily the same. Many Venezuelans hoped that oil-led prosperity might result in a higher standard of living and perhaps a more open political system.

Others recalled with outrage the past attitudes and abuses of the foreign oil companies. Exxon's efforts to "convince the [Venezuelan] public that we are not a big octopus" had little impact, and political demands grew for more oil revenues, more national control over oil, and a more equitable distribution of oil wealth. Oil remained a central issue in Venezuela's national politics from the 1940s into the 1970s as the nation moved haltingly toward a more open and democratic system. Rómulo Betancourt, one of the founders of the AD and a chief proponent of its revolution of 1943, captured the essence of resource nationalism in the title of his influential book *Venezuela's Oil*. In the 1960s and '70s, the AD returned to power and led the way toward nationalization.[17]

The challenge to Exxon's control of Venezuela's oil went forward on two levels: national politics and international co-operation by the oil-producing nations represented by OPEC. In this era, the IOCs managed a global glut of oil by co-operating to hold down oil production through interlocking ownership ties in consortia in the major producing nations. The IOCs reinforced their control over both the amount of oil produced and oil prices by negotiating with only one producer at a time. Such collusion on the part of the IOCs strengthened the OPEC nations' resolve to share information and forge an organization capable of collective action.[18] Venezuela took the lead in creating OPEC in 1960, and it received a critical, if unintended, assist from Exxon. In the fifteen years after the Second World War, the IOCs maintained a measure of control over global oil prices by posting the price they would pay for crude without consulting producers. In August 1960, Exxon unilaterally lowered its posted price, sharply reducing oil revenues for producing nations. Its rationale for the cut was the need to lower oil prices to prevent the loss of market share to expansive Soviet companies. This was, of course, of secondary concern to the OPEC nations, which planned their national budgets around projected oil revenues. A unilateral reduction in the posted price of oil was a hard slap in the face. It reminded Venezuelans and citizens of other major oil-exporting nations once again of their lack of control over their own oil. Shared anger over the price cut, as well as shared memories of historical grievances, hastened these nations' resolve to create an organization capable of presenting a united front in their dealings with the IOCs. By September, OPEC was that organization.

In the 1960s, however, the focus of negotiations between the IOCs and major oil producers remained the individual producing nations. Creole was an obvious target for nationalist sentiment in Venezuela. By 1974, it produced approximately 1.5 million B/D of oil out of total national production of about 3.3 million B/D. Along with the other IOCs in Venezuela, Exxon faced serious problems. Some of these problems were geological. The major IOCs in Venezuela had access to lower-cost, higher-quality crude oil in the younger and larger fields of the Middle East, putting Venezuela at a disadvantage in global markets. Other problems were political. Opposition to foreign oil companies had been a staple of Venezuelan politics for almost forty years. Indeed, Creole's most pressing problem in 1973 was historical. The petroleum law of 1943 had renewed existing leases for forty years, stipulating that these leases would revert to the nation in 1983. The clock was ticking as the IOCs sought ways to retain a strong position in Venezuela.[19]

Early reversion became a key issue in the presidential election of December 1973. The position of the AD's candidate, Carlos Andrés Pérez, was simple: "Venezuela must take over control of this product." In his winning campaign, and later as president, Pérez sought a middle way between the military dictatorships with close ties to the IOCs in Venezuela's past and the Cuban model of socialism. He acknowledged that the nation was not yet ready to manage its own oil industry. It still needed the IOCs' technical assistance and access to markets, at least in the transitional period after the reversion of the leases.[20]

In May 1973, top Creole executives told their superiors in New York that Exxon faced "major uncertainties beyond our control." Yet they also advised that, even if early reversion took place, the corporation could continue to provide important services to the Venezuelan nation "on a mutually satisfactory and profitable basis." By this time, Exxon had little to no leverage. As Howard Kauffmann, Exxon's president at the time, put it, "We recognized they had the right to nationalize that property.... All we wanted [them] to do was pay us a fair price for it, and we wanted to continue to be a customer of theirs.... We realized that losing your temper or showing any animosity was not going to get you anywhere."[21]

After Pérez won election, he moved quickly toward nationalization. In his inaugural speech in March 1974, he promised that the early takeover of foreign oil operations and assets in Venezuela was a certainty. In announcing a two-year deadline to arrive at a national consensus on the early reversion of the 1943 leases, he called for a "coolheaded approach" that would "fulfill the old aspiration of our people, that our oil will be Venezuelan." To help build consensus, in May 1974, Pérez appointed a Reversion Commission made up of more than thirty prominent Venezuelans to recommend government policy on early reversion. According to Creole officials, when the commission at times threatened to get "out of hand, the administration . . . maintained control."[22] The company's co-operation with Pérez reflected the reality that other, more radical oil policies were possible in Venezuela.

Early reversion was now an accepted reality, not a matter of speculation. In 1973, the government handed control over all gasoline service stations and other local markets to CVP, a national oil company created in 1960 to help collect information. It was now asked to manage the transition to Venezuelan control. In April 1974, Creole reported that the foreign companies had been "arbitrarily assigned, by decree, supply and distribution obligations to CVP at very low prices"[14] to provide oil products to subsidize Venezuelan development.[23]

As Venezuela marched toward nationalization, Creole of necessity chose diplomacy over indignation. With no realistic option, it supported and carried out Pérez's policies. When the government called for the drastic reduction of natural gas flaring, Creole launched a "very aggressive program to install additional gas compression capacity" designed to "raise Creole's gas utilization in Lake Maracaibo to essentially 100 percent." When the government sought to cut back production to conserve reserves, Creole accelerated its efforts to save oil by making its own operations more efficient.[24] Venezuelan officials could be excused for wondering why one of the world's leading oil companies with a reputation for engineering excellence had not previously taken such measures on its own.

Amid growing tensions, Jack Clarke, a central figure in the company's negotiating team, sought the counsel of Howard Page, who had handled similar talks for Exxon from the 1950s through the early 1970s. Recounting the frustration of negotiating from weakness in these years, Page noted a crucial difference after 1973: "In my day, when I was negotiating, I at least had the appearance of having a gun. You fellows don't have anything."²⁵ Lacking power to impose a solution, the company made a final accommodation: it co-operated in its own nationalization, hoping to retain a profitable presence in a new Venezuela in which the government controlled the nation's oil.

Legislation passed in July 1975 called for the early reversion of the 1943 leases on 1 January 1976; it also announced the framework for the newly organized Venezuelan oil industry. Six months earlier, the president of Creole had sent a discouraging letter to New York decrying the lack of input on the part of the IOCs on this key issue. He noted that Creole's personnel had taken part in "many technical discussions [about the law] underway at government request, between their representatives and industry professionals concerning refining, computing, technology, research, etc." The Reversion Commission, however, included no representatives of the major foreign oil companies. Creole's president complained that "no high level discussions between industry and government have taken place in over half a year."²⁶ Venezuelans, not Exxon managers, would make the decisions about reversion.

The law asserted control over the nation's oil, but despite fierce political opposition, President Pérez stood by his position that Venezuela was not yet ready to manage the industry without assistance from the IOCs. To facilitate a smooth transition to national ownership, the new law grouped all existing Venezuelan oil companies into four firms, Lagoven (built around Creole), Maraven (built around the holdings of Shell), Meneven (built around the holdings of Gulf Oil), and Corproven (created around CVP). Smaller companies would be folded into these four entities. This approach retained as much as possible of the organization, the Venezuelan personnel, and the professionalism of the three major IOCs. Sitting on top of the four competitors was the newly created Petróleos de Venezuela, S. A. (PDVSA), which initially exercised oversight of the operating companies but evolved into a strong national oil company. Exxon felt that the new organizational framework, which embodied well-developed ties between Creole and the Venezuelan government, might pave the way for future co-operation.²⁷

These historical ties would not much matter to Exxon, however, unless it retained access to large quantities of crude while also earning a reasonable profit on the technical, marketing, and managerial services it contracted to provide to the new companies. The reversion law allowed the foreign oil companies to sign "two-year renewable technical assistance contracts—to include marketing—with the government in order to continue providing essential support services after nationalization."[21] The IOCs and the government vigorously negotiated all aspects of these contracts, which now took the place of the direct ownership of oil that Creole had enjoyed under the old lease system. The contracts specified payments per barrel of oil for different services. Amounts ranged from 10 to 20 cents per barrel, but such small sums quickly added up when a company processed a million barrels of oil a day. Creole and the government also bargained hard to establish a pricing system flexible enough to reflect changes in global markets. The two parties also had to find a compromise on the amount of oil that would be made available to Exxon. Short of crude, the company wanted the largest quantity of oil acceptable to Venezuelan officials; seeking to limit exports, the government wanted the smallest quantity acceptable to Exxon. Just days after the official nationalization, on 1 January 1976, Exxon signed a contract with the government to purchase an annual average of 965,000 B/D of crude, at least temporarily fulfilling its major strategic objective in Venezuela—continued access to large, relatively secure supplies of crude at prices that were reasonable in the context of rising oil prices in the mid-1970s. The one-time king of Venezuelan oil had become a contractor.[28]

The attainment of Creole's second strategic objective, fair compensation for its nationalized properties, proved much more difficult. The Venezuelan government awarded about $1 billion in compensation to all nationalized oil companies, with Creole receiving about half of this sum. As called for in the law of reversion, compensation reflected the net book value of the companies on which taxes had been based, not the total amount invested by the companies, which the IOCs claimed totalled approximately $5 billion. The foreign companies had only sixty days to accept the government's compensation offer. Creole had no realistic option. It accepted the government's take-it-or-leave-it offer, and its properties reverted to the state on 1 January 1976.[29]

Only months after the deal had been done, however, the Venezuelan government filed a suit against Creole for disputed back taxes from 1970. The sum involved was $231 million, almost half of the compensation payment received by Exxon. As far as the company's managers were concerned, the total was not as important as the principle involved. They had accepted the government's offer because it seemed as close to fair and timely compensation as it could obtain. In this context, the tax claim appeared to be an end run around the agreement. Throughout its history, Exxon has fought long and hard in the courts on issues of principle—in the process sending a message to other potential litigants that the company would not settle out of court. Believing the "claims as without legal foundation," Exxon's lawyers vowed that they "would be resisted vigorously in the courts." Another top executive warned that "failure to reach equitable settlement of the outstanding nationalization issues could result in phasing out of our Venezuelan activities." Negotiations droned on until 1986, when those working on the tax issue advised Exxon CEO Cliff Garvin that "the best deal we are going to get is to call it even." Garvin, who had led the company throughout the reversion process in Venezuela, swallowed hard and replied, "I don't like it, but okay." This end game foreshadowed things to come for Exxon in Venezuela, where long-term investment opportunities beckoned it while political risks pushed it away.[30]

Looking back, nationalization seems inevitable, but the timing was uncertain. From the 1940s onward, Exxon's management strategy of choosing accommodation over resistance probably enabled the company to extend its run as a major leaseholder in Venezuela.[31] The fundamental limit to accommodation was Venezuela's desire to control its own resources, and events in the early 1970s allowed the nation to just that. Exxon had no practical option except to work with the Venezuelan government to move the nation as smoothly as possible toward state ownership of petroleum. Despite intense political pressure to use the process of nationalization to demonize and punish the foreign oil companies, the government chose instead to accept their assistance and then to move gradually toward more independence in its operations. Lacking the power to impose a better outcome, Exxon co-operated with the government and then with PDVSA in these transition years, to the benefit of Venezuela and consumers of petroleum around the world.

In and Out in the 1990s and 2000s

Far-reaching changes in the global oil industry in the 1970s shaped Venezuela's success in nationalizing Exxon and other foreign oil companies throughout the decade. Within individual producing nations, politicians of all shades supported the strong nationalistic urge to take control of valuable national resources from foreign oil companies. Across national borders, oil-producing nations shared knowledge about the inner workings of the international petroleum industry. The increased oil revenues brought by OPEC's assertion of control over oil prices after 1973 dramatically enhanced producer power. This revenue bonanza, coupled with a shared sense of historical grievances against the IOCs, became the glue binding together the diverse member nations of OPEC. The completion of nationalization and the rise of OPEC did not, however, ensure the success of each national oil company or the prosperity of each oil-exporting nation. Because its oil fields were relatively old and its heavy oil were expensive to produce in comparison to Middle Eastern oil, Venezuela faced difficult challenges in carving out a place for itself in a highly competitive global oil industry during a lengthy period of low oil prices.

As the Venezuelan economy stagnated in the early 1990s, the country's political leaders looked for ways to jump-start growth. Petroleum remained the primary engine of growth for Venezuela, and the government decided to try to foster growth by inviting foreign oil companies to return.[32] Ironically, the leader of this new opening to foreign oil companies was Carlos Andrés Pérez, who was re-elected president in 1989, ten years after the end of his first term in office. As in the 1970s, Pérez represented the reformist wing of Venezuelan politics, and he still believed that the nation needed the capital, the access to markets, and the advanced technology of the IOCs to help develop its oil fields. In the twenty years since the nationalizations, the global oil industries had added numerous strong new competitors, including both national oil companies and a more diverse group of IOCs. Many of these companies responded to Pérez's invitation. From their perspective, Venezuela was a promising oil frontier. It had relatively manageable political risks and held out the prospect of being a part of one of the most touted oil booms of the era—namely, the development of the nation's vast heavy oil reserves in the Orinoco River Basin.

Since the 1970s, the oil industry had made headway in developing technologies to unlock the great potential riches of the heavy oil deposits in the Orinoco region. By the early 1990s, estimates of the nation's recoverable conventional oil reserves had reached a respectable 90 billion barrels, but its heavy oil belt held as many as 250 billion more barrels of recoverable reserves—if ways could be found to develop this oil at prices competitive with conventional oil. Exxon's previous experience with Canadian oil sands and heavy oil deposits, along with its research in the 1970s and '80s on synthetic fuels, made it a logical company to develop Venezuela's heavy oil.[33]

Even though the Pérez government offered attractive terms to the IOCs, Exxon initially hesitated to return to Venezuela. This was hardly surprising given the bad memories of retroactive taxes levied against the company after the nationalization. In addition, the company had a long commitment to financial discipline, and it already had large investments that came with high political risks in Russia and West Africa. Violent coup attempts in Venezuela in 1992, one involving then Colonel Hugo Chávez, put Exxon and other potential investors on notice that Pérez and the nation's still fragile democratic institutions were in danger. As Exxon studied the situation in Venezuela, it had to look ahead to the coming presidential election of 1998 and handicap the direction of political change. The company also considered the economics behind Venezuela's new overtures to foreign oil companies. In an era of low oil prices, the government lacked the revenue needed to develop its heavy oil reserves. Would this remain true over the long period required to develop heavy oil? In short, did long-term political and economic trends merit large investments in a nation whose modern history had been shaped by recurring periods of confrontation with IOCs?

Exxon took a stake in one traditional oil project in Venezuela in the late 1990s, but it did not enter the heavy oil sector in the first round of contracts. Many of its competitors signed thirty-five-year contracts that stipulated low royalties and tax rates. These projects planned to produce the region's very thick heavy oil and then upgrade it to a lighter syncrude through refining. This would take place in existing plants owned by the foreign companies—at times in joint ventures with PDVSA—on the Texas-Louisiana Gulf Coast and in new plants built in Venezuela. Mobil's

Cerro Negro project (which came to Exxon through its merger with Mobil in 1999) involved potential production of 120,000 B/D by 2001, with most of the upgrading to be done at a Chalmette, Louisiana, refinery jointly owned by Mobil and PDVSA. Mobil, the operator, had about 42 per cent ownership.[34] The low tax and royalty rates on these heavy oil projects made them attractive despite the prevailing depressed prices for oil.

Though not a partner in any of the original heavy oil projects, Exxon continued negotiations for Hamaca Este, a project designed to produce about 170,000 B/D of syncrude by upgrading heavy oil from Venezuela in the company's Baytown or Baton Rouge refineries. Exxon also continued planning for a $3 billion petrochemical complex in Venezuela with Pequiven, the state-owned petrochemical company. Finally, it took part in the latest proposal for the Cristobal Colon LNG project that had emerged in the 1970s and then reemerged in the early 1990s.

Unfortunately for the company, Chávez won the presidential election in 1998, after which he quickly moved to consolidate his political power. His self-styled Bolivarian Revolution put in place a variety of programs to improve the education, health, and welfare of the poorest segments of society—paid for largely by increased payments by foreign oil companies. In essence, this was a more radical version of sowing the petroleum, with the assumption that PDVSA would serve as a cash cow that could be milked to provide the funding for extensive social programs in Venezuela and other nations. Chávez backed these programs with aggressive rhetoric against US foreign policy. His message to the IOCs was clear: they could stay in Venezuela only on his terms.[35]

A turning point in the Chávez regime was his dramatic showdown with PDVSA. When President Chávez sought to tie PDVSA's goals more closely to his own, the company's leaders resisted. Tensions came to a head in a strike by much of PDVSA's workforce in December 2002. Chávez fired some eighteen thousand strikers, replacing many of the company's professional oil specialists with people whose major qualification was their loyalty to him. He proclaimed, "Previously, PDVSA was managed as a multinational company, with criteria that did not consider our social reality. Now it is a national company that has allowed us to deploy, for the first time, our plan." Almost overnight, an efficient oil company run by experienced engineers became an organization run by Chávez loyalists with limited experience in the oil industry. Long-standing ties between the IOCs and PDVSA were severed in the process, as many experienced oil technicians left home for oil-related jobs in Calgary and Houston.[36]

Direct challenges to the foreign oil companies followed. Increases in oil prices generated higher government revenues, encouraging Chávez's resource nationalism. The speeches of the president and his spokesmen heated up, with pointed references to the deals president Pérez had cut with the IOCs in the mid-1990s as "criminal" and "treasonous giveaways."[37] The government backed its rhetoric by revising the terms of contracts for conventional oil projects written in the 1990s and giving PDVSA increased authority in managing the joint ventures involved in these projects. After threatening to take its grievances against Chávez to international arbitration, Exxon decided instead to sell its holdings.[38]

The Chávez regime moved on to heavy oil in 2004 by unilaterally raising the royalty rate on the Orinoco projects. In 2006, Chávez altered the original thirty-five-year contracts to significantly increase taxes and royalties and give PDVSA majority control of each project. The companies involved faced a difficult choice: accept these changes or leave Venezuela. Collectively, they had already invested an estimated $11 billion in Venezuela's heavy oil fields and in refineries needed to upgrade the approximately 600,000 B/D of syncrudes flowing or scheduled to flow from their projects. Much of this investment, including advanced technology being used to transform heavy oil into useful products, could not be moved out of Venezuela.

ExxonMobil had backed away from a threat of international arbitration after the earlier round of royalty increases, but it held its ground in 2006. With oil prices rising steadily, the Venezuelan government also stood firm. After ExxonMobil indicated that it could not make an adequate return under the proposed new taxes, the Venezuelan oil minister responded with disdain. If the company preferred to leave rather than to adjust, he said, "we don't want them to be here then. . . . [If] we need them, we'll call them." The minister reminded Exxon that plenty of other oil companies from around the world, particularly national oil companies, had expressed their interest in Venezuela's heavy oil.[39] With the growth of competition and the prevailing high prices for oil, Venezuela no longer needed Exxon as it had in the 1970s.

After almost a year of this war of words, Exxon announced its decision to leave Venezuela. Conoco was the only other foreign company in the heavy oil projects that made the same choice. Before Exxon's departure, Chávez proclaimed that "the Orinoco belt is still a living symbol of what was an important part of the oil opening. We must eliminate this symbol." Chávez punctuated his subsequent political victory by standing up to Exxon, the global symbol of Big Oil and a ready villain for politicians hoping to rally support. The company took this dispute to arbitration, but after more than five years of hearings, it received only a small portion of the claims it had made on the Chávez regime.[40]

This was not a case of Exxon reverting to its earlier rigidity on the sanctity of contracts. The company knew that governments would and could alter the terms of contracts. Instead, this was a decision based on considerable experience during the difficult search for non-OPEC oil after the 1970s. Some political risks simply were not worth taking. Top management concluded that doing business with Chávez over the long term was a losing game; the heavy oil projects were becoming increasingly expensive; it would take decades to recoup investments. Better to avoid large investments in Venezuela, cut its losses, and try to recover its previous investments through arbitration than to face the uncertainty of life with Chávez. No doubt, the company walked away in anger over its treatment by Chávez, but shorn of pride, the decision to leave Venezuela made economic sense for Exxon.

Exxon paid a high price for its decision to resist Chávez. It sold one traditional oil field in Venezuela and lost its stake in the Cerro Negro heavy oil project. In addition, it lost the chance to pursue a $3 billion petrochemical project and an even larger LNG project in Venezuela. Its highly publicized confrontation with Chávez yielded some long-term benefit by announcing once again that the company believed strongly in the sanctity of contracts and was willing to stand up for its principles. Re-entry into Venezuela had looked interesting for a moment in the mid-1990s, but events after the election of Chávez in 1998 showed how quickly political risks could mount, particularly in times of rising oil prices.

Exxon's departure from Chávez's Venezuela shows that the company's choices were shaped by various considerations beyond the politics of an individual nation. The price of oil and the company's access or lack thereof to alternative sources of crude also entered into its decisions, as did the long time required to make profits on the large investments that had become the primary business of big oil companies. Geopolitics constrained some choices during the Second World War and the Cold War, but the fall of the Soviet Union and the "triumph" of capitalism in the 1990s opened new horizons for the company, notably in Russia, the breakaway Soviet republics, and China.

History also shaped Exxon's choices. The behaviours and attitudes it brought to Venezuela in the early twentieth century left lasting impressions that proved difficult to alter. Memories of the early years of unabashed exploitation—passed down from generation to generation and embodied in political rhetoric—fuelled the zeal of reformers. During almost a century in Venezuela, the company modified its attitudes and behaviours in response to the rise of producer power. It stretched itself to its limits in its efforts to change while remaining profitable. In juggling the demands of accommodation, Exxon gradually became a new company, one with a broader vision of its social and political environment. It also gained a clearer understanding of a central reality of the twenty-first-century oil industry: the giant, expensive projects that had become the norm for the major IOCs required them to remain in producing nations for decades. To do so required a heightened sense of social responsibility and good corporate citizenship so that the companies could form lasting relationships with the governments and citizens of the producing nations.

When history happened to Exxon in the 1970s, the company tested the limits of accommodation and co-operation, but it could not avoid nationalization. When Hugo Chávez pushed the company to the wall in the early twenty-first century, it had enough experience with extreme political risks to recognize that it was time to seek opportunities elsewhere. Throughout its history in Venezuela, Exxon's learning curve was steep and at times painful. But the company emerged with a clearer sense of the limits of its own power and the need for close co-operation with governments. In Venezuela, as in other parts of the Americas, the road to producer power was long and rough, but the destination was ultimately reached. The lesson learned by the IOCs and the producer nations was simple: it was only natural for oil-producing nations to seek to control their resources. And for the major IOCs, it was only natural to learn to adapt to an ever-changing world.

NOTES

1. The company known as ExxonMobil since 1999 has undergone numerous name changes throughout its long history. It began as part of John D. Rockefeller's Standard Oil Company. Under the name Standard Oil of New Jersey, it served as the holding company for Standard Oil. After the breakup of Standard Oil by the US Supreme Court in 1911, Standard Oil of New Jersey emerged as the largest of the resulting companies. It often was referred to as "Esso" or Jersey Standard. In 1972, it took the name Exxon. I use that name to refer to the company throughout this chapter.

2. For overviews of oil-led development in Venezuela, see Juan Carlos Boué, *Venezuela: The Political Economy of Oil* (Oxford: Oxford Institute for Energy Studies, 1993), and Jorge Salazar-Carrillo and Bernadette West, *Oil and Development in Venezuela during the 20th Century* (Westport, CT: Praeger, 2004).

3. Sweeping views of the rise of producer power can be found in Anthony Sampson, *The Seven Sisters: The Great Oil Companies and the World They Shaped* (New York: Viking Press, 1975), and Daniel Yergin, *The Prize: The Epic Quest for Oil, Money and Power* (New York: Simon & Schuster, 1992). Terry Lynn Karl analyzes the difficulties in oil-led development in *The Paradox of Plenty: Oil Booms and Petro-States* (Berkeley: University of California Press, 1997).

4. Exxon has sponsored an ongoing corporate history since the Second World War. The project has now published five volumes, each covering about twenty-five years of the company's history. The general title of the series is History of Standard Oil Company (New Jersey). The five volumes are as follows: Ralph W. Hidy and Muriel Hidy, *Pioneering in Big Business, 1882–1911* (New York: Harper & Brothers, 1955); George S. Gibb and Evelyn H. Knowlton, *The Resurgent Years, 1911–1927* (New York: Harper & Brothers, 1956); Henrietta M. Larson, Evelyn H. Knowlton, and Charles S. Popple, *New Horizons, 1927–1950* (New York: Harper and Row, 1971); Bennett H. Wall, *Growth in a Changing Environment: A History of Standard Oil Company (New Jersey), Exxon Corporation, 1950–1975* (New York: McGraw-Hill, 1988); and Joseph A. Pratt with William E. Hale, *Exxon: Transforming Energy, 1973–2005* (Austin: Dolph Briscoe Center for American History, University of Texas Press, 2013).

5. For an overview of Exxon's responses to producer power, see Joseph A. Pratt, "Exxon and the Control of Oil," *Journal of American History* 99, no. 1 (2012): 145–54.

6. In this section, I make extensive use of Exxon's five-volume history. These books were written under contract by professional historians who had editorial control, access to internal records, and the opportunity to interview personnel. They provide useful insights into the internal life of the corporation and proved helpful in reconstructing the company's view of events. I have tried to place this internal view in a broad historical context, both in this chapter and in the fifth volume of the Exxon history. The remainder of this chapter draws primarily from my research in Exxon records while completing my recently published volume of the Exxon history, which covers the years from 1973 to 2005. All five volumes are cited in footnote 4.

7. Gibb and Knowlton, *The Resurgent Years*, 3.

8   Gibb and Knowlton, *The Resurgent Years*, 386-390; Larson, Knowlton, and Popple, *New Horizons*, 133-41.
9   Larson, Knowlton, and Popple, *New Horizons*, 140-4.
10 Larson, Knowlton, and Popple, *New Horizons*, 481-4.
11 Larson, Knowlton, and Popple, *New Horizons*, 479-88; Wall, *Growth in a Changing Environment*, 401.
12 Wall, *Growth in a Changing Environment*, 142-3. For more on welfare capitalism at Exxon, see Henrietta M. Larson and Kenneth Wiggins Porter, *History of Humble Oil & Refining Company: A Study in Industrial Growth* (New York: Harper & Brothers, 1959), 290-318, 350-89.
13 Larson and Porter, *History of Humble Oil*, 484.
14 Jack Clarke, interview by Joseph Pratt, Orlando, Florida, 3 January 2007, 13, Exxon Oral History Collection, ExxonMobil Archive, Dolph Briscoe Center for American History, University of Texas at Austin.
15 Larson, *New Horizons*, 728-30.
16 For production statistics, see Larson, Knowlton, and Popple, *New Horizons*, 486; Wall, *Growth in a Changing Environment*, 402; and Pratt, *Exxon*, 77. For a quote on Creole's labour system, see Wall, *Growth in a Changing Environment*, 396.
17 Rómulo Betancourt, *Venezuela's Oil*, trans. Donald Peck (London: Allen & Unwin, 1978); Wall, *Growth in a Changing Environment*, 403.
18 Wall, *Growth in a Changing Environment*, 600-21.
19 Wall, *Growth in a Changing Environment*, 396-430.
20 Most of the quotes on nationalization in the 1970s are from Pratt, *Exxon*, 26-36; *Oil and Gas Journal*, no. 71 (1 December 1973), various items; Exxon Management Committee Records (hereafter, XMC), Report from Robert Dolph to Management Committee, May 5, 1973, and May, 8, 1973, Irving, Texas, Exxon Archives. These records are destined for deposit at the Briscoe Center for American History. See also "Venezuela's Pérez Promises Take-Over of Oil in 2 years," *Oil and Gas Journal*, 25 February 1974, 29; "Venezuela Starts Down Road to Nationalization," *Oil and Gas Journal*, 27 May 1974, 33.
21 Quoted in Pratt, *Exxon*, 31.
22 Creole Petroleum to Exxon Management Committee, Fall 1974 CEO Letters, 26 September 1974, 1 and 2, XMC.
23 Dolph to Exxon Management Committee, 24 April 1974, XMC.
24 Exxon Management Committee, 25 April 1974, XMC.
25 Page is quoted in the interview with Jack Clarke cited in note 14.
26 Robert Dolph to Management Committee, 28 January 1975, XMC.
27 Emma Brossard, *Petroleum Research and Venezuela's INTEVEP: The Clash of the Giants* (Houston: PennWell Books/INTEVEP, 1993), 108-14.

28 "Venezuela Take-Over Set Jan. 1 for 21 Private Oil Companies," *Oil and Gas Journal*, 8 September 1975, 25.

29 "Creole Petroleum in Venezuelan Pact," *New York Times*, 13 November 1975, 61.

30 Pratt, *Exxon*, 33–4.

31 Wall, *Growth in a Changing Environment*, 430.

32 Most of the quotes about Exxon's entry to and exit from Venezuela in the 1990s and 2000s are taken from Pratt, *Exxon*, 328–34.

33 For a history of Exxon's development of heavy oil and oil sands, see Pratt, *Exxon*, ch. 4.

34 Thi Chang, "Upgrading and Refining Essential Parts of Orinoco Development," *Oil and Gas Journal*, 19 October 1998, 67; Pratt, *Exxon*, 330–3.

35 For a lively account of Hugo Chávez's years in office from 1998 to 2007, see Tina Rosenberg, "The New Nationalization: Where Hugo Chávez's 'Oil Socialism' Could be Taking the Developed World," *New York Times Magazine*, 4 November 2007, 45.

36 Rosenberg, "The New Nationalization," 48–9.

37 Brian Ellsworth, "Chavez Views '90s Oil Deals as Criminal," *Houston Chronicle*, 19 April 2006, D-6.

38 "Exxon Mobil Pays Price for Balking," *Houston Chronicle*, 8 February 2006, D-4.

39 "Venezuela Takes on ExxonMobil," Associated Press, 30 March 2006.

40 Russell Gold, "Exxon, Conoco Exit Venezuela Under Pressure," *Wall Street Journal*, 27 June 2007, A-9; Kristen Hats and John Otis, "Two Oil Giants Defy Chavez," *Houston Chronicle*, 27 June 2007, D-1 and D-5; Peter Howard Wertheim, "Venezuela to Nationalize Orinoco Oil Operations," *Oil and Gas Journal*, 15 January 2007, 41.

Current Concerns: Canadian–United States Energy Relations and the St. Lawrence and Niagara Megaprojects

Daniel Macfarlane

Until the 1950s, Canadian-US energy relations predominantly revolved around hydroelectricity exports from Ontario. The transnational construction of the Niagara and St. Lawrence hydroelectric megaprojects in the 1950s represents a significant watershed in North America's shared electricity history. The St. Lawrence and Niagara Rivers are international rivers, bisecting the state of New York and the province of Ontario, which necessitated the involvement of various federal governments and subnational entities (i.e., state and provincial governments and their respective power utilities), the utilization of many of the same engineers and workers, and oversight by the International Joint Commission.

The St. Lawrence Seaway and Power Project, built between 1954 and 1959, was the product of half a century of negotiations. It is one of the largest transborder projects ever undertaken by two countries and is considered one of the great civil engineering achievements of the twentieth century. The seaway technically runs 181.5 miles, from Montreal to Lake Erie, and features numerous dams, two of which generate hydroelectricity. Its importance was not restricted to its physical scale. In 1961 political scientist James Eayrs labelled the St. Lawrence negotiations one of the "most difficult and most momentous" issues for Canadian foreign policy.[1] It was the longest continually running issue in US congressional history. As the authors of a text on Canadian-US relations declared, "nothing represents the bilateral [Canada-US] relationship during the cold war better than that seaway."[2] Schemes to remake Niagara Falls were part of the St. Lawrence negotiations in the first half of the twentieth century. The 1950 Niagara Diversion Treaty was the result of several decades of binational attempts to plumb Niagara Falls for greater hydro production while "enhancing" the waterfall's appearance. This treaty authorized bilateral engineering works that enabled huge amounts of water to be diverted and used at downstream hydroelectric power plants while also manipulating the river and waterfalls in order to maintain their scenic appeal.

Important conceptual differences had tangible impacts on how Canada and the United States approached the creation and distribution of electricity from these border waters of the Great Lakes–St. Lawrence Basin.[3] In this chapter I argue that the history of the Niagara and St. Lawrence power projects, in addition to demonstrating the importance of hydroelectricity for the evolution of North American domestic and transborder energy forms, relations, and exports over the first half of the twentieth century, reveals important similarities and differences in Canadian and US conceptions of the interrelationship between identity, electricity, natural resources, technology, and nation—and province—building.[4] The role of private versus public development, and the involvement of subnational governments and actors, are also a key factor in the historical development of energy regimes in the Americas. Canadian nationalism and identity attached a different significance to hydroelectric developments and exports than did their US variants, and I suggest that a Canadian "hydraulic nationalism" is apparent in the intertwined evolution of these two projects.

This hydraulic nationalism shared many elements with the various forms of Latin American resource nationalism, generally linked to fossil fuels, identified in this volume (and in the Canadian hydroelectric case, energy has been most commonly treated as a common and/or political good, according to the typologies that Heidrich identifies in chapter 1 of this volume).[5] Moreover, as was the case with Canadian hydroelectricity, the United States directly and indirectly shaped the energy regimes of many Latin American countries. At various times, a number of nations in the Americas were subject to US energy imperialism; however, we should not overstate the one-sided nature of such relationships, since many countries concluded that it was in their best interests to integrate or trade with the United States.

How does the materiality of hydro-power production and distribution distinguish it from fossil fuels, and affect the trajectory of Canadian and Latin American energy regimes? One way to bridge the gap between energy types is by invoking Timothy Mitchell's notion of "carbon democracy"—the idea that the materiality of fossil fuels has shaped democracy and political economy in various countries. Here, I borrow from Mitchell to suggest "hydro democracy" as a concept for considering Canada's hydroelectric relationship with the United States.

Developing Hydroelectricity

Hydroelectricity in North America dates to the end of the nineteenth century. Niagara Falls quickly became the focal point of continental hydro production and distribution on a large scale: a number of private hydroelectric plants were in place before the end of the century on both sides of the border, aided by technological improvements (e.g., alternating current) that allowed electricity to be transmitted over longer distances. The world's first international electricity interconnection occurred here in 1901.[6] The United States outpaced Canada in terms of initial industrial and hydroelectric development around Niagara; in reaction to the heavier industrialization on the New York side, the US public was more vocal about the degradation of the Falls' vista than their Canadian neighbours.[7] US concerns about preserving scenic beauty also stemmed from a desire to preserve the country's hydro monopoly at the Falls, and from worries that the Canadian side of the cataract was more attractive than its US counterpart.[8] Given coal shortages in Ontario in the early twentieth century, that provinces was less concerned about the scenic beauty of the Niagara Falls and more focused on its potential for power. In this period, however, Ontario did not have the capacity to fully develop its own hydroelectric resources but relied on US capital and technology. This reliance foreshadowed US involvement in future Canadian and Latin American oil and petroleum developments, as Pratt and others in this volume show. But here the story diverges, for Ontario did quickly develop the capacity, though it kept exporting much of its electricity to the United States. This, too, mirrors aspects of Canada-US and Latin America–US fossil fuel relations, as well as aspects of oil development in Western Canada, for hydroelectric development in Central/Eastern Canada also involved a unique intermingling of public and private entities (e.g., state involvement, regulation of marketing of private industry). Much like the future continental oil trade that Chastko describes in this volume, infrastructure bound Canada and the United States together physically when it came to electricity trade—and in this context, it is worth noting that the politics of the Keystone XL pipeline have been compared with the leadup to the St. Lawrence Seaway.[9] Moreover, both hydroelectric and fossil fuel developments have been central to federalism and nation/province/state building in the Americas.

The first powerhouse on the Canadian side at Niagara was completed in 1901, and two others were completed within a few years. These were subsidiaries of US companies, and the majority of the electricity produced at these plants was sent across the river to the United States. Indeed, much of the electricity was exported because there was little market for it in Canada at that point.[10] Several other cross-border interconnections soon followed, each involving the long-term exportation of electricity from Canada to one isolated customer on the US side (e.g., an eighty-five-year export contract for 56 megawatts to the Aluminum Company of America from the Les Cedres generating station on the St. Lawrence in Quebec).[11] Under the Liberal government of Wilfrid Laurier, Canada adopted a laissez-faire approach to electricity exports, and by 1910 about one-third of Canada's electricity was being exported.[12]

Many Canadians resented this state of affairs, however, and the desire to keep power and develop industry helped lead to the creation in 1906 of a provincially owned power utility, the Hydro-Electric Power Commission of Ontario (also known as HEPCO or Ontario Hydro). This commission would begin with the distribution of electricity, but over the following decades, Ontario Hydro subsequently acquired the aforementioned private Niagara generating stations, built several of its own massive hydroelectric facilities along the Niagara River, and expanded the hydroelectric transmission network throughout Ontario (while still continuing exports to the United States).

The same concerns that led to the creation of HEPCO were also linked to the federal passage of the Exportation of Power and Fluids and Importation of Gas Act of 1907. The act required Canadian power exporters to secure an annual licence, gave the federal Parliament the authority to levy an export duty on hydroelectricity, prohibited hydro power from being sold at a lower price in the United States, and featured a recall clause allowing exports to be quickly revoked if the power was required in Canada. The 1907 act would undergo minor modifications in 1925 and 1955, with the export duty abolished in 1963.[13] South of the border, the US president had the power to authorize the construction of border facilities that could be used to export electricity, but it was not until 1935, when the Federal Power Act created the Federal Power Commission (Federal Energy Regulatory Commission as of 1977), that the US government was given the authority to license exports.

Public discontent with the despoiling of the Niagara landscape had led the US Congress to enact the 1906 Burton Act limiting Niagara diversions to 15,600 cubic feet per second (CFS). Concerns about Niagara and St. Lawrence developments also contributed to the formation of the Boundary Waters Treaty of 1909, which created the International Joint Commission (IJC) and put further limits on Niagara diversions; henceforth, water could be diverted from above the Falls at a rate of 36,000 CFS by Ontario and 20,000 CFS by New York.[14]

During the First World War, the limits on the diversion of Niagara water imposed by the United States via the Burton Act were lifted and all the water that could be utilized was made available for power diversion. Domestic Canadian opposition to electricity exports to the United States reached a fever pitch during the war, resulting in what Karl Froschauer has called the "Repatriation Crisis," which involved various studies into the nature of Canadian electrical development and exports, such as the Drayton Report.[15] Internal opposition continued during the interwar period, but the Canadian government was reluctant to take any strong action because the country still depended on coal imported from the United States. In 1925, the Mackenzie King government enacted a minor duty on electricity sold to the United States. Though this duty "was too low to have immediate repercussions on the ability of companies to export hydro-electric power," according to Janet Martin-Nielsen, "it marked the beginning of a gradual change in the style of Canadian electricity exports. As the Canadian and U.S. electricity grids became increasingly interconnected in the interwar years, electricity trade between the two countries changed from unidirectional firm power sales from Canada to the United States to interruptible power sales in both directions."[16]

Hydro Democracy

As of 1920, hydro represented 97 per cent of the electricity produced in Canada and 20 per cent in the United States. Mexico, of course, also shares border waters with the United States, and those two nations had also developed formal transboundary water governance institutions. Yet Mexico shares only a handful of cross-border interconnections with the United States, and it has not integrated its electricity grid with the United States to nearly the same extent as has Canada. This is in part a function of Mexico's comparative lack of hydroelectric developments and its much smaller available electrical generating capacity; as a result, the US-Mexico energy relationship is much more heavily predicated on petroleum, as Linda B. Hall's chapter in this volume shows.[17] While Canada and the United States take turns at their border being the upstream/downstream riparian, or have major water bodies such as the Great Lakes that form rather than cross this border, the United States is in a more powerful position than Mexico when it comes to these countries' shared waters.[18]

Electricity is restricted to movement via a physical grid, whereas other energy stocks such as fossil fuels can move via various intermodal transport mechanisms. This means that although a country like Venezuela needs the appropriate infrastructure to move petroleum to the United States or Canada, this is much easier than constructing the infrastructure for international electricity transmission. The practical result is that there are no electricity imports or exports between the United States and Latin American nations outside of Mexico.

Energy is a commodity unlike any other; electricity and fossil fuels are the magic elixirs of modern society. Energy scholars have separated energy regimes into "stocks" and "flows," with the latter generally consisting of "organic" energy—e.g., wood, water, and human/animal muscle power—while stocks (coal, petroleum, electricity) are generally also considered "mineral" energy forms.[19] Unlike carbon sources of energy, such as coal and petroleum, which are non-renewable stocks of fossil fuels, society harnesses the renewable flows of hydro power from rivers and transforms them into electricity.[20] Since it involves both water and electricity, the material aspects and realities of producing hydroelectricity make it a hybrid energy regime: both flow and stock, both mineral and organic.[21]

In *Carbon Democracy: Political Power in the Age of Oil*, Timothy Mitchell argues that the ways we access energy flows and stocks (in his case, coal and then oil) substantially shape governing structures.[22] According to Mitchell, coal was a catalyst for democracy because worker control of the mine environment allowed unions to exercise political agency and make democratic claims. Along with oil, coal broke the ecological constraints of an organic energy economy and allowed for the belief in unlimited economic growth.[23] Unlike coal, however, the spatial and material aspects of oil lent themselves to less democratic and more elite control. Granted, as Mitchell—along with scholars such as Christopher Jones, Andreas Malm, and Ruth Sandwell—makes clear, energy transitions are highly contingent.[24]

Hydro power enhanced democracy in Canada in certain ways, both tangible and symbolic, while undermining or negating it in other ways. The public control of hydro power provided the energy-based affluence for a growth society—i.e., cheap power—and this allowed individuals to increase their material and economic positions (and arguably escape the "resource curse," or at least aspects of it; see Triner's chapter in this volume) and better participate in a liberal democratic society; this, in turn, helped create the platform for social democratic governance that enjoyed wide public consent for interventionist policies that claimed to fairly, and liberally, apportion resources.[25] Moreover, most of Canada's early hydro power came from its border with the United States, and integration with the United States initiated a unique type of energy diplomacy that had profound implications for democracy and political economy.[26] At the same time, hydro power gave Canada the ability to domestically produce the necessary electricity, which meant it did not need to rely as heavily on foreign energy, such as American coal. Akin to energy and hydroelectric production in countries like Brazil, in the Canadian case hydro-power development was part of enhancing autonomy and "natural security," even if out of self-interest the country continued to tie itself, energy-wise, to the United States.[27]

The material realities of working with water and electricity shaped democratic opportunities: for example, as the technological and spatial scale of hydroelectric projects increased, hydro democracy also served as a means of limiting the rights and claims of those situated closest to hydro developments, particularly Indigenous groups, ostensibly in the name of the greater good and wider public interest. Hydroelectric development involved sacrificing hinterland watershed environments for metropolitan benefits. Indeed, First Peoples have borne the disproportionate brunt of hydroelectric development, and energy development and extraction in general, across the Americas.[28] In the case of Canadian hydro power, this "hydraulic imperialism" partly stems from the fact that water sites that attracted Indigenous groups for such things as fishing and settlement also make for viable hydroelectric installations. But the bigger factor is settler society's propensity to view Indigenous groups as second-class citizens whose disenfranchisement—always framed in terms of "progress"—is to the collective benefit of the nation. Conversely, in other parts of the Americas, this resource imperialism often comes from foreign governments and companies.

Like fossil fuel networks, the environmental transformations required to build hydroelectric systems involved significant initial capital investments to construct and maintain technological infrastructures, such as dams, generating stations, and electric grids.[29] Hydro power, like coal and oil energy networks, attracted investors and financiers with the availability of large rents, and these individuals used their economic influence to shape the development of governing structures.[30] In Canada, this significant investment, and the attendant risks, often necessitated state involvement in hydroelectric development as hydro installations grew in size.

Megaprojects

The 1920 Federal Power Water Act moved the limits of the United States' Niagara diversion to those set by the Boundary Waters Treaty. While some limitations were instituted on the volume of diversions between the two world wars, further expansion of hydro production facilities on both sides of the Niagara Gorge took place, including the construction of lengthy diversion conduits. Canada and the United States accelerated their various undertakings, transnational boards, and studies aimed at maintaining or increasing power diversions without sacrificing the great cataract's scenic appeal. The Canada-US Niagara Convention and Protocol was signed in 1929, outlining remedial works that would disperse water to insure an unbroken crestline in all seasons while enshrining hydro diversions. However, it did not receive congressional assent in the United States.

Serious governmental consideration of a bilaterally constructed deep waterway in the St. Lawrence also dates back to the end of the nineteenth century. After its formation, HEPCO forwarded a number of different plans for hydroelectric dams on the St. Lawrence, as did various private and public entities in the United States. Binational engineering studies conducted after the First World War solidified such schemes, and the idea of a deep waterway became intertwined with power development. However, in Canada this was caught up in provincial-federal disputes about constitutional rights around hydro-power development. Moreover, between 1926 and 1931, Ontario signed a series of contracts with different Quebec power companies to furnish the province with electricity. As a result, both the Quebec and Ontario governments were uninterested in developing hydroelectric power from the St. Lawrence as long as these contracts remained in effect. There were similar disputes in the United States over which level of government held the rights to the electricity harvested from the St. Lawrence. At Governor Franklin D. Roosevelt's instigation, the New York legislature created the Power Authority of the State of New York (PASNY) in 1931. The following year, Canada and the United States signed the Great Lakes Waterway Treaty, a comprehensive agreement outlining not only the St. Lawrence project but also a range of other border water issues in the Great Lakes–St. Lawrence Basin. The treaty, however, failed to pass the US Congress due to the range of interests opposed to the project, such as railways, utilities, private power, and port cities on the East Coast and Gulf of Mexico.

The new Ontario premier, Mitch Hepburn, was opposed to development of the St. Lawrence, but he did seek power through additional diversions at Niagara Falls. Despite Franklin Roosevelt's continued desire for a St. Lawrence development after he became US president, Ontario and Quebec's opposition forestalled any progress until the Second World War. With the war rendering the need for electricity acute, Canada and the United States arrived at an executive agreement, rather than a treaty, that covered much of the same ground as the 1932 St. Lawrence accord, including terms for Niagara Falls. But the United States' entry into the war prevented this agreement from coming to fruition. Nonetheless, the two countries agreed that the limits on the amount of water diverted at Niagara Falls for wartime needs could be temporarily increased outside of the agreement. By June 1941, the first of this extra water was being diverted, and further withdrawals were subsequently allowed during the war, rising to a total diversion of 54,000 CFS for Canada and 32,500 CFS for the United States. In early January 1942, both countries agreed to split the cost of constructing a stone-filled weir—a submerged dam—in the Chippawa–Grass Island Pool about a mile above the Falls.

In the immediate postwar years, a variety of economic and defence factors further emphasized the necessity of a seaway and power project on the St. Lawrence. These included the need for hydroelectricity for industrial and defence production; the ability of a deep waterway to transport the recently discovered iron ore deposits from the Ungava district in Labrador and Northern Quebec to Great Lakes steel mills; the possibility of protected inland shipbuilding on the Great Lakes; and the economic and trade stimulation that a seaway would bring.[31] But the 1941 St. Lawrence agreement remained stalled in the US Congress. In 1949, with Ontario experiencing major power shortages, the Liberal government of Louis St. Laurent realized that an "all-Canadian" waterway might be viable and would not need the permission of the Congress. But the cost of an all-Canadian seaway was only feasible if it was built in conjunction with an Ontario–New York power dam. In 1948, New York and Ontario had each asked their respective federal governments for permission to forward to the IJC a "power priority plan" whereby the province and state would build a hydro dam separate from a deep waterway system. This scheme had initially been opposed by both President Harry Truman and Prime Minister St. Laurent. But the Canadians reversed their position, since this Ontario–New York plan would accommodate the all-Canadian waterway approach.

Ottawa began taking steps to condition public opinion on both sides of the border for the possibility of an all-Canadian seaway. A waterway entirely in Canadian territory quickly resonated with the Canadian public and continued to build momentum throughout the 1950s; in fact, the proposal soon boomeranged, with the St. Laurent government feeling strong pressure to pursue a wholly Canadian waterway in order to satisfy popular demand for such a system. An all-Canadian seaway, however, clearly threatened important US national security and economic interests. Truman was opposed to any St. Lawrence project that was not a joint Canada-US endeavour.[32] Although the St. Lawrence waterway would certainly further Canadian-US integration when completed, the environmental diplomacy leading to the St. Lawrence Seaway and Power Project demonstrates the asymmetry and conflicting national interests that often characterized the Canada-US relationship, even in the early Cold War.

In the 1940s, hydro was still responsible for about 90 per cent of the electricity generated in Canada. Canada has traditionally been among the top—if not at the top—of global per capita users of energy in general and electricity specifically. Today, Canada is said to be the third-largest producer of hydroelectricity in the world, behind only China and another country from the Americas: Brazil. Granted, we should not forget that prior to the Second World War, though hydro power was the source of most of the electricity consumed in Canada and Ontario, this was primarily by industry and manufacturing; hydroelectricity still accounted for a fairly minor percentage of the energy consumed in *households* across the nation, especially outside of urban areas, which remained reliant on power derived from the organic energy regime (i.e., coal and wood) much longer than was the case in, say, the United States and the United Kingdom, though not for as long as in Latin American countries.[33] Indeed, hydro power's influence on Ontario's political economy and statist evolution has been out of proportion to its actual statistical significance in the province's energy portfolio.[34]

The wartime diversions from the Niagara River had continued on a temporary basis after the end of the war. With the need for energy reaching acute levels, the two countries sought to arrive at a permanent accord. Consequently, the Niagara Diversion Treaty was signed in 1950.[35] The accord called for remedial works—jointly built by HEPCO, PASNY, and the US Army Corps of Engineers, and approved by the IJC—and virtually equalized water diversions while restricting the flow of water over Niagara Falls to no less than 100,000 CFS during daylight hours (of what the treaty deemed the tourist season: 8:00 a.m. to 10:00 p.m. from April to mid-September, and from 8:00 a.m. to 8:00 p.m. during the fall), and no less than 50,000 CFS during the remainder of the year. This meant that either half, or only a quarter, of the Niagara River's water would henceforth go over the Falls. Construction of the remedial works began in earnest in early 1954. A 1,550-foot control structure was built into the river from the Canadian shore, featuring thirteen sluices equipped with control gates. The purpose of this structure was to control water levels in the Chippawa–Grass Island Pool in order to adequately supply the water intake works for both countries' diversions; it also sought to spread out the water for aesthetic purposes and because flows concentrated in certain places caused more erosion damage.

The Horseshoe Falls were designated for significant modification too. Excavation took place along the flanks (64,000 cubic yards of rock on the Canadian flank; 24,000 cubic yards on the US flank) in order to create a better distribution of flow and an unbroken crestline at all times. To compensate for erosion, crest fills (100 feet on the Canadian shore and 300 feet on the US side) were undertaken, parts of which would be fenced and landscaped in order to provide prime public vantage points. On the Ontario side, the diverted water went to the enormous reservoir feeding the newly completed Sir Adam Beck No. 2 Generating Station, which was beside Beck No. 1 station. By 1961, New York had completed the controversial Robert Moses Niagara Power Plant across the gorge (which generated 2.4 megawatts—the largest at the time in the Western world).

The overarching goal was to create an uninterrupted "curtain of water" over the precipice that displayed a pleasing consistency and colour. The remedial works were also intended to reduce "spray problems" as excessive mist had apparently been scaring off visitors to the tunnels behind

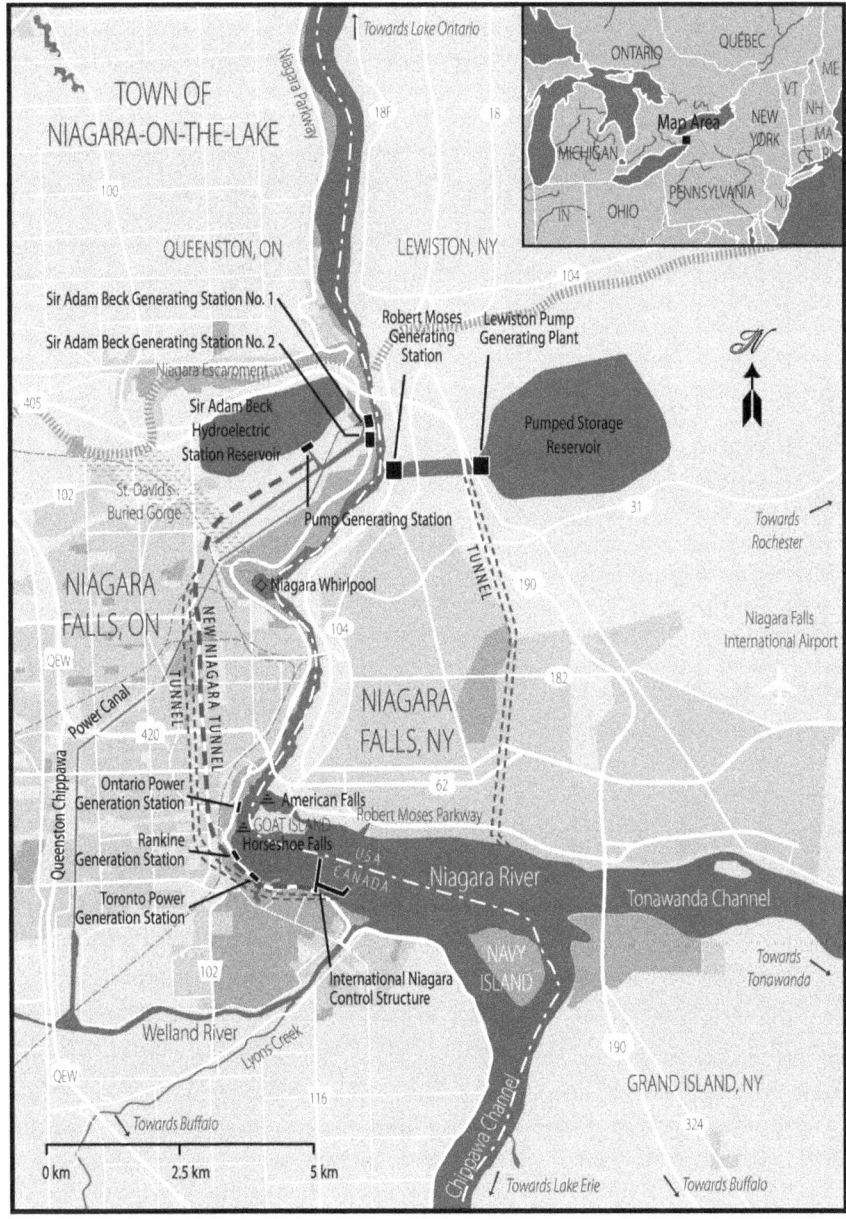

Figure 5.1 Hydroelectric Landscape of Niagara Falls.

Source: Created by Rajiv Rawat, Anders Sandberg, and Daniel Macfarlane.

Figure 5.2 Beck Stations (left) and Moses Station (right)
Source: Photo by author.

the Horseshoe Falls. This speaks to the commodification of the Niagara experience, a process that was inextricably intertwined with the other tourist trappings prevalent at Niagara Falls: nature should be sanitized, made predictable and orderly, and packaged for easy consumption.

Returning to the St. Lawrence impasse, which continued while work got underway at the Falls, the New York share of the St. Lawrence hydro works, to be built by PASNY, needed a licence from the US Federal Power Commission (FPC). But the FPC refused to license the undertaking. Although the body was supposedly free of partisan political influence, its commissioners were presidential appointees. It was clear that the White House was impacting the FPC's decision, and that it would continue to do so. To be fair, US interference was also partially the result of Washington's misreading of Canada's intentions to proceed alone with the waterway, a situation to which Ottawa had contributed by sending mixed messages about its commitment to proceed unilaterally. Since the hydroelectric works were needed in order to make a Canadian waterway a reality, Ottawa was essentially caught in a catch-22. The Canadian government tentatively left the door open to US participation in the hopes that this would allow the hydro aspect to commence. Dwight Eisenhower, who became president in January 1953, was non-committal about the seaway until several months into his term. In May 1953, his cabinet finally came out in favour of US involvement, primarily for defence reasons. The FPC, unsurprisingly, did a volte-face and quickly approved a licence for New York. However, sectional and regional interests then conspired to exploit the appeals process so as to further delay a start on the St. Lawrence project until 1954, when Congress finally approved US participation via the Wiley-Dondero Bills.

In the end, the Canadian prime minister consented to US involvement chiefly because of the negative ramifications for the Canadian-US relationship that would likely result if Canada resisted. Through a 1954 bilateral St. Lawrence agreement, rather than a treaty, Canada reluctantly acquiesced in the construction of a joint project, although not before it extracted concessions from the United States during the ensuing negotiations, such as the placement of the Iroquois lock and Ottawa's right to later build an all-Canadian seaway. Really, the two nations were agreeing to build separate facilities that would function together.

The construction of the St. Lawrence Seaway and Power Project wrought huge changes in the St. Lawrence Basin. The Moses-Saunders powerhouse, a gravity power dam with thirty-two turbine/generator units, was a bilateral project, with the Canadian and US halves meeting in the middle, that generated a combined 1.8 megawatts. The Beauharnois power dam, which had been finished in the early 1930s, became part of the St. Lawrence project. The seaway cost $470.3 million (with Canada paying $336.5 million and the United States $133.8 million) and, including the cost of the power phase, the bill for the entire project was over $1 billion. Lake St. Lawrence inundated some 20,000 acres of land on the Canadian side, along with another 18,000 acres on the US shore, flooding out many communities and a wide range of infrastructure.

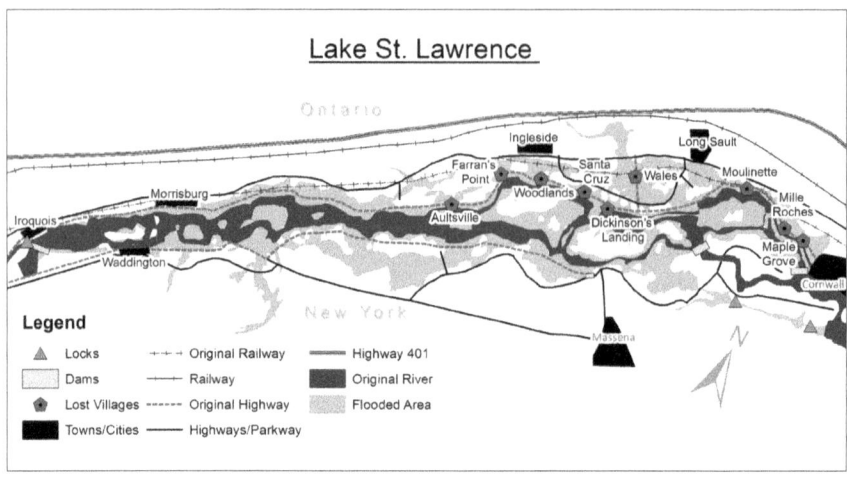

Figure 5.3 Lake St. Lawrence
Source: By the author.

Figure 5.4 Moses-Saunders Powerhouse
Source: Photo by the author

The creation of Lake St. Lawrence, which served as the reservoir for the Moses-Saunders hydroelectric dam while also deepening the water for navigation, required the largest rehabilitation project in Canadian history. On the Canadian side of the International Rapids section, 225 farms, a number of communities (often referred to as the Lost Villages), 18 cemeteries, approximately 1,000 cottages, and over 100 kilometres of the main east–west highway and main line railway were relocated, and major works (e.g., bridges) were required in the river at Montreal. So as not to create navigation and other difficulties in the new lake, everything had to be moved, razed, or flattened, including trees and, as mentioned, cemeteries.[36] Many people chose to transport their residences via special vehicles to the new communities created to house the displaced residents.

For many, mass displacement in the St. Lawrence Valley was a small price to pay for the production of electricity and the increased accessibility of iron ore deposits. Flooding out thousands of people in the Lost Villages and surrounding rural areas (including Mohawk reserves) was justified in the name of progress and for the benefit of the wider nation. The reorganization and resettlement of those affected by the power development would be for their own benefit as they would be placed in consolidated new towns—instead of scattered about in inefficient villages, hamlets, and farms—with modern living standards and services. Instead of the previous towns spread along the waterfront—set out in a long and narrow grid—the new communities were based on the latest planning principles and utilized curved streets and crescents, with the major services and amenities grouped strategically together in centralized plazas, with schools, churches, and parks placed to facilitate easier and safer access.[37]

Ontario Hydro repeatedly went door-to-door and held numerous public and town hall meetings.[38] The utility compromised on certain aspects of the relocation—the most prominent example being the concession to use house-movers so that people could keep their original residence (granted, the Ontario Hydro chairman was keen to do this because moving houses was also cheaper than building new ones).[39] At the insistence of the provincial government, the amount of compensation for forceful taking was increased and a commission for appeals established (though it usually reflected Ontario Hydro's assessments).[40] Nevertheless, there was a societal deference to government, which in turn reflected a deference to experts and engineers. For the involved governments, as well as for the general public, the idea that it was all a sacrifice worth making was pervasive. There were certainly those who resisted in various ways, but for many the project carried an aura of inevitability. Moreover, those dislocated by the power pool generally expected that the St. Lawrence project would bring with it great prosperity, and therefore bought into the general logic of progress.

The Canadian and US governments used the St. Lawrence and Niagara projects as spectacles to demonstrate their power and legitimacy to the citizenry. Sampling, polling, surveying, testing, and modelling were extensively used, for, as fundamental techniques of a high modernist approach, they allowed the state to control information, set the terms of debate, and manufacture consent; if people knew the facts, the thinking went, the rationality of the project would inevitably compel them to accept its logic.[41] The residents of the Lost Villages were repeatedly promised that the Upper St. Lawrence region would become a great industrial area, even though this proved to be an empty promise. Ontario Hydro created observation platforms and millions of people came to watch the construction. Many residents of the area acquired employment on the project. On the New York side, the head of PASNY, the infamous planner Robert Moses, made a deal with Alcoa for about one-quarter of the power from the eponymous powerhouse, and Reynolds Metal and General Motors opened factories in the area and signed power supply contracts. These three industries cumulatively accounted for over half of the US share of power from the St. Lawrence development.

Government experts viewed nature as something to be controlled and ordered through technology, with little to no consideration of the wider environmental impact. Because of the engineer's cultural prestige, this view extended to the state and society. The rhetoric used by experts and governments focused on defeating, dominating, exploiting, and mastering the river. A megaproject ethos is also revealed by the language that was *not* used: namely, acknowledgement of the environmental limits and repercussions inherent in a project on the scale of the St. Lawrence Seaway and Power Project.

The engineering prowess and brute force used to radically reconfigure a riparian landscape may have made the St. Lawrence Seaway and Power

Project seem like a human-made artifact, but in reality its transformation forged a new enviro-technical system: the St. Lawrence (and Niagara Falls) was now both artificial and natural, a technology and an environment.[42] There have been enormous environmental repercussions since the 1950s. Water flowing downriver became more polluted after the creation of the seaway. Along with pollution caused directly by construction, large amounts of decomposing plant life released mercury into the water, and water released methane into the atmosphere. Submerged infrastructure also leeched various types of toxins, such as oil, fertilizers, and other contaminants. The St. Lawrence Seaway and Power Project reconfigured the local ecosystem and disrupted its aquaculture by restricting the mobility of certain species. Biologist Richard Carignan even contends that the project created three separate channels or ecosystems along the river around Montreal, in contrast to the unified habitat that existed before construction began.[43] Dams blocked the movement of eels, which could no longer traverse the length of the river until authorities added eel ladders to the Moses-Saunders dam in 1974 and the Beauharnois dam in 1994.

For both the Niagara and St. Lawrence projects, engineers employed scale hydraulic models that replicated long stretches of rivers in minute detail: the topography, the shoreline, the river channels and contours, the cataracts and rapids, and the turbulence and velocity of the currents. This appears to be the first time that such models were used this extensively for a civil engineering project in Canada. Building on the Niagara modelling experience, the same agencies and many of the same engineers were moved to the St. Lawrence models. The reliance on models was emblematic of a faith in high modernist technology; yet there were many model mistakes, and when extrapolated onto a larger scale, seemingly small errors could have significant ramifications.[44]

The Niagara and the St. Lawrence hydroelectric developments had a tremendous impact on Canadian electricity exports to the United States. Since the Second World War, non-firm (i.e., interruptible) power sales have characterized the Canada-US electricity trade, with some exceptions.[45] Up to the 1960s, the majority of the power exported from Canada to the United States was via Ontario, and St. Lawrence and Niagara power had played the leading role in shaping the Ontario and federal governments' approaches to electricity exports. These two megaprojects thus entrenched

Canadian-US energy relations and paved the way for the development of transborder electricity grids that proliferated in the 1960s (as of 1975, there were sixty-five international interconnections, with a total transfer capability of over 6,000 megawatts) and the Canadian allowance of long-term firm power (as part of the Columbia River Treaty arrangements).[46] Moreover, electricity exchanges between Canada and the United States helped pave the way for the oil and gas trade to move from what Paul Chastko calls "informal continentalism" to the contemporary "integrated, harmonized, and liberalized energy trade."[47]

Conclusion

When imagining the landscape changes that tend to result from energy development, most picture the despoiled fossil fuel zones spread across the Americas and discussed in many other contributions to this volume, rather than tourist locales such as the Niagara and St. Lawrence Rivers. But both were "energy landscapes" since fundamental aspects of their shape and appearance were determined by the exigencies of producing hydro power, and thus even these major tourist draws are in some ways sacrifice zones for energy production.

Both the Niagara and St. Lawrence river systems are important sites of Canada's historical development and nation building vis-à-vis the United States, and they figure heavily in the transportation and industrial development of the Canada-US borderlands. The creation of the St. Lawrence and Niagara projects speaks to transborder ideas about technology and the environment, but also to the ways that national identities were bound up in such ideas. Canadian and US identities have strong ties to their respective landscapes and environmental-determinist forms of explanatory development paradigms (e.g., the frontier thesis in the United States, the metropolitan-hinterland, staples, and Laurentian theses in Canada). Yet it has been suggested that Canadians tend to see nature in more antagonistic terms. Some commentators argue that this stems from Canadians' conception of themselves as a small population struggling against a vast, foreboding, cold, and hostile landscape,[48] and other factors that serve as partial explanations for different Canadian and US views of nature can be identified.[49]

Hydroelectricity in particular was seen as a means of delivering Canada from its "hewer of wood servitude to American industry and its bondage to American coal."[50] US Americans have a longer history of using technology to dominate the natural environment. By comparison, technology was historically seen by many Canadian nationalists as the means by which the United States could dominate and control Canada. However, technology was a "double-edged sword," for by the mid-twentieth century Canadian access to modern technology—which could be used to conquer the hostile environment—held out the potential for the nation to evolve independently of the United States, rather than further integrating the two countries.[51] Many Latin American countries have been similarly ambivalent about aligning their energy resources with the United States, though the past century suggests they had greater reason to fear American encroachment than did Canada.

The St. Lawrence River was historically seen as a national, rather than a shared, river (further enabled by the fact that the river's lower section is wholly within Canada). This view of the St. Lawrence as a strictly "Canadian" river manifested itself in the attempts for an all-Canadian seaway. The St. Lawrence River holds an exalted and iconic place in the Canadian national imagination, as the waterway served as the crucible of Canadian settlement and development.[52] Canadian historiography, particularly of the Anglo-Canadian variety, is replete with notions of the river narrative and aquatic symbolism.[53] The Laurentian thesis, for example, holds that the St. Lawrence River was the dominant element shaping the physical, political, economic, and cultural evolution of Canada. At the height of its popularity in the 1950s, the Laurentian thesis helped sustain the conception of the St. Lawrence watershed as the defining and fundamental aspect of Canadian history and identity, and for this reason it infused the notion of an all-Canadian seaway with the same nationalist importance and symbolism.[54] The seaway effectively served as a conduit for many different expressions of Canadian nationalism, which can be subsumed under the term "hydraulic nationalism."[55]

Hydraulic and technological nationalisms were also apparent in the Niagara projects. Niagara appealed to Canadian nationalists for various reasons (many of which could equally apply to the St. Lawrence), including Niagara's proximity to the Canadian heartland, its connection to the

St. Lawrence–Great Lakes system, its proximity to many sites of Canadian resistance to US encroachment in the War of 1812, and because of uniquely Canadian views of the environment. Put another way, Niagara Falls was Canada's front door, and America's back door; the same metaphor could apply to the St. Lawrence.[56] The US federal government and the State of New York were, like the Canadian and Ontario governments, most attracted by the power they could get from Niagara, though this had stronger nationalist motivations for Canada and more imperialist motivations for the United States. It was the technological control of Niagara Falls for hydroelectric development that resonated most strongly with Canadian nationalists. As was the case with the St. Lawrence, the hydro power of the Niagara River was a strong nationalist expression, the full usage of the nation's natural birthright. Though the Niagara works were a joint undertaking with the United States, this was as much a legal and practical necessity as the result of a desire to co-operate. For some Canadians, such technological development and resource exploitation would allow for greater integration with the United States; others, however, saw this as a means to make Canada more fully self-sufficient and no longer reliant on the United States.

The vitality of publicly operated hydroelectric utilities helped condition Canadians for an interventionist state. It also appears that hydroelectricity, at least in the public imagination, allowed for more effective claims for a just and egalitarian world than did oil, even if it did become, like fossil fuels, a mode of governance that employed popular consent as a means of limiting claims for greater equality and justice by dividing up common resources. Because hydro power in Canada was mostly produced by the state, it was able to resist certain facets of neoliberalism—for example, privatization and deregulation—longer than fossil fuels.[57] During the twentieth century, hydro power was the only energy system in Canada that rivalled the mineral energy of fossil fuels.[58] Both hydro power and fossil fuels involved elaborate socio-technical systems, which in turn influenced the governance of the countries that developed and shared them. Canada in the twenty-first century has been labelled a "Petro state";[59] however, it might be said that Canada (Central Canada especially) was first a "hydro state."

NOTES

1. James Eayrs, *The Art of the Possible: Government and Foreign Policy in Canada* (Toronto: University of Toronto Press, 1961), 157.

2. John Herd Thompson and Stephen J. Randall, *Canada and the United States: Ambivalent Allies*, 3rd ed. (Montreal: McGill-Queen's University Press, 2002), 213.

3. Quebec also exported electricity, both from within and outside the St. Lawrence Basin, and in the second half of the twentieth century "hydraulic nationalism" may well have been most clearly on display in that province.

4. For a comparative elaboration, see Daniel Macfarlane, "Dam the Consequences: Hydropolitics, Nationalism, and the Niagara-St. Lawrence Projects," in *Border Flows: A Century of the Canadian-American Water Relationship*, ed. Lynne Heasley and Daniel Macfarlane (Calgary: University of Calgary Press, 2016), 123–50.

5. Similar to Latin American countries such as Colombia, in the last few decades hydroelectric production in Ontario has taken the route of neoliberalism and privatization, whereas Quebec and British Columbia have maintained public hydroelectric utilities, and Latin American countries such as Peru, Mexico, and Argentina have shifted to energy as a common good.

6. J. C. Molburg, J. A. Kavicky, and K. C. Picel, *The Design, Construction, and Operation of Long-Distance High Voltage Electricity Transmission Technologies* (Lemont, IL: Argonne National Laboratory, 2007).

7. Alfred Runte, "Beyond the Spectacular: The Niagara Falls Preservation Campaign," *New York Historical Society Quarterly*, no. 57 (January 1973): 30–50.

8. H. V. Nelles, *The Politics of Development: Forests, Mines, and Hydro-Electric Power in Ontario*, 2nd ed. (Montreal: McGill-Queen's University Press, 2005), 312–13, 374–5.

9. Graeme Wynn, foreword to *Negotiating a River: Canada, the US, and the Creation of the St. Lawrence Seaway*, by Daniel Macfarlane (Vancouver: UBC Press, 2014), xxiii.

10. Mark Perlgut, *Electricity across the Border: the U.S.-Canadian Experience* (New York: C. D. Howe Research Institute, 1978), 10.

11. Perlgut, *Electricity across the Border*, 11–12.

12. Janet Martin-Nielsen, "South over the Wires: Hydroelectricity Exports from Canada, 1900–1925," *Water History* 1, no. 2 (2009): 109–29.

13. For more on the 1907 act and its subsequent modifications, see Martin-Nielsen, "South over the Wires," and Perlgut, *Electricity across the Border*.

14. The apparent Canadian advantage reflected US-owned plants and their exportation of electricity to the United States. See John N. Jackson with John Burtniak and Gregory P. Stein, *The Mighty Niagara: One River—Two Frontiers* (Amherst, NY: Prometheus Books, 2003), 212.

15. Karl Froschauer, *White Gold: Hydroelectric Power in Canada* (Vancouver: UBC Press, 1999).

16 Martin-Nielsen, "South over the Wires," 126–7. See also A. E. D. Grauer, "The Export of Electricity from Canada" in *Canadian Issues: Essays in Honour of Henry F. Angus*, ed. R. M. Clark (Toronto: University of Toronto Press, 1961), 276.

17 For a statistical overview of electricity generation and exchange within and between the United States, Canada, and Mexico, see United States Congressional Research Service, "Cross-Border Energy Trade in North America: Present and Potential," EveryCRSReport.com, 30 January 2017, https://www.everycrsreport.com/reports/R44747.html#_Toc473645486.

18 This is exemplified by the initial US application of the Harmon Doctrine, followed by the quick abandonment of this judicial principle, in the country's water relations with Canada, as well as by the history of Colorado River allocations.

19 Christopher Jones treats hydroelectricity as stock and part of the mineral energy regime, whereas R. W. Sandwell, emphasizing its renewable and flowing features, places it within the organic energy regime. Christopher F. Jones, *Routes of Power: Energy and Modern America* (Cambridge, MA: Harvard University Press, 2014); R. W. Sandwell, ed., *Powering Up Canada: The History of Power, Fuel, and Energy from 1600* (Montreal: McGill-Queen's University Press, 2016); E. A. Wrigley, *Energy and the English Industrial Revolution* (Cambridge: Cambridge University Press, 2010).

20 Owing to spatio-temporal realities, flowing water produces power that needs to be used on demand and at a scale that justifies the construction and maintenance of the system designed to convert and deliver that power as electricity. Fossil fuels can be removed from their place of origin and then burned and utilized at a desired location. But hydroelectricity typically has to be generated at the site of falling water, and the resulting electricity can only be transported if and where transmission wires make that possible (granted, hydro power generally isn't exposed to the same supply problems as fossil fuels). Water volumes and flow rates cap the amount of energy that could be produced by any particular hydro station, though the spread of massive electricity grids have allowed electricity to be pooled over large swaths of North America. Daniel Macfarlane and Andrew Watson, "Hydro Democracy: Water Power and Political Power in Ontario," *Scientia Canadensis* 40, no. 1 (2018): 1–18.

21 For an elaboration on the concept of "hydro democracy" with a focus on Ontario, see Macfarlane and Watson, "Hydro Democracy."

22 Timothy Mitchell, *Carbon Democracy: Political Power in the Age of Oil* (New York: Verso, 2011).

23 Wrigley, *Energy and the English Industrial Revolution*; E. A. Wrigley, *The Path to Sustained Growth: England's Transition from an Organic Economy to an Industrial Revolution* (Cambridge: Cambridge University Press, 2016).

24 Jones, *Routes of Power*; Andreas Malm, *Fossil Capital: The Rise of Steam Power and the Roots of Global Warming* (New York: Verso, 2016); R. W. Sandwell, "Pedagogies of the Unimpressed: Re-educating Ontario Women for the Modern Energy Regime, 1900–1940," *Ontario History* 107, no. 1 (Spring 2015): 36–59; and R. W. Sandwell, "People, Place and Power: Rural Electrification in Canada, 1890–1950," in *Transforming the Countryside: the Electrification of Rural Britain*, ed. Paul Brassley, Jeremy Burchardt, and Karen Sayer (New York: Routledge, 2017), 178–204.

25 In this sense, our adoption of Mitchell's concept of carbon democracy contributes to a wider historiographical debate on the nature and influence of liberalism in Canada. See Ian McKay, "The Liberal Order Framework: A Prospectus for a Reconnaissance of Canadian History," *Canadian Historical Review* 81, no. 4 (2000): 617–45; Stephane Castonguay and Darin Kinsey, "The Nature of the Liberal Order: State Formation, Conservation, and the Government of Non-humans in Canada," in *Liberalism and Hegemony: Debating the Canadian Liberal Revolution*, ed. Jean-Francois Constant and Michel Ducharme (Toronto: University of Toronto Press, 2009), 221–45; James Murton, *Creating a Modern Countryside: Liberalism and Land Resettlement in British Columbia* (Vancouver: UBC Press, 2007); Shannon Stunden Bower, *Wet Prairie: People, Land, and Water in Agricultural Manitoba* (Vancouver: UBC Press, 2011); Macfarlane, *Negotiating a River*.

26 Heasley and Macfarlane, *Border Flows*; Froschauer, *White Gold*.

27 The concept of "natural security" is taken from Daniel Macfarlane, "Natural Security: Canada-US Environmental Diplomacy," in *Undiplomatic History: The New Study of Canada and the World*, ed. Asa McKercher and Philip Van Huizen (Montreal: McGill-Queens University Press, 2019), 107–36.

28 A number of historians in Canada have explored the relationship between the consequences of hydro-power development for rural and Indigenous communities and environments, and the benefits enjoyed by urban residents and economies. See Brittany Luby, "From Milk-Medicine to Public (Re)Education Programs: An Examination of Anishinabek Mothers' Responses to Hydro-electric Flooding in the Treaty #3 District, 1900–1975," *Canadian Bulletin of Medical History* 32, no. 2 (2015): 363–89; Daniel Macfarlane and Peter Kitay, "Hydraulic Imperialism: Hydro-electric Development and Treaty 9 in the Abitibi Region," *American Review of Canadian Studies* 46, no. 3 (2016): 380–97; Caroline Desbiens, *Power from the North: Territory, Identity, and the Culture of Hydro-electricity in Quebec* (Vancouver: UBC Press, 2014); Matthew Evenden, *Fish versus Power: An Environmental History of the Fraser River* (Cambridge: Cambridge University Press, 2004); Matthew Evenden, *Allied Power: Mobilizing Hydro-electricity during Canada's Second World War* (Toronto: University of Toronto Press, 2015); Tina Loo and Meg Stanley, "An Environmental History of Progress: Damming the Peace and Columbia Rivers," *Canadian Historical Review* 92, no. 3 (September 2011): 399–427.

29 Thomas Park Hughes, *Networks of Power: Electrification in Western Society, 1880–1930* (Baltimore: Johns Hopkins University Press, 1993); David E. Nye, *Electrifying America: Social Meanings of a New Technology, 1880–1940*, new ed. (Cambridge, MA: MIT Press, 1992); David E. Nye, *American Technological Sublime* (Cambridge, MA: MIT Press, 1996); Harold L. Platt, *The Electric City: Energy and the Growth of the Chicago Area, 1880–1930* (Chicago: University of Chicago Press, 1991); Paul Hirt, *The Wired Northwest: The History of Electric Power, 1870s–1970s* (Lawrence: University Press of Kansas, 2012); Gretchen Bakke, *The Grid: The Fraying Wires between Americans and Our Energy Future* (New York: Bloomsbury, 2016); Julie A. Cohn, *The Grid: Biography of an American Technology* (Cambridge, MA: MIT Press, 2017).

30 Once the up-front capital costs were paid off, hydro power tended to be even cheaper per unit of production than coal and oil.

31 On the history of the St. Lawrence Seaway and Power Project, see Macfarlane, *Negotiating a River*.

32 Dwight D. Eisenhower Library and Archives, Columbia University Oral History Project, OH 177, Oral History Interview with N. R. Danielian (1972), 15; NARA II, RG 59, file 711.42157 SA 29/11-148 to 711.4216/10-1447, box 3304, Memorandum from Harry Truman to George C. Marshall, 3 December 1948.

33 In 1941, oil represented 17 per cent, coal 53 per cent, and electricity 6 per cent of total energy consumed. See Richard W. Unger and John Thistle, *Energy Consumption in Canada in the 19th and 20th Centuries: A Statistical Outline* (Naples: Consiglio Nazionale delle Riecerche-Instituto di Studi sulle Società del Mediterraneo, 2013). In terms of household rather than total national consumption, data from the Dominion Bureau of Statistics shows that (unlike the United States) Canadians were consuming very little electricity in their homes before the Second World War. On wood and biomass use for energy, see Joshua MacFadyen, "Hewers of Wood: A History of Wood Energy in Canada," in *Powering Up Canada: The History of Power, Fuel, and Energy from 1600*, ed. R. W. Sandwell (Montreal: McGill-Queen's University Press, 2016), 129–61. As Ruth Sandwell argues, Canada was an outlier compared to other industrialized countries because of the extent to which Canadians had "free" and widespread access to the organic energy regime through the generous homesteading system, cheap and often marginal agricultural lands at great distances from state surveillance, and the persistence of a dominant rural population more interested in "getting by" than in "getting rich." See R. W. Sandwell, *Canada's Rural Majority: Households, Environments, and Economies, 1870–1940* (Toronto: University of Toronto Press, 2016); R. W. Sandwell, introduction to *Powering Up Canada*; R. W. Sandwell, "Mapping Fuel Use in Canada: Exploring the Social History of Canadians' Great Fuel Transformation," in *Historical GIS in Canada*, ed. Jennifer Bonnell and Marcel Fortin (Calgary: University of Calgary Press, 2014), 239–70.

34 Macfarlane and Watson, "Hydro Democracy."

35 For the full history of the modern remaking of Niagara Falls for the purposes of both energy and beauty, see Daniel Macfarlane, *Fixing Niagara Falls: Environment, Energy, and Engineers at the World's Most Famous Waterfall* (Vancouver: UBC Press, 2020).

36 Ontario's process of rehabilitation evolved over several years. For an example of considerations about how to handle the Lost Villages, see Hydro-Electric Power Commission of Ontario (HEPCO), SPP Series, *Report of Meeting in Morrisburg (August 9, 1956), Outstanding Problems Related to the Rehabilitation Problem in the St. Lawrence Seaway Valley* (Toronto: Ontario Department of Planning and Development, August 31, 1956); Government of Ontario, RG 34-3, container 27R, file: St. Lawrence Waterway, file: St. Lawrence Seaway, 1948–June 1954, Memorandum to Bunnell, Subject: Preliminary Survey, St. Lawrence Area (September 13, 14, 15, 16, 17, 1954), September 23, 1954.

37 Writing as the St. Lawrence project was completed, Peter Stokes, who was critical of many elements of the rehabilitation, contends that the "the improvement of the loop streets are unappreciated since the previous towns weren't large enough to appreciate the traffic hazards of the old grid system." See Peter Stokes, "St. Lawrence, a Criticism," *Canadian Architect* 3, no. 2 (February 1958): 43–8. See also Sarah Bowser, "The Planner's Part," *Canadian Architect* 3, no. 2 (February 1958): 38–40.

38 For example, HEPCO, SPP series, St. Lawrence Rehabilitation: Meeting at Osnabruck, November 23, 1954; HEPCO, SPP series, St. Lawrence Rehabilitation: Meeting at Osnabruck, November 23, 1954.

39 HEPCO, SPP series, Report on the Acquisition of Lands and Related Matters for the St. Lawrence Power Project (By Property Office), 1955–56; HEPCO, SPP series, Supplementary Report to James S. Duncan (Chairman, and HEPCO Commissioners), "The Acquisition of Lands and Related Matters for the St. Lawrence Power Project," January 2, 1957.

40 Government of Ontario, RG 19-61-1—Municipal Affairs, Research Branch—Special Studies, St. Lawrence Seaway Study, Box 21, file 14.1.5—Minutes of Meetings—St. Lawrence Seaway #1, Memorandum of Meeting Re: Iroquois, December 21, 1954; HEPCO, SPP series, Report on the Acquisition of Lands and Related Matters for the St. Lawrence Power Project (By Property Office), 1955–56.

41 HEPCO, SPP series, Memorandum to Lamport: House to House Survey—Village of Farran's Point, February 10, 1955; HEPCO, SPP series, Memorandum to Carrick: Property Transactions—St. Lawrence Seaway, July 12, 1954. See also Tina Loo, "People in the Way: Modernity, Environment, and Society on the Arrow Lakes," *BC Studies*, nos. 142/143 (Summer/Autumn 2004): 169–71; Loo and Stanley, "An Environmental History of Progress," 399–427.

42 Sara B. Pritchard and Thomas Zeller, "The Nature of Industrialization," in *The Illusory Boundary: Environment and Technology in History*, ed. Stephen Cutcliffe and Martin Reuss (Charlottesville: University of Virginia Press, 2010), 70; Sara B. Pritchard, *Confluence: The Nature of Technology and the Remaking of the Rhône* (Cambridge, MA: Harvard University Press, 2011).

43 Richard Carignan, "Dynamiques écologiques/Ecosystem Dynamics, Panel: Rivières & Fleuves/Rivers" (paper presented to the conference Positionner le Québec dans l'histoire environnementale mondiale/Positioning Quebec in Global Environmental History, Montreal, 3 September 2005); Gregory G. Beck and Bruce Littlejohn, *Voices for the Watershed: Environmental Issues in the Great Lakes–St. Lawrence Drainage Basin* (Montreal: McGill-Queen's University Press, 2000).

44 For more on the engineering and model process, see Macfarlane, *Negotiating a River*, ch. 6.

45 Martin-Nielsen, "South over the Wires," 126–7.

46 Perlgut, *Electricity across the Border*, 11. See also Cohn, *The Grid*.

47 Paul Chastko, *Developing Alberta's Oil Sands: From Karl Clark to Kyoto* (Calgary: University of Calgary Press, 2004), ch. 8.

48 In a chapter on Canadian-US differences, Donald Worster cites Marilyn Dubasak, Margaret Atwood, and Northrop Frye in support of this hostility argument. See Donald Worster, "Wild, Tame, and Free: Comparing Canadian and U.S. Views of Nature," in *Parallel Destinies: Canadian-American Relations West of the Rockies*, ed. John M. Findlay and Kenneth S. Coates (Montreal: McGill-Queen's Press, 2002), 246–75.

49 These include cultural differences (e.g., the fusion between freedom/liberty and wilderness in US thinking), the greater Canadian reliance on extractive industries, a relatively greater abundance of wilderness, and lack of federal control over land in Canada. See Worster, "Wild, Tame, and Free," 257–60, and George Altmeyer, "Three Ideas of Nature in Canada, 1893–1914," in *Consuming Canada: Readings in Environmental History*, ed. Chad Gaffield and Pam Gaffield (Toronto: Copp Clark, 1995), 96–118.

50 Christopher Armstrong and H. V. Nelles, *Monopoly's Moment: The Organization and Regulation of Canadian Utilities, 1830–1930* (Philadelphia: Temple University Press, 1986), 237–8.

51 R. Douglas Francis, *The Technological Imperative in Canada: An Intellectual History* (Vancouver: UBC Press, 2009), 2; Marco Adria, *Technology and Nationalism* (Montreal: McGill-Queen's University Press, 2010), 45.

52 Carolyn Johns, Introduction to *Canadian Water Politics: Conflicts and Institutions*, ed. Mark Sproule-Jones, Carolyn Johns, and B. Timothy Heinmiller (Montreal: McGill-Queen's University Press, 2008), 4; Jean Manore, "Rivers as Text: From Pre-modern to Post-modern Understandings of Development, Technology and the Environment in Canada and Abroad," in *A History of Water*, vol. 3, *The World of Water*, ed. Terje Tvedt and Eva Jakobsson (London: I. B. Tauris, 2006), 229.

53 Johns, Introduction to *Canadian Water Politics*, 4; Manore, "Rivers as Text," 229.

54 The sense of identification with, and ownership of, the St. Lawrence resulted in Canadians' fear of US encroachment on the river, particularly in the context of nationalist reactions against their nation's subservient role as a mere raw material exporter to the United States. An all-Canadian seaway project, along with other contemporary transportation projects such as the Trans-Canada Highway, were framed as nation-building parallels to the transcontinental railways of the late nineteenth century.

55 Andrew Biro uses the term "hydrological nationalism." See his "Half-Empty or Half-Full? Water Politics and the Canadian National Imaginary," in *Eau Canada: The Future of Canada's Water*, ed. Karen Bakker (Vancouver: UBC Press, 2007), 323.

56 Some of these, including the "door" metaphor, are taken from Patrick McGreevy, *The Wall of Mirrors: Nationalism and Perceptions of the Border at Niagara Falls* (Orono, ME: Canadian-American Center, University of Maine, 1991), 1–3; See also McGreevy, *Imagining Niagara*.

57 Matthew Huber, *Lifeblood: Oil, Freedom and the Forces of Capital* (Minneapolis: University of Minnesota Press, 2013), 5.

58 Unger and Thistle, *Energy Consumption in Canada*, appendix 1; Sam H. Schurr and Bruce C. Netchert, *Energy in the American Economy, 1850–1922* (Baltimore: John Hopkins University Press, 1960), 22.

59 According to the *Collins Dictionary*, "petro state" is a derogatory term for a small oil-rich country in which institutions are weak, and wealth and power are concentrated in the hands of a few; I prefer to use the term in reference to any state in which oil plays an outsized role in politics and political economy.

Tellico Dam, Dickey Dam, and Endangered Species Law in the United States during the 1970s

Michael Camp

In the late 1970s, the United States Army Corps of Engineers spent two summers and thousands of dollars scouring the banks of the St. John River in Maine, searching for undiscovered populations of an unexceptional wildflower named the Furbish lousewort. It did so because in peril was a massive hydroelectric project that would have brought energy to the New England region, which had long suffered frigid winters and needed robust sources of power. The corps needed to find new populations of the lousewort in order to allow the dam's construction to go forward, and it spent significant amounts of time and money to do so. The national news magazine *Time* was outraged, castigating the corps for its quixotic quest and lampooning the idea that a mundane wildflower should impede a multi-million-dollar construction project.[1] How had the state of Maine—and the United States more generally—gotten to this strange moment?

This regional situation had its roots in developments a few years earlier. The 1973 oil embargo, instituted by oil-producing nations as punishment for covert US support for Israel in its war against a coalition of Arab states, was a major event in the political history of the late twentieth century. The embargo caused oil prices to skyrocket and created lines and fist fights at gasoline stations as Americans waited hours to fill their gas tanks.

The US presidents of the 1970s—Richard Nixon, Gerald Ford, and Jimmy Carter—pursued energy policies that would increase domestic production to replace foreign oil, including coal, nuclear power, and alternative technologies.[2]

As it was for all domestic energy sources, the mid-1970s was therefore a moment that held the potential for dynamic change in the hydroelectric economy of the United States. Keynoting the 1976 annual convention of the Colorado River Water Users Association (a group of representatives and officials from Western states and Native American tribes), US Bureau of Reclamation commissioner Gilbert Stamm declared emphatically that hydro power was significantly underdeveloped in the United States, with untold numbers of rivers primed and ready for useful hydroelectric construction. He optimistically predicted that remedying this problem of underuse could help solve the nation's energy woes, dependence on foreign oil foremost among them. Citing the key role of hydro power in the historical development of the American West, Stamm warned that "we would be grossly irresponsible if we ignored its undeveloped potential in planning for future generations." And noting that only a third of the nation's identified hydroelectric capacity had been exploited, Stamm extolled water's potential to make an "important and unique" contribution to energy security.[3] Though Commissioner Stamm specifically touted the untapped hydro capacity of the Colorado River Basin in the West, he also expressed broader optimism about flowing water's potential to solve the nation's energy problems. If the numberless rivers criss-crossing the country could be harnessed for human use, the nation's dependence on oil from across the world—especially the Middle East, but also places like Venezuela, which was in the process of nationalizing its oil industry, as Joseph Pratt describes elsewhere in this volume—would dissipate.

Not all observers shared Stamm's zeal for hydroelectricity. The mid-1970s witnessed tense debates surrounding several large hydroelectric projects, whose potential effects on the landscape and wildlife in a proposed construction area generated controversy. Environmentalists often mobilized to block the construction of these huge structures, which brought them into conflict with public agencies funding and supporting the projects. Environmentalist opponents of the dams were often unable to prevent the construction of hydroelectric projects by appealing to general environmental sensibilities. Instead, they resorted to using a relatively new piece of regulatory legislation, the Endangered Species Act (ESA), to preserve undeveloped wilderness areas.

Passed in 1973 as a key piece of a broader wave of environmental legislation in the United States during this era, the ESA was meant to protect imperilled animal and plant species. Supporters of the law argued that allowing species to go extinct was short-sighted. One pragmatic reason given was that these species might provide some yet unknown benefit to humans in the future, and another was that they had an inherent right to exist and humans did not hold the moral authority to wipe them out.[4] Once passed, the ESA prevented federal agencies from taking any action that would kill endangered animal or plant species or destroy their habitats. Though the law passed with virtually universal acclaim from the public, several facets quickly became controversial once it was put into practice. Chief among them was the fact that the law protected endangered species indiscriminately with no regard for their relative usefulness to humans. This provision at first seemed uncontroversial. How can one compare the inherent monetary value of one endangered species relative to another? Yet the ESA's enforcement soon irritated many Americans who came to believe that it was too broad. Not long after the law's passage, several of these endangered species—which often had negligible differences setting them apart from similar species whose populations were abundant—delayed or halted massive, multi-million-dollar energy projects.

Endangered species' ability to dominate and marginalize all the other facets and issues embedded within an otherwise complex debate soon made many observers question the scope and power of the law. Even publications that may have had mixed feelings about a given economic project came to opine that such debates should pivot around weightier concerns than one seemingly un-notable species. This chapter examines two controversies that unfolded from the mid-1960s through the 1970s, both related to hydroelectric projects, and that imparted this pessimistic notion to diverse constituencies and interest groups.

The two cases, Tellico Dam in East Tennessee and Dickey Dam in northern Maine, each unfolded over more than a decade, with stops and starts in funding allocations based on sporadic environmental litigation. But while the Tellico Dam was finished and its gates closed to impound the Little Tennessee River, the Dickey Dam was never built—in fact, wilderness land was never even cleared to prepare the area, and families living on the dam's proposed site who had faced forced relocation remained on their land. There were also differences in the dynamics of public-private alliances in the two cases. While Tellico witnessed co-operation between the quasi-public Tennessee Valley Authority (TVA) and the Boeing Corporation to develop land around the Little Tennessee, in the case of Dickey Dam, the Army Corps of Engineers clashed with private power companies who detested public competition in electricity generation.

Yet even with these significant differences in play, each project was at one point imperilled by the ESA. A small fish called the snail darter delayed the Tellico project and for a time put its eventual completion at risk. The dispute over the dam made its way to the US Supreme Court, which ruled in favour of the tiny fish. Likewise, a few clumps of the Furbish lousewort jeopardized the future of the Dickey Dam in Maine. The two endangered species' ability to dominate public debate and supersede all other concerns about the future of the two projects made many observers, including individual citizens and national periodicals, come to believe that the act protecting them was too powerful. These cases turned many Americans against the idea of environmental regulation, as numerous observers came to believe that regulations, while admirable in the abstract, did not in practice adequately take into account the imperatives of human need.

The Tellico story has already received significant attention from historians and political scientists. Such analysis generally focuses on narrow aspects of the story, such as the history of legal litigation on the dam or the internal discussions among TVA officials as the story played out. This chapter instead places Tellico into the larger unfolding story about the declining political power of environmentalism after the 1973 oil embargo, a story that also includes the never built and much less well-known Dickey Dam. When environmental guidelines did not seriously endanger Americans' standard of living, they were relatively uncontroversial. But when environmental values and energy production came into conflict, some Americans came to believe that recent regulations were unfairly predisposed, against the dictates of common sense, to favour the former at the expense of the latter. The Tellico and Dickey controversies led to the deterioration of the ESA's legal power. With it, the reputation of environmentalism in the United States suffered a serious blow, as energy production was firmly established as the more pressing public policy problem in the post–oil embargo United States.

The Tennessee Valley and Riverfront Development

The Tellico Dam project, as an initiative of the quasi-public TVA, had deep historical roots. By the mid-1960s, the time of the project's inception, the agency had developed a central and nearly mythical position in the history of the US Southeast. During the New Deal years, many of President Franklin Roosevelt's top advisers had developed a theory to explain the seemingly insurmountable poverty of the American South, which, in terms of wealth, persistently lagged behind the industrial centres of the Northeast and Midwest. They concluded that urban industrial hubs in other parts of the nation had kept the "resource-rich hinterlands" of the South in a perpetual state of underdevelopment by appropriating the region's raw resources with little concern for its residents. The southern states had exhausted their soils and forest resources to produce material—mainly cotton—for refining and processing in urban industrial centres. To equalize incomes between farm and factory, therefore, meant that agricultural regions must "retain the right to their own resources" and use them effectively. New Dealers also decided that the federal government would have to be the agent of change, as the South, focused intently on preserving strict nineteenth-century racial hierarchies through maintenance of a farm-based economy, lacked the political will to achieve its own forward-thinking economic uplift.[5]

As historian Sarah T. Phillips has argued, no single New Deal initiative better embodied this thinking than the TVA, a government corporation created during FDR's first hundred days. Created to "restore and develop the resources of an entire watershed area," according to Phillips, the TVA built multi-purpose dams, supplied hydroelectric power to farms and small towns, and began to repair the South's damaged forests and soil.[6] Though some New Deal programs were either ineffective or were ruled unconstitutional, the TVA emerged as one of the most prominent symbols of the successes of New Deal liberalism. In 1933, when the TVA was established, per capita income in the Tennessee Valley was a mere 45 per cent of the national average. By 1972, the ratio stood at a greatly increased 75 per cent, a figure of which the TVA was exceedingly proud. The agency attributed much of the difference to its own activities in the region, and it used the irrefutable economic progress of the past decades to push for an expanded mission in the near future.[7]

The agency had a practical reason for wanting to expand the scope of its mission in the Tennessee Valley. It had relied on consistent funding from Congress to pay for the construction of power-generation facilities for the first quarter-century of its existence, as the subsidized electric rates offered to impoverished valley residents did not in turn provide sufficient revenue to the authority for its daily operations. During the Eisenhower administration, however, Congress began to withhold dollars, channelling money instead to the task of waging the burgeoning Cold War with the Soviet Union. Aubrey Wagner, TVA board chairman from 1962 to 1978, recognized that the TVA's current formula—relying on power generation, navigation, and flood control—was insufficient to financially sustain the agency; it needed to expand its role in the region so as to multiply its sources of revenue. Wagner decided that including more direct local economic-development initiatives within the TVA's mission could attract additional congressional appropriations, as members of Congress from the Tennessee Valley would be eager to steer federal funds that would generate local jobs. The TVA had long used dams to generate electricity for residents of the valley. The chairman decided that building entirely new communities around the reservoirs created by these dams provided the path forward.[8]

In 1962, the first year of Wagner's chairmanship, the TVA began a fierce push for increased riverfront development. It explained to the US Congress why federal support for these projects would be beneficial. First and foremost, it would help develop industry in the region. The Tennessee Valley had numerous navigable waterways that, in theory, could be used for easy transport of industrial products to other areas of the nation for consumption. The only problem was that the region, focused on maintaining the romantic ideal of the independent rural farmer, had largely failed to develop industrial sites along these promising rivers. The TVA, the agency's leaders claimed, could and should rectify this shortsightedness.

There was also a more pressing practical reason for this course of action. Due to robust population growth, Tennessee's labour force was outpacing job opportunities in the state's stagnant farming economy. A failure to diversify the region's economy would soon lead to structural economic disaster.[9] In the TVA's estimation, riverfront development would continue to create low-cost hydroelectric power for the valley, but it would also provide a way to encourage capital investment and industrial development in the resource-rich region.[10] However, as the TVA found, the new environmental legislation of the late 1960s and early 1970s created a formidable obstacle to its riverfront development plans.

The Tellico Project

The TVA's inaugural effort to pursue this new mission centred on constructing a dam on the Little Tennessee River, about twenty-five miles southwest of the TVA headquarters in Knoxville, and then building a new industrial community around the hydroelectric structure. The site seemed to be ideal, as it was a rural and impoverished area desperately in need of an economic jolt. Following Wagner's lead, in April 1963 the TVA board voted to endorse the project and seek congressional funding, which came quickly. Congressional favour led to executive support as well. President Lyndon Johnson's January 1965 budget proposal included nearly $6 million for the project.[11]

In its initial stages, the project proceeded without any apparent problems, as a modernization program for an impoverished rural area seemed to have little obvious downside. Tennessee congressman Joe Evins got a favourable vote for the prospective Tellico Dam from the Appropriations Committee and then the full House in 1966. Initial construction of the project began soon afterward in March 1967. The initiative's main component was the dam on the Little Tennessee River, about a quarter mile above its confluence with the Tennessee. It seemed a perfect location on a river whose utility had already been proven. In its promotional materials, the TVA referred to the Little Tennessee and its tributaries as "a hard-working river system." Indeed, it had already been successfully impounded sixteen times for hydroelectric generation and flood control.[12]

The project also included the creation of a thousand-foot-long canal to divert the waters of the Little Tennessee into the Fort Loudon Reservoir, enabling these waters to pass through the existing hydroelectric units in the Fort Loudon powerhouse. The reservoir created by the dam would prospectively extend over thirty miles upstream, its impressive length allowing its waters to occupy over fifteen thousand acres. In the TVA's boosterish words, this would "create an ideal living, working, and recreation environment . . . [in an area] characterized by low incomes and under-utilization of human and natural resources." Recognizing that "the influx of thousands of people requiring homes and services in an essentially rural area" could result in rapid and uncontrolled sprawl, the TVA planned to create a focused, suburban-style community of single-family homes on the left bank of the reservoir's lower reaches.[13]

In promoting the project, the TVA emphasized a multiplicity of recreational, disaster-preparedness, and energy-production benefits. First and foremost, it would bring money and jobs to an area that sorely needed both. Pointing out that the nearby Great Smoky Mountains National Park received over seven million visits from tourists every year, the TVA claimed that the lake would be a "valuable" supplementary recreational asset that would attract dollars from wealthier areas of the Southeast and the nation. The TVA also projected that the diversion of the reservoir waters through the turbines at Fort Loudon Dam would provide 200 million kilowatt hours of inexpensive electricity for valley residents annually. Emphasizing the environmental benefits of hydroelectric power, the TVA claimed that producing this same amount of electricity in a coal-fired steam plant would require about ninety thousand tons of coal each year, the pollution from which would be mitigated by the turbines' operation.[14]

Within its more traditional mission, the agency also pointed out that the Tellico Dam and Reservoir would provide over a hundred thousand acre-feet of storage for flood control, providing much-needed flood protection for Chattanooga (a city about a hundred miles southwest of Knoxville, on the border with Georgia) as well as myriad communities along the Tennessee River between Chattanooga and the project.[15] To assuage possible concerns about risk to drinking water, the TVA claimed that the project, despite its massive scale, was not expected to adversely affect water quality "to any significant extent." It also downplayed the possible losses of rare and endangered species, claiming that any rare fish or mollusks in the area that might be affected by the construction also existed securely in other locations.[16]

With all of these ostensible benefits, the project received virtually unanimous support from local governments and business interests. The Chamber of Commerce of nearby Lenoir City resolved in 1969 that the dam was "vital to the economy and welfare" of the city's residents and urged that the level of appropriations for the project be increased by such amounts to insure "timely completion." In 1970, the Monroe County Quarterly Court deplored the fact that the project was only 30 per cent complete, and criticized a delay caused by recent budget cutbacks. In 1972, the town of Madisonville exhorted the "economic development and employment opportunities" of the dam, as did Lenoir City's Board of Mayor and Aldermen. The same year, the president of the Knoxville Chamber of Commerce wrote to Governor Winfield Dunn explaining his support, claiming that the dam's creation of a lake with adjacent properties would address the concerns of both environmentalists and urban planners by "providing a place for [growing populations] to live, while at the same time enhancing their environment."[17] To the Chamber of Commerce president it seemed that the concept of environmental quality was synonymous with human recreation, providing a glimpse into how boosters unconvincingly tried to square their support for economic growth with the political power of environmentalism in the early 1970s.

Vague definitions of "environmentalism" aside, not all citizens were persuaded. Local ecologist Edward Clebsch crystallized the environmentalist viewpoint, writing indignantly to the recently created President's Council on Environmental Quality to criticize the TVA's process of land acquisition. He lamented the idea that the financial benefits of the project would be derived from the development of pollution-generating industrial sites. According to Clebsch, the dam's economic proceeds would flow overwhelmingly to the privileged few who owned the industrial sites, with the negative externalities distributed among the general populace. Pointing out that the TVA expected to receive several million dollars in land sales to industry, Clebsch also found it "revolting" that it would use eminent domain to acquire land "and then sell it at an unbelievably high profit to itself."[18]

To the agency's surprise, many local residents were even more vocal against the project, with some allying themselves with environmentalists to oppose the dam. Chairman Wagner encountered this opposition in person, travelling to the nearby town of Greenback in 1964 to sell the idea to locals. He assumed they would embrace an initiative to improve their area's aggregate income and economic standing. Instead, the trip was a disaster. The rural residents loved the idyllic farm life to which they were accustomed and were loath to give up agricultural land for industrial development and suburban-style home building; this was a deeply rooted cultural ideology that Wagner had not considered. Farmers and fishermen from the area were not content to voice their protest against visiting TVA officials, but instead supplemented their localized grumblings by travelling to the nation's capital in 1966 to speak out against the project in congressional hearings, enraging the TVA head.[19]

Even though it included the state governor, this alliance of environmentalists and farmers seemed to matter little. The US Congress generally sided with Wagner and the TVA. Not unimportantly, eminent domain powers backed by Congress gave the TVA the ability to seize farmland against locals' wishes. Private companies also joined the controversy on the side of the TVA and Congress, creating a seemingly unstoppable alliance in favour of the project. As the debate unfolded, the TVA had attracted the support of the Boeing Corporation as a partner to help build the prospective new town of Timberlake on the Tellico Reservoir, a project that was never completed. Also in 1972, the agency received approval of its environmental impact statement, prepared in response to National Environmental Protection Act requirements that federal projects be evaluated for their environmental consequences. Rumours of budget overruns and exploding costs, while providing fodder to those already against the dam, did little to move the opinions of those who favoured it. By 1973, it appeared that the dam would go forward as planned, despite the vehement and diverse opposition.[20] But dam opponents had one more powerful weapon to use against the project: the Endangered Species Act.

Discovering the Snail Darter

In August 1973, zoology professor David Etnier, a Tellico Dam opponent, recognized that the ESA might be the last chance for wishing to stop the project. Though the ESA had been passed with known species threatened by human development in mind, Etnier realized that as yet undiscovered species would fall under the act's provisions too. He therefore went looking for new species in the Little Tennessee River that might require federal protection. Etnier's expedition was indeed fruitful, as he discovered a tiny, previously unidentified fish barely bigger than a paper clip. The find, which became known as the snail darter, gave new life to opponents of the dam. Not unimportantly, the snail darter, while a unique species, was one of over a hundred known species of darter fish, each of which had negligible differences from the others. After extended testimony from both the TVA and the environmental opposition, the Fish and Wildlife Service decided to side with the environmentalists. The service listed the snail darter as an endangered species and designated a part of the Little Tennessee River its "critical habitat." This designation meant that the area could not be altered in a way that might imperil the snail darter's survival. Even though the dam was 90 per cent complete by this point, the fish and its habitat in the Little Tennessee were now protected by the ESA, and TVA could not go forward with the project.[21] Litigation by the agency over the subsequent years advanced within the US court system, and a spring 1978 Supreme Court decision—which saw the Carter administration, especially Attorney General Griffin Bell, siding with TVA against dam opponents—ended with the court ruling that the dam could not be completed.[22]

The Tellico Dam saga indeed played a role in reorienting some of the environmentalist legislation passed a few short years before. In March 1977, the month after Weisman's letter was published, the *Christian Science Monitor* reported that Congress was considering curbing the power of the ESA, specifically the Fish and Wildlife Service's power to safeguard habitats deemed essential to the survival or recovery of an endangered or threatened species. The mere addition of an organism to the endangered species list did not automatically exempt the land it lived on from developmental potential. But since the service had broad authority to designate land a "critical habitat," each new listing held the corresponding possibility to impede or prevent a developmental project. According to the *Monitor*, the service's authority faced a "water[ing] down" at the hands of Congress in multiple ways. For example, the changes under consideration would give the interior secretary unilateral power to exempt a federal project that would otherwise be excluded from a designated critical habitat. Furthermore, the kinds of species that might be eligible for critical habitat protection also faced curtailing, with cold-blooded vertebrates and invertebrates possibly losing habitat protections altogether.[23]

Opposition to the ESA continued to grow in Congress. In April 1978, within the Senate Environmental and Public Works Committee's Resource Protection Subcommittee, John C. Culver, Democrat of Iowa, offered an amendment that would create a review board drawn from seven federal agencies empowered to grant exemptions from the act for some government construction projects. Under certain circumstances, the proposed board could permit construction of a project that would destroy an animal or plant species if the project's benefits to humans "clearly outweigh[ed]" the value of the species.[24]

The amendment offered no scale or metric by which to determine how benefits to humans would compare to the existence or non-existence of a given species, and it seems impossible that any such measure could be reasonably devised, giving the review board wide latitude to make decisions. The board could not override the ESA with a simple majority vote. Instead, it would take five out of seven members to permit a project to proceed in the face of an endangered species objection. The review board would be composed of the secretaries of the interior, agriculture, and the army, the chair of the Council of Economic Advisers, administrators with the Environmental Protection Agency (EPA) and the National Oceanic and Atmospheric Administration, and an individual nominated by the governor of the state in which a project was affected by the ESA. Six of these seven members were presidential appointees. Given such criteria, the practical effect of the panel would be influenced by the ideological orientation of the president making these personnel decisions.

This proposed amendment, while seemingly byzantine in its bureaucratic orientation, represented a major change in the nature of the law. One of the things that made the ESA different from other federal regulations was its locally enforceable curbs on development. Other areas of federal regulation—antitrust, financial, and others—relied on vigorous efforts from law enforcement officials like the president and attorney general to function properly. Presidents who disfavoured regulations often did not need to persuade Congress to roll them back in order to weaken their power; they simply needed to institute lax enforcement of the laws. But the provisions of the ESA allowed local groups to petition local courts to stop an action that might harm endangered species. In the case of Tellico, local groups took their opposition all the way to the Supreme Court, where they took on Jimmy Carter's attorney general, and won. This amendment, by potentially taking power back from local opposition groups and giving it to high-ranking federal officials, represented a major reduction in the enforcement powers of the ESA.

In summer 1978, the US Senate voted overwhelmingly to amend the ESA, creating the proposed interagency review board. Three months later, the House voted for its own version of the ESA amendments, and soon agreed to adopt the Senate version. The *Washington Post* did not mince words that fall, with a September 29 headline declaring simply that the "Endangered Species Act Is Dying." Recognizing the rising unpopularity of the ESA within Congress and the heavy pressure for change, environmentally inclined representative John Dingell, Democrat of Michigan, had reportedly been working non-stop to maintain a "holding action" of offering compromises in Congress and averting moves to gut the act or kill it outright.[25] And in November, in the face of this immense congressional support for the amendments, President Carter reluctantly signed the amendments and made them law.[26]

The irony of the ESA amendments, though, is that although they had largely been spurred to passage by the Tellico Dam saga, they did not resolve the controversy dragging on in East Tennessee. The new exemption committee voted *not* to exempt the Tellico Dam from the act, claiming that the project's economic and social benefits did not "clearly outweigh" the negative impacts. Also ironically, the snail darter was scarcely a factor in the committee's decision. Instead, looking at the hard numbers, the committee decided that the dam would not generate enough economic benefit in the region to justify its multi-million-dollar cost. In other words, it simply was not worth the money.[27] Though the snail darter was barely a consideration, the committee's refusal to grant an exemption meant that the ESA legally prohibited the dam's completion. Dam proponents had one last idea to try to circumvent the snail darter and finish the project, and it required some congressional manoeuvring.[28]

In 1979, on a day when most legislators were absent, Tennessee representative John Duncan attached a rider to the Energy and Water Resources Appropriation exempting Tellico from the ESA, and the appropriation passed with few caring about the exemption. The Senate deleted the amendment in its version, but Duncan—along with Senator Howard Baker, who called in as many favours as possible—ensured its return in conference. After the amendment passed both houses, President Carter, who was under pressure to support energy projects while the Iranian Revolution was causing oil prices to spike, signed it. The TVA finally finished the dam, the environmentalist opposition defeated by an anticlimactic legislative proceeding. In November 1979, the long saga of Tellico came to a quiet and strange conclusion.[29]

The Origins of Dickey Dam

Of all the hydroelectric projects of the 1960s and '70s, the Tellico Dam controversy has received by far the most attention from historians and legal commentators, and for good reason: it was a key event that helped turn public and congressional opinion against the ESA. Yet there was another major but less well-known case, one that involved the prominent senator Edmund Muskie and that also witnessed an extended battle between environmentalists and pro-development advocates. The story of the Dickey Dam, while unfolding with quite different dynamics and within different parameters than the Tellico saga, further helped discredit endangered species legislation in the public arena. Putting the story of Tellico alongside that of Dickey shows that, whether a potential hydroelectric project was actually completed or not, the intrusion of the ESA into the debate helped discredit environmental regulation.

Like Tellico, Dickey began in the mid-1960s as an effort to bring power and jobs to a rural area. In 1965, the US Congress authorized the Army Corps of Engineers to begin construction of the dam—a project the corps supported—on the St. John River in northern Maine, near the Canadian border. New Englanders hoped the project would bring jobs and cheap electricity, much as the TVA had done in the Southeast. In practice the formal authorization had little consequence. Congress refused to appropriate any money for the project, despite the consistent support of the powerful Maine senator Edmund Muskie. Appealing to historical precedent, proponents implored Congress for money to begin preparing the site. Government-produced electricity, they said, would have provided a "yardstick" to shame New England utilities for their perceived exorbitance, again much as the TVA had done in the Southeast. Private power interests, though, fearing government competition, succeeded in holding off construction for the better part of a decade, preserving their dominance in the power market.[30]

The 1973 oil embargo changed the parameters of the public-private controversy. With electricity bills for consumers skyrocketing around the country, especially in the frigid winters of New England, utility executives decided it would be "unseemly" to appear opposed to new energy supplies from any source, and they relented in their opposition. By the middle of 1974, a start to the construction of the project seemed a distinct possibility for the first time in years.[31]

Even with private utilities relaxing their opposition, the contrast between the condition of the proposed site and the magnitude of the prospective project in 1974 was nothing short of astounding. The town of Dickey, after which the dam would be named, consisted merely of a few homes and a Shell gas station. The local post office had long since closed. Slated to stretch nearly ten thousand feet between two mountains and to soar more than three hundred feet above the St. John riverbed, the dam would flood this small group of buildings. Dubbed an "Aswan Dam for Maine" by the *Wall Street Journal* after the massive structure located on the Nile River in Egypt, the dam would be the eleventh largest in the world. Though located in an area that could have hardly been called even sparsely populated, a completed dam would send electricity throughout New England.[32]

Environmentalists expressed vehement opposition. The Friends of St. John, a Boston-based group, argued that the dam and the hundreds of miles of transmission lines would ruin an astonishing 110,800 acres of "the last remaining wilderness area in the northeast." The group's chairman, Paul Swatek, feared that 57 miles of "the best white water canoeing in the northeast" would be lost forever. The effect on wildlife was a concern as well. Swatek pointed to the approximately two thousand deer that spent their winters in the area, as some 13,000 acres that they inhabited during the cold season would be inundated by the dam.[33]

The Friends of St. John critiqued the project on a fiscal basis too. Opponents claimed that the dam's benefits paled in comparison to the costs: Dickey would only be used for peaking power (it would run only in periods of high demand, in other words), since the river contained very little water; one newspaper described it as "a ribbon of rocks through the wilderness." The river's limited flow capacity meant that the dam would operate a mere three hours a day, as the reservoir behind the dam would otherwise get too low in the summer to generate any power at all. The dam's sporadic usefulness, opponents said, was hardly worth the wholesale environmental devastation it would cause. Even more tragic, they said, was the forced relocation of long-time residents from their homes that would have to be carried out.[34]

The Pro-dam Response

A faction calling itself People of the St. John provided several rebuttals to these critiques. The generic-sounding name of the pro-dam group was not accidental. All the members of the group lived in northern Maine, an area that would receive an economic infusion from the project. The group demanded that the elitist, environmentalist "out-of-staters" making up the Friends of St. John remove themselves from the debate and allow locals to make decisions about their own land. While environmentalists saw the wilderness areas of northern Maine as a recreational asset to be shared by all New Englanders, dam proponents were concerned about those who lived nearby. In response to wildlife and landscape concerns, the Army Corps of Engineers asserted that the dam complex would be built carefully to cause minimal impact to native ecosystems. Colonel John H. Mason, the corps' chief engineer for New England, said that public hearings would likely be held to allow environmentalist grievances to be aired. He also promised that his organization would submit an environmental impact statement to the president's Council on Environmental Quality.[35]

Dam supporters conceded that some people would be forced to leave their residences if the structure was built. But few people lived in the immediate area and the entire region would benefit from the dam's power generation, the People of St. John said, arguing that the needs of the many outweighed those of the rural few. On the issue of peaking power, proponents admitted that the dam was not capable of remaining in operation around the clock. But they also said that tallying the number of hours per day the dam would be in operation was misleading and missed the bigger picture: the dam's aggregated use, even for only a few hours each day, would reduce New England's power bill by about $40 million over the course of a year, proponents pointed out, which was the important figure.[36] As Paul Chastko notes in his contribution to this volume, the enormous US demand for energy was sometimes enough to keep even *foreign* energy producers afloat through tough economic times, and the Friends of St. John were unsurprisingly incensed that a needed domestic energy project might be stymied by what they saw as relatively minor concerns.

For some other local supporters, backing for the project emanated from a more pressing worry—namely, the floods that were causing increasing damage to the area's farmland. Robert Jalbert, a lawyer in the nearby town of Fort Kent and a registered Maine wilderness guide, was a representative figure. Having long opposed the dam, in mid-1974 Jalbert shifted his view. His conversion was not attributable to the jobs that would come into the area, but instead the effects of recent changes in the lumber industry. The past handful of years had witnessed the introduction of the "skidder," a large vehicle used for dragging and pushing trees. The technology increased the lumber industry's yield to the point that it was able to completely strip hillsides of trees. When snow came in the winter, not only was there no shade to slow melting, but hillsides could no longer absorb excess water. The quicker, bigger runoff was generating disastrous floods that damaged nearby farms. Jalbert critiqued the lumber industry's irresponsibility—"They believe they have to harvest [the forest] like a garden," he said—but conceded that, within the current system, nothing could be done. "It's a capitalistic system and they own that land," he acknowledged. Though the corps had a plan to flood a series of dikes to protect Fort Kent, Jalbert was not convinced that this would be sufficient. Only damming the St. John's waters would provide lasting protection.[37]

Unexpected Setbacks

In 1977, the contents of the long-awaited, two-years-in-the-making Army Corps of Engineers impact study must have come as a shock to this varied group of dam supporters, and as a gift to environmental opponents. It stated plainly that "there would be a reduction in the long-term productivity" of the area's economic future if the dam was built. Though the nearly two-hundred-page report noted that there would be short-term gains in electric power production and recreational opportunities on the resulting lake, they would be far outweighed by the long-term downsides. As the *New York Times* reported, the statement "painted a grim picture of flooded timberlands, destroyed canoe and fishing rivers and wiped-out deer herds." In the time since construction had become a serious possibility, environmentalist heavyweights like the Sierra Club, Audubon Society, Friends of the Earth, and Greenpeace had joined the Friends of St. John to oppose the project.[38] While dam supporters seemed to have the upper hand in the debate in 1974, the dynamics of political influence had clearly shifted in the intervening years as the more lasting environmental consequences became apparent.

Environmentalists had also found another, more powerful weapon, the same one wielded by opponents of Tennessee's Tellico Dam—the ESA. In 1976, as part of the preparations for the site, the US Army Corps of Engineers hired Maine botanist Charles Richards to identify potential "rare and unusual" plants in the project area. The discovery near the dam site of a few clumps of a greenish-yellow wildflower named the Furbish lousewort (after botanist Kate Furbish), not known to exist anywhere else, threatened to bring the project to a halt and compelled the corps to act. The ESA required that federal agencies not take any action that would jeopardize the continued existence of a listed species or its habitat, which dam construction clearly would. The menace to the project's future was enough to compel the corps to spend $17,000 and two summers scouting a three-hundred-mile stretch of the St. John to try to locate other communities of the flower.[39]

While conceding the broader environmental concerns and doubts about the limited production possibility of the dam, *Time* called the idea that the lousewort alone would hold up the project "downright silly." The magazine seemed quite satisfied to report that the engineers, after their long search, had "proudly announced" the discovery of "no less than five clumps" of lousewort "safely beyond" the proposed dam site. "What is more," *Time* declared triumphantly, the corps had also concluded that "the exotic flower can be cultivated elsewhere."[40] As was clear from the magazine's tone, the ESA was one regulatory measure whose reach seemed far too broad. The idea that a few clumps of flowers would by themselves impede a nearly $700 million project seemed to the periodical to be simply ridiculous. For *Time*, as well as for other national periodicals, the delicate balance between protecting vulnerable species and cultivating development projects to benefit human populations had moved entirely too far in one direction.

And with the project still in the planning stages, it remained susceptible to new strains of criticism. Many government projects see their projected budgets increase steadily as time goes on. The bigger a project is and the longer it takes to complete, the more difficult the final cost is to estimate, which often leads cost assessments to rise over the course of a project's planning. The Dickey Dam, a multi-year project with costs in the hundreds of millions of dollars, was no exception. In the summer of 1979, for example, the House's Public Works Committee voted to kill the project, the first time that the committee had ever voted to end a major water project after substantial sums—$10 million so far—had already been spent. Defying the default urge to support pork-barrel projects, both of Maine's House members, Republicans Olympia Snowe and David Emery, supported de-authorization. So, too, did one of the state's senators, Republican William Cohen. With Senator Muskie's continued support, however, de-authorization faced a challenge on the Senate floor, and the measure indeed failed.[41]

Yet, other events unexpectedly impinged upon this hydroelectric political situation. In 1980, President Carter authorized the secret Operation Eagle Claw, a daring desert rescue involving several helicopters, to liberate the hostages being held in Tehran. Deeming it far too risky, Carter's secretary of state, Cyrus Vance—who had often clashed with the hawkish National Security Adviser Zbigniew Brzezinski—resigned as soon as Carter approved the mission. Vance's concerns turned out to be prophetic. The mission failed spectacularly when one of the copters became engulfed in a dust cloud and crashed into a transport aircraft, killing eight American servicemen. In response, the Iranian government scattered the American hostages across the nation, making another such rescue attempt impossible. Carter tapped Senator Muskie as Vance's replacement, removing the Mainer from the Senate.[42] Maine's governor, Joseph Brennan, appointed George Mitchell, a federal judge on the US District Court for the District of Maine, to serve out Muskie's term. With Muskie's exit from the Senate, the Dickey Dam's future was in serious doubt.[43]

In the spring of 1981, after the election of Ronald Reagan, the Maine delegation submitted legislation to Congress to de-authorize the dam, the projected cost of which had risen another 20 per cent in less than two years and now stood at $900 million. Senator Mitchell was in principle a supporter of the project, "contin[uing] to believe that the entire project merits support" and believing "it will in the future receive the support it deserves." But with Reagan coming to office on the message of deep cutbacks in federal spending, and with local opinion near the St. John turning against the dam, Mitchell agreed to support de-authorization legislation for the time being.[44]

Local opinion had not turned against hydroelectricity in general, but it *had* shifted in favour of a smaller, more focused project, a path also favoured by environmentalists as a compromise measure. The Natural Resources Council of Maine (NRCM), formed in 1959 to oppose large hydroelectric projects, expressed support for the proposed Lincoln School Dam a few miles downriver from the prospective Dickey. Though the Lincoln School Dam would produce only a small fraction of the potential output of the larger dam, it would also affect less than 5,000 acres of wilderness land—compared, of course, with over 110,000 for the Dickey—which made it seem like a worthwhile compromise. More important to locals was the use of the power. Nearly 80 per cent of the Dickey's output would have been transmitted from Maine to other states in New England, but the Lincoln School's power would remain in the area for local use. Though some St. John locals continued to believe in the Dickey's superior potential for economic development, the NRCM and other environmental groups succeeded in turning others against the project by compromising in favour of a more diminutive alternative.[45]

Other Mainers had also been converted to the anti-dam position for fiscal reasons, becoming ever more suspicious as cost estimates grew; politicians, meanwhile, used the issue to garner votes, with no physical construction to show for the money being spent. Contractor Clark McBreaity had once supported the dam but had gradually come to oppose the project. "Every time a candidate ran for office," McBreaity remarked, "he run [sic] up and down New England whooping and hollering" about the dam's potential, using the perpetually un-begun project for their own political gain. As time went on, the hype surrounding the Dickey's economic possibilities faded in the St. John area, replaced instead by suspicion and skepticism. As the *Christian Science Monitor* noted, this independent-minded rural area had always been suspicious of government intervention, and the enchantment of the Dickey's potential had finally run out.[46]

Still another logistical problem had to do with the relocation of the families living on the land potentially affected by the Dickey Dam. The small town of Dickey itself was a Scotch-Irish enclave, but the surrounding countryside was populated largely by French Canadians. The government could have provided money to assist in relocating the Dickey families, but regulations prohibited it from paying to move the 161 Dickey families more than fifty miles, which was not far enough to get them out of French-speaking territory. The Dickey families' reticence to move to an area in which they would be surrounded by speakers of a foreign language also imperiled the dam's future.[47]

The End of the Dam

The final nail in the coffin for the project came when the Interior Department expressed opposition to it. James Watt, Reagan's appointee to head the department, had drawn early and intense fire from environmentalists when he moved to roll back environmental regulations and to expand leasing of federal lands to coal mining companies.[48] But in the midst of the Dickey debate, Watt was on an extended tour of the Western states and was not in day-to-day control of the department. Therefore, when Acting Secretary Donald Hodel expressed opposition to the dam on environmental grounds, it was he who was speaking for the department. In taking a stand against the project, Hodel cited destruction of black duck breeding grounds and the loss of summer foraging areas for moose, as well as the migratory deer areas emphasized by the anti-dam Friends of St. John years earlier. As it turned out, Watt himself was also against the dam, bringing him into rare agreement with environmental activists, although Watt's opposition probably owed more to Reagan's fiscally motivated desires to cut back on federal water projects. Declining energy demand in the early 1980s, which made many energy projects seem much less necessary, did not help Dickey's prospects either. Though the corps made one last appeal to public opinion, officials conceded that the united front presented by Maine's congressional delegation and the Interior Department made the dam's construction "unlikely" to ever happen.[49] Despite the TVA's nearly mythical role in the Southeast, the United States was never on the whole a "hydro democracy" on par with Canada, as Daniel Macfarlane describes the United States' northern neighbour elsewhere in this volume. National pride was not enough to keep expensive hydro projects afloat as their costs continued to balloon.

Indeed, ground was never broken for construction on Dickey Dam, and neither was the smaller Lincoln School alternative built. After years of debate and congressional wrangling, the issue was effectively dead. There were therefore many differences between the Tellico Dam debate in East Tennessee and that of the Dickey in northern Maine. First was the final result. While the gates of Tellico Dam were closed in 1979 after some sneaky legislative manoeuvring by Tennessee representative John Duncan, turning a portion of the Little Tennessee River into a reservoir, Dickey Dam simply faded into obscurity in 1981 when the corps gave up on the project. The Tellico Dam involved intense controversy over the cozy relationship between the quasi-public TVA and private industry in forcing small family farmers from their land, bringing an extra level of scrutiny not present in the Dickey Dam debate, which had instead witnessed a confrontation between public and private interests. Local opposition in East Tennessee against Tellico was also much fiercer than in northern Maine against Dickey, as the area around the proposed site in Maine was largely unpopulated and would not have involved forcing farm families off of their land, as was the case in Tennessee.

There was, however, one important similarity to be found in the two dam sagas, one that overwhelmed all the diverse differences. The Dickey

Dam battle, with a divergent set of circumstances and a different outcome from the controversy over the Tellico Dam, nonetheless witnessed a comparable debate surrounding the ESA. There were many compelling arguments in favour of Dickey, including the economic opportunities to be brought to the St. John area, as well as the electricity that would flow throughout New England. There were also compelling reasons to oppose the dam, such as the negative effects on human recreational opportunities in wilderness areas and the disruptions to both migratory and permanent habitats of extensive varieties of birds and mammals. But national periodicals seemed to agree on one thing: the Furbish lousewort should not be part of the deliberation.

The idea that a few clumps of wildflower should control the fate of Dickey Dam seemed to many observers just as ridiculous as the tiny snail darter's influence on the Tellico in East Tennessee. For these analysts, the reach of the ESA had again proved itself far too broad, protecting small populations of seemingly useless and unneeded species at the expense of projects that otherwise turned on sums in the hundreds of millions of dollars and land areas of thousands of acres. The ESA's ability to assume such a disproportionate power in these debates was, for many commentators, more than unfortunate—it was unjust and unfair. The public may have assumed that Congress was protecting well-known endangered animals like grizzly bears and bighorn sheep when it passed the act in 1973, but with thousands of species listed, it was doing much more than that. In some cases, including those of the Dickey and Tellico Dams, many constituents and interest groups came to think that the act needed to be brought under control.

Endangered Species Law

Though it enjoyed overwhelming popular support at the moment of its passage, the ESA was more controversial in professional circles. Several distinct criticisms, both on scientific and economic grounds, emerged. First, there was the matter of defining exactly what a "species" was, especially in terms of where one began and another ended—itself a tricky epistemological exercise.[50] Second, the broad-reaching and inflexible nature of the law could interfere with other common-sense actions meant to protect the environment. For example, in 1979 a federal judge in Los Angeles barred the EPA from acting to reduce municipal sewage discharges from the city into the Pacific Ocean. Since the EPA's treatment would remove nutrients from the water that supported a fish population around the discharge point, and since the fish provided a vital source of food for both the endangered brown pelican and the endangered grey whale, the judge ruled that the EPA's plan would indirectly jeopardize the two predators. Though an attorney for the National Wildlife Federation called the ruling "absurd on its face," a characterization broadly expressed by other environmental groups, the EPA was nonetheless legally barred from trying to clean up the ocean.[51] As this case demonstrated, the strict terms of the act, which privileged the survival of individual species—sometimes with several degrees of separation from a proposed action—at the expense of the overall health of broader ecosystems, could generate nonsensical outcomes. But by far the most common criticism of the act was that it unfairly impeded seemingly reasonable attempts at economic development, halting projects that could create wealth and improve standards of living merely for the sake of the survival of small animals that many thought useless and barely worth protecting.

Speaking in 1979 about proposed deregulation of the trucking industry, President Carter characterized regulation as a bureaucratic nightmare impeding both common sense and economic efficiency:

> Too many trucks are rattling back and forth empty on the road today, burning up precious diesel fuel because the ICC [Interstate Commerce Commission] rules prohibit two-way hauling. Some trucking firms can deliver all the ingredients necessary to make soup to a factory, but are forbidden from hauling soup away from the factory. Other rules defy human imagination. Some truckers can haul milk; they can't haul butter. They can haul cream; they can't haul cheese. Others can transport paint in 2-gallon cans; they can't haul paint in 5-gallon cans. Some truckers are allowed to haul bananas; they can't haul pineapple. They can haul pineapple and bananas if they are mixed.[52]

There were, of course, significant differences between trucking (and airline and railroad) regulation, on one the hand, and environmental regulation, on the other. The first was designed to protect economic systems from abuse by balancing competing business interests and regulating entry barriers, while the latter was meant to protect people themselves from the actions of business entities.[53] But put in the terms of the trichotomy that Heidrich outlines in this volume, the rhetoric surrounding energy in the United States has overwhelmingly cast it as a market good subject to the same political trends as any other commodity. This was especially true in the transitional economic moment of the mid- to late 1970s. In an era in which regulations of all sorts came under attack as antithetical to efficiency and common sense, environmental regulations affecting energy production were not excepted from the onslaught. Indeed, Carter's characterization of trucking regulation as an anti-common-sense, bureaucratic folly would have been familiar to anyone who had been following the stories of the Tellico and Dickey Dams, in which forgettable animals and plants protected by the ESA threatened the construction of massive development projects. The rhetorical strategies invoked to inveigh against both economic and environmental regulation had become barely distinguishable. Though in popular perception it was Ronald Reagan who inaugurated an era of anti-regulatory, anti-government feeling in the United States, the process of loosening state control over American economic life was well underway during the Carter administration. The weakening of the ESA fit coherently into Carter's broader program of deregulation, an agenda that reached across the trucking, airline, and railroad industries and into the arena of environmental regulation as well. And the desire for cheap and abundant energy after the oil embargo earlier in the decade lay near the heart of these deregulatory impulses.

NOTES

Portions of this chapter were previously published in chapter 4 of my book *Unnatural Resources: Energy and Environmental Politics in Appalachia after the 1973 Oil Embargo* (Pittsburgh, PA: University of Pittsburgh Press, 2019). I am grateful to the University of Pittsburgh Press for permission to reprint this material.

1   "In Search of the Elusive Lousewort," *Time*, 19 September 1977.

2   For the political history of the oil crisis, see Meg Jacobs, *Panic at the Pump: The Energy Crisis and the Transformation of American Politics in the 1970s* (New York: Hill and Wang, 2016).

3   "Reclamation Chief Backs Hydro Power," *Los Angeles Times*, 14 December 1976.

4   On the history of endangered species law from the late 1950s to the early 1970s, see Charles C. Mann and Mark L. Plummer, *Noah's Choice: The Future of Endangered Species* (New York: Alfred A. Knopf, 1995), 149–63.

5   Sarah T. Phillips, *This Land, This Nation: Conservation, Rural America, and the New Deal* (New York: Cambridge University Press, 2007), 78–80.

6   Phillips, *This Land, This Nation*, 78–80.

7   Tennessee Valley Authority, *Environmental Statement: Tellico Project* (Chattanooga, TN: TVA Office of Health and Environmental Science, 1972), I-1-43. The TVA's apparent success in catalyzing economic development in the Tennessee Valley led other nations to pursue similar planning strategies. For example, the agency's influence on Mexican planners is a major topic of Tore Olsson's recent *Agrarian Crossings: Reformers and the Remaking of the U.S. and Mexican Countryside* (Princeton, NJ: Princeton University Press, 2017).

8   Kenneth M. Murchison, *The Snail Darter Case: TVA versus the Endangered Species Act* (Lawrence: University Press of Kansas, 2007), 12–13.

9   "A Program for the Preservation and Development of Industrial Areas Along Tennessee's Waterways" (Nashville: State-Local Waterfront Industrial Site Committee, 1962), 1, found in box 4, TVA Reports, 1933–1973, Special Collections, University of Tennessee.

10 For more on Wagner's reasoning, see William Bruce Wheeler and Michael McDonald, *TVA and the Tellico Dam, 1936–1979: A Bureaucratic Crisis in Post-industrial America* (Knoxville: University of Tennessee Press, 1986), 31–5.

11 Murchison, *The Snail Darter Case*, 7–22.

12 TVA, *Environmental Statement: Tellico Project*, I-1-1, I-1-5; Erwin C. Hargrove, *Prisoners of Myth: The Leadership of the Tennessee Valley Authority, 1933–1990* (Princeton, NJ: Princeton University Press, 1994), 175; "Upper Little Tennessee River Region: Summary of Resources" (Knoxville: Tennessee Valley Authority, 1968), 5, found in box 3, TVA Reports, 1933–1973.

13 TVA, *Environmental Statement: Tellico Project*, I-1-2, I-1-3.

14 TVA, *Environmental Statement: Tellico Project*, I-1-2, I-1-3.

15 TVA, *Environmental Statement: Tellico Project*, I-1-2, I-1-3.

16 TVA, *Environmental Statement: Tellico Project*, I-1-28, I-1-42.

17 Resolution by the Chamber of Commerce—Lenoir City, Tennessee, 1 May 1969, box 10, folder 11, Howard H. Baker Jr. Papers (hereafter HBJ), MPA 101, Howard H. Baker Jr. Center for Public Policy, University of Tennessee; Monroe County Quarterly Court, 20 April 1970, box 10, folder 11, HBJ; Resolution in Support of the Tellico Dam and Reservoir, Town of Madisonville, 14 April 1972, box 10, folder 11, HBJ; Resolution by

the Board of Mayor and Aldermen, City of Lenoir City, Tennessee, 10 April 1972, box 10, folder 11, HBJ; James C. Talley II to Governor Winfield Dunn, 25 January 1972, box 10, folder 11, HBJ.

18 *Environmental Statement: Tellico Project*, I-4-7, I-4-9, I-4-10.

19 Zygmunt J. B. Plater, *The Snail Darter and the Dam: How Pork-Barrel Politics Endangered a Little Fish and Killed a River* (New Haven, CT: Yale University Press, 2013), 20–2.

20 Hargrove, *Prisoners of Myth*, 176.

21 Murchison, *The Snail Darter Case*, 80–107. Though contemporary accounts claimed that Etnier happened to discover the snail darter in the river by accident, later interviews with participants in the case have revealed that Etnier was purposefully looking for species that would fall under the ESA's provisions.

22 Murchison, *The Snail Darter Case*, 108–40; Hargrove, *Prisoners of Myth*, 175–6.

23 "Endangered Species Rules to Be Curbed?" *Christian Science Monitor*, 10 March 1977.

24 "Hearings Open on Amending the Endangered Species Act," *New York Times*, 14 April 1978.

25 "Endangered Species Act Is Dying," *Washington Post*, 29 September 1978.

26 Shannon Petersen, *Acting for Endangered Species: The Statutory Ark* (Lawrence: University Press of Kansas, 2002), 63–4.

27 Petersen, *Acting for Endangered Species*, 65.

28 Patrick Allitt, *A Climate of Crisis: America in the Age of Environmentalism* (New York: Penguin, 2014), 124–7.

29 Allitt, *A Climate of Crisis*, 124–7; Hargrove, *Prisoners of Myth*, 177; Mann and Plummer, *Noah's Choice*, 170–3. Almost a year after the dam was completed, David Etnier, who had originally discovered the snail darter, located another population in a different portion of the Tennessee River, sixty miles downstream from Tellico.

30 "An Aswan Dam for Maine?," *Wall Street Journal*, 25 July 1974.

31 "An Aswan Dam for Maine?"

32 "An Aswan Dam for Maine?"; "Dam Project Forges Strange Alliances," *Washington Post*, 30 June 1974.

33 "Dam Project Forges Strange Alliances."

34 "Dam Project Forges Strange Alliances."

35 "Dam Project Forges Strange Alliances."

36 "Dam Project Forges Strange Alliances."

37 "Maine Dam Project Sparks New Debate," *New York Times*, 26 August 1974.

38 "Study Says Power Dam in Maine Would Damage the Environment," *New York Times*, 2 September 1977. On national environmentalist involvement, see, for example, "Testimony of the National Wildlife Federation at a Public Hearing Conducted by the

US Army Corps of Engineers," 14 November 1977, box 7, folder 10, Senate Office and Committee Staff Files (hereafter MS), Edmund Muskie Papers, Bates College.

39   "In Search of the Elusive Lousewort"; NED Policy Statement on Furbish's Lousewort at Dickey-Lincoln School, 15 November 1976, box 7, folder 11, MS.

40   "In Search of the Elusive Lousewort."

41   "House Panel Votes to Scrap Maine's Dickey Dam Project," *Washington Post*, 27 July 1979.

42   Sean Wilentz, *The Age of Reagan: A History, 1974–2008* (New York: HarperCollins, 2008), 118–19.

43   "US Likely to Pull Plug on Maine's Dickey Dam," *Christian Science Monitor*, 29 September 1981.

44   "US Likely to Pull Plug on Maine's Dickey Dam."

45   "US Likely to Pull Plug on Maine's Dickey Dam." The Lincoln School Dam was projected to produce 202.6 million kilowatt-hours of energy per year, compared to 1.45 billion from the Dickey. The NRCM had, in 1977, opposed both dams, but compromised in favour of the smaller Lincoln after the second energy crisis of the late 1970s. On the NRCM's previous opposition to both projects, see Testimony of Chris Herder (NRCM director) at Augusta Public Hearing, 26 October 1977, box 7, folder 10, MS.

46   "US Likely to Pull Plug on Maine's Dickey Dam."

47   "US Likely to Pull Plug on Maine's Dickey Dam."

48   Samuel P. Hays, *Beauty, Health, and Permanence: Environmental Politics in the United States, 1955–1985* (New York: Cambridge University Press, 1987), 494–5.

49   "Interior Dept. Acts to Halt Controversial Maine Dam," *Washington Post*, 30 September 1981; "Watt Opposes Dam Project in Maine," *Los Angeles Times*, 1 October 1981.

50   Mann and Plummer, *Noah's Choice*, 28–9.

51   "Environmentalists, Like Developers, Find Endangered Species Act Can Delay Plans," *Wall Street Journal*, 21 March 1979.

52   Trucking Industry Regulation Remarks Announcing Proposed Legislation, 21 June 1979, *Public Papers of the Presidents of the United States: Jimmy Carter: 1979* (Washington, DC: Government Printing Office, 1979), book 1, 1114.

53   See Benjamin C. Waterhouse, *Lobbying America: The Politics of Business from Nixon to NAFTA* (Princeton, NJ: Princeton University Press, 2014), 32.

Seismic Innovations: The Digital Revolution in the Search for Oil and Gas

Tyler Priest

During the 1920s, the lion's share of global oil production came from lands that rimmed the Gulf of Mexico and Caribbean Sea, with Texas, Mexico, and Venezuela dominating the world oil market. Nearly one hundred years later, the Gulf-Caribbean continues to yield prodigious amounts of oil and attract huge investments. Although not as dominant as before, this region nevertheless has demonstrated remarkable endurance as an oil province. What explains its staying power?

Obviously, the size of the petroleum resource is a determining factor. But someone still has to extract that petroleum in a cost-effective way and locate new reserves to offset depletion. In recent decades, as chapters by Joseph Pratt and Linda Hall in this volume reveal, resource nationalism in Mexico and Venezuela largely prevented those countries from achieving this. As a result, both have suffered steady production declines. The US portion of the Gulf of Mexico, by contrast, has experienced wave after wave of new discoveries and development, expanding from the shallow "tidelands" out beyond the edge of the continental shelf into 10,000-foot water depths in the middle of the Gulf. The underlying key to this expansion was the application of digital technology to geophysical exploration.

This chapter shifts the focus in this volume away from the role of the state in shaping energy development and outcomes, to the role of business and technological innovation in discovering the largest reserves of conventional petroleum in the recent history of the Americas. Government actions and policies assisted the growth of the US Gulf of Mexico offshore industry through a transparent property rights regime, generous fiscal terms and access, minimal safety and environmental regulation, and import protection.[1] But the driving force in this story was the digital transformation of seismic technology, which increased the accuracy and lowered the costs of finding oil. Long before digitization altered everyday lives through personal computing and the Internet, it reshaped the geoscience of oil exploration. The digital revolution happened earlier in the oil industry than in other established industries, and earlier in geophysical exploration than in any other part of the oil industry.[2] What we now call "Big Data," a term coined in the 1990s to describe the challenge of storing and processing massive amounts of digital information, was something that the oil industry first encountered in the 1960s in trying to harvest digital acoustic data from beneath the surface of the earth.[3]

Petroleum seismology was born on the US Gulf Coast, and subsequent digital advances were all developed in the waters of the US Gulf of Mexico. The commercialization of digital seismic technology could have emerged elsewhere in the world, but the particular geology and marine environment of the Gulf were uniquely conducive to it. The marginal costs of applying novel ideas and expensive new technologies were lower offshore than on land. The gradual slope of the shelf and relatively calm waters allowed for incremental approaches to solving problems. The deep-seated salt domes and sedimentary layers underlaying the coast and continental shelf of the Gulf of Mexico hold vast amounts of petroleum, but they are geologically complex, with massive overlaying salt sheets, highly faulted and steeply dipping beds, and numerous but thin sandstones in which hydrocarbons are difficult to pinpoint. Oil extraction here depended on continuous advances in technology.

As the Gulf yielded riches in the form of hundreds of oil and gas fields of varying size and productivity in gradually deeper waters, exploration technology continued to be refined and improved at a steady pace. Companies operating there became accustomed to seeking technological solutions to exploration challenges.[4] The entrepreneurs who commercialized leading edge technologies, however, were usually not the oil operators themselves; early on, those operators moved away from developing their own seismic instruments and running their own seismic crews. Instead, they purchased these services from geophysical contractors who invested in research to gain their own competitive edge and who interfaced most closely with cutting-edge work coming out of the universities and professional organizations.

Geophysical contractors became a bellwether service industry, the first hired in booms and the first fired in busts. In helping to reduce financial risk for oil firms, geophysical contractors ended up assuming an inordinate amount of that risk themselves. While oil firms jealously nurtured in-house expertise to interpret, reprocess, and correlate ever-larger streams of seismic data, the acquisition and primary processing technologies developed by contractors spread throughout the global oil industry. After leading the charge into the deep waters of the Gulf, advanced digital seismic techniques found successful application elsewhere. In the Americas, this can be seen most spectacularly in the deep waters off Brazil and most recently off Guyana and on the Mexican side of the Gulf of Mexico, which has further extended the life of the Gulf-Caribbean as a major oil-producing region.

The Gulf Coast Origins of Petroleum Seismology

In the 1920s, oil explorers began applying new methods and instruments to search for oil-bearing structures deep in the ground. Most importantly, companies adopted seismology, the practice of measuring acoustic wave velocities through elastic layers in the earth's crust in order to better understand earthquakes. During the First World War, the German military had tested the technology for locating enemy artillery. Afterward, oil companies began deploying a unique new instrument, the refraction seismograph, in a similar way, but with the objective of determining subsurface features that might lead them to oil.[5]

Refraction worked particularly well in locating Gulf Coast salt domes. Salt is impermeable and thus good at trapping oil deposits. In a refraction survey, a charge of dynamite set off near the surface created a sound wave that travelled through the earth and was picked up by a series of distant seismometers, or "geophones." These waves travelled through soft formations, such as sand and shale, in underground arcs at a known velocity. A hard or more compact formation, such as a salt dome, would transmit the waves at a much faster rate, in effect refracting them like a prism. Refracted waves would arrive at the geophone relatively fast, often indicating the presence of salt, and possibly oil.

The most ambitious and successful effort to commercialize seismic exploration came from the Tulsa-based Geophysical Research Corporation (GRC), an Amerada Petroleum affiliate established in 1925 by one of the geophysical industry's founding fathers, Everette DeGolyer.[6] Expanding rapidly and spreading its crews far and wide, Amerada's GRC established itself as the leading seismic contractor in the United States, especially on the Gulf Coast. In the late 1920s, GRC set two important historical precedents for the business of geophysical contracting. The first was the inauguration of marine operations across the swamps, lakes, and open bayous of southern Louisiana. The second was the commercialization of the reflection seismograph.

Reflection seismology offered more seductive possibilities than refraction.[7] It measured the time it took for a wave to travel from the sound source at the surface to an underground layer and back again to the surface. An acoustic wave would be reflected or bounced back toward the surface, much like an echo, from any place where there was a change in the elastic properties of the medium through which the wave travelled. Using a series of recordings and knowledge of wave velocities through various formations, the reflection method made it possible to plot the contour and depth of reflecting layers.[8]

In the 1930s and '40s, reflection seismic surveying transformed the business of petroleum exploration in nearly every oil region in the United States. In 1930, Everette DeGolyer and two associates responsible for the development of the reflection seismograph, John Karcher and Eugene McDermott, left Amerada and GRC to form a new venture, Geophysical Service Inc. (GSI). Still other GRC employees left to start new geophysical companies. During the 1930s, more than thirty US seismic contracting firms appeared, many of which could trace their lineage to GRC or GSI. In

1933, Henry Salvatori left GSI to form the Western Geophysical Company, which would become GSI's chief competitor.[9]

Reflection seismology's greatest economic impact was on the Texas-Louisiana Gulf Coast. Several technical refinements, especially sonograph recording, ultimately gave the reflection seismic method much broader range along the coastal plain and into the Gulf of Mexico.[10] New capabilities for detailed geophysical prospecting accelerated the pace of wildcat leasing and land acquisition all along the Gulf Coast. Seismic surveying did not stop during the Second World War, but military and industrial mobilization diverted scientific minds away from investigating improvements in seismic technology to other priorities. After the war, companies made a big push both to expand surveying offshore in the Gulf of Mexico and to upgrade seismic capabilities.

In the late 1940s and early 1950s, the move from onshore leasing conducted by private and public landowners to offshore leasing by competitive auctions held by state and federal governments placed an even greater premium on geologic and geophysical capabilities, as incentives for speculative leasing were fewer, and costs higher, offshore. Oil firms and service companies had made rapid strides in learning how to drill and log wells. Still, drilling and producing hydrocarbons from deeper water offshore would entail steeply rising development costs, which mandated greater accuracy and economic efficiency in exploration.

Seismic surveying on the water nevertheless promised advantages over surveying on land. For one, companies did not have to contend with individual property holders or imposing topography, giving recording surveys potentially much greater speed and scope. In the early postwar years, operations in the Gulf of Mexico were conducted on modified shrimp boats or war surplus vessels. Establishing accurate shot and geophone positions and handling heavy, bulky geophones and cables designed for land operations, all from small vessels bobbing in offshore swells, proved difficult. By the early 1950s, radio-positioning systems such as "RAYDIST" (for *radio* and *distance*), based on advances made during the Second World War, had enabled accurate surveying, but it also added to the costs of deploying a small fleet of boats.[11]

The economies of surveying improved greatly with the construction of larger, purpose-built ships that combined all shooting, recording, and

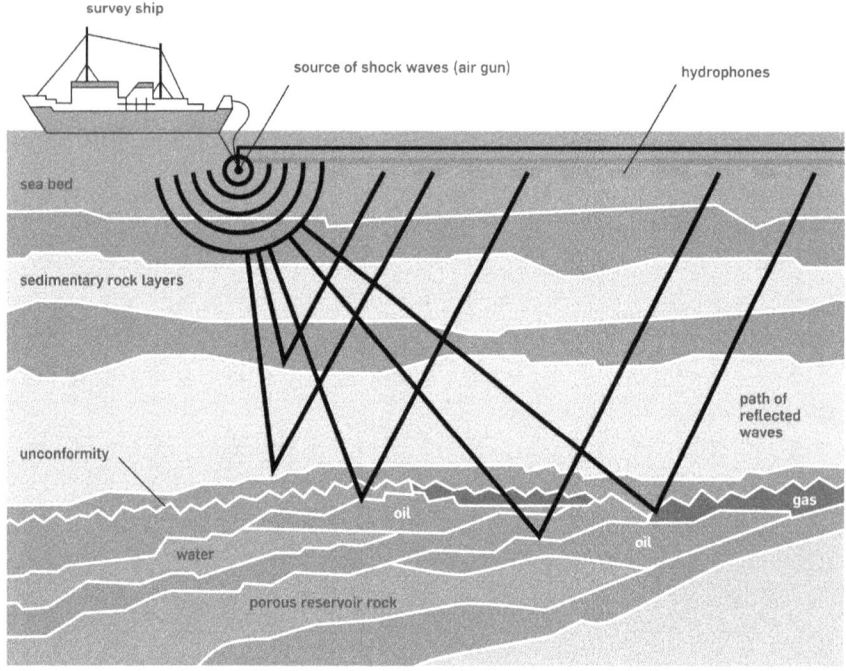

Figure 7.1 Offshore Reflection Seismic Survey Diagram
Source: Image courtesy of Kris Energy

surveying operations in a continuous operation. The breakthrough that made this possible was the oil-filled seismic "streamer," a cable towed behind a boat with electrical wires and "hydrophones" that recorded and relayed seismic data to the vessel. With neutral buoyancy in water, the "Pavey" streamer, named after one of the men who patented it, could be adjusted to any depth. Because of its pressure-sensitive characteristics, the streamers were unaffected by cable motion and could be "yo-yoed" from a storage reel off the end of the boat. This meant that shots could be recorded one after the other from a moving boat, rather than having to stop the boat for each one.[12]

The next logical step was building bigger boats that could perform all the surveying functions continuously through rough waters. The single-ship operation that became the industry standard by the late 1950s could record seismic profiles every one-half to two minutes continuously and cover up to 65 miles per day. This compared to 50 miles covered *per month* on dry land. The cost of a water crew in 1955 far exceeded that for a land crew ($60,000–$100,000/month versus $15,000–$25,000/month), but the higher rate of data acquisition by the new marine exploration techniques yielded a much lower cost per profile obtained, as little as one-third of the land cost by the 1960s. An offshore seismic survey simply offered much greater economies of scale in seismic data acquisition than onshore.[13]

Oil firms both ran their own seismic crews and contracted out for seismic services. The contractors' stock-in-trade was their instruments and the quality of their records. Nearly every company built and used its own instruments. Oil firms hired contractors by the month on "time-and-materials" contracts. Each seismic crew had a person designated as "the computer," someone who managed the seismic sections recorded on photographic paper, which were metre-long strips covered in reflection squiggles. The computer washed and hung the strips to dry, converted time data to depth, made all sorts of corrections for various factors, and then plotted this information profile on a two-dimensional, subsurface cross-section. The cross-section would be handed over to the seismologists, who would draw the geologic inferences on a contour map. All this was extremely tedious and time-consuming, not to mention vulnerable to human error. The successful contractors were those who could provide quality data at the lowest cost per month. But the time-based contract meant there was no incentive to exploit fully the increased productivity (i.e., reduced cost per mile or per profile) made possible by the single-ship operation. Company crews operated on a similar basis.[14]

From 1952 to 1958, geophysical contractors found themselves caught between rising costs and declining revenues.[15] They responded in four possible ways: (1) they went out of business or sold to a competitor; (2) they continued cutting costs to the point of sacrificing quality, which often resulted in the first option; (3) they tried to change the contracting model; or (4) they looked to new technological advances to give them a leg up on competitors. Of the two strongest companies that emerged from this period, Western Geophysical pursued both the third and fourth options, and GSI embraced the fourth in the most ambitious way.

In the mid-1950s, Western Geophysical introduced new ways of contracting that shifted incentives toward productivity and spurred the firm's fantastic growth during the next two decades. Founded in Los Angeles in 1933 by GRC/GSI veteran Henry Salvatori, Western started running marine crews in 1938.[16] In 1956, under the visionary leadership of Vice-President Booth Strange, Western began bidding marine jobs on a "turn-key" basis—on a per-mile cost rather than a per-month cost. This freed Western's crews from client restrictions such as "no overtime." The ships and instruments were still the largest expense, so paying overtime or double-time wages did not appreciably add to overall costs, especially per mile. Oil companies accepted the new arrangement because they received a more concrete estimate for the data acquired and delivered. Meanwhile, Western's productivity and profits soared. The company then invested profits in better equipment and added more personnel, further increasing productivity and lowering the cost per mile.[17]

Not long after the introduction of the new bidding model, Strange persuaded Western's board to approve gathering data without a contract—that is, on a speculative, or "spec," basis. This was in response to growing pressure by some oil companies to do "group shoots," which dramatically reduced contractors' profits.[18] In 1956, at the end of the contract to shoot proprietary data for Union Producing in the Gulf of Mexico, Western made a deal to keep gathering data on a non-exclusive, non-proprietary basis over acreage Union was interested in nominating at the next federal offshore lease sale. Union would pay a fraction of the cost, and Western would be able to resell the data to other interested companies.[19] The price per increment of data to each company would be substantially less than if the job were done on a proprietary basis. Companies started buying, and Western expanded its spec data shooting, selling data for some areas twenty to thirty times.[20]

Western took more commercial risks than competitors such as GSI and made a reputation as the leader in spec data. In addition to being able to resell the data, spec shooting had other benefits. It kept seismic crews working continually, thus cushioning operations against cyclical swings in demand for data from oil companies.[21] Spec shooting also drove

Western to invest more in research and development, because spec data competed not only in price, but also in quality. In 1960, when Salvatori sold the company to Litton Industries, Western gained access to deeper pockets for making these kinds of investments. Booth Strange took over as president, and in 1965 he relocated the company from Los Angeles to Houston, where Western could be closer to the centre of the oil business and focus its operations and research in the booming Gulf of Mexico.[22]

The mid- to late 1950s proved to be the most fertile period of invention perhaps in the entire history of seismic imaging. Inventions came from varied sources, but they combined to lay the ground for the revolutionary move from analogue to digital technology. First, the introduction of continuous velocity well logs (sonic logs)—in which the velocity of sound measurements within a well bore was matched to rock density—allowed for greater precision in locating the origin of seismic reflections. Even more important, starting in 1955, was the replacement of paper records by magnetic tape in seismic recording. Magnetic tape could record signals in analogue over a wide range of frequencies and play them back using different "filters" to adjust for time delays caused by surface effects and path geometry.[23]

Cross-sections prepared from analogue magnetic-tape playback changed the way seismic data were processed as well as collected. Most importantly, magnetic-tape playback provided a means for economically applying the "common-depth-point" (CDP) or "horizontal stacking" method of acquisition and processing. Patented and developed by Harry Mayne of Petty Geophysical, CDP stacking involved taking tapes of individually corrected seismic traces from different sound source and recording stations, each equally offset from the same reflection point or mid-point, and then combining or "compositing" these traces. Stacking enhanced the desired or "primary" reflections and filtered out unwanted "multiple" reflections or "noise." The CDP method dramatically improved the accuracy of seismic surveying and the delivery of quality data.[24] After presenting and marketing the CDP technique at the 1960 international meeting of the Society for Exploration Geophysicists (SEG), Mayne and Petty licensed it to the most technologically advanced oil firms in the industry. Still the main signal-to-noise enhancing technique today, CDP stacking was a watershed that divided previous seismic exploration from all subsequent innovations and paved the way for the conversion to digital technology.[25]

Magnetic recording and CDP shooting led to additional refinements and improvements in seismic acquisition, which, again, found their most productive use offshore in the Gulf of Mexico. Magnetic recording made it possible to employ other sound sources to replace the thousands of tons of dynamite exploded every year in the Gulf. Dynamite was costly, time-consuming, and dangerous to deploy; it also killed or disturbed aquatic life, leading to conflicts with shrimpers, fishermen, and oystermen.[26] Beginning in the late 1950s, many companies experimented with new types of sound sources, such as mechanical/hydraulic vibrating mechanisms and gas exploder devices. By the mid-1960s, air guns, pioneered by a young engineer at Lamont Geological Observatory, Stephen Chelminski, proved to be safest, simplest, and most reliable. They eventually became the source of choice.[27]

The Digital Revolution

Magnetic recording, with its capacity for storing seismic information in reproducible form, generated interest in what one geoscientist referred to in the 1950s as "mechanized automatic means of data processing," or simply "computing." Conventional methods of seismic data processing involved tedious human computational labour. In the mid- to late 1950s, analogue seismic-data-processing computers made their appearance, which relieved the human computer of some of the busy work in processing and plotting cross-sections. Efforts to digitize analogue magnetic recordings soon followed, largely to assist in filtering unwanted noise. The logical extension of this technology was the direct digital recording and processing of seismic data.[28]

The shift from analogue to digital, however, was not immediate or seamless. The transition required companies and contractors to replace outmoded equipment with expensive new computers and adopt entirely new ways of doing things, which oil companies often resisted.[29] But thanks to research breakthroughs and savvy methods of marketing digital technology by GSI, the digital revolution finally transformed the industry during the early 1960s, expanding oil companies' understanding of the subsurface and increasing their accuracy in finding oil and gas. This lowered the considerable risks of exploration in the Gulf of Mexico, where digital seismic technology was commercially introduced.

Investigations into digital seismic surveying began with the Geophysical Analysis Group (GAG), organized in 1952 at the Massachusetts Institute of Technology (MIT). In 1951, a twenty-year-old graduate student in mathematics at MIT, Enders Robinson, applied a time-series analysis to the task of enhancing the quality of seismograph records, something never tried before, and came up with a method of "deconvolution," which was a way of filtering desired seismic signals from other noise signals that corrupted them. The basic problem was that acoustical wavelets were reflected with varying amplitudes from hundreds of subsurface reflecting horizons. Hence, a single seismic trace recorded at the surface consisted of a continuous series of overlapping reflections that were difficult to distinguish from one another. This was an especially troublesome problem in offshore seismic prospecting. Seismic signals tended to reverberate in the water layer between the seabed and water surface, producing a "ringing" noise so strong it often masked the desired reflections from the subsurface. Robinson's study proved that numerical filtering could separate data and noise just like electronic filtering, but in a much more precise and high-powered fashion. What deconvolution did, in essence, was provide better resolution for imaging seismic signals.

Based on this revolutionary discovery, the Office of the President at MIT sponsored GAG, and the following year a consortium of twenty oil and geophysical companies took over funding the group. Between 1952 and 1957, the GAG group attracted some of MIT's brightest graduate students, most of whom subsequently specialized in geophysics. At first, the group mainly used analogue recordings to perform deconvolution. However, having access one hour per week to MIT's first digital computer with stored program architecture, the "Whirlwind," and, later, Raytheon's British Ferranti Mark 1 computer, they found that all analogue methods could be done by digital seismic processing and with much greater accuracy.[30]

The conversion to digital was years away, not least because oil companies were still skeptical about the technology's commercial applications, even after publication of Enders Robinson's path-breaking thesis,

"Predictive Decomposition of Time Series with Application to Seismic Exploration," reproduced as *GAG Report No. 7* in July 1954.[31] In spite of the oil industry's reticence, GSI forged ahead to commercialize digital seismic technology. During the Second World War, GSI had diversified into electronics, becoming a major contractor to the US military as a maker of submarine detection devices, airborne magnetometers, and radar. This led to the creation in 1951 of a new company called Texas Instruments (TI), with GSI reorganized as TI's geophysical subsidiary.[32] That same year, GSI's president, Cecil Green, a towering figure in the geophysics profession who had an eye for spotting talent, worked with Robert R. Shrock of MIT to organize a summer "co-operative program" designed to give selected college students an orientation in applied geophysics working with crews in the field.[33] The combination of GSI's pipeline to MIT and TI's aggressive approach to electronics innovation propelled GSI into the digital vanguard.

Dr. Kenneth Burg, GSI's technical vice-president, grasped the potential of the emerging computer revolution and initiated research into digital seismic processing at TI's Central Research Laboratory in Dallas.[34] To support this effort, Burg hired a large crop of geophysics PhDs from MIT, including former members of GAG. Headed by Mark Smith, GSI launched a special research effort in 1954 to adapt the newly recognized statistical communication theory developed by Robinson to reflection seismology. Milo Backus, one of the MIT PhDs, devised a unique deconvolution solution to the water reverberation problem using something called a "multiple analyzer and eliminator," a crude sort of "digital filter implemented in analog form," as Backus described it, to reduce multiple reflections.[35] According to Mark Smith, "this approach was very successful and helped to give GSI a competitive edge in many important offshore areas."[36]

Between 1956 and 1958, GSI's digital seismic investigations broke important new ground. After testing digital processing methods on a hybrid analogue-digital computer called the *seis*MAC, TI's research department—renamed the Data Systems and Earth Sciences Department—designed and built an analogue-to-digital converter and TI's first digital computer. Programmed for seismic processing, the data analysis and reduction computer used two thousand vacuum tubes and measured six by three by twenty-four feet. As Mark Smith noted, "it began to look to GSI as though the equipment end of the geophysical business was starting to wag the dog, and that the misconception was developing that a major step in hardware alone would substantially change the effectiveness of seismic exploration."[37]

Smith, in turn, instituted a comprehensive R&D program that addressed all aspects of the reflection seismic problem. He focused on locating stratigraphic traps, which were a key objective in the sedimentary basin of the Gulf of Mexico. Stratigraphic traps are features that accumulate oil due to changes in rock character rather than because of structural aspects such as faulting or folding of the rock. Up to that point, reflection seismology was only useful for finding structural traps. GSI-TI's "Stratigraphic Trap Program" aimed to introduce digital recording in the field (instead of recording in analogue and converting to digital) and integrate it with continually improving digital processing software and techniques, so that the recorded seismogram would provide a closer approximation of the particular geology and stratigraphy.[38]

Dovetailing with this effort was the rapid development of another breakthrough technology in the 1950s, the semiconducting transistor, which replaced vacuum tubes, first as a sound amplifier in many kinds of electronic devices, and then as electronic switches in digital computers. Both applications had a pivotal impact on seismic surveying. Transistors fabricated from germanium and eventually silicon were smaller, lighter, and increasingly more powerful than vacuum tubes. Developed and licensed by Bell Laboratories, early transistors were relatively costly and thus found commercial application initially in small, portable, and lower-power-consuming devices, such as hearing aids, radios, and, by 1958, seismic receivers. Transistorized geophysical equipment significantly lightened the load for field crews.[39]

By the late 1950s, thinner, faster, and more reliable transistors enhanced digital computing. In 1954, TI introduced the first commercial silicon transistor and in 1957 became a major supplier of transistors for IBM computers. Then, in 1958, TI pioneered a major advance with the integrated circuit made of a single semiconductor material.[40] By 1960, most new computer designs were fully transistorized with integrated circuits. At TI's seismic branch in Houston, J. Fred Bucy, who would later become president of TI, led the development of the first digital field recording system, the DFS-9000, which was integrated with an all-transistorized computer called the TIAC (Texas Instruments Automatic Computer).[41]

In launching this "total seismic system," as GSI called it, the company faced an uphill climb, first to produce it within TI, and then, as with other seismic innovations, to market it to a dubious oil industry. Even though digital recording promised to eliminate the time and costs of converting analogue data, the front-end costs of the system were much higher, and oil companies and contractors alike preferred tried and true methods of recording in analogue. A digital recording set cost more than $100,000; converting to digital meant completely replacing equipment.[42]

To market the new system and obtain the initial financial support to manufacture the equipment and develop field experience, GSI agreed to give two of the oil companies most interested in the technology, Mobil and Texaco, a two-year contract (1961–3) for exclusive use of GSI digital crews and equipment. If the technology proved itself, Mobil and Texaco would have a jump on competitors. However, seismic software and signal processing were not part of the exclusive agreement, which allowed GSI to make marketing presentations in all the petroleum centres around the United States showing the latest processing developments, thus "whetting the industry's appetite" for the full digital service.[43]

And whet it, it did. After the exclusive period, during which GSI made dramatic improvements to all aspects of the integrated system, company after company signed up for digital crews. GSI had convincingly demonstrated that the greater dynamic range and processing flexibility of digital recording and processing allowed for a much fuller exploitation of CDP shooting and the tremendous seismic signal-to-noise enhancements it provided. In 1964, GSI experienced a 58 per cent growth in revenue, driven largely by the new digital business.[44]

Although some of GSI's digital crews worked on land (mainly for Texaco), the "real bread and butter was in digital marine work," especially in the Gulf of Mexico.[45] GSI's marine business grew fairly quickly to twenty-six crews operating with a fleet of more than fifty seismic vessels.[46] In 1964, GSI opened its first regional TIAC data centre in New Orleans to handle growing business in the Gulf of Mexico.

There were several reasons for the intensive application of digital seismology offshore. First, offshore exploration was already growing at the expense of land work in many areas of the world, and the Gulf of Mexico was a proven oil region with a lot of unexplored territory. The aforementioned economies of scale offshore meant that the increase in marginal cost of digital equipment over analogue was smaller than on land. The higher volume of data acquired offshore was ideal for digital data processing. Most importantly, the digital system brought offshore geology into clear focus in ways that it did not on land. The amazing resolution of high-powered deconvolution allowed geophysicists, for the first time, to pinpoint Gulf region salt domes and stratigraphic traps, the main objective of the digital research program at GSI. "They just came out and hit you in the eyeball," marveled Milo Backus. "The whole structural picture was quite different from what they had seen out there before. That was a major thing in the Gulf of Mexico."[47]

In the mid-1960s, as digital seismic surveying gained industry acceptance, and as a new generation of digital computers emerged, geophysicists acquired ever-improving tools to visualize offshore geology. Existing contractors, such as Western, and new competitors, such as Digicon and Seiscom Delta, quickly developed and marketed their own digital systems and versions of deconvolution.[48] In 1964, IBM introduced its 360 series computer, and the more serious exploration-minded oil companies began installing huge banks of them in newly established data centres. Geoscientists started transferring large volumes of data from bookshelves and filing cabinets into computers, and computer programmers generated new processing algorithms (Milo Backus at GSI was the mastermind behind many of the first ones). As computing costs dropped exponentially during the next several years, oil firms were able to process vast amounts of seismic data at ever-increasing speeds, greatly enhancing their capabilities in geophysical and geological interpretation.

In the late 1960s, these evolving capabilities led to a critical advance in exploration in the Gulf of Mexico. Binary-gain digital recording systems were enabling geophysicists to measure and quantify the "relative wave amplitudes" between seismic traces for the first time.[49] This measurement was sometimes referred to as "true amplitude recovery." Up to that point, seismic techniques only helped delineate structures, stratigraphy, and traps; operators still had to risk sinking a well to determine if oil and gas existed in those features. But the new digital seismic data revealed

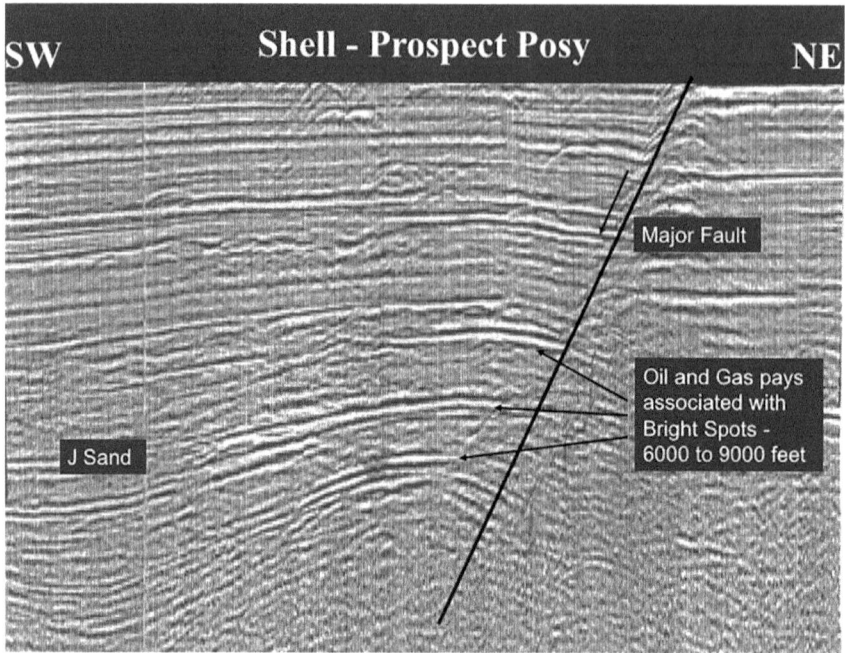

Figure 7.2 Shell Oil Bright Spot Seismic, Posey Prospect, Eugene Island 330 Field

Source: Image courtesy of Mike Forrest

striking "amplitude anomalies" that suggested the tantalizing prospect of "directly detecting" hydrocarbons that might be associated with them. Shell Oil and Mobil Oil were the first companies to identify and quantify such anomalies and factor them into their bids for offshore leases. Mobil referred to them as "hydrocarbon indicators." Shell called them "bright spots," because they seemed to light up on the seismic record.[50] "Direct hydrocarbon indicators" (DHI) has since become the industry's standard technical term.

Once the bright spot interpretation, or DHI, method was refined and disseminated in the early 1970s, it had a giant impact on the business of exploration in the Gulf. Being able literally to "see" hydrocarbons on the seismic section before ever drilling a well eliminated the questions of whether hydrocarbons existed in a certain location or what the drilling targets were. The remaining questions were whether the target was big enough or if the hydrocarbons would come out the ground fast enough. Reducing the "dry hole factor" changed the way companies allocated risk and capital in their general strategic approach to offshore oil. If a bright spot scan reduced the odds of drilling a dry hole on a prospect from three out of five to two out of five, managers could afford to bid more for attractive leases or use the money saved by avoiding dry holes to invest in drilling and production technologies for deeper water. The advances in seismic amplitude analysis were one of the most important products of the digital revolution for the exploration business, moving the industry into 1,000-plus-feet water depths in the 1980s and '90s.

One caveat about bright spots—the technique worked only for certain kinds of geology. The clastic sedimentary rocks found in deltaic regions like the Gulf Coast—and, as oil explorers would later learn, along the Atlantic Ocean margins of Brazil and West Africa—were well-suited to this kind of interpretation. Hard-rock areas elsewhere were not. Bright spot interpretation and the digital seismic revolution helped oil companies overcome the water depth and cost limits that had stalled offshore development in the Gulf. In the late 1970s, the Brazilian state-owned oil firm, Petrobras, which Gail Triner writes about in this volume, also used bright spot amplitude analysis to help identify prospects in the offshore Campos Basin that ultimately contained more than twelve billion barrels of oil. By 1995, Petrobras was producing a million barrels a day from the Campos Basin, establishing Brazil, for the first time, as a major oil-producing nation.[51]

Three Dimensions

The move from two-dimensional (2D) to three-dimensional (3D) seismic technology was decisive confirmation of the revolutionary potential of digital technology in the oil business. The concept of 3D seismology had existed since the earliest days of geophysics. Geoscientists have always sought to visualize the subsurface in three dimensions, not two. All seismic surveys, when they produce a subsurface contour map, are conceived of in three dimensions. By the early 1970s, the arsenal of digital data recording and processing techniques had taken exploration to an unprecedented level of sophistication, but imaging was still 2D.

Exxon claims to have shot the first 3D seismic survey over the Friendswood field south of Houston in 1967. Esso Production Research presented the results at an SEG meeting in 1970.[52] It was a presentation that displayed a model based on data gathered from well logs and 2D seismic surveys, and it used a special fibre optic viewer to simulate depth in three dimensions. Although Exxon later received the Distinguished Achievement Award from the SEG for "inventing" and developing 3D methods, this was not actually 3D technology as it came to be properly understood and practised. As GSI's Robert Graebner put it, "3D involves gathering data in a spatial sense so that you can put together that data from wherever it reflected with another piece that came from that same spot."[53] This means doing 3D "migration." Migration is the geometric repositioning of the return signal to show the exact subsurface location where the seismic wave reflects, as opposed to where it is picked up by the geophone. To position events accurately in three dimensions was a massive computational challenge. It required building a mathematical and physical model governed by the so-called wave equation, which is a hyperbolical partial differential equation that describes the propagation of waves.[54] This is not what Exxon (Esso at the time) was doing in the Friendswood field in 1967.

The density of spatial seismic coverage required to produce a 3D image magnified the computational challenge of migration. A detailed 2D seismic survey might collect data in a grid spaced at one-kilometre intervals, whereas a 3D survey would require a much tighter grid, by at least an order of magnitude, to get any kind of accurate detail. By the early 1970s, computing power and digital seismic acquisition and processing techniques had developed to a point where this was finally possible. But, as with every major step forward with geophysical technology, the constraint on commercializing this concept was cost. And again, it was GSI that pioneered the technology and successfully marketed it to industry.

In early 1972, an important brainstorming session took place at GSI headquarters in Dallas. The principals were research scientist William Schneider, Milo Backus, then director of research, and Robert Graebner and M. E. "Shorty" Trostle, both executives. To fund an experimental survey to test the idea, the GSI executives enlisted the support of six large oil companies—Chevron, Amoco, Texaco, Mobil, Phillips, and Atlantic Richfield. They selected the Bell Lake field in southeastern New Mexico and West Texas, which was "a structural play with nine producers and several dry holes." Bell Lake had sufficient well data so that 3D data could be correlated with subsurface geology.[55] The results of the 3D survey were stunning. They not only confirmed the field's nine producers and three dry holes but also indicated several new drilling prospects in this mature area. As the *Midland Reporter-Telegram* later reported:

> When the petroleum history books are written, Milo Backus, M. E. "Shorty" Trostle, and Bob Graebner (of GSI) [Schneider should also have been mentioned] may stand in significance alongside Howard Hughes and his rotary bit, the Schlumberger brothers and their logging machine, and Earl Halliburton and his idea for pumping cement behind the casing of oil wells. Because when the final tally is made, the impact of 3D on the oil industry will be in the billions.[56]

It took considerable time for the tally to mount. Many oil companies could not justify the cost of the 3D survey. Even a modest sampling of the data acquired in a 3D survey generated a huge number of paper sections to examine and interpret. Computers were limited in power to handle more advanced and accurate algorithms. The commercial viability of 3D seismology for *exploration*—that is, looking for new, wildcat fields—was still in the future. The expense of a 3D survey was prohibitive in an area with a relatively high probability of drilling a dry hole. GSI's Bob Graebner, however, made an increasingly convincing case that the bottom-line results of a 3D survey could be worth the cost for *developing* producing fields and *defining* already discovered reservoirs.[57]

Again, as with the introduction of digital recording and processing, the most value could be added offshore, where the marginal cost of doing a 3D survey was smaller than on land. The Gulf of Mexico, the most mature offshore producing region in the world, was where oil companies and contractors cut their teeth on 3D and devised ways to bring down costs. Better instruments, wider arrays of hydrophone streamers, larger vessels, faster navigation, and on-board processing all reduced costs and improved

Figure 7.3 GSI's 3D Seismic Pioneers
Bill Schneider, Milo Backus, Bob Graebner, and Jack Pizant, co-authors of the 1966 SEG Award-winning paper "A New Marine Processing System."

Source: Photo courtesy of Degolyer Library, Southern Methodist University.

data acquisition. Most importantly, advances in computing power spurred the market for 3D surveys. The emergence of interactive computer workstations permitted geophysicists to see results in computer screen images with three dimensions and reduced the time to interpret a 3D survey from months to weeks.

Before workstations, images produced from a 3D survey were basically "a sandwich of 2D cross sections linked by horizontal slices."[58] Workstations finally rendered seismic images in 3D shapes that corresponded to the subsurface features, and with increasing speed. By the early 1980s, all the major seismic contractors and several major oil companies had developed their own systems. New companies formed to focus entirely on the seismic workstations business, led by Landmark Graphics, GeoQuest, and others associated with Schlumberger and Halliburton.[59] Eventually, these contractors developed special rooms called "visualization centres" that displayed seismic images in three dimensions. Using stereoscopic glasses, viewers could immerse themselves in 3D seismic images constructed from projections on the walls, ceiling, and floor, and actually walk through a moving perspective of the subsurface.[60]

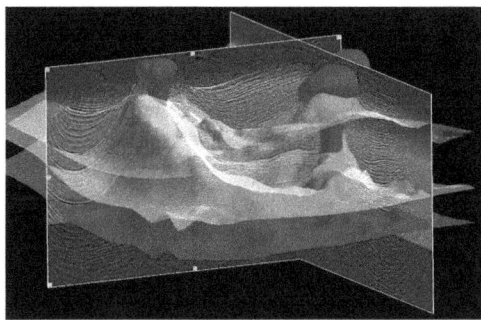

Figure 7.4 3D Seismic Image with Salt Domes in Deep Blue

Source: Photo courtesy of Paradigm.

In the 1990s, the market for 3D surveys exploded, first in the Gulf of Mexico and then in other marine areas such as the North Sea. In 1989, only 5 per cent of the wells drilled in the Gulf relied on 3D; in 1996, nearly 80 per cent did. Companies acquired the majority of that data between 1990 and 1993.[61] Data acquisition was made easier beginning in the early 1990s by the deployment of the US Navy's global positioning system (GPS) in place of conventional radio positioning systems. By the late 1990s, oil firms increasingly used 3D data not only for field development, but for exploration as well. As majors such as Shell began to divest from older producing properties in the shallow waters of the Gulf's continental shelf in favour of new "deepwater" prospects (in water greater than 1,500 feet), smaller firms purchased the older properties and redeveloped them with significant reserve additions using 3D data. Graebner conservatively estimates that 3D *quadrupled* the oil and gas reserves in the Gulf of Mexico.[62]

As the majors moved into deepwater, where a single well could cost $50 million or more, it made perfect sense to have 3D coverage before drilling. However expensive a 3D survey was, that was little more than a rounding error when applied to the overall cost of exploring and producing in deepwater. More significantly, 3D gave oil firms nearly pinpoint accuracy in discovering oil and gas. Wildcatting success rates without 3D were typically no higher than 30 or 40 per cent (three or four out of every ten wells struck pay). By most accounts, 3D boosted wildcat drilling success to 60 or 70 per cent. The savings from drilling three or four fewer $50 million dry holes out of every ten added up very quickly. Investment bank Salomon Smith Barney estimated that 3D technology accounted for 46 per cent of falling exploration and production costs between 1995 and 1997, far more than any other oil field technology.[63]

Ongoing Innovations

Ironically, just as the forty-year effort to exploit the digital potential of seismic exploration was bearing fruit in what *Business Week* called "a Golden Age of technology," the geophysical contractor business took a dive.[64] The demand for seismic crews had been relatively weak since the oil bust in the mid-1980s. The sharp oil price drop and wave of oil company mergers beginning in 1998 further slashed demand. Compounding the problem, contractors found themselves swimming in an excess supply of data—what one analyst described as "data indigestion." The diffusion and commodification of 3D seismic technology generated intense competition. Speculative shooting, pioneered by Western Geophysical, and so-called multi-client surveys, had become the dominant mode of acquiring and selling data, and both became less profitable.

In a multi-client deal, a group of oil customers would fund a seismic shoot in advance, but the real profits were earned over time from reselling the data (after usually a six-month exclusive period). This kind of deal emerged in the Gulf of Mexico during the leasing boom that started in 1995. However, if the data turned out to be of little value, or if demand fell due to slashed exploration budgets, then the seismic contractors operating with less than 100 per cent funding were on the hook. To win business, contractors would agree to lower their "pre-funding" requirements to 35 or 40 per cent, taking on greater risk and essentially subsidizing seismic exploration for the oil companies.[65]

The result was a massive contraction and consolidation in the geophysical contractor business that lasted for a good part of the 1990s. Forty years of innovation could not protect GSI, which was sold to Halliburton in 1988. Six years later, Halliburton sold the remnants of its GSI assets to Western Geophysical, which itself underwent a series of reorganizations and mergers before resurfacing in 2000 as Western Geco, a business unit of Schlumberger. Over the long run, the oil companies, many of whom were initially skeptical about leading-edge innovations in seismic technology, enjoyed most of the benefits from the subsurface vision digitally engineered by firms such as GSI and Western.

While geophysical contractors were the first to be fired in the downturn, they were also the first to be hired in an upturn. During the oil boom that lasted from 2002 to 2014, the marine seismic business recovered and thrived once again. This expansion pushed exploration into new geological frontiers, most spectacularly beneath massive layers of salt in deepwater. The subsalt play began first in the Gulf of Mexico in the late 1990s, and then spread elsewhere, especially offshore of Brazil, spurring successive rounds of innovation in digital seismic acquisition, processing, and interpretation.

Although developed in the 1970s, 3D technology was still in its infancy by the late 1990s, and it matured in many directions. More complex 3D migration algorithms, such as 3D "prestack" time and depth migration and "reverse-time migration," provided ever-greater precision necessary for imaging through wave-distorting bodies of salt. To overcome the data constraints that still inhibited subsalt exploration, contractors introduced "multi-azimuth" (MAZ), "wide-azimuth" (WAZ), and "full-azimuth" (FAZ) seismic surveys, acquiring data from several vessels at a time that recorded data in multiple azimuths (the angle of linear horizontal direction), rather than merely along one narrow azimuth from one vessel. Steadily increasing computing power allowed geophysicists to extract more and different kinds of information from richer sets of data obtained through MAZ, WAZ, and FAZ seismic surveys.[66]

These capabilities combined to propel further advances in data acquisition and processing. Along with the development of high-sensitivity ocean-bottom hydrophones, or "nodes," these advances helped to improve on a kind of seismic amplitude analysis called "amplitude vs. offset," or AVO, which is a way of measuring the variation of seismic reflection amplitudes with a change in distance between the shotpoint and receiver. The advances enabled geophysicists to estimate the velocity of not only "p-waves," but also "s-waves," known variously as secondary, shear, or transverse waves. P-waves travel longitudinally by compression in the same direction as sound; they have the highest velocity and move through both solid rock and fluid. S-waves travel perpendicularly to the direction of sound; they are slower and can only move through solid rock, thus requiring ocean-bottom receivers to be recorded. S-waves can detect important reservoir properties or subtle changes in lithology that p-waves cannot. Improvements in AVO analysis had a major impact on modelling reservoirs found with DHI or bright spots in young, poorly consolidated rocks, such as those in the Gulf of Mexico. In relatively a short time, s-waves enabled oil and gas firms to find hundreds of millions of barrels of oil and tens of billions of cubic feet of gas that could not have been found with p-waves alone.[67]

On top of advanced AVO modelling, technology moved along many different fronts. These include broadband data recording, simultaneous sound sources, wireless systems, higher channel counts, fibre optic streamers, and robotic ocean-bottom nodes. As computing power began to catch up with advances in seismic acquisition, the industry progressed toward "full wave-form inversion" (FWI), in which primary and shear waves, reflections and refractions, all contribute to the creation of a more fine-grained subsurface image from much better estimates of seismic velocity. FWI could obtain quantitative information from seismic data about rock properties, such as porosity, lithology, and fluid saturation, on a detailed scale.[68] Oil explorers closed in on acquiring the power to visualize, literally, the intricacies of subsurface geology before ever drilling a well.

Once again, the Gulf of Mexico was the proving ground for this latest trend in seismic innovation. Explorers used their expanded capabilities to uncover a whole new oil frontier in the subsalt strata, foldbelts, and Lower Tertiary formations of the "ultra-deepwater" (7,000- to 12,000-foot depths) Gulf of Mexico. By 2015, the US Department of the Interior counted 171 deepwater and ultra-deepwater fields discovered in the Gulf since the 1980s, containing an original 13 billion barrels of oil equivalent, with billions more classified as "contingent," awaiting a development commitment from operators.[69]

Beginning in the late 1990s, advanced digital seismic techniques animated other deepwater basins, enabling geophysicists to collect accurate images through the salt and decipher frontier geology. Many major discoveries followed, which helped allay fears about the adequacy of oil supplies for years to come. By 2006, the industry had discovered 60 billion barrels of oil in deepwater worldwide, production from which is still coming on line.[70] From 2007 to 2012, half of the 170 billion barrels of global conventional oil and gas discovered by the industry was in deepwater.[71]

West Africa accounted for a lot of this action, but seismic innovations have also reshaped oil prospects in the Americas. Most spectacularly, as Triner in this volume recounts, Brazil's Petrobras announced in late 2007 that it had discovered 7.5 billion barrels of oil in the "pre-salt" sediments of the Santos offshore basin. The company has since estimated pre-salt reserves across three basins to be 13 billion barrels. In May 2015, ExxonMobil used bright spot amplitudes to make a significant discovery in the Stabroek Block offshore Guyana (population: 770,000).[72] The company followed that up with a string of additional discoveries in even deeper water, based on advanced 3D imaging, that totalled more than 8 billion barrels of oil equivalent by 2020. Geophysical surveying and drilling have also indicated "huge hydrocarbon potential" in the offshore basins of Brazil's equatorial margin.[73] Finally, the expansion of leasing and drilling ever closer to the US-Mexico maritime boundary has played no small part in compelling Mexico in 2013 to end the seventy-five-year-old oil monopoly that barred foreign participation in the nation's oil sector (see Hall in this volume). In January 2018, Mexico sold exploration rights to nineteen deepwater blocks for $500 million. The ongoing digital revolution in seismic technology has illuminated new pockets of hydrocarbon resources across the Americas.

Conclusion

Beginning in the 1950s, technological advances in petroleum seismology transformed oil exploration into a high-tech business and turned the Gulf of Mexico into one of the most active oil-hunting areas in the world. The development of marine geophysical operations and a new model of contracting in the 1950s opened up new offshore vistas. The early introduction of magnetic tape recording and common-depth-point shooting in the late 1950s, closely followed by digital processing and recording in the early 1960s, led to continual improvements in seismic processing and interpretation, from the deconvolution of signals caused by reverberations in water in the late 1950s, to the direct detection of hydrocarbons in the late 1960s, to three-dimensional seismology in the late 1970s, to the emergence of full wave-form inversion in the twenty-first century.

The fifty-year project of digital innovation has had its greatest impact on the water, where the marginal costs of applying novel ideas and expensive new technologies were lower offshore than on land. The proving ground for digital seismic technology was the US Gulf of Mexico. But geophysical techniques pioneered in the Gulf have also helped to open other deepwater basins around the world to petroleum extraction. In the Americas, from the Santos Basin off Brazil to the Mexican side of the Gulf, digital seismic innovations have led explorers to find billions upon billions of barrels of petroleum, much of which has yet to be coaxed from the ocean. This newly discovered offshore petroleum abundance, combined with the spectacular growth of oil and gas production from shale basins in the United States through hydraulic fracturing, which also benefitted from advanced digital seismic technologies, silenced alarms about an impending "peak" in global oil supply that had been so common in the early 2000s.[74]

Ironically, just as the progress in seismic innovations reduced a great deal of the uncertainty in finding oil, other uncertainties arose to cloud the future of offshore exploration. The unreliability of future demand in a world desperately trying to shift away from fossil fuels to mitigate runaway global warming is obviously a big problem. Related to this is the ongoing price volatility of oil in a world without a mechanism to balance supply and demand. This volatility wreaks havoc on the investment decisions companies make in developing resources in high-cost environments like deepwater.[75] The first industry affected in a price downturn, like the one that lasted from 2014 to 2018, remained geophysical contractors. Among other casualties in this shakeout, the long-established French company CCG filed for bankruptcy, and Schlumberger sold off the seismic acquisition business of WesternGeco, whose ancestors, GSI and Western Geophysical, pioneered the digital revolution.[76] The supply and demand for digital data has turned out to behave a lot like oil, subject to endemic cycles of boom and bust.

NOTES

1   Tyler Priest, "Extraction Not Creation: The History of Offshore Petroleum in the Gulf of Mexico," *Enterprise & Society* 8, no. 2 (June 2007): 227–67.

2   Enders A. Robinson, "Geophysical Exploration: Past and Future," *Leading Edge* 25, no. 1 (January 2006): 98.

3   Steve Lohr, "The Origins of 'Big Data': An Etymological Detective Story," *New York Times*, 1 February 2013.

4   Exploration geophysicists have documented the technological milestones in their field, but they do not emphasize the Gulf Coast origins of commercial geophysics or the business contours of its evolution. See, for example, George Elliott Sweet, *The History of Geophysical Prospecting* (Los Angeles: Science Press, 1966); J. E. Brantly, *History of Oil Well Drilling* (Houston: Gulf Publishing, 1971); Rajni K. Verma, *Offshore Seismic Exploration: Data Acquisition, Processing, Interpretation* (Houston: Gulf Publishing, 1986); L. C. Lawyer, Charles C. Bates, and Robert B. Rice, *Geophysics in the Affairs of Mankind: A Personalized History of Exploration Geophysics* (Tulsa: Society of Exploration Geophysicists, 2001); and Mark Mau and Henry Edmundson, *Groundbreakers: The Story of Oilfield Technology and the People Who Made it Happen* (Peterborough, UK: Fast-Print Publishing, 2015).

5   Sweet, *The History of Geophysical Prospecting*; Lawyer, Bates, and Rice, *Geophysics in the Affairs of Mankind*, 1–12.

6   Edgar Wesley Owen, *Trek of the Oil Finders: A History of Exploration for Petroleum* (Tulsa: American Association of Petroleum Geologists, 1975), 505–10; Lawyer, Bates, and Rice, *Geophysics in the Affairs of Mankind*, 15–17.

7   J. A. Klotz, "Geophysical Exploration Methods," *Journal of Petroleum Technology* 4, no. 6 (June 1952): 20–1.

8   R. J. Graebner, G. Steel, and C. B. Wason, "Evolution of Seismic Technology into the 1980s, Pt. 1," *Australian Petroleum Exploration Association (APEA) Journal* 20 (1980): 110–20; "Seismic Technology: Evolution of a Vital Tool for Reservoir Engineers," *Journal of Petroleum Technology* 51, no. 2 (February 1999): 22–8; and Robert J. Graebner, "Meeting the Challenge of Cost-Effective Exploration," address to the Dallas Geophysical Society, 15 May 1987, Texas Instruments Records, DeGolyer Library, Southern Methodist University, Dallas (documents from this collection hereafter cited as TI Records).

9   Sweet, *History of Geophysical Prospecting*, 122–5. Also see "Fifty Years of Trailblazing in the Oil Patch, GSI (1930–1980)," *The Grapevine* 36, no. 2 (1980): 4–17. *The Grapevine* was GSI's internal magazine. A full set can be found in the TI Records, 87–60.

10 D. C. Barton, "Petroleum Potentialities of Gulf Coast Petroleum Province of Texas and Louisiana," *Bulletin of the American Association of Petroleum Geologists* 14, no. 11 (1930): 1380j; Owen, *Trek of the Oil Finders*, 511–14, 794–7; and Lawyer, Bates, and Rice, *Geophysics in the Affairs of Mankind*, 21–4.

11 "A Method of Surveying by Use of Radio Waves," *Oil and Gas Journal*, 7 July 1949, 69–71, 90–1; "Offshore Seismograph Work . . . with a Single Boat," *Oil and Gas Journal*, 13 April 1950, 82–3, 112–13.

12 Jack M. Proffitt, "A History of Innovation in Marine Seismic Data Acquisition," *Geophysics: The Leading Edge of Exploration* 10, no. 3 (March 1991): 27.

13 Curtis A. Johnson and John W. Wilson, "Marine Exploration Comes of Age," *World Oil*, March 1954, 76–7; John W. Wilson, "Single Ship Takes the Place of a Fleet," *World Oil*, June 1954, 163.

14 Society of Exploration Geophysicists (SEG) Wiki, s.v. "Booth Strange," last modified 18 October 2016, 11:08, https://wiki.seg.org/wiki/Booth_Strange; Sam Evans, former

GSI seismologist, interview with the author, 9 April 2002, Houston. This and other oral histories cited in this chapter were collected as part of a six-volume study for the Minerals Management Service of the US Department of the Interior, *History of the Offshore Oil and Gas Industry in Southern Louisiana* (OCS Study MMS 2008-042, New Orleans, September 2008), which can be accessed online at the Bureau of Ocean Energy Management's Environmental Studies Program Information System, https://www.boem.gov/espis. Oral history audio and transcripts can be found at University of Houston Libraries, Oral Histories—Houston History Project, 1996–, Series 7: Energy Development, http://archon.lib.uh.edu/?p=collections/findingaid&id=231&q=&rootcontentid=129960#id129960.

15 "Geophysical Activity Drops Again in '54," *Oil and Gas Journal*, 4 April 1955, 138–47; "Seismic Work Hits a Slump," *Oil and Gas Journal*, 17 March 1958, 176–8; "Firms See Higher Fees as Solution," *Oil and Gas Journal*, 14 July 1958, 72–3.

16 Delores Proubasta, "Henry Salvatori," *Geophysics: The Leading Edge of Exploration* 2, no. 8 (1983): 14–22; and "Henry Salvatori, G.O.P Advisor and Oil Company Founder, 96," *New York Times*, 13 July 1997.

17 SEG Wiki, "Booth B. Strange."

18 Neal Cramer, President of Western Geophysical, 1984–91, interview with the author, 20 August 2002, Houston.

19 Evans, interview.

20 Cramer, interview.

21 Lawyer, Bates, and Rice, *Geophysics in the Affairs of Mankind*, 298.

22 "Western Geophysical, Division of Western Atlass International," *Oil and Gas Online*, 21 September 2000, https://www.oilandgasonline.com/doc/western-geophysical-division-of-western-atlas-0001. Also see various issues of *Western Profile*, the in-house magazine of Western Geophysical, the full set of which is available online at https://seg.org/Publications/Journals/Western-Profile.

23 See Lawyer, Bates, and Rice, *Geophysics in the Affairs of Mankind*, 83–5; "Seismic Technology: Evolution of a Vital Tool," 24.

24 For Mayne's personal account, see W. Harry Mayne, *50 Years of Geophysical Ideas* (Tulsa: SEG, 1989).

25 Mayne, *50 Years of Geophysical Ideas*, 33–7.

26 Proffitt, "A History of Innovation in Marine Seismic Data Acquisition," 27–8.

27 Proffitt, "A History of Innovation in Marine Seismic Data Acquisition," 28–9.

28 "Seismic Technology: Evolution of a Vital Tool." The difference between analogue and digital media has to do with the way the sound is recorded and stored. Analogue refers to recordings where the original sound is modulated onto another physical medium, such as the iron oxide surface of magnetic tape. The physical quality of the medium is directly related, or analogous, to the physical properties of the original sound. A digital recording involves sampling and converting the physical properties of the

original sound into binary digits or numbers, which can then be stored, replayed, and manipulated for various purposes on a computing device.

29   Robert Graebner, interview with the author, 13 June 2002, Dallas.

30   The early history of the MIT GAG is told by Enders A. Robinson, "The MIT Geophysical Analysis Group (GAG) from Inception to 1954," *Geophysics* 70, no. 4 (July–August 2005): 7JA–30JA. For details on the origins of stored-program architecture, the basis for what most people recognize as the modern computer, see Martin Campbell-Kelly and William Aspray, *Computer: A History of the Information Machine* (New York: Basic Books, 1996), 87–104.

31   "Digital Revolutionaries: Technical Advances Reverberated Through the Industry," in *AAPG Explorer Special Issue—A Century* (Tulsa: AAPG, 2000), 51; Robinson, "The MIT Geophysical Analysis Group," 23JA; Enders Robinson, oral history interview by Andrew Goldstein, 6 March 1997, New York, available at Engineering and Technology History Wiki, last modified 26 January 2021, 19:06, https://ethw.org/Oral-History:Enders_Robinson.

32   "Fifty Years of Trailblazing in the Oil Patch, GSI (1930–1980)," 10–12; Caleb Pirtle III, *Engineering the World: Stories from the First 75 Years of Texas Instruments* (Dallas: Southern Methodist University Press, 2005), 1–25.

33   Robert R. Shrock, *A Cooperative Plan in Geophysical Education: The GSI Student Cooperative Plan, the First Fifteen Summers, 1951-1965* (Dallas: Geophysical Service, 1966).

34   For more on Burg, see "Kenneth Edwin Burg," A Profile by Cecil H. Green for Honorary Membership in the SEG, October 1979, Ken Burg folder, Box 4, TI Records.

35   Milo Backus, interview with the author, 12 June 2002, Dallas.

36   Mark Smith, "The Seismic Digital Revolution" (unpublished manuscript provided by Smith to author).

37   Smith, "The Seismic Digital Revolution."

38   Smith, "The Seismic Digital Revolution."

39   Michael Riordan and Lillian Hoddeson, *Crystal Fire: The Birth of the Information Age* (New York: W. W. Norton, 1997).

40   See Pirtle, *Engineering the World*, 27–84.

41   Ken Burg Lecture, 10 April 1964 Revision, "The Total Seismic Exploration System and the Role of Digital Technology," Ken Burg Folder, Box 4, TI Records; GSI, Fact Sheet, Digital Seismic Service Technology and GSI's Systems Approach to Exploration, 9 June 1964, GSI Press Releases, 1964–1966 Folder, Box 1, TI Records.

42   Backus, interview. See also Lawyer, et al., *Geophysics in the Affairs of Mankind*, 114–115.

43   Smith, "The Seismic Digital Revolution."

44   Smith, "The Seismic Digital Revolution."

45   Smith, "The Seismic Digital Revolution."

46   For more on the GSI navy, see Pirtle, *Engineering the World*, 20–5.

47   Backus, interview.

48   Lawyer, Bates, and Rice, *Geophysics in the Affairs of Mankind*, 279–80.

49   "Binary gain refers to a seismic digital-recording system that switches decibel levels (gain) for each seismic channel in steps of two in response to changes in signal energy. This technique allows data recovery with low distortion." F. Reynolds and Robert H. Ray, "Binary-Gain Recording and Processing," *AAPG Bulletin* 51, no. 5 (May 1967): 814.

50   "Direct detection" was based on the principle that the acoustic impedance of a loosely cemented rock filled with hydrocarbons was different from that of a similar water-filled rock, and with advanced digital methods, this difference often could often be detected as an "amplitude anomaly" or "high-amplitude reflection" on the seismic record. Mobil and Shell first bid on offshore leases using bright spots in the December 1970 federal offshore Louisiana lease sale. Tyler Priest, *The Offshore Imperative: Shell Oil's Search for Petroleum in Postwar America* (College Station: Texas A&M University Press, 2007), 124–136; Mike Forrest, interview with the author, 29 June 1999, Houston; Robert Hirsch, interview with the author, 6 November 2003, Navasota.

51   Décio Fabrício Oddone da Costa, Renato Sanches Rodrigues, and Álvaro Felippe Negrão, "The Evolution of Deepwater Drilling in Brazil" (paper presented at the Society of Petroleum Engineers Latin American Petroleum Engineering Conference, Rio de Janeiro, 14–19 October 1990); Tyler Priest, "Petrobras in the History of Offshore Oil," in *New Order and Progress: Development and Democracy in Brazil*, ed. Ben Ross Schneider (New York: Oxford University Press, 2016), 56, 64–7.

52   The presentation resulted in the publication by G. G. Walton, "Three-Dimensional Seismic Method," *Geophysics* 37, no. 3 (June 1972): 417–30.

53   Graebner, interview.

54   Jon F. Claerbout, a Stanford geophysicist and consultant to Chevron, published two seminal papers, in 1970 and 1971, that pioneered the methodology of using the wave equation to perform seismic imaging: "Coarse Grid Calculations of Waves in Inhomogeneous Media with Application to Delineation of Complicated Seismic Structure," *Geophysics* 35, no. 3 (1970): 407–18, and "Toward a Unified Theory of Reflector Mapping," *Geophysics* 36, no. 3 (1971): 467–81. Also see J. Bee Bednar, "A Brief History of Seismic Migration," *Geophysics* 70, no. 3 (May–June 2005): 3MJ–20MJ.

55   William A. Schneider, "3-D Seismic: A Historical Note," *Leading Edge* 17, no. 3 (March 1998): 375.

56   Quoted in Pirtle, *Engineering the World*, 19.

57   C. G. Dahm and R. J. Graebner, "Field Development with Three-Dimensional Seismic Methods in the Gulf of Thailand—A Case History," *Geophysics* 47, no. 2 (February 1982): 149–76.

58   Bob Tippee, "Seismic Progress: Where the Trends Might Lead," *Oil & Gas Journal*, 13 December 1999, https://www.ogj.com/articles/print/volume-97/issue-50/petroleum-in-the-21st-century/upstream-in-the-new-century/seismic-progress-where-the-trends-might-lead.html.

59 Internal memo, Bob Graebner to Bob Tiner, Halliburton research director, "Material for Indonesian Meeting," 17 September 1991, copy provided to author by Graebner. This memo lays out a summary of the major milestones in the use of seismic methods in the petroleum industry. In 1988, Halliburton purchased GSI from TI and merged it with Geosource into Halliburton Geophysical Services.

60 Tippee, "Seismic Progress."

61 "U.S. E&P Surge Hinges on Technology, Not Oil Price," *Oil & Gas Journal*, 13 January 1997, https://www.ogj.com/articles/print/volume-95/issue-2/in-this-issue/general-interest/us-ep-surge-hinges-on-technology-not-oil-price.html.

62 Graebner, interview.

63 "U.S. E&P Surge Hinges on Technology"; "Looking Ahead in Marine and Land Geophysics—A Conversation with Woody Nestvold and Ian Jack," *Leading Edge* 14, no. 10 (October 1995): 1061–7; International Association of Geophysical Contractors, "Industry at a Crossroads: A Message from the Geophysical Industry," *Leading Edge* 22, no. 1 (January 2003): 14–17.

64 "The Cat Scans of the Oil Patch," *Business Week*, 10 June 1991, 66.

65 Nelson Antosh, "Bad Vibrations: Seismic Firms Have Been Unable to Imitate Oil Industry's Rebound," *Houston Chronicle*, 20 February 2000, 1D, 3D; Nigel Ash, "Consolidation Still Needed," *Petroleum Economist*, October 2002, 21–2.

66 David Brown, "Wide Azimuths Combat Salt 'Blur': Resolution Undergoing Revolution," *AAPG Explorer* 29, no. 3 (March 2008): 16–18.

67 Derman Dondurur, *Acquisition and Processing of Marine Seismic Data* (Amsterdam: Elsevier, 2018), 567–9; David Monk, "Technological Advances Bringing New Capabilities to Seismic Data Acquisition," *American Oil & Gas Reporter*, July 2014, https://www.aogr.com/magazine/editors-choice/technological-advances-bringing-new-capabilities-to-seismic-data-acquisitio.

68 Rocky Roden, "The Promise of Full Waveform Inversion," *E&P Magazine*, 3 June 2013, http://www.epmag.com/promise-full-waveform-inversion-694906#p=1.

69 US Department of the Interior, Bureau of Ocean Energy Management, Gulf of Mexico OCS Region, Office of Resource Evaluation, *Deepwater Gulf of Mexico December 31, 2014* (OCS Report BOEM 2016-057, New Orleans, August 2016).

70 Peggy Williams, "Deep Water Delivers," *Oil & Gas Investor* 26, no. 5 (May 2006): 32.

71 Kerry Nelson et al., "Deepwater Operators Look to New Frontiers," *Offshore* 73, no. 5 (May 2013), https://www.offshore-mag.com/articles/print/volume-73/issue-5/international-report/deepwater-operators-look-to-new-frontiers.html.

72 Velda Addison, "ExxonMobil VP Stresses Value of Geophysical Data," *E&P Magazine*, 28 September 2017, https://www.epmag.com/exxonmobil-vp-stresses-value-geophysical-data-1660357#p=full.

73 Karyna Rodriguez, Neil Hodgson, and Richie Miller, "Hydrocarbon Prospectivity in Brazil," *GeoExpro* 15, no. 3 (2018), https://www.geoexpro.com/articles/2018/08/hydrocarbon-prospectivity-in-brazil.

74 Tyler Priest, "Hubbert's Peak: The Great Debate Over the End of Oil," *Historical Studies in the Natural Sciences* 44, no. 1 (February 2014): 37–79.

75 Robert McNally, *Crude Volatility: The History and Future of Boom-Bust Oil Prices* (New York: Columbia University Press, 2017).

76 Bruce Beaubouef, "Seismic Survey Contractors Hoping for Turnaround," *Offshore* 78, no. 3 (March 2018), https://www.offshore-mag.com/articles/print/volume-78/issue-3/seismic-survey-market-outlook/seismic-survey-contractors-hoping-for-turnaround.html. CCG eventually emerged from bankruptcy. Schlumberger sold WesternGeco to Shearwater Geosciences, formed in 2016.

Optimism, Fear, and Free Trade: Canada's Winding Path to a Globalized Petroleum Industry, 1930–2005

Paul Chastko

The Canadian petroleum industry's integration into a globalized world petroleum industry seems self-evident in retrospect. After the twin shocks of the Great Depression and the Second World War, Imperial Oil's discovery of the substantial petroleum and natural gas reserves of the Western Canadian Sedimentary Basin (WCSB) confronted both the Canadian and Alberta governments with an existential question about how to best pursue development of a significant, but nonetheless regional, source of crude operating on the margins of a much larger global oil industry. In an era when governments across the Americas and the Middle East opted for nationalization of natural resources to spur industrial development, successive Canadian governments chose to develop petroleum reserves within the parameters of a market-based system, recognizing the economic and geographic obstacles to quick development, as well as the oil industry's mastery of the necessary technology, methods, and skills for rapid exploitation of the WCSB. The wisdom of that model remained basically unquestioned until the oil shocks of the 1970s, when fear, rather than optimism or self-confidence, prompted the federal government of

Pierre Elliott Trudeau to embark in a decidedly more nationalist direction, culminating with the National Energy Program in 1980. Only after the program failed did Canada resume its trajectory toward globalization by signing the Canada-US Free Trade Agreement.

The continental integration of the North American petroleum industry emerged in the late nineteenth and early twentieth centuries because of proximity, shared values, and similar institutions that facilitated the creation of regulatory, taxation, and royalty provisions. Early in the twentieth century, Canadian petroleum policies reflected elements of pragmatism because Canadian subsidiaries, like Imperial Oil (Standard Oil of New Jersey, now ExxonMobil) and McColl-Frontenac (Texaco), had markets and customers to service but were typically "crude short" (that is, with no substantial domestic source of supply.) Conversely, US-based parent companies had ready access to crude supplies but required markets and customers to service, creating a symbiotic relationship between the Canadian and US petroleum industries. Canadian companies focused their operations on downstream operations (transportation, refining, and marketing) of the crude oil produced by their US corporate parents. At the same time, Canadian companies did not completely abandon upstream (exploration and production) operations and adopted the same business strategies and corporate cultures of their parent companies, who also provided access to capital, technology, and industry knowledge.[1]

Jurisdiction over natural resources in the Canadian context is shared between the provinces and the federal government. Section 109 of the British North America Act granted subsurface mineral rights to the individual provinces, but when Alberta and Saskatchewan entered confederation in 1905, the federal government retained jurisdiction over natural resources until 1930, partly out of the calculation that the two new provinces lacked the capital and population to effectively develop whatever natural resources existed. In 1929, Ottawa set the Crown royalty at 5 per cent of the sale price of oil for the first five years of production before raising it to 10 per cent thereafter. When control over natural resources transitioned from federal to provincial authority on 1 October 1930, the Alberta government assumed full responsibility for the development of resources. Provincial authorities maintained the federal royalty rate until

1935, when they began increasing it in stages; by 1 January 1940, the rate was 12.5 per cent.[2]

After failing to attract Canadian or British investors to build on the success of the second Turner Valley petroleum boom in the 1930s (the first Turner Valley era began in 1914 with discoveries of natural gas), the Province ended the system of imperial preferences and invited capital from anywhere in the world, namely the United States, to invest in Alberta's oil industry. The decision, argued Alberta's deputy minister for mines and resources, Hubert Somerville, ended discriminatory practices and opened Alberta's market to American capital and expertise. "As long as [they] were spending Canadian dollars in Canada and Alberta," noted Somerville, investors would enjoy "the same benefits as though you were a Canadian or a ... British subject."[3] By 1945, American investment comprised fully 95 per cent of the $157 million in foreign direct investment in the Canadian oil industry.[4]

Numerous informal cross-border linkages tightened connections as the free flow of capital, technology, ideas, people, and publications facilitated the evolution of the younger Canadian industry.[5] To stimulate exploration using new technologies and methods, particularly geophysics, the Province expanded lease sizes two times between 1937 and 1941 from 1,920 to 50,000 and then to 600,000 acres (in three blocks of 200,000 acres each).[6] But in 1942, during the wartime emergency, Ottawa assumed control of the province's oil fields in Turner Valley and the Abasand oil sands plant in Fort McMurray. Under the auspices of Wartime Oils Ltd., over the objections of provincial regulators, the federal government drilled twenty-one additional wells in Turner Valley. Production peaked at 9.7 million barrels in 1942 and steadily declined thereafter, in large measure because the wasteful and prolific flaring of the natural gas cap in the 1930s depressurized the field, making it impossible to recover crude oil. Only 100 to 150 million of the estimated 750 million barrels contained in the Turner Valley field were produced.[7] Meanwhile, federal control over the Abasand facility excluded provincial researchers and experts from operations and led to venomous accusations that Ottawa deliberately sabotaged the facility when a fire destroyed it in 1943.

With few domestic sources of petroleum—total Canadian crude production in 1946 was 7.6 million barrels against 77 million barrels of demand—Canada remained dependent on imports of crude and refined products at an annual cost of half a billion dollars.[8] Prospects for increasing oil production in Western Canada remained bleak. California Standard (Chevron) discovered some small fields in southern Alberta and some heavy oil around Lloydminster, but the oil was either of such low quality or insufficient volume to inhibit commercial development. "You couldn't do anything with it," recalled Imperial Oil's Doug Layer. "You couldn't produce it because you'd just lose money every time you turned around."[9]

Developments in the global industry, however, soon transformed the province from a marginal producer of crude and natural gas for local markets into a major destination for international business and capital. The gradual improvement and evolution of geology and geophysics in oil exploration helped transform exploration from an art into a science and led to dramatic increases in the world's proven reserves from 62 billion barrels to 534 billion barrels. All told, the size of the global industry increased by a factor of nine.[10]

Technological change and innovation combined with changing local and national conditions to create a unique set of circumstances. Canadian economic and trade policies were largely influenced by both the need for markets and a near total dependence on two trade partners—the United Kingdom and the United States—to buy Canadian exports. However, British demand for Canadian imports collapsed following the war, contributing to a $500 million trade deficit as Canadian imports from the United States continued to climb. The growing trade deficit and currency crisis—Canada's shortage of US dollars to pay for additional imports—threatened the stability of the entire economy.[11] Fortunately for Canadians, policy-makers and business leaders alike were determined to avoid the mistakes of the 1930s and embraced the US-led liberal world order established at the end of the war and marked by multilateral institutions and organizations like the Bretton Woods system, which established the convertibility of currencies, the World Bank, and the International Monetary Fund. Collectively, joining the multilateral order reflected the optimism that liberal free trade and the market would lead to prosperity and peace. Moreover, Canada's decision to reduce trade barriers with the United States as part of the first "round" of negotiations on the General

Agreement on Tariffs and Trade (GATT) in 1947 opened a number of sectors to increased bilateral trade and strengthened economic relations in the process.[12]

Stated simply, politicians, businesses, and consumers made choices, based in part on history, institutions, and values. Unlike several Latin American examples discussed in this volume, where the export of crude was essential to national economic prosperity, the need to rapidly develop the Canadian petroleum industry was offset by the presence of a large manufacturing and industrial base in Eastern Canada and export markets geared to the United States. Arguably, the burden of driving the postwar Canadian economy lay with auto manufacturing. With comparatively little at stake in terms of national economic priorities, Canadian authorities could—and did—rely on the private sector to guide development by creating favourable conditions for international investment. With an eye toward kick-starting oil exploration, the Alberta government re-examined its regulatory regime beginning with attempts to attract the attention of the majors—and their exploration dollars—by reducing the leasehold requirements. Moreover, the Province established clear and predictable royalty and taxation regimes to provide certainty and predictability.[13] Meanwhile, the federal government offered generous tax incentives that allowed companies to write off up to 40 per cent of losses for exploratory wells and up to 50 per cent of costs for "deep difficult" tests, in addition to waiving import duties on certain drilling equipment brought from the United States. Combined with US tax incentives that encouraged US companies to explore for international supplies, all that remained was to discover a prolific field.

In 1945, a group of Imperial Oil's management and technical people joined Jersey Standard advisers in Toronto to plot the company's next move. Between 1917 and 1946, Imperial Oil spent $23.2 million in exploration and drilled 133 consecutive dry holes in southern Alberta and Saskatchewan. More distressingly, discoveries of natural gas were more prolific and brought with them unwelcome assumption of further financial burdens to cap the well since the market for natural gas was already saturated. These additional—and unwanted—expenditures already prompted Shell Oil to indefinitely shelve exploration plans in the province.[14] As Imperial Oil geologist Doug Layer recalled, the company also launched one final oil exploration effort, "with the chance that maybe this would be the time we might be lucky and find oil." Beginning in 1946, Imperial's seismic crews from Carter Oil—a wholly American subsidiary of Jersey Standard—shifted attention from southern to central Alberta between Edmonton and Leduc. Although the geophysical techniques were still somewhat primitive, they revealed a promising anomaly. Despite the fact that the interpretation of the anomaly was wrong, Imperial went ahead and drilled at Leduc No. 1. Ultimately, the well produced 318,000 barrels of oil until it was abandoned in 1974.[15] The discovery of petroleum at Leduc in February 1947, along with the additions from the more voluminous Redwater field a year later, transformed Alberta into a crucial, but nonetheless regional rather than global, energy source. As the WCSB produced the first of more than 259 million barrels of oil and 415 trillion cubic feet of natural gas, business and political leaders faced a series of important, and long-lasting, choices regarding Alberta's integration into the supply, operations, and infrastructure network of the international petroleum industry that remained fundamentally intact for the next seven decades.[16]

The boom presented both the federal and provincial government with an existential question: How to best develop provincial oil resources? Given the recent experience of state control during the war, the matter hardly seemed predestined. In February 1948, Imperial Oil—whose parent company, Standard Oil of New Jersey, faced the prospect of oil nationalization in other producing countries in the Americas, such as Brazil and Venezuela—began a broad public relations campaign designed to emphasize to the Canadian public how the company's success at Leduc reflected years of risk and investment undertaken in the public interest, and to inform both the public and its employees about the danger posed by "socialistic policies" that might result in a stronger role for the state in natural resource development.[17]

Perhaps Imperial need not have worried, as geography, economics, and politics argued against adopting either the Mexican, Brazilian, or Venezuelan model of national development, but the fact that they did suggests at the least that global developments helped shape some of the public discourse. Regardless, there remained potent political and economic arguments against the recourse to nationalist policies in oil. The pro-business, small-government ethos of Premier Ernest Manning's Social Credit government at the provincial level and the cool pragmatism of American-born C. D. Howe in the federal cabinets of Mackenzie King and Louis St. Laurent ensured the Canadian experience would differ from that of Latin America and hew more closely to the United States' postwar pursuit of market-driven capitalism and free trade liberalization.[18] Scarcity of investment capital and a lack of adequate industry skills and technology also provided a moment of pause. Leduc stood at the crossroads of the modern petroleum industry and the transition of exploration from an art to a science. The operation of rotary rig technology capable of drilling faster and deeper wells than traditional cable tool rigs required skill and sophistication that were lacking in Canada. Transportation costs to ship Alberta crude to the nation's largest refinery in Sarnia, Ontario, were $3.24 a barrel—when world crude prices were $3.55—argued against the pursuit of a national policy. Furthermore, the industry lacked a transportation system capable of moving crude in volume to refining facilities and markets. With only 672 kilometres (418 miles) of pipeline in the nation as a whole, and only a small line from Turner Valley to Calgary, Alberta crude moved by legacy infrastructure (road and rail) to service regional markets. Furthermore, refining facilities on the Prairies were only capable of handling small volumes (less than 10,000 barrels per day) and producing kerosene and some motor gasoline fractions. Creating a national industry would require massive investment of scarce capital, result in economic inefficiencies, displace cheaper offshore crude from Eastern Canadian markets, and higher transportation costs east of Winnipeg would result in lower profits.[19]

The federal government implemented more tangible policies to catalyze the industry by facilitating the transfer of global capital, skills, and technology. Leduc's dramatic discovery placed pressure on the province's labour force as demand for skilled oil field workers and equipment spiked—especially for drill rigs and their crews as the number of wells drilled in the province spiked from 126 in 1946 to over 1,000 in 1950.[20] Canadian and American companies alike turned to the United States to provide labour and equipment. If rigs could not be built in Canada because of material shortages, the federal government allowed the components that could not be manufactured in Canada to be brought into the country duty-free.[21] The Canadian Department of Immigration allowed American workers into the country on temporary work permits but implemented certain restriction and regulations, including stipulations that US rig operators would have to transfer skills by providing technical training to Canadians and that US rig workers could not take another job without federal government approval. The net result was that by May 1949, 28 US companies were drilling in Alberta with 112 rigs, but only 105 US workers operated in the province (all on temporary six-month work permits) compared to 2,103 Canadian roughnecks.[22] Furthermore, American-based Multinational Oil Companies (MNOCs) and their affiliates, like Imperial and British-American, quickly repatriated most of their Canadian personnel from Latin America and the United States, facilitating the transfer of industry knowledge. US drilling, engineering, and seismic crews brought their experiences with the Mid-Continent and Texas fields to Alberta. As Canadian mining engineer Charlie Dunkley later noted, "the type of American these companies transferred up were highly educated, they were all, mostly all technical men so they had either an engineering or geological or legal training."[23] By the mid-1950s, Alberta was second only to Texas in seismic surveying, and this influx of industry experience reduced the time to completion from two to three months in 1947 to between thirty-five and forty-five days in 1948. Canadian and American investors pumped $2.115 billion into the Canadian oil patch—$855 million for capital projects and $1.26 billion in exploration and development—resulting in twelve new producing fields totalling 2.2 billion barrels of oil by 1953, cementing Alberta's status as a major petroleum producer.[24]

With Alberta under Social Credit rule until the early 1970s, relations between provincial officials and industry developed along more informal, "handshake at a barbecue" lines subject to little legislative oversight. Most provincial oil and gas rules and regulations emerged as Orders in Council from the Premier's Office. Industry organizations like the Western Canadian Petroleum Association (later the Canadian Petroleum Association, a precursor to the Canadian Association of Petroleum Producers) enjoyed access to key ministers and influence over legislation.[25] Nathan Tanner, the provincial minister of lands and mines until September 1952, surprised his deputy minister, Hubert Somerville, one day by asking industry representatives to produce their own draft of legislation while the minister's own draft remained tucked away. When industry representatives could not agree between themselves on the wording of the legislation under discussion, Tanner intervened and presented his draft as a compromise, presenting the Province as a partner in development and honest broker between competing corporate ambitions.[26]

Canadian oil's pursuit of markets necessarily involved the federal government. In a speech before the Alberta Chamber of Mines and Resources in early January 1951, Manning speculated daily production might reach 170,000 barrels provided the Province could find a suitable market.[27] Later that year, over 737 producing wells operated within the province, forcing provincial policy-makers to balance the immediate demands of a booming economy while ensuring long-term prosperity by securing market share and attracting investment capital to sustain the economic boom and distribute the benefits to Albertans. The oil boom reversed Alberta's population decline as the province added 600,000 new people and created 22,000 direct new jobs by 1956. Daily crude exports to the United States grew from approximately 900 barrels in 1951 to 40,600 barrels by 1955, earning the Province an estimated $7 million in revenues. To address the problem of growing production but limited market reach, Alberta government adopted a prorationing scheme in 1950 to ensure that all producers, both large and small, "shared the pain" of a limited export market.[28]

Given Canada's small population and the sheer distance separating producers from the main population centres and domestic markets in Eastern Canada, looking toward the United States simply made economic sense. The construction of a continental pipeline network linking Alberta to US markets began in 1950 with the 1,812-kilometre (1,126-mile) Interprovincial (now Enbridge) Pipeline linking Alberta to the Ottawa Valley; the 1,156-kilometre (718-mile) Trans Mountain Pipeline followed in 1953. The two oil pipelines benefited greatly from US investment capital and dramatically enhanced the attractiveness and reach of Canadian crude.[29] Indeed, the Trans Mountain Pipeline linking Alberta producers to the West Coast could hardly be justified by the small volume of oil consumed in the Vancouver market, estimated at 46,000 barrels per day in 1950. However, including the nearby US cities of Seattle, Portland, and Spokane increased the size of the market to 250,000 barrels per day and made the project economically viable. Canadian assumptions about the further integration of the Canadian and US markets dovetailed with those of Washington, such that, by the 1950s, both governments informally considered North America a coherent economic unit. While the Petroleum Administration for Defense (PAD) generally concerned itself with Middle Eastern oil, it also encouraged policies to enhance hemispheric supplies. Considering that the Pacific Northwest in PAD V was then the only major oil-consuming region of the United States not serviced by a pipeline—the region relied on tanker shipments of refined products from California—the PAD facilitated pipeline construction by aiding with the acquisition of scarce steel resources.[30]

The combination of proven reserves, similar language, laws, institutions, and values highlighted the attractiveness of the Canadian market as a destination for US oil companies and investment capital and allowed the composition of the Canadian oil industry to mimic that of the United States. Carl Nickle, the publisher of *Nickle's Daily Oil Bulletin*, estimated that roughly 260 independent companies as well as every major multinational oil company rushed to Alberta.[31] Like in the United States, a handful of majors conducted upstream (exploration and production) and downstream (transportation, refining, and marketing) operations from coast-to-coast. The proliferation of independents—smaller companies focused on the upstream—has imbued the Canadian and US oil industries with a dynamic, entrepreneurial mindset that stimulates innovation and experimentation. With smaller reserves to develop compared to the MNOCs, independents typically spend more time and energy ensuring their reserves are produced in a timely fashion to generate cash flow. Moreover, independents operate in a highly competitive environment, and are therefore more willing to take risks to drill wildcat wells or search for more cost-effective ways of doing business.

Dome Exploration (Western) Limited, headed by John ("Jack") Patrick Gallagher, illustrates the intersection between public policy, private-sector development, and transnational benefits. In 1950, the trustees of the Massachusetts Institute of Technology, as well as the trustees of Harvard and Princeton Universities, decided to invest in the Canadian oil industry. US tax laws allowed American and investors to write off losses incurred anywhere else in the world against their gross income, making Canada an attractive investment opportunity. Ottawa encouraged such perceptions when, on 14 December 1951, the federal government removed all restrictions on funds entering or leaving the country.[32] Furthermore, between 1947 and 1972, Canadian tax laws encouraged the growth of Canada's petroleum producers by allowing companies to deduct provincial royalties, as well as exploration and development expenses, from gross revenue. Companies could either pay income tax on the remaining amount or take an additional depletion allowance of 33.3 per cent before paying taxes. As Dome Petroleum's Charlie Dunkley explained, "as long as you were putting everything that you made back into the business you didn't have to pay tax."[33] Overall US foreign direct investment (FDI) in Canadian oil and gas nearly doubled from $636 million in 1951 to $1.13 billion dollars in 1953. In the two decades between 1954 and 1974, US FDI in the Canadian industry reached $81.57 billion.[34]

Despite continued spending on exploration and steadily increasing proven reserves from the WCSB, by 1955 daily production leveled off to approximately 40,600 barrels per day because of limited market reach. Part of the difficulty stemmed from the election of November 1952, which gave the Republican Party control of both the Congress and the White House. Dwight D. Eisenhower's inauguration brought new priorities in trade and national security issues, particularly a willingness to establish protectionist measures on oil imports, which now accounted for 20 per cent of domestic US consumption. With higher costs of production relative to other crude suppliers—especially the Middle East—Alberta oil remained a price taker rather than a price setter, dependent as it was on a market established by other sources of crude. Between 1953 and 1955, Alberta's shut-in capacity averaged approximately 30 per cent because it was too expensive to displace other sources from the market. The 1956 Suez Crisis doubled Alberta's daily production from 40,600 barrels to 94,000 barrels, with most of the supplies headed via the Trans Mountain Pipeline to California's refineries.[35] At the end of 1957, with only 1.5 per cent of the world's proven reserves, Canada was responsible for 3 per cent of global production.[36] Industry spending (exploration, development, operations, and royalties) in Alberta reached a record $622 million in 1957 before contracting back to $592.2 million in 1958.[37]

The rapid, but nonetheless temporary, expansion of Alberta production and additions to proven reserves in 1956–7 resulted in an oil glut

Figure 8.1 Average Price Alberta Oil versus World Prices ($/bbl), 1947–1961

on the Prairies, abruptly bringing industry growth to a sudden stop as export markets contracted 66 per cent in 1958. Drilling in the Alberta peaked at 1,856 wells in 1956 before contracting to 1,450 wells in 1957.[38] Industry exploration and development budgets that increased to $495.2 million in 1957 shrank to $455.7 million in 1958 and stayed below 1957 levels until 1961. World crude prices temporarily rose from approximately $2.82 barrel in 1956 to $3.07 in January 1957 before returning below $2.97 barrel by 1959. As figure 8.1 illustrates, higher production and transportation costs gave Alberta's oil its defining characteristic as a more expensive crude relative to world prices; between 1948 and 1950, the price of Alberta oil remained nearly 34 per cent higher than world crude prices.[39] But the succession of Middle Eastern crises—Iran in 1953, Suez in 1956, and Iraq in 1958—highlighted the political and military volatility of the Middle East, and starkly underlined the dangers of instability. While Canadian oil served as the marginal barrel—the most expensive barrel of oil to produce in order to replace current inventories—US military and economic planners regarded oil imports from Canada as safe and reliable because of the country's integration into the US transportation and refining network. But the national security argument cut both ways during the Eisenhower years as US independent producers frequently invoked "national security" to restrict oil imports, including those from Canada.[40]

One 1958 State Department policy planning paper listed numerous reasons to exempt Canadian oil from a mandatory program. Pipeline deliveries of Canadian crude to the Pacific Northwest and Mid-continent regions were safer and more reliable than tanker shipments of offshore crude; import restrictions would be contrary to joint Canadian-US plans to share resources in the event of war. US imports were also sufficiently large that they would continue to stimulate further petroleum exploration and development in Canada, indirectly enhancing American security. If the United States restricted imports of Canadian oil, the Canadian industry would search out other markets—perhaps developing the Canadian industry along national (east–west) lines and displacing Venezuelan crude from Eastern Canadian markets. Finally, import restrictions might undermine global perceptions about American commitments to free trade and the open door. Taken together, these arguments pointed to the conclusion that preferential treatment for Canadian oil "is of such importance to the foreign economic policy of the United States that it should be justified personally to representatives of affected countries and to the GATT by the President."[41]

Faced with mounting pressure from Alberta's own independent oil producers, Premier Manning lobbied the new federal Conservative government of John Diefenbaker for relief and, at the behest of Alberta's independent producers, proposed the adoption of a national (east–west) energy strategy with the extension of the Interprovincial Pipeline to Montreal refineries. If approved, the new pipeline would displace offshore crude imports from Eastern Canadian markets, much to the consternation of the Canadian affiliates of US-based companies with international sources of production.[42] On 3 February 1958, a Royal Commission headed by Robert Borden began hearings in Calgary about Canada's oil and gas industry, energy exports, and the potential responsibilities of a soon-to-be created National Energy Board (NEB). Three years later, in 1961, the Diefenbaker government implemented the National Oil Policy (NOP).

The NOP created the NEB with advisory and regulatory powers over the Canadian oil industry. Moreover, the policy divided Canada's domestic market at the Ottawa Valley. Alberta oil would service expanded "natural" markets—the territory west of the Ottawa Valley and into the portions of the Western and Midwestern United States—while markets east of the Ottawa valley would rely on foreign imports from the United States, Venezuela, and the Middle East. Over the next decade, Alberta's crude production doubled from 519,000 barrels per day in 1960 to over 1.1 million barrels per day in 1969. The success of the NOP remained inextricably linked to increased consumption in the United States. Canadian exports grew an average of 20 per cent per year and passed 1 million daily barrels by 1972 despite an (ineffective) informal agreement to limit annual growth of Canadian exports to 5 per cent.[43] The fundamental assumptions underpinning the NOP—low world crude prices, increasing additions to proven reserves, excess production in Alberta, and continued access to the US export market—all came to an end in the early 1970s with the onset of the energy crisis, and an increasingly assertive brand of Canadian nationalism created new problems and challenges for the Canadian petroleum industry. Over the course of the 1970s, federal energy policies increasingly became more assertive and ignored the cross-border ties underpinning the Canadian industry, as well as its dependence on access to international markets and investment capital.[44]

Canadian energy policy shifted because of complex domestic and international issues that included questions about US economic and political leadership in the wake of the Vietnam War and Washington's commitment to international economic prosperity following President Nixon's 1971 unilateral decision to bring down the Bretton Woods system, impose wage and price controls, and establish a 10 per cent tax on imports to protect domestic producers, thereby shifting US trade policy in a decidedly more protectionist direction and sending Canadians scrambling to find new trade partners. President Nixon's April 1972 speech before the Canadian Parliament seemed to deliver the eulogy for the special Canada-US relationship that underpinned Canada's post–Second World War economic growth. As Nixon put it, "It is time for us to recognize that we have very separate identities; that we have significant differences, and that nobody's interests are furthered when these realities are obscured."[45]

At the national level, the NEB dominated oil and gas policy-making but remained highly dependent on the information provided by the industry itself, as the NEB lacked the capacity to gather geological, technical, economic, or financial data independently.[46] As world crude prices began to rise slowly in the early 1970s, concerns emerged about declining Canadian reserves from the WCSB and their implications for the ability of the Canadian industry to supply future domestic needs, let alone sustain continued exports to the United States. (Canada remained a net exporter of petroleum until 1975.[47]) In 1972, the NEB examined Canadian production and reserves data and concluded that future production from all Canadian sources were insufficient to supply demand of both the export and domestic markets after 1973, and it recommended that Ottawa impose direct controls on crude oil exports. On 4 September 1973, the federal government introduced a series of ad hoc measures to reduce Canadian dependence on foreign imports of crude by asking Alberta's producers to freeze prices below world levels, cut 10 per cent of the 1 million barrels of Canadian oil exports to the United States, and levy a 40 cent tax on every remaining barrel exported—the exact difference between the "made in Canada" price and world prices. This triggered an increasingly sharp response from Premier Peter Lougheed. Two days later the Yom Kippur War started, and two weeks after that OPEC's Arab member states began their embargo, bringing the first dramatic increase in world crude prices and radically changing both the context and dynamics of the federal-provincial dispute over the capture of windfall profits.

Domestic and international factors thus prompted a shift in Canadian energy policy in a more protectionist direction. The decade-long battle between the Province and the federal government for control of natural resource rents, plus the commanding American presence in the Canadian oil industry (estimated by the federal government in 1973 to amount to 91 per cent share of the industry) made it easier for the Trudeau government to impose price controls, just as Nixon had in response to the currency crisis a few years before. The federal government then entered a pricing agreement with the Province that fixed Canadian wellhead prices below world levels and established the Foreign Investment Review Agency (FIRA), which required businesses investing in Canada to demonstrate that a "significant benefit" would accrue to the country. FIRA squeezed out international investors and made middle- and upper-income Canadians the principal source of investment capital, averaging at least $1 billion per year over the five-year period between 1976 and 1981. Like Mexico and Brazil, Canada also joined the growing global trend of creating a state-owned oil company, Petro-Canada, in 1974 to supplement the private sector, provide better information, increase the Canadian presence in the energy sector, serve as Ottawa's "window" on the industry, address the problem of underinvestment, and help develop Canada's energy "frontiers"—the oil sands, the Arctic, and offshore—to replace the declining reserves of the WCSB. Although the creation of a Crown corporation rankled Calgary's free-market enthusiasts, the Province created its own entity, Alberta Energy Company, in 1973 to stimulate capital investment and lessen dependence on foreign crude.[48] The oil shocks produced different policy decisions across the Americas, where the price increases acted as a de facto tax on consumers, equal to 2 per cent of GDP throughout the industrial West.[49] In Venezuela, increased confidence and rising oil and gas revenues provided the impetus to launch a grand development program with the nationalization of its petroleum industry and creation of Petróleos de Venezuela S. A. (PDVSA) on 1 January 1976. In Canada, fear—of growing provincial power and wealth, of economic stagnation brought on by shortages of petroleum, of freezing in the dark—drove federal policies toward greater state intervention. Collectively, the policies assumed both that US-owned multinationals operating in the Canadian oil patch could no longer be trusted to serve the national interest and that world oil prices would continue to rise. They also assumed that the federal government needed to serve as a catalyst to ensure that Canadian natural resources, particularly the higher-cost projects on the energy frontiers, would be developed for the benefit of Canadians.[50]

Cumulatively, energy policies in the 1970s self-consciously pushed the Canadian industry away from continued integration with the United States and toward self-sufficiency. Symbolically, this meant industry operations shifted away from the low-cost but declining conventional reserves to bigger and ultimately riskier "megaprojects" with high upfront costs and long-term investment horizons only economically feasible given higher crude prices attained in the post-embargo world. In the United States, President Richard Nixon introduced price controls, encouraged conservation, and launched Project Independence to attain energy independence by 1980.[51] Under Trudeau, the Canadian Science Council invested nearly $600 million in renewable energy programs, like solar energy, at the same time that federal dollars helped diversify the Canadian oil industry's sources of supply by joining with the Province of Alberta to bail out the Syncrude oil sands project.[52] Federal subsidies and tax breaks during the prolonged boom between 1947 and 1972 encouraged producers to invest in exploration and development so that companies (and their investors) would not have to pay taxes. Dome's Charlie Dunkley noted that the system worked so long as companies spent their money wisely, deferring the payment of dividends to avoid taxes by turning profits back into exploration and development. "By the time 1972 came along, oil companies who had pursued the same policies that Dome had of ploughing everything back into the business, they were starting to pay tax because they couldn't spend their money prudently." Companies took greater risks or paid too much for land and wound up drilling dry holes in the process. "We [at Dome]," conceded Dunkley, "got sloppy in our exploration."[53]

Federal and provincial policies combined to drastically alter the economics of petroleum exploration in the 1970s because four factors—rising crude prices, growing inflation, a rapidly changing regulatory and royalty environment, and the perception that the reserves of the WCSB were in decline—made it cheaper for companies with adequate cash reserves to acquire production through mergers and acquisitions. For Canadian companies that continued to develop their own reserves, federal polices encouraged them to pursue the more expensive and technologically complex "frontier areas" of the Arctic and offshore Newfoundland and Nova Scotia, where production costs were substantially greater because of harsher environmental conditions and shorter drilling seasons. To pursue his Arctic dream, Dome Petroleum's Jack Gallagher assembled a team of naval architects and engineers to build thirty-three ships of various sizes and classes for a cool $600 million before drilling for a single barrel of oil from the Beaufort Sea. "If the gamble comes off," wrote *Maclean's* magazine, "Gallagher will have created in Canada an internationally ranked oil company. . . . If it fails, Gallagher's lifework could be endangered . . . and, incidentally, Canada's economic future will be that much bleaker."[54]

Despite record crude prices, the economics of the project remained dubious in the absence of significant subsidies that distorted markets and placed government in the position of picking winners and losers. In 1977, at the urging of Jack Gallagher, Ottawa introduced a federal tax incentive known as "super-depletion" to stimulate frontier exploration. Super-depletion allowed companies to write off 166.66 per cent of their expenses from gross income above the standard 33.33 per cent depletion allowance. Dome eventually struck oil at Kanopar in 1979, where it produced 12,000 barrels per day. But even with super-depletion the project remained uneconomical because production costs were prohibitively high, a point Gallagher later conceded. "When you have over $600 million up there which is inactive two-thirds of the year [this] drastically increases the costs." Dome's executives later estimated that each well drilled in the Arctic had to produce a minimum of 400 million barrels simply to break even.[55]

The apex of nationalization came in the aftermath of the second price shock in the wake of the 1978–9 Iranian Revolution, which resulted in the removal of a million daily barrels from world markets and created a panic that drove prices above $40 per barrel. Internationally, higher prices accelerated fears of shortages, raising the stakes for consuming states seeking to attain secure supplies. Polling completed for the Canadian Petroleum Association in the autumn of 1980 revealed that Canadians saw energy as the second most important issue confronting the nation after inflation. Half of Canadians thought the country would suffer energy shortages within a year and more than half were willing to pay more to secure energy supplies. The poll also clearly showed that Canadians trusted the federal government more than industry, with an overwhelming majority—75 per cent—favouring government regulation to increase Canadian control and ownership of the petroleum industry.[56] Combined with the return to power of Pierre Trudeau's Liberals after a short-lived Conservative minority government under Joe Clark, the October 1980 announcement of the NEP offered the prime minister one last chance to wrestle with the troublesome energy question, quell public fears about the energy crisis, and reassert diminished federal authority at the hands of the provinces.[57]Crafted in secret, and completed without consulting either the industry or the provincial governments, the NEP attempted a dramatic restructuring of industry economics, taxation, and operations. The NEP's formal unveiling as part of the federal budget on 26 October 1980 struck a defiantly nationalist tone, establishing three objectives for federal policy:

- It must establish the basis for Canadians to seize control of their own energy future through *security* of supply and ultimate independence from the world oil market.

- It must offer to Canadians, all Canadians, the real *opportunity* to participate in the energy industry in general and the petroleum industry in particular, and to share in the benefits of industry expansion.

- It must establish a petroleum pricing and revenue-sharing regime that recognizes the requirement of *fairness* to all Canadians no matter where they live.[58]

Anticipating oil shortages as early as 1985, and believing that world prices no longer reflected adherence to market fundamentals of supply and demand, the NEP announcement made it clear that "any country able to dissociate itself from the world oil market of the 1980s should do so, and quickly. Canada is one of the few that can."[59] At an estimated cost of $11.6 billion, the NEP promised to achieve energy self-sufficiency and create conditions to realize the government's goal of achieving at least 50 per cent Canadian ownership by 1990. Altogether, the Department of Energy, Mines and Resources anticipated that the bevy of new taxes and programs would generate at least $24 billion in revenues for the federal government.[60]

To generate greater revenues for the federal government, the NEP launched the Petroleum and Gas Revenue Tax (PGRT). Loathed in industry circles as little more than a royalty on gross revenue, the PGRT established a flat 8 per cent tax on operating revenues and eliminated deductions for exploration and development expenses.[61] Some funds would be returned to the industry via Petroleum Incentives Payments (PIP), but the PGRT would raise government revenues. Capitalized at $5 billion for the 1981–5 period, PIP grants replaced writeoffs of exploration costs and the earned depletion allowance (that included a further one-third of exploration and development costs against resource income up to 25 per cent) as the principal federal means of stimulating petroleum exploration, changing the industry's economics in the process. Prior to the NEP, profits from production typically financed exploration budgets—if a company was producing and selling oil and natural gas, it would invest in exploration. PIP grants became the chief means of stimulating exploration, and they rewarded businesses with at least 50 per cent Canadian ownership (as determined by the newly created Petroleum Monitoring Agency and enforced by FIRA) with payments equal to 10 per cent of costs for oil and gas exploration anywhere in Canada; the PIP increased to 35 per cent when the Canadian ownership level was 75 per cent or greater. The real incentive, however, lay in exploration and production on the frontiers, where all projects qualified for a 25 per cent PIP grant, but this increased to 80 per cent if the company was more than 74 per cent Canadian-owned, meaning that the government would spend "$4 for every $1 the firm is able to invest."[62]

To advance its nationalist agenda, and to administer the PIP grants, Ottawa created the Canada Oil and Gas Lands Administration (COGLA) to manage the approval process for exploration and development on the frontier projects like the Beaufort Sea and offshore Newfoundland and the Canadian Ownership Account (COA). COGLA regulations stipulated that exploration on federally controlled land be done with Canadian labour and equipment when possible and that companies had to have a minimum Canadian ownership of 50 per cent and effectively were the only way that the federal government could cap PIP expenditures that by 1983 were already $1 billion beyond projections.[63] The COA established taxes on all oil and gas consumption in Canada and would be "used solely to finance and increase of public ownership in the energy sector."[64] One of the most controversial nationalist measures, though, gave Petro-Canada an automatic 25 per cent ownership stake in projects undertaken on Crown lands.[65] In a nod to Canada's postwar legacy of multilateralism, the NEP allocated $250 million for the creation of Petro-Canada International to "seek joint-ventures opportunities with other state-owned oil companies in the western world." Toward that end, the government announced that preliminary discussions with Pemex in Mexico and PDVSA in Venezuela had already begun in pursuit of regional oil and gas development.[66] Unsurprisingly, given its explicitly nationalist aims and the incentives toward Canadianization, the NEP triggered a renewed round of industry mergers and acquisitions by Canadian oil companies, who believed they could buy oil in the ground cheaper than they could find it via exploration. They were also eager to capitalize on the new federal Canadianization incentives. A few months after the announcement of the NEP, Petro-Canada kicked off a fifteen-month industry-wide buying spree lasting from February 1981 to August 1982 in which it paid $1.7 billion to acquire Petrofina Canada, the subsidiary of Belgium's Petrofina S. A. Altogether, fourteen additional major mergers and acquisitions (valued at $43 million or more) took place at a total cost of $7.67 billion. Arguably, the frenzy of nationalist mergers and acquisitions climaxed with Dome Canada's $2 billion purchase of Connecticut-based Conoco's 53 per cent stake of Hudson's Bay Oil and Gas (HBOG) in the summer of 1981. While most media and public attention focused on the majors, hundreds of independents operating in the Canadian oil patch also got in on the act, "farming-in" (paying a portion of exploration costs) on lands controlled by foreign-owned firms.[67] Most of the buyouts were paid for in US dollars, financed on the basis of short-term loans, or, in the case of Petro-Canada and the Canadian Development Corporation, taxpayer money. The sheer volume of acquisitions drove up inflation and resulted in the devaluation of the Canadian dollar that, five years before, in 1976, traded at par with the US greenback. By mid-1981, however, just as the orgy of Canadianization reached a crescendo with Dome's acquisition of Conoco's stake in HBOG, the value of the Canadian dollar plunged to $0.76 against the US dollar and the inflation rate hit 12.9 per cent. The grim news prompted Finance Minister Alan MacEachen to instruct Canadian banks to stop lending to oil companies hoping to finance further mergers and acquisitions.[68] To restore flagging confidence in the Canadian dollar, the Bank of Canada raised interest rates in August 1981 to a staggering 21.03 per cent—its highest level in history—and the Canadian government borrowed from the banks to back the dollar.[69]

The NEP also kick-started negotiations between the federal and provincial governments to reach a new agreement on pricing and revenue sharing signed by Lougheed and Trudeau on 1 September 1981. The agreement forecast that world crude prices would rise and established the base price of "made in Canada" oil—by fiat—at $16.75 per barrel, approximately 85 per cent of world levels. Over the next decade, the deal projected crude prices would increase 13 per cent a year to reach $67 per barrel by 1 July 1990. Ottawa and Edmonton fully expected the deal would produce oil and gas revenues of $212.8 billion dollars over its five-year term. But instead of rising, world crude prices began declining months later in March 1982 when OPEC cut its prices by $5 per barrel. Globally, petroleum consumption reached 63.1 million daily barrels in 1980 before declining to 58.7 million in 1983 as a result of more effective conservation measures and the beginning of a recession in the Western economies in 1982. Furthermore, overproduction, both by OPEC and non-OPEC producers, resulted in a sizable glut on the world market, placing gradual downward pressure on prices until the elimination of supply overhangs.[70]

The decision to divorce Canadian oil from world prices and encourage development of the energy frontiers produced different problems. The federal government discovered that estimates for the PIP grants severely underestimated costs. The June 1982 budget saw the federal deficit climb to $19.6 billion, $9.1 billion over the $10.5 billion deficit forecast just seven months earlier.[71] As world crude prices declined, the gap between world and domestic prices widened, making frontier projects envisioned to provide future supplies unprofitable. By early 1983, the "made in Canada" price of $43.88 per barrel for "new oil" proved substantially higher than the world market price of $29 per barrel. Moreover, federal restrictions on oil exports to the United States transformed Canada from a net oil exporter to a net importer by 1976.[72] Between 1972 and 1984, Canadian oil dropped from supplying 50 per cent of US crude imports to about 7 per cent. Because softening world crude prices made imports cheaper for Canadian consumers, the combination effectively shut in Alberta oil. In a period when the NEP forecast supply shortfalls and promised to make Canada energy self-sufficient, Alberta's crude production declined every year between 1980 and 1982, when production totals were 20.6 per cent lower than those in 1979. Daily production increased slightly to 1.03 million barrels in 1984 before dropping to 914,722 barrels in 1986.[73]

Meanwhile, the wave of industry nationalizations in 1981 transformed the energy crisis into a financial one because of the investment decisions of Canada's major banks to finance Canadianization. Dome financed its post-NEP expansion with high-interest short-term loans, and by early

1982 Dome faced the prospect of paying off a crippling debt of $6.3 billion to creditors with few liquid assets or revenue sources, transforming the issue of Dome's survival from an energy question to one implicating the solvency of Canada's financial system because three of Canada's big banks—Toronto Dominion, the Bank of Montreal, and the Commerce— each loaned Dome over $1 billion. If the company defaulted on those loans, policy-makers feared it might bring down the nation's banking system. Facing few good alternatives, the federal government contributed $500 million to a $1 billion bailout package that also forced Jack Gallagher to step down as Dome's chairman in 1983.[74]

Perhaps the greatest irony of Trudeau's nationalization program was that it found itself increasingly at odds with emerging economic policies in the United Kingdom and the United States that reasserted interdependence and globalization after state interventions in the economy failed to slay the twin demons of stagnant economic growth and inflation. Starting with the 1979 election of Margaret Thatcher, followed by Ronald Reagan's inauguration as president in 1981, the neoliberal revolution revivified global capitalism. Characterized by reduced taxes, privatization of state-run enterprises, cutbacks to public-sector spending, the pursuit of free trade, and deregulation, the policies pursued by the US and UK governments during this period kick-started two and a half decades of unprecedented economic expansion. Bowing to the reality that federal energy policies failed to achieve their objectives, in July 1984, the new Canadian prime minister, John Turner, announced that the federal government would re-examine aspects of the NEP. Accordingly, it began dismantling the unpopular program months before the 17 September federal election brought Brian Mulroney's Progressive Conservatives to power. Armed with a more pragmatic neoliberal approach than either Prime Minister Thatcher or President Reagan, Mulroney nevertheless advocated a free market approach and a liberalized trade agenda that emphasized improved relations with the United States, accessing greater volumes of international capital, and reliance on market forces to allocate resources.[75]

Conservative energy policies predated Mulroney's election when energy critic Pat Carney began consulting with industry groups to help formulate the Conservative's oil and gas policies. Mulroney's Conservatives sought to reduce the role of government, re-establish investor confidence, and ensure equity of prices and supply.[76] The Western Accord (June 1985) deregulated oil and gas pricing established during the Trudeau years, replaced the PIP grants with tax incentives available to any company, and abolished export restrictions adopted during the oil shocks.[77] Gone were the more overtly nationalist overtones of FIRA; in its stead came Investment Canada, with its mandate to attract foreign investment and capital.[78]

The path pushing Canada toward interdependence and globalization passed, once again, through the United States. In 1984, even after the nationalist interventions of the previous decade, 75.6 per cent of Canadian exports went to the United States and the Liberal government initiated a study by Donald Macdonald that concluded that Canadians would benefit greatly from reducing trade barriers with the United States. Negotiations began between Canadian and American representatives toward a free trade agreement in May 1986. Ratification of the Canada-US Free Trade Agreement (CUFTA) in 1988 signalled the formal transformation of North American energy markets to interdependence, with market forces lowering transaction costs, reducing the need for lengthy hearings, and determining both prices and the volume of trade.[79] Significantly, the energy provisions within the CUFTA provided Canadian energy producers with security of market while simultaneously guaranteeing the United States security of supply. Perhaps most important of all in the aftermath of the NEP, the agreement prevented either government from enacting discriminatory measures against the other. Further steps included the privatization of Petro-Canada in 1990. As a result, the United States began importing ever-larger volumes of crude oil and natural gas from Canada. Access to American markets fuelled the expansion of the Canadian industry. Canada tripled the volume of oil exported to the United States between 1985 and 2007, becoming the single largest exporter of crude oil to the United States in 2004. Meanwhile, over the same period, natural gas exports quadrupled and supplied approximately 16.5 per cent of US annual natural gas demand.[80]

Clearly, the globalization and integration of the Canadian and US petroleum industries was far from straightforward. Certainly, proximity, cross-border ties, shared values and beliefs, as well as common institutions and regulatory frameworks, made integration easier, but they did

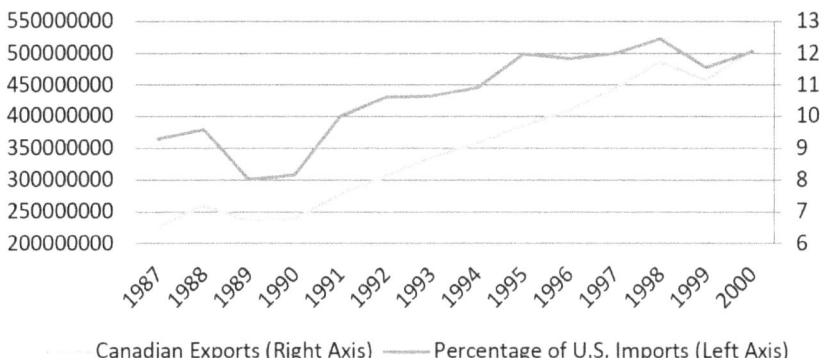

Figure 8.2 US Imports of Canadian Crude, 1987–2000 (bbl)

not make it inevitable, or, I hasten to add, permanent. At crucial points—like with the import quota programs of the 1950s or the Canadianization drive of the 1970s—one state or the other stepped back from further integration. Current petroleum policies, buffeted as they are by domestic affairs, developments within the global industry, technological change, and environmental concerns, are bound to remain dynamic.

NOTES

1   Ralph Hidy and Muriel Hidy, *Pioneering in Big Business, 1882–1911*, vol. 1 of *The History of Standard Oil Company (New Jersey)* (New York: Harper, 1955), 463–4; George Sweet Gibb and Evelyn H. Knowlton, *The Resurgent Years, 1911–1927*, vol. 2 of *The History of Standard Oil Company (New Jersey)* (New York: Harper & Brothers, 1956), 195–6; Graham Taylor, "From Branch Operation to Integrated Subsidiary: The Reorganization of Imperial Oil under Walter Teagle, 1911–1917," *Business History* 34, no. 3 (1992): 51; J. D. House, "The Social organization of Multinational Corporations: Canadian Subsidiaries in the Oil Industry," *Canadian Review of Social Anthropology*, 14, no. 1 (January 1977): 5–6; Oliver Knight, "Oil: Canada's New Wealth," *Business History Review* 30, no. 3 (1956): 306.

2   Hubert Somerville, interview by S. A. Kerr, 19 July 1984, Glenbow Archives ("GA" hereafter), Petroleum Industry Oral History Project fonds ("POH" hereafter), interview RCT-657 (GAPOH Hubert Somerville). (Interviews from this project will appear in shortened citations with the initials "GAPOH" and the interviewee's name.)

3   GAPOH Hubert Somerville; James Bamberg, *British Petroleum and Global Oil, 1950-1975: The Challenge of Nationalism* (Cambridge: Cambridge University Press, 2000), 126.

4   Gibb and Knowlton, *The Resurgent Years, 1911-1927*, 251; Michael Bliss, *Northern Enterprise: Five Centuries of Canadian Business* (Toronto: McClelland & Stewart, 1987); John Herd Thompson and Stephen J. Randall, *Canada and the United States: Ambivalent Allies*, 4th ed. (Montreal: McGill-Queens University Press, 2008); W. B. Whitham, "Les investissements américains et les origines de l'industrie pétrolière canadiennne," *Actualité économique* 44, no. 4 (January–March 1969): 702; Bamberg, *British Petroleum and Global Oil*, 100, 125-9; Stephen Howarth and Joost Jonker, *Powering the Hydrocarbon Revolution, 1939-1973*, vol. 2 of *A History of Royal Dutch Shell* (Oxford: Oxford University Press, 2007); Tammy Lynne Nemeth, "Canada-U.S. Oil and Gas Relations, 1958 to 1974," (PhD diss., University of British Columbia, 2007), 32.

5   Sandy Gow, *Roughnecks, Rock Bits, and Rigs: The Evolution of Oil Well Drilling Technology in Alberta, 1883-1970* (Calgary: University of Calgary Press, 2006).

6   Dale Jordan, "Evolution of Alberta's Petroleum and Natural Gas Land Regulations," *Journal of Canadian Petroleum Technology* 20, no. 2 (1981): 102.

7   GAPOH Hubert Somerville; Douglas Layer, interview by Nadine Mackenzie, 12 July 1983, GA, POH, interview RCT-521 (GAPOH Doug Layer).

8   Earle Gray, *The Great Canadian Oil Patch*, 2nd ed. (Toronto: June Warren Publishing, 2005), 133.

9   GAPOH Doug Layer.

10 Francisco Para, *Oil Politics: A Modern History of Petroleum* (London: I. B. Taurus, 2003), 33; Daniel Yergin, *The Prize: The Epic Quest for Oil, Money and Power* (New York: Simon & Schuster, 1992), 499-500.

11 Norman Hillmer and J. L. Granatstein, *Empire to Umpire: Canada and the World to the 1990s* (Toronto: Copp-Clark Longman, 1994), 194-6; Michael Hart, *A Trading Nation: Canadian Trade Policy from Colonialism to Globalization* (Vancouver: UBC Press, 2003), 148; Thompson and Randall, *Ambivalent Allies*, 186-95.

12 Thomas W. Zeiler, "Opening Doors in the World Economy," in *Global Interdependence: The World after 1945*, ed. Akira Iriye (Cambridge, MA: Belknap Press of Harvard University, 2014), 213; Dimitry Anastakis, "Multilateralism, Nationalism and Bilateral Free Trade: Competing Visions of Canadian Economic and Trade Policy, 1945-70," in *Creating Postwar Canada: Community, Diversity, and Dissent, 1945-75*, ed. Magda Fahrni and Robert Rutherdale (Vancouver: UBC Press, 2008), 137-61.

13 *The Financial Post Survey of Oils, 1949* (Montreal: Maclean-Hunter Publishing, 1949), 33.

14   Aubrey Kerr, *Redwater* (Winnipeg: Kromar Printing, 1994), 9.

15   GAPOH Doug Layer; David H. Breen, *Alberta's Petroleum Industry and the Conservation Board* (Edmonton: University of Alberta Press, 1993), 250; Aubrey Kerr, *Leduc* (Altona, AB: Friesen Printers, 1991), 21–32.

16   Breen, *Alberta's Petroleum Industry*, 250; Kerr, *Leduc*, 21–32; Alberta Geological Survey, *Geological Atlas of the Western Canada Sedimentary Basin* (Edmonton: Canadian Society of Petroleum Geologists-Alberta Research Council, 1994).

17   "Public Relations Aspects of the Leduc Oil Discovery," February 1948, GA, Imperial Oil Limited fonds (IOL), IOLpub-1a-3.

18   Robert Bothwell, Ian Drummond, and John English, *Canada since 1945*, rev. ed. (Toronto: University of Toronto Press, 1993), 61; Kenneth Norrie, Douglas Owram, and J. C. Herbert Emery, *A History of the Canadian Economy*, 4th ed. (Toronto: Nelson, 2008).

19   Larry Kohler, "Canadian/American Oil Diplomacy: The Adjustment of Conflicting National Oil Policies, 1955–1973" (PhD diss., Johns Hopkins University, 1983), 98; Gray, *Great Canadian Oil Patch*, 249; Alvin Finkel, *The Social Credit Phenomenon in Alberta* (Toronto: University of Toronto Press, 1989), 116–117; Allan MacFadyen and G. Campbell Watkins, *Petropolitics: Petroleum Development, Markets and Regulations, Alberta as an Illustrative History* (Calgary: University of Calgary Press, 2014), 111–12.

20   Breen, *Alberta's Petroleum Industry*, 571.

21   Ray Tull, interview by Susan Birley, January 1985, GA, POH, interview RCT-682 (GAPOH Ray Tull).

22   Gow, *Roughnecks*, 75.

23   Charlie Dunkley, interview by Susan Birley, 14 May 1984, GA, POH, interview RCT-658 (GAPOH Charlie Dunkley).

24   Knight, "Oil: Canada's New Wealth," 302; Breen, *Alberta's Petroleum Industry*, 571; Gow, *Roughnecks*, 75.

25   Kenneth H. Norrie, "A Regional Economic Overview of the West since 1945," in *The Making of the Modern West: Western Canada since 1945*, ed. A. W. Rasporich (Calgary: University of Calgary Press, 1984), 64.

26   Breen, *Alberta's Petroleum Industry*, 251–68; GAPOH Hubert Somerville.

27   Doug Owram, "1951: Oil's Magic Wand," in *Alberta Formed: Alberta Transformed*, ed. Michael Payne, Donald Wetherell, and Catherine Cavanaugh (Calgary: University of Calgary Press, 2006), 2:567.

28   Canadian Association of Petroleum Producers (CAPP), "Annual Statistical Review"; John J. Barr, "The Impact of Oil on Alberta: Retrospect and Prospect," in *The Making of the Modern West: Western Canada since 1945*, ed. A. W. Rasporich (Calgary: University of Calgary Press, 1984), 98.

29   John N. McDougall, *Fuels and the National Policy* (Toronto: Butterworths, 1982), 56–65; Henrietta M. Larson, Evelyn H. Knowlton, and Charles S. Popple, *New Horizons: 1927–1950* (New York: Harper and Row, 1971), 744–6.

30 Privy Council Office, *Royal Commission on Energy—Second Report* (Ottawa: Privy Council Office, 1959), 15, 27; Theodore Binnema, "Making Way for Canadian Oil: United States Policy, 1947–1959," *Alberta History* 45, no. 3 (1997): 17; G. Bruce Doern and Glen B. Toner, *The Politics of Energy: The Development and Implementation of the NEP* (Toronto: Methuen, 1985), 71; Stephen J. Randall, *United States Foreign Oil Policy since World War I: For Profits and Security* (Montreal: McGill-Queen's University Press, 2005), 256, 266; Gray, *Great Canadian Oil Patch*, 262; Nemeth, "Canada-U.S. Oil and Gas Relations," 37, 86.

31 Carl Nickle, "Western Canada's Oil and Gas: Part of Canada's Progress, and North America's Security," Address to Society of Petroleum Engineers Annual Meeting, San Francisco, 16 February 1959 (in author's possession).

32 J. P. Gallagher, interview by Nadine Mackenzie, 10 May 1984, GAPOH, interview RCT 612-1 (GAPOH J. P. Gallagher); J. P. Gallagher, "Proposals for a More Prosperous Canada: Excerpts from an Address to the Canadian Society of New York, January 18, 1979" (New York: Dome Petroleum Limited, 1979).

33 GAPOH Charlie Dunkley.

34 Statistics Canada, "G227-243 Foreign Direct Investment in Canada All Countries and by Major Areas, By Industry, Selected Year Ends, 1926–1974," https://www.statcan.gc.ca/pub/11-516-x/sectiong/G227_243b-eng.csv.

35 Letter from the Director of the Office of Defense Mobilization (Flemming) to the Oil Importing Companies, Washington, 29 October 1955, in *Foreign Relations of the United States, 1955–1957*, vol. 10, *Foreign Aid and Economic Defense Policy* [henceforth cited as *FRUS*], ed. Robert J. McMahon, William F. Sanford, and Sherrill B. Wells (Washington, DC: US Government Printing Office, 1989), document 207; Memorandum for the Files, by the Officer in Charge of Economic Organization Affairs, Office of European Regional Affairs (Moline), 9 December 1957, in *FRUS, 1955–1957*, vol. 10, document 280.

36 Breen, *Alberta's Petroleum Industry*, 422.

37 CAPP, "Annual Statistical Review."

38 CAPP, "Wells and Metres Drilled in Western Canada, 1947–2005."

39 "History of Refineries 1950" (unpublished manuscript, 1950), GA, IOL, IOLpub-1a-5; CAPP, "Table 5.1. Western Canada Average Prices of Crude Oil and Natural Gas"; British Petroleum, *Statistical Review of World Energy, 2015* (London: British Petroleum, 2015).

40 Memorandum from the Assistant Secretary of State for Economic Affairs (Waugh) to the Chairman of the Council on Foreign Economic Policy (Dodge), Washington, 16 March 1955, in *FRUS, 1955–1957*, vol. 10, document 198; Minutes of a Cabinet Meeting, Laurel Cottage, Camp David, Maryland, 22 November 1955, in *FRUS, 1955–1957*, vol. 10. document 210; Richard H. K. Vietor, *Energy Policy in America since 1945: A Study of Government-Business Relations* (Cambridge: Cambridge University Press, 1984), 104.

41 Memorandum from the Secretary of the Council on Foreign Economic Policy (Cullen) to the Chairman of the Council (Randall), 18 December 1958, in *FRUS, 1958–1960*, vol.

4, *Foreign Economic Policy*, ed. Suzanne E. Coffman, Edward C. Keefer, and Harriet Dashiell Schwar (Washington, DC: US Government Printing Office, 1992), document 290.

42 McDougall, *Fuels and the National Policy*, 80.

43 CAPP, "Statistical Handbook 2014," and author's calculations; Nemeth, "Canada-U.S. Oil and Gas Relations," 233.

44 Robert N. McRae, "A Survey of Canadian Energy Policy, 1974–1983," *Energy Journal* 6, no. 4 (1985): 49–64.

45 Richard Nixon, "Address to a Joint Meeting of the Canadian Parliament, April 14, 1972," The American Presidency Project, https://www.presidency.ucsb.edu/node/254646 (accessed 8 February 2021).

46 Doern and Toner, *The Politics of Energy*, 131.

47 Department of Energy, Mines and Resources (DEMR), *National Energy Program 1980* (Ottawa: Energy, Mines and Resources Canada, 1980), 8.

48 "Tax Measures to Stimulate Oil and Gas Activity in Canada," 17 December 1982, GA, Independent Petroleum Association of Canada fonds (IPAC), Box 105, File 1621; MacFadyen and Watkins, *Petropolitics*, 251–64; Dean Goodermote and Richard B. Mancke, "Nationalizing Oil in the 1970s," *Energy Journal* 4, no. 4 (October 1983): 67–80; John English, *Just Watch Me: The Life of Pierre Elliott Trudeau, 1968–2000* (Toronto: Knopf Canada, 2009), 224–7; DEMR, *An Energy Strategy for Canada: Policies for Self-Reliance* (Ottawa: Energy, Mines and Resources Canada, 1976), 27.

49 Jeffry A. Frieden, *Global Capitalism: Its Fall and Rise in the Twentieth Century* (New York: W. W. Norton, 2006), 366.

50 DEMR, *An Energy Strategy for Canada*, 27.

51 Richard Nixon, "Address to the Nation about National Energy Policy, November 25, 1973," The American Presidency Project, https://www.presidency.ucsb.edu/node/255623 (accessed 8 February 2021).

52 Henry Trim, "Planning for the Future: The Conserver Society and Canadian Sustainability," *Canadian Historical Review* 96, no. 3 (September 2015): 375–404; Paul Chastko, *Developing Alberta's Oil Sands: From Karl Clark to Kyoto* (Calgary: University of Calgary Press, 2004).

53 GAPOH Charlie Dunkley.

54 David Crane, "Capturing the Benefits of Our Oil, Gas," *Toronto Star*, 16 December 1987, A27; Peter Bakogeorge, "Dome Petroleum Started with Modest Resources and . . ." *CanWest News*, 8 June 1988, 1; "Dome, Oil, and the Arctic: Tales of a True Believer," *Maclean's*, 27 June 1977, 43.

55 Peter Foster, *The Sorcerer's Apprentices: Canada's Superbureaucrats and the Energy Mess* (Toronto: Collins, 1982), 219; GAPOH J. P. Gallagher, RCT-612-3; Anthony McCallum, "Dome, Panarctic Sold on Frontier's Prospects," *Globe and Mail*, 8 March 1982, R3.

56 Discussion Paper #3, "Banff Planning Session October 23, 1983: The Selling of the National Energy Program and a Marketing Approach for the Alternative Oil and Gas Policy," GA, Canadian Petroleum Association fonds (CPA), Box 106, File 1623, 3.

57 English, *Just Watch Me*, 545–6.

58 DEMR, *National Energy Program 1980*, 2; emphasis in the original.

59 DEMR, *National Energy Program 1980*, 7.

60 DEMR, *National Energy Program 1980*, 89, 112.

61 DEMR, *National Energy Program 1980*, 38.

62 DEMR, *National Energy Program 1980*, 39–41, 96, 103, 108.

63 G. Bruce Doern, "The Liberals and the Opposition: Ideas, Priorities and the Imperatives of Governing Canada in the 1980s," in G. Bruce Doern, ed., *How Ottawa Spends: The Liberals, the Opposition & Federal Priorities, 1983* (Toronto: James Lorimer & Company, 1983), 27–9.

64 DEMR, *National Energy Program 1980*, 51.

65 DEMR, *National Energy Program 1980*, 47.

66 DEMR, *National Energy Program 1980*, 53.

67 DEMR, *National Energy Program Update 1982* (Ottawa: Energy, Mines and Resources Canada, 1982), 48.

68 "Historical Spot Exchange Rates for USD to CAD," PoundSterling Live, https://www.poundsterlinglive.com/bank-of-england-spot/historical-spot-exchange-rates/usd/USD-to-CAD (accessed 10 February 2021); "Inflation Canada 1981," Inflation.eu, https://www.inflation.eu/inflation-rates/canada/historic-inflation/cpi-inflation-canada-1981.aspx (accessed 10 February 2021); Irving Lutsky, "Canadian Dollar Hits 50-year Low," *Washington Post*, 1 August 1981; Foster, *The Sorcerer's Apprentices*, 159.

69 Bank of Canada, "Selected Historical Interest Rates, 1935–," https://www.bankofcanada.ca/wp-content/uploads/2010/09/selected_historical_v122530.pdf (accessed 10 February 2021).

70 Energy Information Agency, "International Energy Statistics," https://www.eia.gov/beta/international/data/browser/#/?c=4100000002000060000000000000g000200000000000000001&vs=INTL.44-1-AFRC-QBTU.A&vo=0&v=H&end=2015 (accessed 10 February 2021).

71 Alan MacEachen, "The Budget," 28 June 1982 (Ottawa: Department of Finance, 1982), 4, available at http://publications.gc.ca/collections/collection_2016/fin/F1-23-3-1982-eng.pdf.

72 DEMR, *National Energy Program 1980*, 8.

73 CAPP, "Statistical Handbook 2014."

74 Paul Taylor, "Investors Wary but Some Analysts Like Dome Canada," *Globe and Mail*, 17 May 1982, B11; Jennifer Lewington, "Dome Problems Evident in SEC Filing," *Globe and Mail*, 27 May 1982, B9; Doern, *How Ottawa Spends 1983*, 26; Peter Foster, *Other*

People's Money: The Banks, the Government and Dome (Toronto: Collins, 1983), 120–4; Adam Mayers, "Here's How Toppled Giant Tried to Rise from the Financial Dead," *Toronto Star*, 25 July 1987, C1.

75   Denis Stairs, "Architects or Engineers? The Conservatives and Foreign Policy," in *Diplomatic Departures: The Conservative Era in Canadian Foreign Policy, 1984-1993*, ed. Nelson Michaud and Kim Richard Nossal (Vancouver: UBC Press, 2001), 29; David Pollock and Grant Manuge, "The Mulroney Doctrine," *International Perspectives*, January–February 1985, 5.

76   Tammy Lynn Nemeth, "Pat Carney and the Dismantling of the National Energy Program" (MA thesis, University of Alberta, 1997), 61–2.

77   Stairs, "Architects or Engineers?," 31.

78   Nemeth, "Pat Carney," 87–123; David Finch, *Pumped: Everyone's Guide to the Oil Patch* (Calgary: Fifth House, 2008), 79.

79   André Plourde, "The Changing Nature of National and Continental Energy Markets," in *Canadian Energy Policy and the Struggle for Sustainable Development*, ed. G. Bruce Doern (Toronto: University of Toronto Press, 2005), 51, 56.

80   Monica Gattinger, "Canada-United States Energy Relations: From Domestic to North American Energy Policies," in *Policy: From Ideas to Implementation, in Honour of Professor G. Bruce Doern*, ed. Glen Toner, Leslie A. Pal, and Michael J. Prince (Montreal: McGill-Queens University Press, 2010), 210–11; Energy Information Agency, "International Energy Statistics," https://www.eia.gov/beta/international/data/browser/#/?c=4100000002000060000000000000g000200000000000000001&vs=INTL.44-1-AFRC-QBTU.A&vo=0&v=H&end=2015 (accessed 10 February 2021).

The New Political Economy of Petroleum in Brazil: Back to the Future?

Gail D. Triner

One of the most important recent changes to the energy scenario in the Americas has been the discovery of large reserves of petroleum in the pre-salt layer of the Atlantic Ocean bed off the coast of Brazil. These reserves have the possibility to significantly improve material conditions for the Brazilian population. The subject of petroleum within Brazilian political economy has always been highly fraught. During the 1970s and '80s, Brazil was the largest oil importer among developing countries. Subsequently, discoveries of large offshore deposits nurtured the probability of oil self-sufficiency. The more recent confirmation of the pre-salt deposits has encouraged the expectation that the nation could emerge in the twenty-first century as an important exporter. Along a parallel trajectory, in the 1990s the Brazilian political economy regime underwent a fundamental transition, from the highly managed protectionist and state-directed system that prevailed from the 1940s to one of relative openness to global markets. The transition entailed important changes in the economic role of the state. This chapter argues that the pre-salt petroleum sector demonstrates the fragility of macroeconomic regime change.[1]

Globally, the "resource curse," or the inability to use natural-resource-derived wealth to generate broadly based and sustained economic growth, has most strongly attached to oil.[2] Three characteristics define this curse: Dutch disease, rent-seeking, and the diversion of externalities from natural resources to specific economic actors. "Dutch disease" refers to structural shifts that favour the production and export of raw commodities (in this case, petroleum) to the detriment of domestic (industrial) sectors of the economy because of the increasing value of local currency as global revenues enter the economy. In the modern literature, this process results in deindustrialization.[3] Extraction of profits in excess of "normal" profits, necessary to maintain investment, defines rent-seeking. Finally, the positive externalities (or "spillover effects") creating opportunities that could accrue beyond petroleum producers to generate technological growth and profits to support industries can respond to market conditions, or industrial policy can direct the beneficiaries and distort costs.

With respect to other commodities, Brazilians do not have a history of escaping the resource curse. Periodic generation of wealth from the production of primary commodities—sugar, coffee, rubber, iron ore, soybeans, etc.—has not contributed to widely distributed and sustained well-being among the population. The transition during the 1990s toward an open economy would lead theorists to expect the Brazilian government to mitigate the effects of the resource curse, at least with respect to the incentives to control rent-seeking and manage externalities. The shift from treating petroleum as a protected and centrally managed good to a market-driven commodity proceeded relatively smoothly in Brazil during the 1990s and first decade of the twenty-first century, until the discovery of the pre-salt deposits. While it is too early to know with confidence if Brazil will suffer from Dutch disease with respect to petroleum, some analysts have noted an association between deindustrialization and the recent export booms.[4] This chapter focuses on actions that have been central to rent-seeking and industrial policy, with a time frame that continues through the first decade of the twenty-first century.[5]

Straddling the lines between historical and policy analysis, the chapter analyzes the political-economic history of petroleum in Brazil in order to examine the emerging rules of petroleum governance. It concludes that recent governance reforms have changed the actors and permissible actions without mitigating the deeply entrenched ambitions that originally governed the structure of the sector: energy security, sophisticated industrialization, national control of the industry, and public-sector financial gains. As petroleum wealth has loomed larger on the Brazilian horizon, nationalist industrial policies have re-emerged and explicit rent-seeking has consumed much energy in the midst of inconsistent reconciliation of governing rules.[6] Brazil is not unique in generating inconsistencies in governance because of potential natural resource wealth. Neither is petroleum unique within Brazil as a venue for governance struggles. Its importance derives from the potential size of the sector and the depth of its implications for the Brazilian economy.

Petroleum and the State in Brazil, Updated

Petroleum policy was in place long before the discovery of oil. Small deposits in the province of Bahia in 1864 were of interest for their potential in the manufacture of kerosene, mostly for lighting.[7] Active exploration began in 1892, and industrial ambitions motivated further interest. Petroleum arose as a national issue in the early 1930s. The political rhetoric of national sovereignty with respect to control and ownership shaped the controversy that surrounded oil. Brazil's history as a commodity-export-producing colony, along with its subsequent vulnerability to global demand trends and reliance on imports for manufactured goods, provided the backstory that justified "economic nationalism." Framing its importance in terms of national defence and economic security,[8] the Brazilian military and industrial sectors sought a means to finance petroleum exploration. They based their arguments for direct state participation on the externalities of petroleum development. The substance was necessary to fuel the large-scale modern industrial sector that was integral to their concept of Brazil's future. This perspective assumed the status of accepted wisdom at the highest levels of government. In 1939, President Vargas announced that "It remains for us now to industrialize petroleum and install large steel, which we will do soon. . . . Iron, coal and petroleum are the mainstays of any country's economic emancipation."[9] These ideas underpinned the state's role within the petroleum sector.

In 1953, the Petroleum Law provided for the formation of Petróleo Brasileiro S. A. (Petrobras) with public-sector capital; the law also mandated national control.[10] This solution to the nagging concerns over the need to provide support for industry consolidated strategies of state-driven economic nationalism.[11] The state stepped in to substitute for private-sector capital of foreign or domestic origin.[12] Petrobras based its legitimacy on the state's claims to property rights to extracted oil and the firm-ownership model of earlier state-owned enterprises (overwhelming ownership and control by the federal government, but organized as limited liability companies with shares tradable on the Brazilian stock exchange).[13] Petrobras became a central player in an activist growth strategy that relied on import substitution industrialization. The firm had three functions within this strategy. First, it was responsible for maintaining the supply of petroleum for the Brazilian economy. Second, by virtue of the price differential between imported crude and refined petroleum derivatives, Petrobras refineries provided significant foreign exchange savings for an economy in chronic deficit. Finally, externalities of the petroleum sector spurred further industrial development through both the local demand that Petrobras generated for industrial goods and the physical infrastructure that the firm constructed. The anticipated externalities included directing the supply and allocation of petroleum at government-regulated prices and advancing industrialization by creating domestic demand for sophisticated manufactured products for its own operations. Through most of the twentieth century, the goals of petroleum policy were to support growth and minimize the financial drain and economic vulnerability of oil's prominence in the total basket of imports (see figure 9.1). Until the discovery of offshore deposits in the 1970s, Petrobras focused on refining, domestic distribution, and international expansion to secure supply, while serving as a conduit for national industrial policy.

Two factors fundamentally reshaped Brazilian ambitions within the petroleum sector. The energy crises of the 1970s highlighted the benefit of energy independence at the same time that Brazilians were discovering rich offshore deposits of petroleum. The global oil shocks of 1973–4 and 1978–9 reoriented the political economy of petroleum in Brazil.[14] Global petroleum embargoes, with associated price increases, escalated the cost of continued reliance on imports (see figure 9.2). Nevertheless, the Brazilian state continued its aggressive industrial policy. The resulting increase of sovereign debt and deterioration of balance of payments generated by oil price increases motivated new strategies for oil policy. Domestic

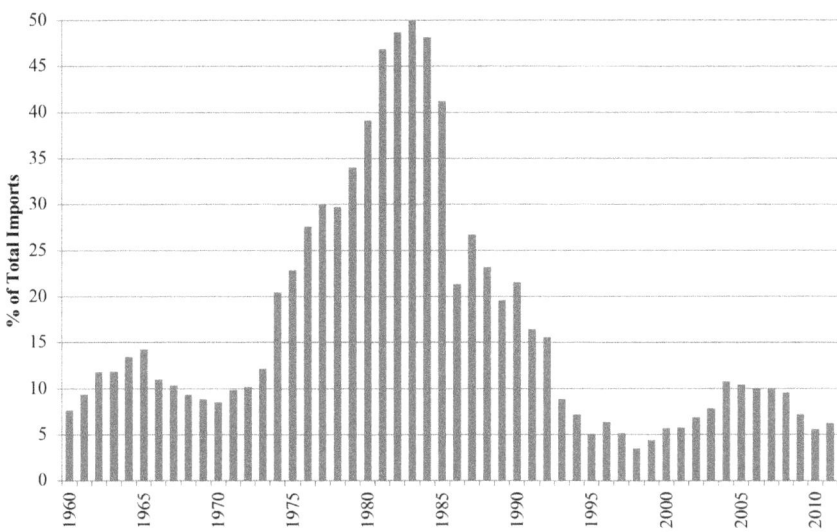

Figure 9.1 Crude Petroleum Imports (Value) % of Total, 1960–2011

Source: UN Comtrade, http://comtrade.un.org, and UN Statistical Office, *International Trade Statistics Yearbook* (New York: United Nations, various years).

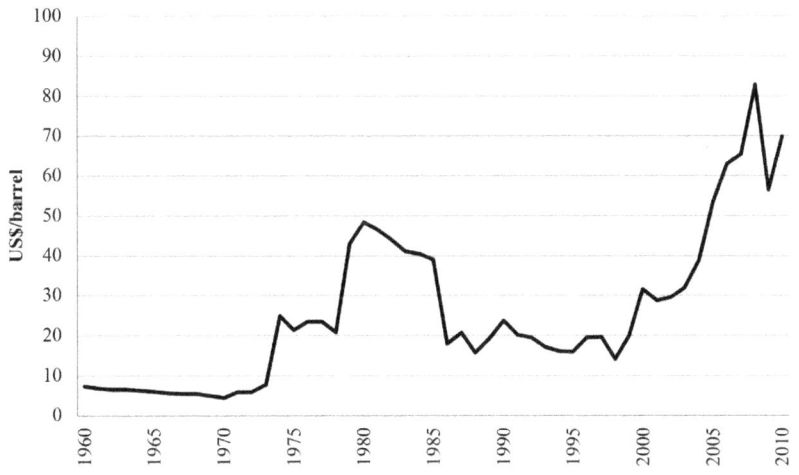

Figure 9.2 World Petroleum Prices, 1960–2010 Real (2005)

Source: World Bank Open Data, https://data.worldbank.org/

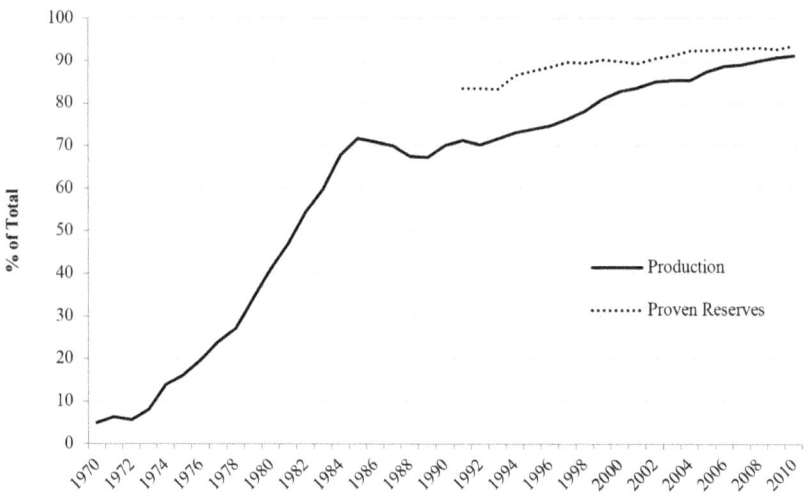

Figure 9.3 Oil Production and Reserves, % from Offshore, 1970–2010

Sources: Instituto Brasileiro de Geografia e Estatística and Conselho Nacional de Estatística, *Anuário Estatístico do Brasil* (Brasília: Imprensa Nacional, various years).

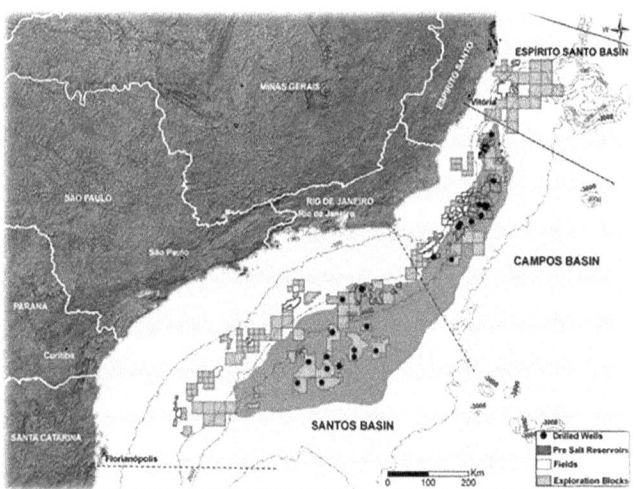

Figure 9.4 Offshore and Pre-salt Petroleum Reserves in Brazil

Source: "Brazil: Petrobras Discovers Oil in BM-S-17 Santos Basin Block," *Energypedia News*, 16 December 2009.

Table 9.1 Global Petroleum Reserves (Year-End 2009; Billions Barrels of Oil Equivalent)

Global Petroleum Reserves	
(year-end 2009; billions barrels of oil equivalent)	
Brazil	106
Pre-salt	90
Other	16
Top 5 Producers (2009)	
Saudi Arabia	264.6
Venezuela	172.3
Iran	137.6
Iraq	115
Kuwait	101.5
Total, Top 5	791
Brazil, % Top 5	**13.4**

Sources: Agência Nacional de Petróleo, *Anuário Estatístico* (Rio de Janeiro: Agência Nacional de Petróleo, 2014), table 1.1; Paulo César Ribeiro Lima, *Pré-Sal: O novo marco legal e a capitalização da Petrobras* (Rio de Janeiro: Synergia Editora, 2011), for the estimate of 2009 pre-salt reserves.

exploration regained priority status in national energy policy. Petrobras found new reserves in the early 1970s, primarily in offshore locations (see figure 9.4), and new wells began operation throughout the decade.[15] State investment in exploration activities tripled between 1973 and 1979.[16] With time, Brazilian oil deposits proved richest in offshore locations. Subsequently, production more than tripled from 1979 to 1987. Offshore production rose from less than 6 per cent of total production in 1970 to 91 per cent in 2009 (see figure 9.3).

Petrobras confirmed its discovery of pre-salt deposits in 2007. The newly discovered reserves have created the opportunity for an additional commodity to assume a major role within the domestic economy. The pre-salt deposits have transformed the goal of self-sufficiency into an expectation of a strong new source of export revenues. At the time, the proven reserves of Brazilian deposits was the equivalent of 13 per cent of the combined proven reserves within the five largest global producers, and the pre-salt reserves accounted for 85 per cent of Brazilian holdings (table 9.1). By another estimate, at the end of 2011 predictions of the volume of these reserves ranged between 50 billion and 123 billion barrels of petroleum equivalent.[17] Through the 2010s, the first-order impact of these deposits has been small, but rapidly increasing. Production from the pre-salt deposits began in 2008 and accounted for 0.4 per cent of total output; by 2013, the pre-salt was the source of 15 per cent of crude oil production.[18]

Industrial Policy and Petroleum

One of the first and strongest signals about the state's preoccupation with oil occurred when the Mining Code began to treat hydrocarbons differently from subsoil minerals in 1937. In contrast to minerals, the oil itself was to be the property of the state. This distinction removed petroleum from private ownership claims. Opposition to foreign ownership was behind the prohibition of private ownership.[19] As a result, the scope for developing the oil sector in a manner consistent with dynamic market conditions capable of attracting sufficient private capital narrowed considerably.[20] By the late 1940s, Juarez Távora, the minister of agriculture, where regulatory authority for oil and minerals resided, understood both that continued exploration would require large-scale state intervention (he phrased it as "monopoly") and that a state monopoly was politically infeasible.[21] Constituting Petrobras as a state-owned enterprise in 1953, with a monopoly for prospecting (and anticipatorily, producing) and refining petroleum was a major break with earlier principles.[22]

By the late 1950s, petroleum policy needed to grapple with the tangible problems of supply and distribution. The mandate and rules for operations expanded, and vertical integration of production processes occurred at a rapid pace through the 1960s. In 1963, the monopoly was widened to include transport as well as the import and export of crude petroleum and its refined derivatives. Petrobras also took on responsibility for the broader policy of overall energy self-sufficiency.[23] It became one of the most complicated conglomerate firms in the developing world. Throughout the decade, the company created subsidiaries for petrochemicals (mostly fertilizers for agro-industrial application, rubber-based products, and plastics), retail distribution and international expansion for commodity trading, overseas exploration, and currency management.[24] With the exception of retail distribution, the state-owned enterprise had monopoly rights in each of these areas. The economic policies that most affected Petrobras were those that defined the company's role in the macro-economy and its position within the industrial policy of import substitution. These included price and currency controls, output allocation and distribution to critical consumers or deficit regions, and pricing and trade preferences. In all of these fields, Petrobras received preferences and exemptions to further the goal of increasing petroleum availability through imports of crude oil, which Petrobras would refine. The firm also adopted pricing, distribution, and contracting practices in coordination with national industrial policy.[25]

The model of state ownership faced pressure as early as the 1970s and '80s. Closed capital markets compounded the problems of international supply uncertainty (the oil shocks described above) as well as financial and fiscal crises.[26] Given the hostile economic environment, the state was incapable of investing sufficiently in its premier enterprise. Financial constraints arose simultaneously with the discovery and development of large offshore deposits. The technology and logistics for offshore production (transportation of equipment, personnel, and output between sites and the coast, maintenance of drilling platforms, etc.) were capital-intensive. Channeling increased investment to basic exploration constrained other aspects of the firm's development and maintenance.

How was Petrobras able to implement the expansion of exploration and technology that was necessary to explore and drill the offshore discoveries needed to transform Brazil from major importer to self-sufficiency?

Rethinking the relationship with foreign actors, Petrobras began to structure mechanisms to tap the capital, operational capability, and technology of major oil producers. The firm entered into joint ventures (termed "risk-sharing contracts") with multinational oil-producing and servicing enterprises. The change reversed the earlier strong prohibitions against foreign presence in Brazil. Prior to the first risk-sharing contracts in 1975, federal concessions to Petrobras determined its exploration and production rights. The firm negotiated contracts with foreign and domestic entities to provide goods and services for fixed fees.[27] All of the risks and potential profits remained with Petrobras, and by extension with the Brazilian state. Through joint ventures, Petrobras created partnerships with its providers that divided the risks and potential profits. Risk sharing provided a means to attract the capital and technology required to develop newly discovered offshore deposits. Simultaneously, it maintained industrial policy, the formality of the Petrobras monopoly, and the public domain of the petroleum. Petrobras retained its monopoly of supply as well as control of all stages of production.[28]

By the end of the 1970s, Petrobras had joint ventures with twenty firms, primarily to develop the offshore deposits of the Campos Basin (see figure 9.4). The ability to partner with foreign and domestic companies opened the way for private actors to explore, produce, and profit from Brazilian petroleum.[29] Industry participants interpreted the introduction of joint ventures as the first step away from the tightly controlled Petrobras monopoly and toward global market competition in supply and production.[30]

Macroeconomic Regime Change

Disruptions in financial markets resulting from the oil shocks focused at least as much attention on the link between macroeconomic policy and the state's entrepreneurial role as they did on petroleum policy.[31] Lack of public-sector capital for investment in the light of fiscal crisis, excessive debt burden, inflation, and political uncertainty left Petrobras and other state-owned enterprises underfinanced. Aligning policy to minimize these detrimental circumstances, and to benefit from globalizing practices that had transformed other economies during the decade required, loosening the grip of import substitution industrial policy.

The Brazilian economy began to introduce many neoliberal reforms that addressed the prevailing crises and aligned governance more closely with global trends by the late 1980s. Doing so reversed the broad industrial policies that prevailed throughout the mid-twentieth century. The pillars of the new strategy were the privatization of many state-owned enterprises and the liberalization of commerce. In the international sphere, liberalizing commerce meant reducing trade barriers and emphasizing global business and trade partnerships. The Constitution of 1988 remodelled the state's economic role to include regulating, planning, and incentivizing private enterprise, mandating the privatization of state-owned enterprises.[32] The Constitution also continued to treat humanly produced goods differently from non-renewable natural resources. Petroleum, natural gas, other hydrocarbons, and nuclear minerals remained property of the state, and Petrobras remained a protected state monopoly.[33]

Although privatization was never seriously considered as a strategy for Petrobras, the sector undertook significant policy reform. Petrobras and energy policy-makers faced strong incentives to open the firm to large outside investment as they tried to balance rapidly escalating capital needs to extend and deepen offshore capability within the limits of strong fiscal constraint and prohibition against competition. The state's response was to "flexibilize" the monopoly with a constitutional amendment in 1995.[34] In this framework, the state retained resource ownership while private actors, including foreign companies, could obtain exploration and production rights.[35] In addition, the Petroleum Law of 1997, which operationalized the amendment, opened other activities, such as refining and transportation, to private (including foreign) investors. The law required open access to pipelines, maritime tankers, and other transport; producers could not operate proprietary facilities.[36] Opening the sector to private participants was politically contentious and necessitated a wide range of regulatory changes; but it did not challenge Petrobras. By 2006, Petrobras still retained 95 per cent of the domestic market in petroleum-derivative products.

Beyond broadening the sector's actors, these reforms supported Petrobras's ability to raise capital in private equity markets, offering a second avenue to the overarching goal of building the capital and technology of the petroleum sector. Doing so supported the firm's growth without requiring public-sector resources. However, the crucial caveat that the state would retain a majority share of Petrobras (minimally, 50 per cent plus one ordinary share) remained in place. Issuing equity on the São Paulo stock exchange raised the equivalent of US$807 million in 2001. Even more radically, Petrobras raised US$5.1 billion by selling equity shares on the New York Stock Exchange in 2002. Opening the enterprise to private capital allowed it to grow extremely rapidly while maintaining the state's control.

Capital expansion had important implications for both petroleum and capital markets. For Petrobras, the new capital financed the company's ever-increasing offshore production and technology development through larger partnerships as well as its own development investments. Increased capital was a crucial factor that contributed to positioning Petrobras as a major global petroleum company in all aspects of production and technology development. Although not the topic of this chapter, the governance practices and procedures for financial capital within Brazil were, arguably, more affected by the Petrobras stock issuance than the first-order effects on the firm. Raising capital from Brazilian investors on the São Paulo exchange aided the promotion of pension fund, mutual fund, and individual investment. International markets (the New York Stock Exchange) bound Petrobras to international corporate governance standards with respect to financial transparency and such operational areas as safety, human resources, and environmental protections.[37]

Back to the Future: Rent-Seeking and Industrial Policy

The confirmation of pre-salt deposits in 2007 motivated another overhaul in the governance of the petroleum sector. The revamped approach, legislated in 2010, applies both to production and to the rents captured by the state. The cornerstone of the reform has been to treat deposits in the pre-salt layers differently from onshore or post-salt (offshore, but not pre-salt) oil. Separating the pre-salt from traditional petroleum paved the way for changing the relationship between producers and the state.

Profit-sharing (also known as production-sharing) contracts shape the relationship between producers and the state, rather than fixed concessionary leases.[38] Profit-sharing is a major break with the history of non-renewable resource management in Brazil. Fixed concessions, compensated by royalty payments, had served to allocate access to non-renewable natural resources since the earliest Portuguese settlement.[39] The Petroleum Law of 1997 maintained this practice while opening the sector to foreign participants through joint ventures. With the 2010 legislation,[40] the federal government will receive a portion of its compensation for production and exploration rights in the form of a share of the pre-salt projects' profits, and payment will be in oil.[41] As a result, both project profitability and global oil prices will determine the state's financial benefits. The state's proportion of profit is not fixed; it is one variable in each auction bid. The motivation for changing allocation practices derived from the extent and certainty of pre-salt reserves. Instituting a discriminatory contractual format indicates the extent to which the Brazilian government believes itself to be in a seller's market with respect to its new reserves.

RENT-SEEKING

Explicit rent-seeking, the attempt of the public sector to extract maximum revenues from petroleum production, was new with the opening of the Brazilian economy in the 1990s. The state had no incentive to extract rent from a fully state-owned monopoly (in contrast to private-sector actors extracting a favoured position in receiving benefits from that monopoly). The increased revenues promised by the pre-salt discoveries, combined with the potential presence of many private-sector producers, has strongly promoted rent-seeking in the forms of royalties and the manner in which the state plans to protect its financial interests in the sector.

Royalties are an additional form of compensation, after profit-sharing, that producers will pay to the Brazilian state for production rights. The federal government, states, and municipalities have displayed rent-seeking behaviour and have politicized the use of their potential pre-salt royalties. Separating the pre-salt sector from other petroleum and instituting production-sharing as the basis for entering exploration and production leases paved the way for differential royalty schedules. Traditional operations typically compensate the state with 5 per cent of the value of production (increased to 10 per cent for especially rich deposits). Royalties from leases governed by production-sharing contracts will be 15 per cent of "profit oil" (the volume of oil produced, after deducting the costs of production).[42]

When enacted in 1985, covering the traditional oil sector, royalties were fully distributed to the states and municipalities associated with extraction.[43] The distribution of royalties from profit-sharing contracts (i.e., the pre-salt deposits) has motivated a larger number of claimants to step forward. Arguments on the grounds of property rights, natural resource theory, and pecuniary interests have easily become conflated. The Constitution of 1988 and subsequent pre-salt-related law clearly delineate petroleum as strategic property belonging to the nation of Brazil (commonly interpreted to be the government, as representative of all Brazilian citizens).[44] Theories associated with the extraction of non-renewable natural resources prioritize intergenerational transfer in considering both the level and distribution of royalties. These economic ideas have long held that, once extracted, the potential wealth is no longer available to future generations, and therefore, excess returns (above normal return on capital) on the resources should be invested for the benefit of future generations.[45] Local governing agencies argue for royalties as compensation for the costs of rapid development of physical and social infrastructure to support the industry, as well as environmental protection. In practice, the costs of supporting extraction and local interests often render the economic definition subordinate to political interests.

Claimants for royalties include municipalities and states hosting the pre-salt exploration and production facilities. These are a very few municipalities, most notably Campos dos Goytacazes and Macaé in the state of Rio de Janeiro, followed very distantly by towns in the states of Espírito Santo and São Paulo.[46] In the 2010 legislation, federal agencies also laid claim to royalties for naval support and an environmental defence fund. Non-producing states and municipalities received a small portion and the federal government claimed the remaining 30 per cent of royalty payments. Intergenerational wealth transfer away from future owners of the resource (all Brazilians), which would have directed royalty payments toward human and social capital investments, was not recognized.[47] Reflecting the contentious and political nature of these decisions, a subsequent re-specification of the royalty legislation shifted the allocation toward the federal government and non-producing state/municipal governments.[48] Almost immediately the producing states challenged the 2012 agreement, and subjected it to Supreme Court review in 2013. A restated law of March 2014 confirmed the transfer of royalties allocated to the federal domain and non-producing regions (see table 9.2). The still largely unrealized pool of funds from royalties to the federal government also became a political tool, with the distribution again open to legislative change. In 2013, in response to widespread street demonstrations against the expense and disruptions caused by the country's preparations for the 2014 World Cup and 2016 Olympic Games, the federal government committed to allocate

Table 9.2 Petroleum Royalties

	On-shore	Off-shore	Special Participation (4) On-shore	Special Participation (4) Off-shore	Pre-salt Original	Pre-salt, Amended Concessions	Pre-salt, Amended Profit-sharing
Year royalties became effective	1991		1998		2010	2013 (5)	
Royalty Rate (%) (1)	5	5	5	5	10	10	15
Distribution (% of royalty revenues)							
Producing states	70		52.5	22.5	26.25	26.25	25
Producing municipalities	20		15	22.5	26.25	26.25	6
Affected municipalities (2)	10	10	7.5	7.5	8.75	8.75	3
States-adjacent to wells		30					
Municipalities-adjacent wells		30					
Navy		20		15			
Special fund (3)		10		7.5	8.75	8.75	22
Science & technology Ministry			25	25			
Federal Treasury					30	30	44

Source: Agência Nacional de Petróleo, http://www.anp.gov.br/?pg=74395&m=royalties&t1=&t2=royalties&t3=&t4=&ar=0&ps=1&1427840784440.

NOTES
1. % of value of production for all categories, except pre-salt profit-sharing. For Pre-salt profit-sharing projects, royalties are calculated and paid as a share of volume of production.
2. Special fund: to non-producing states and municipalities.
3. Affected municipalities have facilities that are not directly "producing." For offshore wells, these are embarkation points.
4. Special participation is the incremental royalty paid on "very productive" wells.
5. The law was approved in 2013; as of April 2015, ANP has not had royalty rates different from the rates effective from 1998.

   Federal Treasury's revenues from all pre-salt profit-sharing projects, Profit shares, Share of royalties, Signing bonus

75 per cent of its pre-salt royalty revenues to education and the remaining 25 per cent to public health in underserved communities.[49]

In addition, the federal government has formed Pré-Sal Petróleo S. A. (PPSA) to protect and maximize the profits the state earns from the profit-sharing projects.[50] Its mandates are to mitigate information asymmetries between the state and oil companies and to serve as a trading company in global markets for the oil that the state receives as its share of profits.[51] PPSA is a wholly state-owned limited liability company under the jurisdiction of the regulatory authority, the National Petroleum Agency (Agência Nacional de Petróleo, or ANP.) This arrangement creates a situation in which the regulator regulates itself and gives the state a direct mechanism for controlling the operations of petroleum producers. No provisions suggesting that resolving potential conflicts of interest between PPSA, ANP, and Petrobras can be achieved in a manner that assures a third party of regulatory independence.[52]

Several criticisms of the profit-sharing mechanisms leave them open to challenge.[53] One major weakness of profit-sharing has been that the bases for calculating the profit to be shared are complicated and obscure. No limit on the share of gross output that recovers costs minimizes the incentive for productivity, just as it creates incentive to overstate costs. Further, the state's share of profits is incremental to the signing bonus and royalty payments. Other petroleum-producing nations using these arrangements accept profit-shares as full compensation for depleting the supply of a non-renewable natural resource, replacing royalties.[54] Beyond the economic and financial concerns, jurists have challenged the constitutionality of PPSA's potential conflicts between the government's regulatory responsibilities and pecuniary interests.[55]

INDUSTRIAL POLICY

Many of the concepts that underpinned early industrial policies supporting import substitution industrialization have re-emerged, with both old and new practices. Overt protection of Petrobras, maintaining an overall energy policy with Petrobras, and directing beneficial externalities to domestic firms were among the most important practices from earlier periods. The most important new tool of industrial policy that the state has invoked is to channel public-sector equity investment to Petrobras through the National Development Bank (BNDES). Petrobras is, once again, both an agent and a beneficiary of industrial policy.

In the most straightforward of the sectoral reforms, the state redefined a very privileged position for Petrobras. The company purchased the exclusive rights (*cessão oneroso*) to five billion barrels of petroleum equivalent in the pre-salt deposits.[56] Although it accounted for less than 6 per cent of the then-anticipated pre-salt reserves, the size of the concession was notable. At the time, the value of the unextracted oil that the contract covered was estimated at US$42.5 billion.[57] The state has recently awarded a second exclusive concession to Petrobras, for 9.6 to 15.2 billion barrels in a newly discovered field.[58] Furthermore, the reforms of 2010 guarantee—or require—a 30 per cent share and lead management of all pre-salt projects to Petrobras.[59]

Significant commitments offset Petrobras's protected access to pre-salt oil. The firm's responsibilities in maintaining the broad-based national energy policy remain in place. The overall goal of national energy policy has always been self-sufficiency, both in petroleum and in total energy supplies, while also supporting rapid economic growth. Petrobras's operation of this policy continues to include the development of biofuels (especially ethanol), investment in pipelines to service the most remote (and hence most costly) regions of the nation, and compliance with price restrictions on retail distribution of gasoline. Prior to pre-salt discoveries (as early as 2003) the federal government rearticulated its expectation that, given Petrobras's dominant position in the Brazilian energy sector, the firm would maintain commitments to regional and social development while also maintaining its international competitiveness.[60]

Further, Petrobras has led the way in establishing norms for domestic content commitments in pre-salt exploration and production.[61] Local content had been one of the key mechanisms for realizing the externalities that early economic nationalists actively promoted: increasing the demand for domestically produced industrial goods and services, developing human capital, and building technological capability. As a traditional state-owned enterprise with monopoly rights, Petrobras highlighted its efforts to enhance the domestic content of its operations.[62] As the practices of auctioning production and exploration leases developed, one variable in evaluating bids for offshore concessions was the bidding company's or consortium's commitment to local content. The regulatory authority, rather than legislative action, determines acceptable levels of local content.[63] In a nominally open market, commitment to maintain local content has become problematic because the policies constrain profit-maximization goals of private firms.

The attempt to foment externalities has evolved. The needs for infrastructure, support goods and services, and technological development in the pre-salt sector increased dramatically the potential impact of mandated local content provisions. Drilling equipment, platforms and refineries, shipping freighters, pipelines, and servicing provisions are the major capital-intensive items subject to local content regulation, as well as sources of skilled job creation.[64] The first contract for pre-salt rights, the exclusive concession, provided that local content of goods and services during the development phase of the project would be 37 per cent and 55 to 65 per cent during production. Petrobras may have established a high threshold in the commitments of its exclusive contract at the same time that it demonstrated the continued political interests in using the petroleum industry as a tool of domestic industrial policy.[65] The standards for determining and calculating local content remain murky.[66] To date, estimates of the short-term cost effects of requiring local, rather than the most cost-efficient, content are not available. Producers and the sector's professional association (Instituto Brasileiro de Petróleo) complain that this form of protection for other domestic industrial sectors slows their operations and increases their costs.[67]

Local content provisions for petroleum-related goods and services have very serious implications beyond the distortion of production and exploration costs. Beginning in 2014, a corruption scandal revealing kickbacks from Petrobras, generated by the governing political party's skimming and rigging of contracts, decimated the management, reputation, and financial value of Petrobras. The entire Board of Directors was replaced in March 2015; Moody's downgraded the creditworthiness of the company's bonds to the status of "junk" (not worthy of investment) in February 2015. The scandal has led Petrobras's partners to anticipate significant delays in pre-salt exploration and production, because of management distraction, bankruptcies, and business bans on contractors enmeshed in the investigations and, possibly, looming capital and credit shortages.[68] Estimates

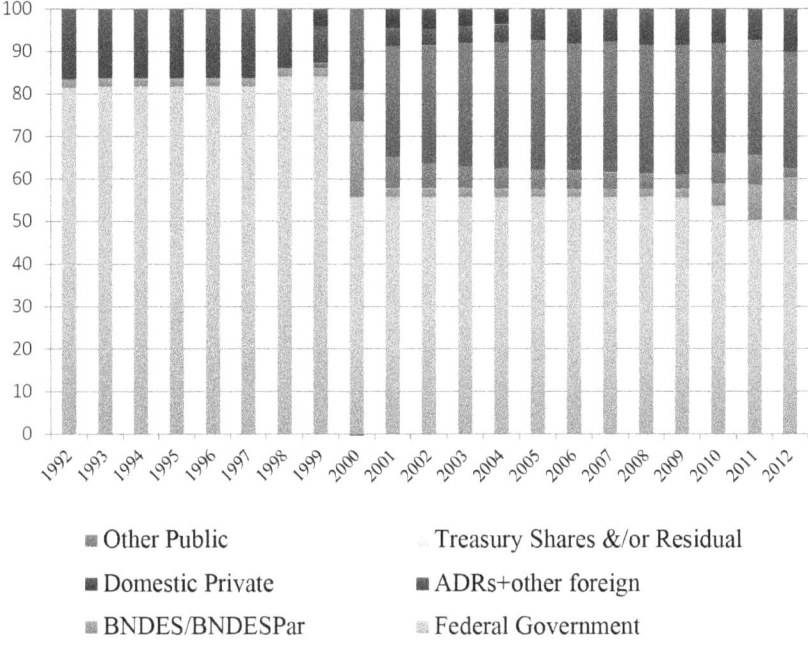

- Other Public
- Domestic Private
- BNDES/BNDESPar
- Treasury Shares &/or Residual
- ADRs+other foreign
- Federal Government

Figure 9.5a Ordinary Shares Distributed by Ownership (%)

Source: Petrobras, "Relatório anual/Annual Report" (various years), https://www.investidorpetrobras.com.br/resultados-e-comunicados/relatorios-anuais/.

of the extent to which Petrobras will provide for losses reach as high as US$20 billion, or about 1 per cent of Brazil's GDP in 2014.[69] Contract tampering and kickbacks are not confined to the pre-salt sector. Nevertheless, a large share of Petrobras's increased operating expenses, and 53 per cent of its investment plan for the 2014–18 period, are targeted for the pre-salt, linking a very large share of contracting to pre-salt development.

The newly emerging industrial policy has emphasized Petrobras's protected position within the petroleum sector from another perspective, which serves to emphasize the state's willingness to remodel its role in the economy. During the 1990s, BNDES received the mandate to operate the federal privatization program. The bank executed valuation surveys and

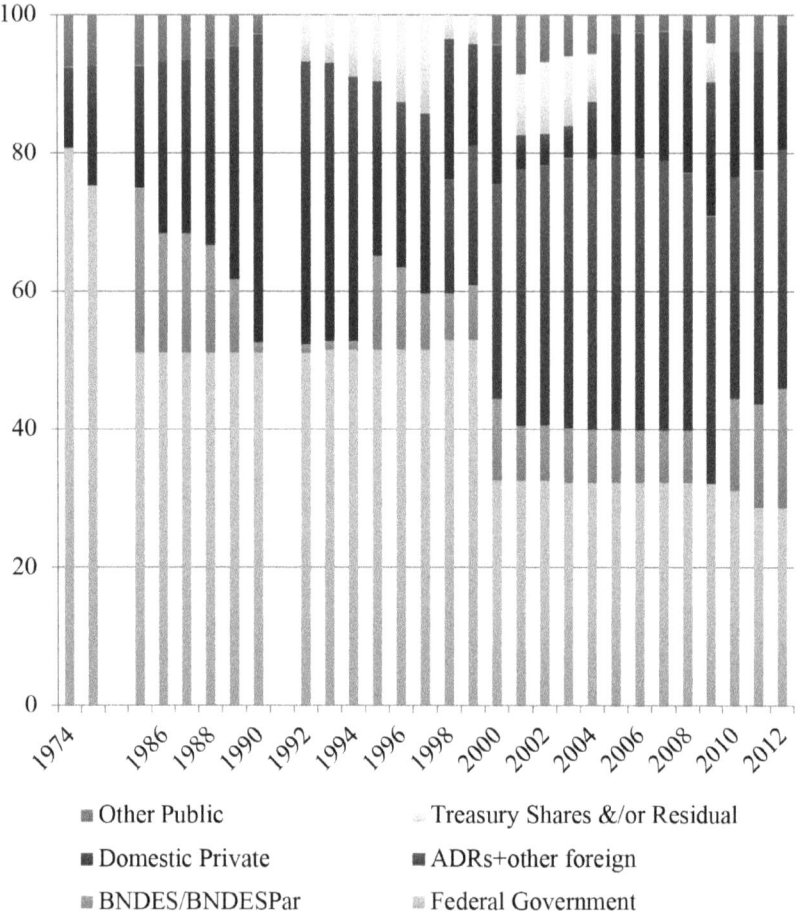

Figure 9.5b Total Shares (Ordinary + Preferred) Distributed by Ownership

Note: BNDES held shares of Petrobras until 1990; thereafter, BNDESPar has been owner of the shares.

Source: Petrobras, "Relatório anual/Annual Report" (various years), https://www.investidorpetrobras.com.br/resultados-e-comunicados/relatorios-anuais/.

sales of equity shares. It also issued loans to some purchasers, potentially influencing the pool of buyers. For its own profit account, BNDES also organized an equity participation subsidiary (BNDESPar), enabling the bank to buy equity shares. BNDESPar offers an updated and opaque avenue for public-sector ownership of firms.[70] As an agency of the federal government and a state-owned enterprise, BNDESPar instituted a strategy of investing in "national champions." Petrobras is the largest "champion" in which the bank has invested. BNDESPar is the largest single owner of Petrobras's preferred and ordinary equity (excluding the federal government's mandated majority ownership of ordinary shares.) BNDESPar notably increased its shareholding during 2010, as a major purchaser of the US$69.6 billion share issue on the New York Stock Exchange.[71] At the end of 2012, the national Treasury and BNDES combined owned 60 per cent of Petrobras's ordinary shares and 46 per cent of all shares (see figures 9.5a and 9.5b).[72]

Protecting Petrobras's share of the petroleum market (at less than 100 per cent), building an ownership position through the development bank, and contractual commitments to local content are modified forms of industrial policy, which allow for a wider range of participants than policy had accommodated in earlier years. These tools sacrifice the intent of macroeconomic regime change formalized in the Constitution of 1988 and its 1995 amendment for petroleum. Similarly, Petrobras's share in development and production consortia circumvents requirements for competitive public bidding for all government contracts, giving the firm the ability to veto any project for any reason. The state makes the case that exemptions for national strategic interests cover the special conditions accorded to Petrobras.[73]

Conclusion

This chapter has considered that, with a short interlude from the late 1990s through the first decade of the twenty-first century, the issues accompanying the development of the petroleum sector in Brazil have never been solely concerned with petroleum. Oil and Petrobras, the vehicle that the Brazilian state created as its conduit, were central to a much broader industrial policy. This position was explicit from the 1950s through the early 1990s; since the discovery of the pre-salt deposits, a return to activist industrial policy has occurred more circuitously. Early practices favouring Petrobras and emphasizing the economic development effects of local content have re-emerged, if in somewhat different forms. Petrobras's use as a tool of macroeconomic policy has waned; while using the National Development Bank as a means to capitalize the firm has become common practice. Explicit rent-seeking is new. Prior to discovering the pre-salt deposits, the state's objectives with petroleum were development and self-subsistence; the beneficiaries of the managed industry were recipients of less expensive and more secure (if artificially managed) supplies. The potential of significant wealth has ignited the state's interest in expanding its take from pre-salt production: increased royalties, instituting profit-sharing, and signing bonuses. At the same time, social conflict over the allocation of future royalties has evolved into a game of political football.

If the goals of governance practices are to establish consistent and transparent "rules of the game," recent Brazilian experience deserves attention. The industrial policy aspects of recent regulation are as opaque as their predecessors. The rent-seeking practices are transparent, even if the expedient of separating the practices for pre-salt and traditional production sacrifices the concept of consistency. Further, situating the profit-seeking portion of the government's oil activity (PPSA) within the regulatory agency (ANP) raises important questions about regulatory independence and the potential for conflicts of interest. Beyond the scope of this chapter, ongoing practices and political contestation, since 2010, suggest that the struggle for regulatory practice and business control within the sector continues, and reflects the experiences of other sectors.[74]

Over the long run, Brazil's success as an oil producer in the pre-salt sector will rely on a wide array of factors. Some considerations, especially global oil price trends and the emergence of alternative sources of supply (such as shale oil), are outside of the control of the Brazilian government. However, the challenges presented by governance concerns will determine both whether other participants in the industry are willing to operate within Brazil and whether Brazilians can accommodate the range of claimants on the sector's potential wealth.

The relevant conclusion from this analysis is neither that state management of production nor market-oriented management offer better governance mechanisms. Rather, the inconsistency of seeking maximum returns through market-based institutions while also implementing strong policies of state management has resulted in inconsistent regulatory structures and uncertainty, and it has (perhaps) facilitated corruption. The governance framework for the pre-salt deposits is also not in accord with the intent of the Brazilian Constitution or its amendment for petroleum. This dissonance has not been specifically addressed by political, legislative, or judicial bodies.

NOTES

This chapter draws heavily on Gail D. Triner, "Regulatory Regimes for Petroleum Production in Brazil," in *Regulation of Natural Resources since 1830*, ed. Pål Thonstad Sandvik and Espen Storli, 139–61 (Vancouver: UBC Press, 2019).

1   Brazil is not unique; some authors see a general re-emergence of "resource nationalism" throughout Latin America. See Allyson Lucinda Benton, "Political Institutions, Hydrocarbons Resources and Economic Policy Divergence in Latin America" (paper presented at the annual meeting of the American Political Science Association, Boston, 28–31 August 2008).

2   See, for example, Thad Dunning, *Crude Democracy: Natural Resource Wealth and Political Regimes* (New York: Cambridge University Press, 2008); Michael L. Ross, *The Oil Curse: How Petroleum Wealth Shapes the Development of Nations* (Princeton, NJ: Princeton University Press, 2012); Terry Lynn Karl, *The Paradox of Plenty: Oil Booms and Petro-states* (Berkeley: University of California Press, 1997); Steven Lee Solnick, *Stealing the State: Control and Collapse in Soviet Institutions* (Cambridge, MA: Harvard University Press, 1998); Benjamin B. Smith, *Hard Times in the Lands of Plenty: Oil Politics in Iran and Indonesia* (Ithaca, NY: Cornell University Press, 2007).

3   Jeffrey G. Williamson, *Trade and Poverty: When the Third World Fell Behind* (Cambridge, MA: MIT Press, 2011), chs. 1 and 4.

4   Luiz Carlos Bresser-Pereira, "Desindustrialização e doença holandesa," *Folha de S.Paulo*, 9 April 2007; Luiz Carlos Bresser-Pereira, "Taxa de câmbio, doença holandesa, e industrialização" (paper presented at Seminário patrocinado por FGV Projetos e pela Escola de Economia de São Paulo da Fundação Getúlio Vargas, São Paulo, 2010). Evidence is also accumulating that increased oil revenues (especially royalties) are not resulting in increased local standards of living. See Francesco Caselli and Guy Michaels, "Do Oil Windfalls Improve Living Standards? Evidence from Brazil" (working paper, London School of Economics, London, 2012).

5   Rapid, ongoing adjustments in the regulatory parameters of the petroleum sector, in response to material, business, and political actions, make it infeasible to declare the subject "closed"—or even up-to-date.

6   See, for example, Rafael Rosas, "Lobão defende mudança na legislação do setor de petróleo para aumentar repasses ao Governo," *Valor Econômico*, 17 April 2008.

7   José Luciano de Mattos Dias and Maria Ana Quaglino, *A questão do petróleo no Brasil: Uma história da Petrobrás* (Rio de Janeiro: CPDOC/SERINST Fundação Getúlio Vargas—Petrobras, 1993).

8   Peter Seaborn Smith, "Petrobrás: The Politicizing of a State Company, 1953–1964," *Business History Review* 46, no. 2 (1972): 183–201.

9   Getúlio Vargas, "Discurso em Leopoldina, Minas, 24 Outubro 1939," in *A política nacionalista do petróleo no Brasil* (Rio de Janeiro: Tempo Brasileiro, 1964), 54–5.

10 Brazil. Congresso Nacional, "Coleção das Leis e Decretos," Lei 2004 (3 October 1953). The law was first introduced for debate in the Congress in 1951, and the final version included such additional provisions as the ability to expropriate land deemed necessary for petroleum exploration.

11 Edelmira del Carmen Alveal Contreras, *Os desbravadores: A Petrobrás e a construção do Brasil industrial* (Rio de Janeiro: Relume Dumará/ANPOCS, 1993), 71.

12 See Gail D. Triner, *Mining and the State in Brazilian Development* (London: Pickering and Chatto, 2011), chs. 5 and 7. According to Mario Bittencourt Sampaio, a major participant in drafting the Petroleum Law of 1953, neither the Conselho Nacional de Petróleo (National Petroleum Council) nor the Treasury believed that sufficient capital could be accumulated from domestic sources to finance a successful petroleum enterprise. Mario Bittencourt Sampaio, interview by Cláudia Maria Cavalcanti de Barros Guimarães and Maria Ana Quaglino, 16 September 1987, Centro de Pesquisa e Documentação de História Contemporânea do Brasil/Fundação Getúlio Vargas (CPDOC/FGV), Memória do setor petrolífero no Brasil: A história da Petrobrás, 13–14, http://www.fgv.br/cpdoc/historal/arq/Entrevista174.pdf; Maria Antonieta P. Leopoldi, "O difícil caminho do meio: Estado, burguesia e industrialização no Segundo Governo Vargas (1951–1954)," in *Vargas e a crise dos anos 50*, ed. Angela de Castro Gomes (Rio de Janeiro: Relume Dumaná, 1994), 178.

13 A very small portion of shares remained in the hands of private owners and was tradable on the stock exchange.

14 Hsu Yuet Heung O'Keefe, *A crise do petróleo e a economia brasileira* (São Paulo: Instituto de Pesquisas Econômicas, 1984).

15 The first offshore discoveries came in 1968. See Humberto Quintas and Luiz Cezar P. Quintans, *A história do petróleo no Brasil e no mundo* (Rio de Janeiro: IBP/Freitas Bastos Editora, 2009), 70.

16 Ilmar Penna Marinho Jr., *Petróleo: Política e poder—um novo choque do petróleo?* (Rio de Janeiro: José Olympio Editora, 1989), 389.

17 Brian W. Blades, "Production, Politics, and Pre-salt: Transitioning to a PSC Regime in Brazil," *Texas Journal of Oil, Gas and Energy Law* 7, no. 1 (2011): 32. Updated estimates offer a similarly wide range, reflecting the continuing exploration activity.

18 Brazil. Agência Nacional de Petróleo (ANP), *Anuário Estatístico* (Rio de Janeiro: ANP, 2014).

19 See Juarez Távora, "O Código de Minas e o desenvolvimento da mineração no Brasil," *Geologia e Metallurgia* no. 14 (1956): 164–5; CPDOC/FGV: ANc 1928.0202, letter to Goés Monteiro from Monteiro Lobato, 3 May 1940.

20 Maria Augusta Tibiriçá Miranda, *O petróleo é nosso: A luta contra o'entreguismo,' pelo monopólio estatal, 1947–1953, 1953–1981* (Petrópolis: Vozes, 1983), 28.

21 Paulo Roberto de Almeida, "Monteiro Lobato e a emergência da política do petróleo no Brasil," in *Potência Brasil: Gás natural, energia limpa para um futuro sustentável*, ed. Omar L. de Barros Filho and Sylvia Bojunga (Porto Alegre: Laser Press, 2008), 14.

22 Thomas J. Trebat, *Brazil's State-Owned Enterprises: A Case Study of the State as Entrepreneur* (Cambridge: Cambridge University Press, 1983), 42; Luis Cezar P. Quintans, *Contratos de petróleo: Concessão e partilha—propostas e leis para o Pré-sal* (Rio de Janeiro: Benício Biz/Instituto Brasileiro de Petróleo, 2011), 77.

23 In this role, development and production of ethanol became a Petrobras project. See Penna Marinho Jr., *Petróleo: Política e poder*, 366.

24 Petrobras, "Relatório Anual/Annual Report" (Rio de Janeiro: Petrobras, 1999), http://www.investidorpetrobras.com.br; Alveal Contreras, *Os desbravadores*, 72–100.

25 Laura Randall, *The Political Economy of Brazilian Oil* (Westport, CT: Praeger, 1993); Dias and Quaglino, *A questão do petróleo no Brasil*.

26 For a discussion of the macroeconomic problems created by the oil shocks and the concurrent management of the economy, see Albert Fishlow, "Lessons from the Past: Capital Markets during the Nineteenth Century and the Interwar Period," *International Organizations* 39, no. 3 (1985): 381–439; Werner Baer, *The Brazilian Economy: Growth and Development*, 4th ed. (Westport, CT: Praeger, 1995).

27 These contracts usually provided for technology transfer and personnel training. CPDOC/FGV, Memória do setor petrolífero, Artur Levy, interview by Valentina da Rocha Lima and Margareth Guimarães Martins, 24 July 1987, 92–8; Antonio Seabra Moggi, interview by José Luciano de Mattos Dias e Margareth Guimarães Martins, 5 February 1988, 40–79, 2 March 1988, 129–30, 31 August 1988, 259–61.

28 Fausto Cupertino, *Os contratos de risco e a Petrobrás: O petróleo é nosso e o risco deles?* (Rio de Janeiro: Civilização Brasileira, 1976), 15–18.

29 Luiz Cezar P. Quintans, *Direito do petróleo: Conteúdo local—a evolução do modelo de contrato e o conteúdo local nas atividades de E&P no Brasil* (Rio de Janeiro: IBP/Freitas Bastos Editora, 2011), 29–31, 50.

30 Getúlio Carvalho, *Petrobras: Do monopólio aos contratos de risco* (Rio de Janeiro: Forense-Univeristária, 1977).

31 Armando Castelar Pinheiro and Fabio Giambiagi, "The Macroeconomic Background and Institutional Framework of Brazilian Privatization" (paper presented at the conferece Privatization in Brazil: The Case of Public Utilities, Rio de Janeiro, 1999).

32 The new Constitution supported the re-emergence of civilian rule after the military regimes of 1964–85.

33 Brazil, "Constituição da República Federativa do Brasil" (5 October 1988), article 176, http://pdba.georgetown.edu/Constitutions/Brazil/brazil88.html. On petroleum, see Cláudio A. Pinho, *Pré-sal: História, doutrina e comentários às leis* (Belo Horizonte: Editora Legal, 2010), 29.; see also William Freire, *Comentários ao Código de Mineração* (Rio de Janeiro: Aide Editora/Comércio de Livros, 1995), 168; Gilberto Bercovici, *Direito econômico do petróleo e dos recursos minerais* (São Paulo: Editora Quartier Latin do Brasil, 2011), 244.

34 Constitutional amendment 09 (9 November 1995) and the Petroleum Law enabled the constitutional amendment (Lei 9478, 6 August 1997). Amaury de Souza and Carlos Pereira, "A flexibilização do monopólio do petróleo no contexto das reformas dos anos 1990," in *Petróleo: Reforma e contrarreforma do setor petrolífero brasileiro*, ed. Fabio Giambiagi and Luiz Paulo Vellozo Lucas (Rio de Janeiro: Elsevier, 2013), 50.

35 To date, only one Brazilian company has engaged in oil exploration (OBX, primarily owned by Eike Batista; it declared bankruptcy in 2013), although a number of Brazilian firms participate in many aspects of petroleum servicing.

36 Paulo Valois Pires, *A evolução do monopólio estatal do petróleo* (Rio de Janeiro: Editora Lumen Juris, 2000), 129; Edna Maria B. Gama Coutinho et al., "O que mudou na indústria do petróleo?," *Informe Infra-estrutura: Área de projetos de infra-estrutura* no. 29 (December 1998): 3–4; Ricardo Pinto Pinheiro, *Abastecimento nacional de combustíveis no ambiente de flexibilização do monopólio de petróleo* (Rio de Janeiro: Ministério de Minas e Energia, 1996).

37 Henri Philippe Reichstul, interview with author, 11 June 2012, São Paulo. In order to issue ADRs on the New York Stock Exchange, foreign firms must comply with the financial disclosure requirements of the US Security and Exchange Commission and meet US GAAP (generally accepted accounting practices) standards.

38 Lei 12351, 22 December 2010; Congresso Nacional, "Coleção das Leis e Decretos."

39 Legal debates sometimes challenged the exact nature of the state's claim to concession granting authority, but the practices involved remained constant, with the exception of the forty-three-year period when subsoil rights were conjoined to the rights of land ownership (1891–1934). See Triner, *Mining and the State*, ch. 2.

40 All existing concessions have been grandfathered; profit-sharing will apply to future operations. The new principles for allocating rights also ignore that many analysts believed that the concessionary system was successful. Luiz Paulo Vellozo Lucas asserts that "there was a consensus in the technical sphere that reform was not necessary."See Vellozo Lucas, "A derrota de um modelo de successo," in *Petróleo: Reforma e contrarreforma do setor petrolífero brasileiro*, ed. Fabio Giambiagi and Luiz Paulo Vellozo Lucas (Rio de Janeiro: Elsevier, 2013), 139; see also Adriano Pires and Rafael Schechtman, "Os resultados da reforma: Uma estratégia vencedora," in *Petróleo: Reforma e contrarreforma do setor petrolífero brasileiro*, ed. Fabio Giambiagi and Luiz Paulo Vellozo Lucas (Rio de Janeiro: Elsevier, 2013).

41 Paulo César Ribeiro Lima, *Pré-Sal: O novo marco legal e a capitalização da Petrobras* (Rio de Janeiro: Synergia Editora, 2011), 30.

42 Ernst & Young, *Global Oil and Gas Tax Guide 2014* (London: EY, 2014).

43 José Roberto Rodrigues Afonso and Sérgio Wulff Gobetti, "Rendas de petróleo no Brasil: Alguns aspectos fiscais e federativos," *Revista do BNDES* 15, no. 30 (2008): 231–69.

44 Brazil, "Constituição 1988," Lei 12531/2010.

45 Harold Hotelling, "The Economics of Exhaustible Resources," *Journal of Political Economy* 39, no. 2 (1931): 137–75.

46 Currently, 79 per cent of proven reserves are located in the deposits attributed to the territorial area of the state of Rio de Janeiro. Gobetti makes the case that Brazil is unique among federally organized oil-producing states in allocating such a heavy proportion of royalties from offshore locations to sub-sovereign localities. Agência Nacional de Petróleo, *Anuário Estatístico*, Table 2.4; Sérgio Wulff Gobetti, *Federalismo fiscal e petróleo no Brasil e no mundo*, Texto para discussão #1669 (Brasília: Instituto de Pesquisa Econômica Aplicada IPEA, 2011).

47 Gobetti, "Federalismo fiscal"; José Roberto Rodrigues Afonso and Sérgio Wulff Gobetti, "Rendas de Petróleo no Brasil: Alguns Aspectos Fiscais e Federativos," *Revista do BNDES* 15, no. 30 (2008): 231–69. These provisions have not been implemented as of April 2015.

48 Lei 12734 (2012); Fernanda Fernandes Maia, Denise Cunha Tavares Terra, and Ludmila Gonçalves da Matta, "A nova sistema de partilha dos royalties do petróleo: Avaliando o debate na mídia," *Petróleo Royalties & Região* 12, no. 45 (2014): 4–7.

49 Sandra Manfrini, "Lei que destina royalties do petróleo para educação e saúde é publicada" *O Estado de São Paulo*, 10 September 2013, http://economia.estadao.com.br/noticias/negocios,lei-que-destina-royalties-do-petroleo-para-educacao-e-saude-e-publicada,164282; Ângela Bittencourt, "Petrobras, A polivalente" *Valor Econômico*, 23 September 2013, http://www.valor.com.br/valor-investe/casa-das-caldeiras/3476316/petrobras-polivalente.

50 Lei 12304 (2 August 2010).

51 PPSA assumes the commercial and price risks of the petroleum received as the state's share of profit. The company appoints one-half of the operating oversight committee for each pre-salt consortium, including the president of each committee, who has veto power on the committee's decisions. Ministério das Minas e Energia, "Novo Marco Regulatório: Pré-sal e áreas estratégicas," (Rio de Janeiro, 2009), 24; Quintans, *Contratos de petróleo*, 99.

52 Fernando Facury Scaff, "Impasses Regulatórios do Pré-Sal e o Plano de Negógios da Petrobras," *Petróleo Royalties & Região* 12, no. 46 (2014): 6–7.

53 Ribeiro Lima, *Pré-Sal*, ch. 3; Antônio Luís de Miranda Ferreira, "Problemas e inconsistências jurídicas de novo marco regulatório: A ótica dos princípios constitucionais da livre iniciativa, da economia de mercado e do direito comercial," in *Petróleo: Reforma e contrarreforma do setor petrolífero brasileiro*, ed. Fabio Giambiagi and Luiz Paulo Vellozo Lucas (Rio de Janeiro: Elsevier, 2013), 185–6.

54 Quintans, *Contratos de petróleo*, 98; Blades, "Production, Politics, and Pre-salt," 38–41.

55 Ferreira, "Problemas e inconsistências jurídicas de novo marco regulatório."

56 Lei 12276 (30 June 2010).

57 An outside valuation determined the signing bonus that Petrobras paid to the state. The value of the "signing bonus" was determined on the basis a forty-year contract and an estimated value for the undrilled oil of US$8.51 per barrel of oil equivalent. While advocates for state intervention in petroleum believed the state's compensation was too low, financial analysts opined that Petrobras had overcompensated the state for the transaction. To finance the signing bonus, firm expansion and technological development necessary for large-scale access to the pre-salt, Petrobras issued equity, for a value of US$69.6 billion on the New York Stock Exchange in September 2010, the largest equity issue in global stock exchange history. Petrobras, "Relatório anual/Annual Report," 2010.

58 The stated purpose of expanding the exclusive concession is to accelerate the development of unexpectedly rich reserves in the Libra Field. "CNPE Ruling Brings Uncertainty to the Exploration and Production Market," *International Law Office Newsletter*, 26 August 2014, http://www.internationallawoffice.com/newsletters/detail.aspx?g=246b85e4-40a1-4736-b40a-bd15ab5c0483; Adriano Pires, "É preciso tirar a Petrobrás do palanque," *O Estado de São Paulo*, 14 Jul 2014, http://economia.estadao.com.br/noticias/geral,e-preciso-tirar-a-petrobras-do-palanque-imp-,1528294.

59 Lei 12351 (22 December 2010). Conceivably, the veneer of open competitive bidding for production sites could be maintained by the firm participating in multiple consortia competing for a particular concession, but this preference ensures a dominant position for Petrobras.

60 Mansueto Almeida, Renato Lima de Oliveira, and Ben Ross Schneider, *Política industrial e empresas estatais no Brasil: BNDES e Petrobras*, Texto para discussão 2013 (Brasília: IPEA, 2014), 20–5.

61 Local, or domestic, content is the share of production inputs (goods, services, labour) that a firm obtains from domestic, rather than imported, sources.

62 Every year in its Annual Report, Petrobras cites the extent of its local content and calculates its contribution to the federal Treasury. Petrobras, "Relatório anual/Annual Report" (various years).

63 Blades, "Production, Politics, and Pre-salt," 50–1. While the CNPE and the production-sharing law define the term "local content" with respect to pre-salt operations, the ANP has the authority to determine the level of the requirement.

64 Perhaps the most contentious application of local content considerations have occurred with respect to the efforts of Brazilian industry and the navy to develop floating production, storage, and offloading facilities, rather than contracting for existing technology and production from British and South Korean providers.

65 Quintans, *Direito do petróleo: Conteúdo local*.

66 Almeida, Lima de Oliveira, and Schneider, "Política industrial e empresas estatais no Brasil."

67 Quintans, *Direito do petróleo: Conteúdo local*; João Augusto de Castro Neves (Eurasia Group), interview with author, 9 November 2012, Washington, DC.

68 Ron Bousso, "Galp Sees Delays in Brazil from Petrobras Graft Probe," *Reuters*, 11 March 2015, http://www.reuters.com/article/email/idUSL5N0WD3KO20150311. The scandal has also seriously impeded the functioning of the federal government. As of mid-March 2015, fifty-four accused participants have been arrested and large mass demonstrations are calling for the impeachment of the president of Brazil. See Simon Romero, "Protests Continue in Brazil against Dilma Rousseff," *New York Times*, 17 March 2015.

69 Rafael Rosas, "Petrobras reitera que não há data definida para divulgação de balanço," *Valor Econômico*, 2 April 2015.

70 For more on this topic, see Sérgio G. Lazzarini and Aldo Musacchio, *Reinventing State Capitalism: Leviathan in Business, Brazil and Beyond* (Cambridge, MA: Harvard University Press, 2014), ch. 9; Almeida, Lima de Oliveira, and Schneider, "Política industrial e empresas estatais no Brasil."

71 This share issuance was intended to finance the signing bonus for the exclusive concession and the research and development necessary to access the pre-salt developments. This issuance was the largest offering in global financial history, to that point.

72 The end of 2012 was chosen as the benchmark year because it is prior to any emerging rumours of the kickback scandal.

73 Blades, "Production, Politics, and Pre-salt," 42.

74 Government regime change has impacted the pre-salt petroleum sector by eliminating mandatory participation by Petrobras, reducing local content requirements, and reducing profit-sharing requirements. The durability of these changes has yet to be proven. On the regulatory similarities among sectors, see Gail D. Triner, "From Regulatory State to Entrepreneurial State? Brazilian Political Economy in the Wake of Privatization" (paper presented at the XVIII World Economic History Congress, Cambridge, MA, 1 August 2018).

The Expropriation of YPF in Historical Perspective: Limits of State Power Intervention in Argentina, 1989–2015

Esteban Serrani

Law No. 26,471 of *Soberanía Hidrocarburífera* (Hydrocarbons Law), enacted on 3 May 2012, represented a transcendental change of the dominant conception in Argentina regarding the exploitation of natural resources in general, and oil and gas in particular. This law declared both the achievement of internal energy supply as well as the activities regarding exploitation and industrialization of hydrocarbons in various segments of the industry to be of national public interest, in order to ensure "economic development with social equity." In this context, hydrocarbons became a strategic resource for the country's productive activities. They had been regarded as a simple exportable commodity "uncoupled" from the dynamics of local production (which were governed by the logic of the international market). In this sense, the law ordered the expropriation of 51 per cent of the assets of YPF (Yacimientos Petrolíferos Fiscales), the continent's first state oil company and one of Argentina's most important businesses for seventy years. The main objective of this chapter is to analyze YPF from its privatization in 1989 until its renationalization in 2012. It analyzes national particularities to explain why YPF was completely privatized in the 1990s (contrary to the regional experience in Mexico, Venezuela, and Brazil), and how, only twenty years later, the same company came back under a process of expropriation and state control, a reversal that had vast popular and parliamentary support. In this regard, this chapter analyzes the consequences of deregulation and financial liberalization of the oil industry from the acquisition of YPF by the Spanish multinational Repsol in 1999, until its nationalization in 2012.

Brief Description of Yacimientos Petrolíferos Fiscales

The early search for oil in Argentina is a paradigmatic example of the industry's roots in Latin America. The first efforts date back to the mid-nineteenth century (1855), when the federal government asked the French geologist Antonio Martin de Moussy to conduct a study on the country's mineral characteristics and fossil fuel potential. However, it was not until 1907 that the first oil fields in Comodoro Rivadavia were found, thanks to the federal government's interest in developing a vital industry to sustain the growth of both agricultural and transportation industries and industrialization.[1] This is how, in 1922, the federal government established the first state oil company in the continent, Yacimientos Petrolíferos Fiscales, which was vertically integrated in the oil supply chain. YPF was developed as a public oligopoly, increasing its production as the participation of private companies, which had operated in the country since the late nineteenth century, gradually decreased. The state's control over the oil sector through YPF deepened to the extent that the process of import substitution industrialization—a trade and economic policy that required a permanent energy supply at low cost—was consolidated after the Second World War.

The development of YPF was favoured by the advent of Peronism and the rapid increase of internal oil demand. However, the route taken by the state oil company was not free of controversy, whether that was from supporters of a full state monopoly or those who defended the participation of private oil companies in the market.[2] Following the military coup against Juan Perón in 1955, this tension was expressed strongly under the government of Arturo Frondizi, well-known for his program of "developmentalism." Frondizi, in order to expand oil exploration, signed a set of construction and service contracts with several of the most important multinational companies in the country, such as Standard Oil of California, Exxon, and Shell. In 1967, after the coups against Frondizi in 1962 and Arthur Umberto Illia in 1966, General Juan Carlos Onganía sanctioned the Hydrocarbons Law No. 17,319, which was still in force in 2012.

Yet the liberalization of the sector only began in earnest in 1976 with the sixth civilian-military coup in Argentina's history. At this time, the peripheral privatization of YPF began, through the increasing participation of local companies in the operation of the oil fields and service contracts to perform tasks that YPF executed at a lower cost.[3] Furthermore, the process gave rise to a policy of unfavourable prices for YPF. The company's use as holder of foreign loans for financial investments in the domestic market left it with a critical debt situation when democracy returned in 1983. In this way, the debt was established as the reason for starting a policy of openness toward the private sector, as the oil plans (Huergo; Houston; Olivos; Petroplán) established by constitutional president Raúl Alfonsín demonstrated.[4] Despite the increasing liberalization of the domestic oil sector and the privatization of important peripheral activities, YPF remained toward the end of the 1980s a key instrument for energy planning and the control of prices and domestic supply. However, the 1990s brought new ideas and the government's decision to restructure the company.[5]

Neoliberal Reforms and the Privatization of YPF, 1989–2001

After the premature departure of President Raúl Alfonsín early in 1989, a process of deep social change took place in Argentina, accelerated by the economic and energy crisis, as well as hyperinflation. At this time, some mainstream economists argued that much of the economic crisis of the 1980s in the region was due to the existence of an inefficient state unable to regulate monopolistic forms of economic action.[6] In order to sustain public spending, the state had to resort repeatedly to the reprinting of paper money, gradually reproducing the inflationary spiral. In accordance with the neoliberal ideology dominant in economics at the time, as well as the design of state policies, structural reforms in Argentina were carried out. In line with the definition offered by Pablo Heidrich in this volume, the policies deployed in this period took energy as a "market good." This differed from the Brazilian experience with Petrobras in the 1990s (see Gail D. Triner in this volume). The privatization of YPF was the largest sale of a public company in the history of Argentina, not only because of the magnitude of its worth, but also because of the depth of both the macroeconomic and social impacts.[7] In this sense, it is possible to organize the analysis of YPF's privatization in three stages, differentiated mainly by the various qualitative components. The first stage extends from the enactment of the first laws of structural reform to the implementation of domestic price deregulation (September 1989–December 1990); the second goes from the domestic deregulation of fuel prices to the privatization of YPF SE (January 1991–August 1992); and the third is the actual privatization of YPF (starting in September 1992 and lasting until May 1999).

From September 1989 to December 1990, both the federal government and private oil companies had no doubts about the need to advance toward a full deregulation and privatization of YPF. However, the question in those days was what assets to privatize from YPF and how. To do this, a set of laws and decrees allowing further deregulation of the sector was established. These changes in the sector-specific legislation fitted out the conversion of oil contracts with the private agents YPF had so far (many of them originated during the last military dictatorship and the government of Raúl Alfonsín between 1976 and 1989). The State Reform Act of 1989 (Law No. 23,696) initiated the structural transformation of the sector that enabled the renegotiation of oil contracts. The new legislation assured the private agents greater power to decide over the reserves of oil fields already tendered.

Additionally, the old contracts for extraction and exploitation of oil were converted into concessions and associations for a twenty-five-year period, to which was added the additional advantage of the free disposition of the products obtained. Concurrently, the Economic Emergency Law of 1989 (No. 23,697) deepened the structural changes in the sector, suspending allowances and tariff discounts to the industry, affecting the National Energy Fund, and discouraging the state control over prices until the market was fully deregulated. Finally, this law set the general guidelines on oil royalties that the state would receive once YPF was privatized. The government of President Carlos Menem issued three decrees specific to the oil industry just a few days after taking office in 1989, paving the way for the privatization of YPF. The first was Decree No. 1,055 of 1989, which defined the need to increase the productivity of oil exploitation through a "necessary deregulation." In this way, the state ceased to have any strategic influence over the sector by transferring the mechanisms of control over supply and pricing to the "market." In addition, the decree initiated the process of concession to private companies in secondary areas and association in the core areas of YPF.

Decree No. 1,212 of 1989 deepened the dismantling of YPF by reconverting the concession contracts and extending the offer of free availability. The federal government transferred the "private oligopoly"—the authority of assigning the price, the amounts allocated per company, and the values of transfers and subsidies—to the actors involved in the industry, thereby increasing the deregulation. Moreover, sought to adjust domestic prices to international prices and allow the fluctuation of the former to reflect the evolution of the latter. It also ratified the freedom to import and export oil. Finally, Decree No. 1,589 of 1989 consolidated the previous provisions and extended certain deregulatory mechanisms, ensuring the elimination of tariffs and export duties, and the free availability of 70 per cent of the foreign exchange obtained from the sale in the international market.

In the second stage, from the deregulation of prices to the beginning of the privatization of YPF (January 1991–August 1992), the federal government sought to restructure the company along the lines of a private firm. To achieve this objective, the company was divided into different business units by selling assets considered non-strategic for the new business structure desired for YPF. Decree No. 2,778 of 1990 propelled the "Plan of Comprehensive Transformation" that transformed the state oil corporation into a public company for which a timetable was established for the sale of its assets. In article 18, the market was reconfigured so as to distinguish between two types of units to tender: the primary and the secondary market. The valuation of YPF's oil and gas reserves was left to the international consulting firm Gaffney, Cline and Associates, which undervalued the price by 28 per cent.[8] The process of analysis and the proposed transformation of YPF were delegated to the international consulting firm McKinsey & Company. This project included the sale of company assets and partnerships with private companies to exploit some areas and to achieve the rationalization of the oil industry's workforce. Of the 51,000 workers (direct and indirect) employed by YPF at the end of 1990, only 7,500 remained three years later, resulting in a payroll reduction from $51 million to $17 million by the end of 1993.[9]

The advent of oil businessman José Estenssoro's directorship of YPF in August 1990 deepened the pro-market transformation of the state enterprise.[10] The measures taken by Estenssoro a few months after he took over direction of the company were aimed to denationalize forms of organization and internal management and restructure the production chain. It was necessary then to resize YPF through disinvestment in certain assets, which according to McKinsey & Company were "non-strategic."

Specifically in the primary market segment, important assets of the central areas of YPF (where there were the highest reserves) were transferred to the private sector. Through Decree No. 1,216 of 1990, private companies were called to a prequalification to access in partnership with YPF the 50 per cent of recoverable oil and gas reserves in the four core areas. Four consortiums were awarded with contracts of association, three of which were formed by some of the same firms that had served as contractors since the beginning of YPF's peripheral privatization, although this time they were associated with major multinationals.[11] Yet, far from receiving the minimum of $800 million projected from the sale of the four main oil areas tendered, the federal government only received about $550 million. The loss of about $250 million was a direct result of the pricing policy implemented by YPF.[12] Instead of placing the oil in the local market for $20 per barrel (international prices), it was sold for $14. At the same time, between 1990 and 1991, 86 other marginal areas (in addition to the 105 existing) were adjudicated for a total of $470 million.[13] In the secondary market segment, all the country's refineries were privatized, including San Lorenzo, Dock Sud, Campo Durán, Luján de Cuyo, La Plata, and Plaza Huincul. Important assets of the naval fleet, naval workshops, ports, and other state oil plants were transferred as well. This process of transferring stocks and the sale of non-strategic assets from YPF meant revenue for the state of $2.059 billion, and a decline of 40 per cent in YPF reserves and 25 per cent in oil extraction between 1991 and 1993.[14]

Finally, the third stage relates to the very process of YPF's privatization (September 1992–May 1999). Once the state company had been restructured to resemble a private oil company, the only thing remaining was "to close" the process by trading YPF shares on the stock market. At that time, the government of Carlos Menem, pressured by the weight of the foreign debt, expected that the sale of YPF would allow the cancellation of pension debt by using assets to pay current liabilities. After many twists and turns regarding the official privatization project, in September 1992 the Law No. 24,145, the Federalization of Hydrocarbons Law, was enacted. From this law, the federal government reserved 51 per cent of the shares of the new corporation that would replace the state company. On 29 June 1993, YPF shares began trading on the local stock exchange. For 43.5 per cent of the shares, $3.04 billion were received at a rate of $19 per share. Of the total sales, the federal government received $1.7 billion, and the rest was for the shareholding provinces, company staff, and bondholders of pension liabilities. After the initial public offering, the shares were structured so that 45.3 per cent were held by the private sector and 54 per cent by the federal government, provinces, and the company personnel; the distribution by nationality was 34 per cent for foreign shareholders and 66 per cent for Argentine shareholders.

One unique technical aspect of the privatization of the state oil company was the fact that the revenue from the sale was not intended to cover expenses or deficits but to consolidate public debt. By cancelling provisional debt and the purchase of debt, the so called bonds of security debt consolidation and other debts in cash, for a nominal value of nearly 3 billion Argentine pesos, were rescued.[15] However, considering the valuation that the Ministry of Economy set for every action, there is no doubt that they were heavily undervalued.[16] In this manner, the state gave away 80 per cent of its shares over time (despite the law passed in 1993 stipulating that the state should reserve for itself 51 per cent of the shares). The decoupling of public agencies from the oil company was progressive until 1999, when Spanish multinational Repsol bought a 98.23 per cent stake in YPF, taking immediate control over the company's business strategies.

The 2000s and the Reorientation of Oil Policies

After the traumatic events of December 2001 and the crisis of democratic institutions—five presidents were elected between December 2001 and January 2002—the Legislative Assembly appointed as interim president Eduardo Duhalde, a Peronist who at the time served as senator for the province of Buenos Aires. A few days after taking office, the new government enacted the Law of Public Emergency and Exchange System Reform No. 25,561, which marked—through the devaluation of the national currency—the end of the exchange convertibility of "1 Argentine peso equal to 1 US dollar." This measure changed the structure of costs and internal relative prices, deepening the financial crisis by bringing about a 10 per cent drop in gross domestic product, with a marked loss of employee purchasing power of around 30 per cent on the profits of large companies because of the "pesofication" of dollar debts. Finally, the law gave special powers to the executive to run the economy, given the situation of systemic crisis throughout the country.

However, it was not until the governments of Néstor Kirchner and Cristina Fernández de Kirchner that a shift in state intervention in the economy became evident. This reorientation, which aimed to boost productive processes, led to a rate of economic growth rarely seen in the history of Argentina; this was especially the case between 2003 and 2008. An aggressive policy of job creation and wage recovery energized the domestic market while substantially reducing rates of poverty and destitution. This dynamic economic structure was safeguarded by macroeconomic balance (fiscal and trade surpluses) in addition to a successful restructuring of the defaulted debt carried out in 2005 and 2010.[17] However, the central part of the oligopolistic economic structure of large price makers and the concentration and foreign ownership of the economy changed little from previous decades. This structure had a strong impact on the dynamics of the oil industry and decision-making in the sector. In this sense, the change in governmental orientation in energy policy, prone as it was to practise state intervention in the economy, transformed the conception of energy from a "market good" to a "common good," to once again borrow Pablo Heidrich's definition (see his chapter in this volume). Far from considering energy a "political good," with a state monopoly over the entire sector, Argentina faced constant energy crises in 2003, due to at least two concurrent processes: the sustained growth in domestic demand for energy, and the establishment of private oligopolistic control throughout the YPF supply chain and in the energy sector in general.

As for oil policy, the 2000s marked a change in the role of the state in the dispute over rent with private companies, as well as an end to the completely unregulated market of the 1990s. First, a fiscal policy of income capture was developed, accompanied by internal pricing management. With Decree No. 310 of 2002, the federal government re-established export duties of 20 per cent on crude oil and 5 per cent for refined products. This tax was modified in May 2004, when export duties were increased to 25 per cent (Resolution No. 337 of 2004), and then again in August of that year, when it became "movable." This meant that if the price of West Texas Intermediate (WTI) was below $32 per barrel, the aliquots were 25 per cent, but if the international price was above $32 per barrel, the aliquots were between 3 and 20 per cent. In January 2007, the government enacted Law No. 26,217, which extended for five years the validity of the export duty on mineral oils. Thus, there was a new scheme, much more aggressive in terms of oil rent capture, based on three fluctuating determinants: (1) if the international oil price (WTI) is between $45 and $61 per barrel, the export duty is 45 per cent; (2) if the oil price is lower than $45, the federal government has ninety days to define a new system of aliquots; (2) if the international price exceeds $61 per barrel, the formula assumes that no matter the increase of the price per barrel in the international market, exporters receive only $42 per exported barrel (value cut-off), with the difference being captured by the federal government.

Second, it carried out a deepening of provincial control over the deposits. In October 2006, the "Federal Oil Agreement" was reached, which resulted in the enactment of Law No. 26,197, the Federal Hydrocarbons Law, in December of that year. The Federal Hydrocarbon Agreement was settled with the signature of the president of the nation and those of the governors of the producing provinces. This was done in order to enforce the second paragraph of article 124 of the Constitution (which had already been extended by Decree No. 564 of 2003), where the domain of the provinces over natural resources in the case of hydrocarbons is enshrined.[18]

In this way, both the agreement and the law deepened the policy of fragmented sovereignty regarding the decision-making and policy guidance on oil, which started with the constitutional reform of 1994.

In the third place, fiscal incentives to productivity in the context of a prolonged decline were implemented in both oil extraction and private investment in exploration. In November 2008, the government, under Decree No. 2,014 of 2008, launched the "Oil Plus" and "Refining Plus" programs, seeking to stimulate investments in exploration, mining, and refining, and to promote the incorporation of reserves. The first plan, Oil Plus, looked for new investments that increased the levels of production and reserves. Tax incentives would be used to cancel export duties. The aim was for the transfer of the costs of production to indirectly impact the improvement in end crude oil prices for the domestic market. Meanwhile, Refining Plus sought to expand idle oil refining capacity, stagnant for many decades. This plan also fostered tax incentives for new refineries or the expansion of refining capacity in diesel and premium gasoline. Additionally, a special regime of benefits for small non-integrated refiners was established. However, these goals went unrealized due to the reluctance of private companies to risk investments in infrastructure while seeking to explore in areas with proven reserves, discovered by YPF.[19]

Finally, the federal government sought an extension of state participation and the "Argentinization" of public services. With the intention of restarting state participation in productive activities in the oil industry, the company Energía Argentina Corp. (ENARSA) was established by Law No. 25,943 in December 2004. ENARSA was granted the ownership of exploration permits and concessions for all offshore blocks in order to attract venture investment strategically associated with the new state company. Nonetheless, according to company information, by the end of 2012, the three consortiums formed for all offshore oil exploration have not yet achieved the main goal of expanding proven oil and gas reserves. At the same time, toward the end of 2007 and the beginning of 2008, boosted by the federal government, the Petersen Group Corp., owned by the Eskenazi family, bought 14.9 per cent of the shares of YPF, with an option to acquire an additional 10 per cent within five years (by the end of 2011). The operation was performed for a total of $2.235 billion (the group contributed $100 million). It was funded almost entirely by debts contracted by the buyers, $1.017 billion through a loan from Repsol itself, and another loan of $1.018 billion from a pool of banks that included Credit Suisse, Goldman Sachs, BNP Paribas, and Itaú.

The resulting Argentinization of YPF shares with the Petersen Group's entry was a bid to halt the industry's decline. The government considered it easier to discuss, discipline, and negotiate with domestic entrepreneurs.[20] However, Repsol had already begun disinvestment in YPF, and the Petersen Group's entry with a large debt assumed by the company of which it was now shareholder contributed to the draining short-term profit-seeking strategies by which the company sought to assume financial commitments, fund investments that Repsol had elsewhere (which were considered strategic), and transfer much of the profits to the shareholders. Clearly, the efforts of the Eskenazi family ended up failing, generating huge financial costs for YPF. So, what course did YPF chart under the management of the Spanish Repsol?

Repsol in Argentina and the Dismantling of YPF, 1999–2012

The analysis of Repsol's performance in Argentina allows us to understand and explain a central part of the course and outcome of YPF. The purchase in 1999 of the entire stake enabled Repsol to integrate a large stock of hydrocarbon reserves that in turn enabled it not only to vertically integrate (balancing its upstream business with the downstream), but also to position itself as one of the world's ten largest oil companies in terms of reserves and market capitalization.[21] However, the arrival of the Spanish company meant an aggressive restructuring plan of strategic assets and a set of planned disinvestments in order to capitalize Repsol's headquarters in Spain, which was highly indebted, to the detriment of companies that it now controlled around the world. From an analysis of the company's balance sheets from 1999 onwards, it can be said that YPF developed two major mechanisms of capitalization via the asset disinvestment that Repsol considered "non-strategic." The first was the transfer of assets from controlled companies to its headquarters; and the second was the sale of assets to third parties that would end up representing revenues of $3.5 billion for the Spanish company. Regarding the first mechanism, between 1999 and 2001, Repsol-YPF successfully transferred to its Spanish headquarters holdings in Peru (YPF Peru and Refiners of Peru) and Brazil (YPF Brazil Corp.), as well as those in Ecuador and Colombia, totalling approximately $535 million. Repsol-YPF also disposed of its assets in Venezuela through Maxus Venezuela and Maxus Guarapiche, totalling $70 million. Finally, Repsol-YPF transferred in 2002 its investments in Bolivia (Andina and Maxus Bolivia), for a total of almost $900 million.

Regarding the second mechanism, in 2001 Repsol got rid of the YPF stake in Crescendo Resources L. P., a US gas-producing company, for $624 million. The assets that YPF had in Chile (the Trans Andean Pipeline) were also sold for $66 million. The same happened to YPF shares in International Canada when the Bitech Petroleum Corporation was sold to the Russian Lukoil, and in Indonesia when the company got rid of its holdings in YPF Blora, YPF Maxus Southeast Sumatra, Java Baratlaut YPF, YPF Madura Barat, YPF Poleng, and PT IIAPCO Services, which in 2003 sold YPF Indonesia for $139 million. In Argentina, it first sold YPF's stake in Electricidad Argentina Corp. and then transferred to Eg3 investments (assets leased at Petrobras), such as PBB Polisur Corp. and Petroquímica Ensenada Corp.

Both mechanisms resulted in a decrease in the capitalization of YPF and the end of its international integration strategy (expanded during the 1990s since the administration of former president José Estenssoro). Through YPF, Repsol reflected the development of a strategy for over-exploitation of natural resources as a mechanism of capital accumulation in Argentina deployed by transnational capital. This strategy can be translated into concrete terms. In relation to oil drilling between 1999 and 2011, it fell 39,637 barrels per day (32 per cent), while YPF's extraction suffered a decline of 20,126 barrels per day (40 per cent). In this sense, Repsol-YPF explains the 51 per cent decline overall of extraction since Repsol-YPF took control.

During the same period and taking into consideration the natural gas market, while the country increased its production by 466 cubic feet per day, the production of Repsol-YPF fell 221 cubic feet per day. That is, if the performance of Repsol-YPF in the period is excluded, the remaining companies of the Argentine gas market increased production at 689 cubic feet per day (26 per cent). Between 1999 and 2011, the country lost 31 per cent of its proven oil reserves (963 million barrels), while YPF's proven oil reserves fell 45 per cent (344 million barrels). The downfall of YPF's proven oil reserves explains the 36 per cent drop in the country's total reserves. In this sense, if in 1999 YPF represented 25 per cent of total proven oil reserves, in 2011 it only accounted for 20 per cent.

The maturation of the company's main sources could explain part of the decline in production and reserves. But if this geological factor was not associated with the strategy of capital accumulation deployed by Repsol-YPF in the short term (extracting at a higher rate than reserves stocks were replenished), no one could explain the declining performance of the company in the long run. Associated with these processes, between 1999 and 2011, YPF invested in an average of 11 exploration wells per year, compared to an annual average of 110 wells during the 1980s (for a 90 per cent reduction).[22] Finally, the jolts to the YPF imports meant a very high cost in terms of the surplus oil trade balance, and energy in general, which would worsen as time went on. According to official statistics from the Ministry of Energy, while YPF did not import energy products in 1988, ten years later it had imported energy products worth $96 million. In 2011, the amount rose to $1.18 billion (a 1,125 per cent increase between 1999 and 2011). Indeed, the country's largest oil company developed a scheduled disinvestment in extraction and exploration, resulting in a significant reduction of reserves not only for the company but for the market as a whole. Much of YPF's strategy was focused on the most profitable segments of the industry, such as sales of liquid fuels to the domestic market (especially expensive fuels such as premium gasoline and diesel), in which it controlled at least 50 per cent of total sales. The systematic decline in oil extraction, refining, and investment in exploration was compounded by the pressure exerted by energy imports on the national trade balance. In 2011, this totalled $9.397 billion, an amount almost equal to the total trade surplus. Also, the relationship between imports and exports of energy ended up being negative, at $2.931 billion in 2011. In this sense, the decline in energy production, the impact of the deterioration of the trade balance, and the renewed political power of the federal government, which obtained 54 per cent of the votes in the 2011 elections, were circumstances that hastened the economic course already adopted. President Kirchner could then take steps to reverse the decline of the productive sector. In this context, the state recovered YPF, its historic flagship company, and regained the ability to exert sovereignty over energy resources.

The Expropriation of YPF and the Road to Energy Self-Sufficiency

The ongoing transformations in the national oil sector reflect the revitalization of the state's role in planning and economic development. After twenty years of structural reforms in the oil industry, which included the sale of the most important state company in Argentina's history, the laws and decrees enacted since late 2011 represent an attempt to reverse the neoliberal trend of full deregulation in the field of hydrocarbons. The way to end the institutionalized privileges accorded to oil companies in the process of capital accumulation, the result of the neoliberal structural reforms described above, began in October 2011 with the enactment of Decree No. 1,722. The decree ended the differential regime, which since 1989 exempted the settlement of up to 70 per cent of foreign exchange earned from commodity exports of mining and oil activities. Having changed the circumstances that gave rise to the tax exemptions, it was necessary to re-establish mandatory income and trading on the exchange market for all foreign exchange coming from export operations of oil and mining companies, in accordance with Decree No. 2,581 of 1964. This policy was of the utmost importance since the projections of capital flight for 2011 were estimated to reach the historical record of 2008, close to $23.165 billion, almost half of the reserves of the Central Bank.

Several studies demonstrate that the objective of the private energy companies in the country, after the deregulation and privatization of hydrocarbons, has been to favour the maximization of profits in the short term and the remission of profits abroad.[23] This logic of capital accumulation is structurally incompatible with the need to have enough energy available to ensure the development of national production, at a cost that ensures the competitive advantage of products produced in the country both in the domestic market and abroad. To meet these goals requires national long-term planning and the rational exploitation of resources, the search for new energy sources, and energy diversification ensuring these sources' future availability. As part of these social and economic concerns, two transcendent laws were sanctioned in order to reverse the pro-market organization of the industry.

Law No. 26,741, the Hydrocarbons Law, was approved in May 2012 with the support of a large majority in both parliamentary chambers. This law declared the achievement of "self-sufficiency in oil and exploration, exploitation, processing, transportation and marketing of hydrocarbons seeking to ensure economic development with social equity, the creation of jobs, increased competitiveness of the different economic sectors, and the equitable and sustainable growth of all provinces and regions" of national public interest for the country. Overall, the priorities and the principles of the national oil policy established by the law sought to reverse the long cycle of neoliberal dominance in the exploitation of hydrocarbon resources in Argentina, giving the state a central role in the organization and development of this industry. The same law declared the expropriation of 51 per cent of the assets of YPF and YPF Gas (owned by Repsol).[24] YPF is a state instrument to revive entrepreneurial activities in the sector, in line with other major industrial countries in the region (Brazil and Mexico), as well as the rest of the countries with reserves of oil and gas (Ecuador, Bolivia, Venezuela, and Colombia). At the same time, a Federal Board of Hydrocarbons composed of the Ministry of Economy, the Ministry of Federal Planning, Public Investment and Services, the Ministry of Labour, the Ministry of Industry, and the provinces, was created for the federal development of a national energy policy. According to the federal government, it was necessary to reverse the trend toward venture investment in oil exploration shown by the private oil companies, especially those controlled by Repsol-YPF.

Thus, in June 2012, Decree No. 1,277 was sanctioned. It sought to regulate Law No. 26,741, and to advance an issue that that law had not addressed. In order to comply with the principles of the new rules in the national oil industry, the Commission for Strategic Planning and Coordination of the National Hydrocarbons Investment Plan was established to carry forward its work. The commission was tasked with ensuring and promoting the necessary investments to reach self-sufficiency in hydrocarbons and establishing measures to control domestic prices. Up until the enactment of the law that expropriated 51 per cent of YPF, domestic prices were set by the logic of the oligopolized operation of private firms. The commission seeks to integrate public and private, national and international capital in strategic alliances aimed at the exploration and exploitation of conventional and unconventional hydrocarbons. It is tasked with the promotion of industrialization, the marketing of hydrocarbons with high added value, and the protection of consumer interests when it comes to the price, quality, and availability of hydrocarbon derivatives. In short, the new orientation of the national hydrocarbon policy entails the enormous challenge of reversing two decades of full decline in the performance indicators of the industry and over-exploitation of hydrocarbon resources as a strategy of accumulation for private enterprises. In the very short term, however, the new legal structure of the oil market and the shareholding structure of YPF have resulted in some attenuation of previous trends. If YPF oil extraction fell, between 1999 and 2011, at an annual cumulative rate of -4.1 per cent (higher than the -3.0 per cent for the whole country), the extraction of YPF rose +4.5 per cent between 2012 and 2015 (while the other companies fell at a rate of -4.2 per cent per annum), thereby breaking the downward trend of the thirteen previous years since Repsol's arrival. As for the extraction of natural gas, between 1999 and 2011, the decline in YPF was -1.5 per cent per annum (when the country's total was -0.9 per cent), but since 2012, the trend has reversed. Between 2012 and 2015, YPF's natural gas production grew at an average annual rate of 8.4 per cent (showing a clear change of direction as the rest of the companies in the local market fell -4.0 per cent per annum in the same period).

Limits of State Energy Intervention

Economic development is closely linked to the availability of energy to power the production sector. To sustain accelerated growth rates, it is necessary to have abundant energy. At the same time, this energy must be provided at costs that allow for a transformation of the energy equation in a vector of competitiveness for the rest of the economy. In the 1990s, it was argued that globalization needed a minimum level of state intervention in the economy to expand the market logic, which will allow the internationalization of companies and the opening of national economic boundaries for increased trade, greater global integration, and higher levels of development. Far from fulfilling these "prophecies," financial globalization allowed the advance of multinational companies from the core countries over peripheral markets, implying a deterioration of national states' capacity to control large corporations. In this sense, Spanish companies found an opportunity to extend their reach by participating in the privatization of public companies in various Latin American countries. The case of YPF's purchase by Repsol is a perfect example of this process. No doubt, when the federal government lost control of YPF, it was failing to comply with the strategic production objectives that gave rise to it. Since it was created in 1922, YPF had managed to expand oil extraction and the supply of energy in all its forms, developing a robust industrial and technological production system that was recognized not only nationally, but also regionally. It was also responsible for expanding the national hydrocarbon border after decades of exploration investment. In addition, YPF acted as a witness company in all segments of the oil industry, controlling domestic prices and seeking energy self-sufficiency, which was achieved for the first time in the early 1980s. Neoliberalism left its mark on the national oil industry and the region. After the obvious failure of the model of private management in Argentina, the country is again facing a double challenge: first, to achieve energy self-sufficiency and sustain industrial demand, resolving the deficit in the balance of trade and sustaining economic growth; and second, to discipline private companies that developed a system of sub-scanning and exploitation, based on the new guidelines of the national hydrocarbon policy.

After the expropriation of YPF, did the federal government take strategic control of this industry? No. YPF was able to reverse the decline of its production and, with strong state support, deploy an extensive process of profit reinvestment to reverse its poor sector performance indicators, while the company embarked on a learning curve aimed at shale resources exploitation. However, YPF's performance was not matched by the rest of the private oil companies, which together continued to diminish their production, thereby slowing the recovery of the sector. With the change of government in December 2015, the new state administration abandoned energy self-sufficiency as a priority objective of the energy sector, and returned to the logic of free trade liberalization and sector deregulation. Again, the pendulum has swung in the Argentine political system, leading to the denationalization of the main and most important companies in Argentina. Economic power and the lack of stability in the orientation of public policies has emerged as a (old and persistent) structural obstacle to economic development.

NOTES

This chapter has been translated by David Barrios Giraldo, with the assistance of Andrew Wiley. An earlier version was published as "Transformaciones recientes en la industria petrolera argentina: El caso de Yacimientos Petrolíferos Fiscales, 1989-2012," *Revista de Gestión Pública* 2, no. 1 (January-June 2013): 247-80.

1   Comodoro Rivadavia is a city located in the province of Chubut, in the southern part of the country. This city is well-known as the capital of the Argentine oil industry.

2   Ignacio Sabbatella and Esteban Serrani, "A 20 años de la privatización de YPF. Balance y perspectivas," *Voces en el Fénix* 2 no. 10 (July-December, 2011): 8.

3   Ana Castellani and Esteban Serrani, "La persistencia de los ámbitos privilegiados de acumulación en la economía argentina. El caso del mercado de hidrocarburos entre 1977 y 1999," *H-Industri@* 4, no. 6, (January-June 2010): 12.

4   Gonzalo Calleja, "La política energética del gobierno de Alfonsín (II)," *Realidad Económica*, no. 214 (2005): 114-17.

5   This chapter only analyzes the transformations of the Argentine oil market. For a comparative analysis of the major changes in the Latin American oil matrix generated by the structural reforms of the 1980s, and their economic and institutional impacts, see Esteban Serrani, "América Latina y su política petrolera frente a las últimas tendencias internacionales. Perspectivas regionales a partir del análisis de Brasil y Argentina," *Foro Internacional* 53, no. 1 (January-March 2013): 182-213.

6   World Bank, *World Development Report 1987* (New York: World Bank/Oxford University Press, 1987).

7   For a detailed analysis of the macroeconomic impacts, see Esteban Serrani, "Estado, empresarios y acumulación de privilegio. Análisis de la industria petrolera argentina, 1988-2008" (PhD diss., Universidad de Buenos Aires, 2012), and Mariano Barrera, Ignacio Sabbatella, and Esteban Serrani, *Historia de una privatización: Cómo y por qué se perdió YPF* (Buenos Aires: Capital Intelectual, 2012). Regarding the social and employment impacts, see Hernán Palermo, *Cadenas de oro negro en el esplendor y ocaso de YPF* (Buenos Aires: Antropofagia, 2012).

8   The concessions of YPF deposits represented less revenue than the actual cost of the company. YPF's assets were estimated at $20 billion, despite the fact that the consultant valued them between $3 and $4 billion. However, Decree No. 2,778 of 1990 estimated only $1.17 billion, significantly less than the consulting firm Gaffney, Cline and Associates. See Roberto Kozulj and Víctor Bravo, *La política de desregulación petrolera*

     argentina. Antecedentes e impactos (Buenos Aires: Centro Editor de América Latina, 1993).

9   YPF, *Memoria de YPF 1993* (Buenos Aires: Library of the Ministry of Economy, 1994). Note: all dollar figures given in this chapter refer to US currency.

10   José Estenssoro was related to Bolivian president Víctor Paz Estenssoro, who carried out a deep reform of that country's oil industry in 1955, the so-called Petroleum Code that allowed the entry of private capital into the oil business.

11   The Vizcacheras site in Mendoza was adjudicated to Perez Companc (in partnership with Occidental Exploration of Argentina); El Tordillo in Chubut to Tecpetrol (with Santa Fe Energy); and Puesto Hernández in Neuquén and Mendoza, and Astra (in partnership with REPSOL). The remaining site, El Huemul (Santa Cruz) was left to Austral Total (of France).

12   More prudent investigations assured that the four areas, representing only 18 per cent of the total production of the contracts converted, generated a loss of $150 million for the state. Nicolás Gadano and Federico Sturzenegger, "La privatización de reservas en el sector hidrocarburífero. El caso de Argentina," *Revista de Análisis Económico* 13, no. 1 (June 1998): 75–115. Besides the $150 million in the most conservative projections, or $250 million in the least conservative ones, it is clear that the strong undervaluation of state assets held by the various interest groups represented a net income transfer to the players concentrated in the industry.

13   Roberto Kozulj, *Balance de la privatización de la industria petrolera en Argentina y su impacto sobre las inversiones y la competencia en los mercados minoristas* (Santiago de Chile: CEPAL, 2002)

14   Kozulj, *Balance de la privatización de la industria petrolera en Argentina*; and YPF, *Memoria de YPF 1993.*

15   YPF, *Memoria de YPF 1993.*

16   Mariano Barrera, "Subexploración y sobreexplotación: La lógica de acumulación del sector hidrocarburífero en Argentina," *Apuntes para el cambio*, no. 2 (March–April 2012): 22–5; Kozulj, *Balance de la privatización de la industria petrolera en Argentina*, 22–4; Daniel Montamat, *La energía argentina. Otra víctima del desarrollo ausente* (Buenos Aires: Editorial El Ateneo, 2005); Ignacio Sabbatella, "La política petrolera de la posconvertibilidad: De la herencia neoliberal a la expropiación de YPF," *Argumentos*, no. 14 (January–June 2012): 168–9; Serrani, "América Latina y su política petrolera," 198–9. In fact, the clearest sign of the undervaluation of shares in YPF was the fact that a day after the initial public offering, they cost 13.9 per cent more, reaching $21.87 per share on the New York Stock Exchange. This meant an immediate net transfer of resources to the new YPF shareholders of about $420 million.

17   In both restructuring processes (2005 and 2010), the Argentine government managed to normalize the situation with 92.4 per cent of default debt. However, the remaining 7.6 per cent, mostly "vulture funds," were henceforth litigated in the New York courts, and they were able to deploy their lobbying power to collect 100 per cent of their claims plus interest, even though they bought default bonds at auction price. In 2015, a New York court ruled against Argentina, and in an unprecedented interpretation of the *pari*

passu clause—it granted the vulture funds the right to collect 100 per cent of their claim plus interest, even against the other 92.4 per cent of the creditors who had accepted a withdrawal, interest reduction, and extension of terms in the debt restructuring of 2005 and 2010—allowed it to collect nearly $10.5 billion—that is, a global return of up to 1,270 per cent compared to its initial investment.

18 These hydrocarbon-producing provinces are Tierra del Fuego, Antártida e Islas del Atlántico Sur, Santa Cruz, Chubut, Río Negro, La Pampa, Neuquén, Mendoza, Salta, Formosa, and Jujuy.

19 Serrani, "Estado, empresarios y acumulación de privilegio," ch. 5. However, none of these surplus production incentive schemes were effective, as they failed to halt the decline in domestic supply that led to the loss of self-sufficiency in 2011.

20 Alice Amsden, "Diffusion of Development: The Late-Industrializing Model and Greater East Asia," *American Economic Review* 81, no. 2 (May 1991): 282–6; Robert Wade, *El mercado dirigido: La teoría económica y la función del gobierno en la industrialización del este de Asia*, trans. Mónica Utrilla de Neira (Mexico City: Fondo de Cultura Económica, 1999).

21 The business network that acquired the capital stock of Repsol Spain allowed it access to $15.5 billion worth of credit for the purchase of YPF, which was offered by a consortium of financial institutions, many of them shareholders of the Spanish company, such as the BBV and La Caixa, along with others like Goldman Sachs, Merrill Lynch, Citigroup, and Union Bank of Switzerland.

22 While YPF was still a state company.

23 Barrera, "Subexploración y sobreexplotación," 32–3; Kozulj, *Balance de la privatización de la industria petrolera en Argentina*, 74–6; Sabbatella, "La política petrolera de la posconvertibilidad," 155; Serrani, "Estado, empresarios y acumulación de privilegio," chs. 5 and 7; Serrani, "América Latina y su política petrolera," 201–3.

24 The expropriation of YPF did not imply a strong public discussion about the negative impacts on the environment or climate change of an energy matrix with strong dependence on fossil fuels: around 85 per cent of primary energy is produced by hydrocarbon sources. However, since the expropriation of YPF in 2012, environmental issues linked to the oil industry were underscored by two situations. The first was raised by the minister of economy, Axel Kicillof (2012–15), who in April 2012 initiated a public discussion about the environmental liabilities that Repsol had left in Argentina. However, an ex-post analysis shows that the Argentine government used the claim regarding environmental liabilities as an instrument to discuss the price of compensation to be paid to Repsol for the expropriation. In the second case, while the federal government was seeking to regain energy sovereignty, in 2013 it encouraged YPF to sign a strategic agreement with Chevron for the development of the field named Vaca Muerta (one of the world's largest unconventional reservoirs). Opposition deputies in the Legislative Assembly denounced the agreement because the text of the agreement was not public (the text was only known by the two companies), and because it could imply damages for the country, as Chevron had caused, years ago, in the Ecuadorian Amazon. The complaint was resolved by the Supreme Court, which forced YPF to publish the agreement. The company objected that the contract had "confidential

information and sensitive operational data, and its publication could harm YPF's economic performance on the market." In a paradox of history, one of the Opposition deputies who in 2014 had filed a complaint against YPF, was nominated, after the change of government in 2015, to run the Anti-Corruption Office. From her new position in government, she blocked the publication of the contract, now employing the same arguments that YPF presented in 2014.

Coming Full Circle: Mexican Oil, 1917–2018

Linda B. Hall

During the 1910s, petroleum had begun to be the most important energy resource, in industry as in war. Mexico and Venezuela emerged as key producers of that significant resource; Mexico's oil, next door to the United States and just at the edge of the Gulf of Mexico, poured out during those years, but with very little recompense, as it was recovered and sent to the United States, while Venezuela, under dictator General Juan Vicente Gómez, increased its petroleum production, particularly with the help of Shell Oil and then Gulf. Venezuela was only 3,500 miles from Britain, while Mexico was 5,000 miles away, but uncomfortably close to the United States. During the 1920s and '30s, Venezuela began to produce huge amounts of oil; Mexico tried to recover and save its resources (see Brian S. McBeth in this volume). Argentina's government, hoping to be a contender, set up the first vertically integrated state petroleum company in Latin America, Yacimientos Petrolíferos Fiscales (YPF), yet Argentina was not able to produce high volumes of oil (see Esteban Serrani in this volume). Initially, the two contenders in Latin America were Mexico and Venezuela, but Mexico was looking for something quite different.

Between 1910 and 1917, Mexico experienced a violent revolution, and in the immediate aftermath of the turmoil, its winners focused almost exclusively upon the creation of a new constitution. These leaders, no less than their followers, strongly objected to injustices regarding land and subsoil resources provided to foreign investors by the previous dictator, Porfirio Díaz; they fixated on the protection of these resources, and this fixation included an emphasis on economic nationalism. The most important section of the Constitution they produced in 1917, article 27, concentrated on land and natural resources, affirming on a legal basis that all such assets would be considered the property and patrimony of the state and its people. The sector most affected for our purposes was the modern petroleum industry, which began precisely during these seven years of revolution with the first major discoveries of oil within Mexican territory. Interests from the United States and Great Britain, taking advantage of the chaotic and violent situation, had quickly established dominant positions in exploration and extraction, distributing oil directly out of coastal ports on the Gulf of Mexico. At the same time, industrial and military entities across the world, rapidly recognizing the immense promise of oil, were quickly taking advantage of this viable new fuel source. Venustiano Carranza, the first chief of the revolution and then first president, followed by subsequent presidents from 1920 to 1940, was determined to ensure that this valuable resource would preserve its benefits, in the near and long term, for the Mexican nation and its populace. Ninety-seven years later, these legalities were eliminated in favour of permitting foreign and private subsoil rights. These major constitutional protections, long considered as a basis of the nation's patrimony, were for a time abandoned.

This sentiment reached its apogee in 1938, when Mexico's president, Lázaro Cárdenas, nationalized the entire oil industry—a formative event in post-revolutionary Mexican political history. In the decades that followed, the notion of reintroducing private or other foreign ownership of the country's "oil patrimony" was politically anathema. However, first in the 1990s, amidst the advent of the North American Free Trade Agreement (NAFTA) and other market-focused legislation, and then with greater speed in late 2000, a series of presidential regimes trained by elite (usually US) institutions in economics and business and public administration began to crack open the door to private and foreign interests. In recent years these efforts have gained even stronger momentum, and finally, in 2014, the national Congress altered the Constitution to legally sanction this participation. As a result, a series of nationally sponsored auctions were scheduled for mid- to late 2015 to allow new kinds of exploration and production operations. These auctions represent important political and economic changes in Mexico's natural resource regime, shifting the state's political ideology significantly over a period of almost a hundred years.

The Mexican Constitution of 1917 was a bold document. President Carranza and his cohort had a clear mandate from the Mexican populace to make radical transformations, and they took advantage of his faction's military and political victories to do so. Specifically, article 27 stated that all "lands and waters" were vested in the nation itself and were to be used for the well-being of its entirety. While article 27 did recognize in some cases that private property could be created by the conveyance of title to individuals by the nation, rights to the subsoil could *not* be so conveyed; rather, these were held in "direct dominion" by the Mexican government itself. Critically, all rights to the exploitation of the subsoil became concessions from the nation.[1] Carranza and the rest of Mexico's revolutionary leadership were well aware of the value of the country's oil fields; at the same time, the US and British oilmen who had already exploited those fields were concerned about their access remaining open. For Carranza's government, like that of his successor, Álvaro Obregón, revenue from petroleum represented the only viable resource with which to re-establish government functions and to develop new programs.

Even before Carranza had become president, he had tried, in his role as first chief, to tax oil production. After his inauguration as president, and now recognized by US president Woodrow Wilson, he further attempted to charge royalties, invoking the principle in the new Constitution that subsoil resources belonged to the nation. Still, he was unable to implement the decree, as foreign oil companies did not comply and Carranza had no power to compel them to do so. His administration then began to issue less restrictive drilling permits at the end of 1918, in an attempt to encourage compliance. When Obregón became president in late 1920, he likewise tried to control his nation's own resources via its newly established constitutional powers. At the same time, he had to proceed carefully because there was not enough capital—public or private—within Mexico at the end of the revolution to develop the oil fields. Meanwhile, new US president Warren Harding, inaugurated in March 1921, refused to recognize Obregón's administration in order to maintain leverage on a series of issues between the two countries, especially a dispute involving former US senator Albert Fall, who had become Harding's secretary of the interior and who had taken over his portfolio on oil issues. In 1919 and 1920, Fall had directed "the investigation of Mexican affairs" in the Senate and then attacked its government; then, in December 1920, he tried to bribe Alvaro Obregón just as he was about to be inaugurated president. Obregón refused, and Fall became an implacable enemy to Obregón and his administration. This lack of recognition, and in turn this lack of capital, slowed the process of economic recovery as the Mexican administration struggled to pull the country out of years of economic disaster. Petroleum was the only sector that might generate sufficient revenues to this end; agriculture and mining had largely been destroyed, and it would take time and great effort to bring them back to productivity. Meanwhile the British, with the end of the First World War, re-established ties with US companies in Mexico and then largely deferred to them in regard to further oil questions.

In May and June 1921, shortly after he had taken office, President Obregón instituted taxes on petroleum—a production tax of 10 per cent at US (rather than wellhead) prices and an export tax. The second levy, as much political as economic, emphasized the importance of Mexican oil holdings to the world market. These taxes were tied to economic development, to conservation, and to addressing environmental damage caused by exploration and extraction.[2] The US Association of Petroleum Producers in Mexico reacted by quickly cutting off oil shipments. However, a modus vivendi was soon reached after discussions in the late summer of 1921 between Mexican secretary of finance Adolfo de la Huerta and leaders of five of the most powerful US oil companies operating in Mexico, including E. L. Doheny and Harry Sinclair. The petroleum magnates were eager to come to a long-term understanding on taxes so that they could make "definite sales commitments over considerable periods of time," with reasonable information in pricing decisions. Further, they wanted to continue seeking new sources of supply and, in general, to avoid pesky regulations.[3] The result was that production taxes were continued for future yields only, with the question of rents and royalties left to the courts. An agreement was also made concerning export taxes, allowing the Americans to pay with Mexican government bonds discounted at 50 percent, left over from the counter-revolutionary presidency of Victoriano Huerta in the mid-1910s. The petroleum companies had obtained an agreement they could live with, while the Mexican government had solved two problems: taxes would in fact be paid, albeit at a reduced rate; and the Treasury could begin the important work of retiring the foreign debt, thanks to the acceptance of the Huerta bonds for tax exports.[4]

A little over two years later, with the intention of finalizing a more permanent agreement and with Obregón's government still unrecognized, Mexicans and US negotiators met again—this time under the aegis, albeit somewhat unofficial, of both governments. On this occasion, the auguries for success were better thanks to some extenuating circumstances. Secretary of the Interior Fall at that time had been forced to resign from Harding's cabinet after a scandal involving the Elk Hills and Teapot Dome oil reserves and US oilmen Doheny and Sinclair (both also involved in Mexican oil), just as Obregón and Harding were becoming more amenable to an agreement on Mexican petroleum.[5]

With Fall neutralized and then out of the way, both administrations were ready to move forward. To this end, they began in 1923 to discuss the so-called Bucareli agreements, named for the mansion in Mexico City where the talks were held. None of the negotiators were officials of their specific countries, and no treaty was discussed, as the fragile Obregón administration could not politically admit what seemed to be a demand from the United States. Rather, it was regarded as a "gentlemen's agreement." At this point, the oil companies were concerned that rights held previous to the 1917 Constitution were at risk and that article 27 might be applied retroactively. On the Mexican side, a remarkable series of memoranda lets us know precisely how Obregón's administration were informing their intermediaries in response to US queries and demands.[6] These documents made clear that the Mexicans were eager to continue and expand US investment. Yet they would not accept any binding changes in the principles of article 27, nor would they brook anything less than the full retention of authority vested in the Mexican courts concerning claims on land and subsoil rights.

The crucial document was Memorandum #8, which insisted that the major nations of the world accepted the principle that such rights belonged to the country in which they were located; certainly neither Obregón nor anybody else believed that this argument would be decisive with US negotiators, but it helped frame Mexico within a global context for the purpose of these negotiations. Moreover, in a tactic that would become common in the Mexican system when politicians negotiated either externally or internally, they changed the terms. "Confiscation" (*confiscación*) was not occurring; to the contrary, it was a mere "adjustment" (*ajuste*). Though this approach, too, would never fly with the United States, it was a first step in the crucial Mexican insistence on the broad notion of government concessions as opposed to absolute rights on the part of property owners or leaseholders. Yet the Mexicans tried to reassure the US representatives (and thus the US companies) that they would have rights of their own, emphasizing that if evidence had been provided or some sort of contract had implied an agreement to work on the subsoil, rights thus acquired would be protected.[7]

When these points were actually discussed by the Bucareli negotiators, they were quickly agreed upon, indicating that very likely there had already been an understanding about petroleum before the meetings began. The finalized agreement turned on the question of "positive acts": that is, if almost any kind of action had been taken on the land, such as the drilling or even simply fencing, that action would be taken as proof that development of the land for economically useful purposes was intended. Leases themselves were taken as evidence of prior rights that would accrue to those who had undertaken these transactions. Land itself, however, was another matter, as some of the companies had bought extensions of land on which they had not begun to work, and therefore there were no positive acts. Still, an agreement was possible in these cases as well. If the price paid for a property was high enough so that it was clearly intended for the production of subsoil resources rather than for agriculture, the negotiators agreed that this kind of evidence would indicate positive acts. Thus, the Mexicans indicated that they would acknowledge preferential rights for these owners of the surface property. The Mexican delegates therefore provided a level of comfort that the rights of US property holders would be preserved—at least for the moment.[8]

Two weeks after the Bucareli meetings began, the discussion moved to the agrarian question, by far the knottiest problem to face the negotiators and a topic that is outside the scope of this chapter.[9] By 15 August 1923, however, they had agreed to drafts on all crucial matters that, though not binding, involved the certification of the minutes of the meeting. Recognition from the United States quickly followed on September 3.[10] The process had been helped along by a brief visit to Mexico by William Randolph Hearst, the powerful newspaper owner, who on his return to the United States expressed his conviction that the talks would lead to official recognition of the Obregón presidency along with improved economic conditions and commercial relations.

The Bucareli agreements were later attacked by Obregón's political opponents as giving away Mexican oil and giving in to the United States; however, because they set the basis for continued drilling and oil extraction, the agreements permitted oil to flow again and thus subsequent tax revenues to make their way into the Mexican exchequer. At the same time, the agreements re-established that rights to control the subsoil belonged to the nation. Each subsequent Mexican administration extended these rights still further, until finally, in 1938, President Lázaro Cárdenas shocked the world by taking the radical step of expropriating almost all the foreign oil companies still operating in Mexico. While disagreements between the two nations emerged on petroleum issues from time to time, the intractable behaviour of foreign oil adventurers faded into the past.

Cárdenas established a single government entity to control oil-related activity in the country: Petróleos Mexicanos, or Pemex. Since the formation of Pemex and until very recently, the Mexican government has enjoyed, at least in theory and much in practice, exclusive control of the basic petroleum business, including exploration and production, refining, and retail sales. However, over the last two and a half decades, beginning particularly in 1991, attempts have been made to dismantle the two major rallying points of the Mexican revolutionary Constitution of 1917—rallying points that Cárdenas skillfully invoked in his campaign to nationalize the oil industry: the more equitable distribution of land, and the use of the subsoil beneath it as belonging to the nation's populace.

The significance of protecting these resources was intertwined with Mexico's national identity, and any attempt to move back in the direction of privatization was for decades impossible. Efforts to rewrite the revolutionary script appeared from time to time, but in the early 1990s, this push finally began in earnest, and it has accelerated over time. This new vision, advanced particularly by Mexican presidents no longer interested in the revolution's precepts, involved efforts to gain for the country more international respect, particularly in economic terms. The various presidents involved were influenced by their own backgrounds and foreign training. The changes they advocated necessarily reduced the social content of legal protection while opening access to various kinds of private investment. A very important moment came in 1991 when then President Carlos Salinas de Gortari (who had attended Harvard) changed the status of communally held properties, known as *ejidos*, by declaring that land distribution would immediately cease and that the land reform program was over. Despite a good deal of pushback from the public, Salinas's government formally submitted legislation to the Mexican Congress in November of that year, seeking to modernize the agrarian sector (as the administration explained) by opening it to other kinds of domestic and foreign investment.[11] In December, Mexico's Chamber of Deputies voted 387 to 250 to amend article 27, such that limits on the size of landholdings were moved significantly higher. Demonstrations against the measures continued for some time, but that portion of the Constitution of 1917, which previously had been untouchable, was significantly compromised. President Salinas insisted that his action had been necessary to protect Mexican agriculture from potentially negative effects stemming from NAFTA, the proposed agreement with Canada and the United States that, ironically, he himself vigorously supported. Opponents were not mollified, and sporadic obstruction is still used in an attempt to protect *ejido* land against government or other projects.[12]

Another portent had already occurred two years earlier: the arrest and imprisonment in January 1989 of Joaquín Hernández Galicia, the head of the powerful oil workers' union, just over a month after Salinas had come into office. This action indicated that from the very first days of his administration, Salinas had had the intention of making a move on subsoil rights, particularly petroleum. He viewed Hernández Galicia as an impediment to the implementation of private participation. However, scandals that unfolded over several years involving Salinas's brother Raúl concerning embezzlement, money laundering, and even murder, derailed the president's ability to move forward.[13] Nevertheless, minor—and in some cases, not so minor—changes continued in the energy sector. Yet in 1994, as Salinas was concluding his six-year presidential term (known as a *sexenio*), Mexico's political landscape was thrown into turmoil by the assassination of the Partido Revolucionario Institucional (Institutional Revolutionary Party, or PRI) candidate chosen to succeed him, Luis Colosio (who had attended the University of Pennsylvania). Ernesto Zedillo, a colourless PRI official with a PhD in economics (this time from Yale) was chosen to replace the murdered candidate. During Zedillo's *sexenio*, he avoided major shifts in oil politics, and even opted to amnesty Hernández Galicia in 1997. No movement of any consequence concerning property rights and the energy sector occurred while he was in the presidency.

In 2000, the political landscape in Mexico changed significantly, as Vicente Fox (Harvard), the candidate of the relatively conservative Partido de Acción Nacional (National Action Party, or PAN) became president. Until that election, the PRI had been in power for seven decades, though it had changed names occasionally along the way. Both Fox and his successor, Felipe Calderón (Harvard), also from the PAN, tried to make significant changes in regard to subsoil rights. The Fox administration attempted major modifications to modernize the energy sector and Pemex itself. In a particularly blatant move, Fox, just a few weeks after his inauguration, named four extremely wealthy corporate leaders to the Board of Directors of the state-run oil company, most notably Carlos Slim Helú, chairperson of communications giant Telmex and one of the richest men in the world.[14] Public outrage began immediately, and Fox quickly reconsidered the appointments. In May, he shifted these members off the board and created a less controversial eight-person advisory committee instead.[15]

Other new initiatives in the energy sector involved the storage and processing of liquefied natural gas. President Fox, who had hoped to avoid some of the issues surrounding petroleum by focusing on natural gas instead, began in 2002 to issue multiple-service contracts (*contratos de servicios múltiples*, or CSMs) to attract private capital to explore, extract, and liquefy that resource. In 2004, Fox came in for criticism for holding secret discussions with Chevron Texaco for a liquefaction plant in the Coronado Islands, off the coast of Baja California, at the same time that the Bolivian government suggested selling natural gas to Mexico. Shortly thereafter, the Chamber of Deputies declined to pursue a constitutional challenge to these arrangements, largely because of the internal failure to produce adequate natural gas, despite what were assumed to be huge holdings and reserves within Mexico itself. More inflammatory, perhaps, was the accusation that foreign companies, through Pemex itself, were illegally operating Mexican retail gas stations.[16]

Meanwhile Fox, in meetings with Russian premier Vladimir Putin, began to negotiate arrangements for Russian investment in Mexico's energy sector, including the possibility of a liquefaction plant, once more in Baja California. Again, the Mexican public reacted negatively. Fox shifted focus slightly when he decided in July to bring the country into Mercosur, the Southern Cone common market, though in an "associate" status. With this new affiliation in hand, he then approached Petrobras, the Brazilian national oil company, seeking to help Pemex with deepwater drilling technology.[17] At the same time, problems of corruption and even fuel theft plagued Pemex, as they still do.[18] Finally, in 2005, in the penultimate year of Fox's term, the Mexican government fined six former Pemex officials for diverting funds to the PRI's presidential campaign. Some senators suggested that attention given to the case was designed to deflect criticism from First Lady Marta Sahagún's two sons, who had been accused of using their connections in the Fox administration to obtain 2.5 billion Mexican pesos in construction projects.[19]

Though objections to Fox's programs continued to roil the political atmosphere through the end of his term, his successor also attempted changes in oil policy. As President-Elect Calderón (Harvard) was coming into power in the autumn of 2006, the Congress overwhelmingly voted to overhaul Pemex; it also permitted the *paraestatal* to hire private foreign companies for fundamental activities in the oil sector. Further, Pemex, which had been giving a very large proportion of its revenues to the government, gained a bit more control over these funds. Mexico's third major political party, the Partido de la Revolución Democrática (the Party of the Democratic Revolution, or PRD), led by former presidential candidate Andrés Manuel López Obrador, opposed any form of private participation in Pemex. Despite this intense opposition, legislators produced an initiative that would limit private-sector participation in the oil sector but not exclude it. One PRD senator overstated the case when he said that "no one disagrees with the participation of the private sector"; even so, this conciliatory comment was indicative of some movement in legislation and practice. A reminder of the still emotional nature of the proposals, however, was the decision to hold the 23 October 2008 Senate vote away from its normal meeting place to avoid López Obrador's threats to disrupt the proceedings. When the ballot in the Chamber of Deputies was held in its own normal meeting room several days later, a small number of legislators from the PRD and another party, the Partido del Trabajo, took the podium to disrupt the proceedings, though they were ultimately unable to stop the overwhelmingly positive vote.[20] The new legislation, backed particularly by the PRI and the PAN and supported by some in the PRD, also established a new form of integrated service contract, replacing Fox's CSMs, which had largely failed to attract interest from the private sector. These instruments offered more financial incentives, including the promise of flat per-barrel fees and reimbursement of some recovery costs. After a series of challenges, the Mexican Supreme Court validated these private contracts, though this decision also attracted criticism, including an accusation that the justices "had amnesia about history."[21]

Two years later, new refineries that would include partnerships with private companies were announced, with Calderón underlining the positive implications for job creation. At the same time, he heralded the discovery of new deposits in the shallower waters of the Gulf of Mexico, important because the rate of depletion for Mexico's oil fields ran ahead of its reserves.[22] A troubling note was injected into the discussions in the same year (2010), when a report from Transparency International, based in Berlin, reported that Mexico ranked 98th out of the 178 countries on its Corruption Perceptions Index. One of the institutions considered most difficult to control was, unsurprisingly, Pemex.[23] In the following year, Pemex awarded contracts for exploration and extraction in several fields in Tabasco state to both foreign and Mexican private enterprises, the first that had ever been approved in this way. Unsurprisingly, many objected, claiming that the changes violated article 27.[24]

The most extreme change, finally, came with the return of the PRI to the presidency in 2012 in the person of Enrique Peña Nieto (Instituto Tecnológico y de Estudios Superiores de Monterrey/Monterrey Institute of Technology). Sensing the battle to come, López Obrador broke away from the PRD, the political party that had sponsored his candidacy for the presidency in the previous election, to build a separate "citizen movement," which he had initially formed in 2011, known as the Movimiento Regeneración Nacional (the National Regeneration Movement, or Morena). While there was some concern that this new group might seriously divide the Left, López Obrador asked his followers to be sure to take only actions that "do not harm third parties," and his withdrawal from the PRD did not at first take on a "vengeful" character.[25]

Peña Nieto very early in his administration showed that he would not tolerate obstructive behaviour by leaders of Mexico's unions when he arrested the long-time head of the teachers' union, Elba Esther Gordillo, on charges of corruption. This action echoed President Salinas's jailing of the head of the oil workers' union at the beginning of his *sexenio*.[26] Peña Nieto was equally eager to move on to petroleum reforms. The president was aided in his efforts by a huge explosion in the Mexico City headquarters of Pemex that cast doubt on the ability of the company to provide a safe environment for its workers, including those in administrative jobs.[27] In early August 2013, almost a year into his administration, Peña Nieto proposed changes to the regulatory plan that had previously limited the access of external and private companies to investment in Mexican petroleum. As the *Christian Science Monitor* reported, "Analysts say Mexico's economic future—and the competitiveness of North America in the global economy—is at stake." The article estimated that Pemex had only ten years of oil reserves remaining, as its shallow-water fields in the Gulf of Mexico had begun to run out. It emphasized that the company lacked the technological know-how to exploit deepwater discoveries, and that although Mexico was believed to have significant amounts of shale oil and natural gas, it lacked expertise and capital as well. The president's initiative suggested that appropriate examples for Mexico to follow would be those of Brazil, Colombia, and Norway: all had state-owned oil companies accepting various kinds of partnership arrangements.[28] In presenting his program in a series of television advertisements, Peña Nieto took care to invoke the image of Lázaro Cárdenas, who as president had expropriated the foreign oil companies in 1938 and was widely hailed at the time as the great defender of Mexican patrimony. Cuauhtémoc Cárdenas, the former president's son and a long-serving leader in the PRD, expressed his disgust at this historically manipulated tactic.[29]

Meanwhile, by late August 2013, all three of the major governing parties had made a number of public proposals for an overhaul of the energy sector. While agreeing on the goal—enough capital to modernize the parastatal energy companies, primarily Pemex—they differed as to the means. The PRI and the PAN wanted to permit private and other foreign investment, while the PRD preferred to see Pemex keep a larger share of its profits for reinvestment. A further proposal shared by all three parties was the creation of a national-level office to administer the future profits of oil and gas. The difference in emphasis was significant, with the PRD's proposal envisioning much greater government oversight of Pemex. In an effort toward transparency, the PRD's proposal recommended the removal of almost all government and petroleum union officials from the Pemex board.[30] Public opinion polls on the issues varied significantly, depending on who was taking them, whom they were asking, and how the questions were framed. At the same time the PRD and Morena pushed for a citizen referendum on the issue, hoping to get a fairer measure of the public voice.[31] Coincidentally and symbolically, Hernández Galicia died in November 2013 at the age of ninety-one.[32] Just a few weeks later, the PRD withdrew from the coalition with the PAN and the PRI that was considering various reforms that might have led to a joint proposal; the issue at hand was said to be secret meetings that PAN and PRI leaders were holding without PRD involvement.[33]

Amid these political gyrations, in an informative and startling interview in November 2013, widely respected Houston energy expert George Baker predicted that Pemex would become "a new company of mixed capital, as a State-majority owned enterprise with minority shares on the New York Stock Exchange." The principal advantage would be that "it could enter into commercial alliances with other oil companies." Still, however, little could be done in the event that Pemex, as a partner in a consortium, would refuse to accept responsibilities for environmental problems, a stance it had taken in the litigation in Texas following the infamous Ixtoc-1 blowout in 1979. Such new associations, Baker suggested, could be established either inside or outside Mexico, including within US waters of the Gulf of Mexico, where several state-owned oil companies already owned drilling rights. In Baker's opinion, the government should "take . . . the oil regime outside the Constitution," a notion he characterized as "an important and long overdue step."[34]

In mid-December 2013, the PRI's initiative passed easily with support from the PAN and two other smaller parties over the opposition of the PRD and López Obrador's Morena. Shortly before the proposal came up in Congress, the Morena leader suffered a heart attack, keeping him from organizing his normally enthusiastic street rallies. A few showed up anyway; estimates ranged from a thousand to three thousand demonstrators "at the peak of the protests," far fewer than the Morena organization had anticipated. Even Cuauhtémoc Cárdenas, however, who served as an important spokesperson for the PRD's opposition to the legislation, had discouraged street demonstrations, insisting that they would not be effective. Meanwhile, immediately after congressional passage of Peña Nieto's legislation, seventeen states, more than half the total, provided the approval that was required for the modifications to the Mexican Constitution. All these states had majority PRI and/or PAN membership in their legislatures.[35]

Despite a setback from a major financial scandal in March 2014 involving Oceanografía, a private shipping company heavily contracted by Pemex, and its loans for millions of dollars based on fraudulent documentation from Mexico's largest bank, Grupo Financiero Banamex, the energy legislation continued to move forward. The PRI was able to avoid major blame for the scandal, as the fraud itself occurred while the PAN controlled the presidency.[36] Almost simultaneously, a new law, the *Ley de Consulta Popular*, made it possible for citizens to call for a referendum, but it was not easy. In the event that voters rather than legislators wanted to initiate such a procedure, huge numbers of signatures were required; 2 per cent of those voters registered would have to sign the relevant petitions. The PRD pushed briefly for a referendum before the secondary laws were presented, though the rapid changes the PRI and the PAN pushed forward made calls for a referendum moot.[37]

In an indication of the degree to which popular attention was focused on the debate concerning energy reforms, Alfonso Cuarón, within a few months of winning the Academy Award for directing the film *Gravity*, insisted in a full-page paid advertisement in the Mexico City newspapers *Reforma* and *La Jornada* that the government answer questions revolving around two major issues in the petroleum equation: corruption and the environment. The PRI and the PAN responded to neither, with the exception of some vague messages on social media, and Peña Nieto sent along the secondary laws that would permit implementation of his proposals to Congress.[38] Though the controversy about the new laws continued through the summer months, in mid-July these pieces of legislation passed with "overwhelming support." These changes concerned reforms to articles 25 and 28 of the Constitution, as well as article 27.[39]

Among the 250 modifications that were made in the drafts of these laws on the way to passage, the word *expropiación* (expropriation) was changed to *ocupación temporal* (temporary occupation) in an attempt to make the package seem less threatening to rural landowners who feared that they would lose their holdings. The PRD, in opposition, called the new laws *despojo* (dispossession). Yet a senator for the PAN argued that there would be recompense for whatever damage occurred to the land, along with some payment to the landholders in the event that hydrocarbons were discovered that could be exploited commercially. While the speaker insisted that "rural people and owners of the land will be enormously benefited by all the riches of their lands," there were many who doubted this claim. However, not even the percentage of profits from the extraction and sale of hydrocarbons that would accrue to landholders would be fixed by the law; rather, as an article in *La Jornada* explained, that determination would be made by the Secretariat of Energy (SENER), which would "establish the methodologies, parameters, and guidelines which could serve as a reference to determine the percentage." Later, another PAN spokesperson explained that these might range from 0.5 per cent to 1.5 per cent of the profits, though skeptics—including this author—believed that given the potential for manipulation of the financial accounts, landholders would get little or nothing. Further, "ejidatarios, comuneros, y productores privados" (ejido owners, commoners, and private producers) would be required to deliver their properties, including "lands, woods, and waters," to concessionaires in legal easements, with payments to be negotiated by the Sedatu (Secretaría de Desarrollo Agrario, Territorial y Urbano) in the event the landholders rejected their offers. In response, apparently, to the doubts of questioners, the PAN's commentator continued to insist that the present landowners might even become, to their benefit, "employees" (*empleados*) of the contracting company.

Further, the landowners, along with their family members and residents of the affected communities, would be protected by the Procuraduría Agraria, a part of Sedatu itself, should they need assistance. Doubts, of course, remained. Emailed responses to press reports of these clauses in the proposed legislation and the PAN and PRI responses indicated not only skepticism but outrage. Some protested that these changes signified a return to the time of President Porfirio Díaz, before the revolution and certainly before article 27. One particular response objected that the legislation amounted to "a blank check, everything for sale, everything given over to the counterrevolution. . . . When will we see the pendulum effect? How can we go back? A sold-out government . . . everything for sale . . . cynicism and shamelessness. When will we be a people with a decent government?"[40]

Nevertheless, the approval process continued through mid-August, with the PRI, the PAN, and two smaller parties voting in favour. On 11 August 2014, President Peña Nieto enacted the secondary laws for his program of energy reform. Still, the PRD and Morena continued in opposition, yet small payments to landowners for the oil and natural gas from their properties quickly became part of the law. Perhaps more importantly, a larger percentage of profits was earmarked for state and municipal governments, as opposed to the national Treasury, which would see its tax revenues from hydrocarbons diminish significantly. Estimates claimed that by 2025, Mexico's oil production could return to 3.5 million barrels a day (BPD), as it had been in 2004 before dropping to 2.5 million BPD in 2013. Fears about fracking and its potential environmental damage also roiled the political atmosphere, but the presidents of the PAN and PRI celebrated "the triumph of consensus" (*el triunfo del consenso*) while at the same time publicly claiming credit for the "victory" (*victoria*) of the new legislation's passage. At the same time, the secretary of finance, Luis Videgaray, stated that Pemex would see a "historic reduction" in its taxes, from 71.5 per cent to 65 per cent, and that it would also enjoy complete control over the use of its own resources. Still, he emphasized, government revenues would increase, "given that there will be more participants in the industry investing and extracting hydrocarbons."[41]

Two days later, the press made clear that the large majority of currently active oil fields (83 per cent) were set aside for Pemex, though others along with Pemex would be permitted to bid on the remaining 17 per cent. The company's chief executive, thirty-nine-year-old former investment banker Emilio Lozoya, announced that competition would help the company. He anticipated that Pemex would soon return to its previous status as the largest oil company in Latin America, a pride of place that recently had been taken over by Brazil's Petrobras. Mexican officials indicated their hopes that the bidding for available concessions would start in 2015. Some officials also said they believed that the most appealing concessions, to US companies in particular, might be those in the deep waters of the Gulf of Mexico. Others believed that some of the shallow water concessions would be preferred—in particular those that had been identified for the initial round of the phase one bidding process in 2015, with phases two and three to appear later that year. The share reserved for Pemex of "proven and probable reserves" amounted to 20.6 billion barrels of crude oil equivalent—that is, 15.5 years of continuous output at "current production levels."[42] Only a few days after the promulgation of the laws, Pemex announced that it was creating its own drilling, logistic, and electricity affiliates, a move that had certainly been planned earlier. Its previous four divisions were reduced to two: the first involved exploration and production, the second "industrial transformation," which is to say petrochemical and refining operations. No longer would Pemex be expected to carry out development projects that did not benefit the company, according to Lozoya. "Our objective is to make money," he announced.[43]

Meanwhile, on August 15, new laws toward private and foreign companies were announced, opening the Mexican petroleum sector for the first time since 1938. The government insisted that the new provisions would add US$590 billion to the Treasury's coffers, and that these funds would be made available for important infrastructure projects, especially related to transportation. In particular, new airports and new passenger train lines were mentioned, as well as upgrades and the doubling of the country's port capacity. At the same time, on August 20, Energy Minister Pedro Joaquín Coldwell insisted that Pemex would be remaining 100 per cent in state hands, and it would have significantly greater powers to control its own business strategy. Still, the problem was acute: government funding across the board, including for infrastructure projects, had shrunk significantly in the prior ten years due in large part to Pemex's sharply reduced figures. In recent decades, Pemex had typically provided up to a third of the funding of the entire federal budget. Even as production slipped sharply after 2004, the number of Pemex employees soared, from 110,000 to 160,000, putting greater strain on Pemex and federal finances.[44]

Only a few months later, all of Mexico's forecasts were shattered as global oil prices plunged from US$100 a barrel to around US$60—and the price seemed poised to plummet even further. The administration's earlier optimism suddenly slumped, and it announced on 31 January 2015 that its budget would be cut by 124.3 billion Mexican pesos (US$8.4 billion) through the year. Substantial portions of the previous plans concerning energy and transportation were reduced by the government's budget, including Pemex, which lost US$4.2 billion of its budget; and the construction of the high-speed rail from the Mexico City to Querétaro was postponed. At the same time, Pemex service contractors quickly began dropping employees, indicating that 10,000 had already been laid off; Pemex employees themselves were spared. Meanwhile, economic analysts in the city of Ciudad del Carmen, in the gulf state of Campeche, where a significant portion of oil employees were based, expected to lose 50,000 jobs as a result of the Pemex losses.[45]

On 14 March 2015, the *New York Times* reported that expectations of initial bids during the upcoming Mexican auctions would still be strong, despite the fall in oil prices. When, in August 2014, oil was at US$100 a barrel, the Mexican administration had been claiming that the new petroleum investments from foreign and private companies would be making US$12 billion a year over four years, and that oil production would be a half million barrels a day greater than it was at present. Now with oil prices sagging and his budget lowered, Pemex director Lozoya reported that the company had to cut back its expansion plans for the Gulf of Mexico, though he still hoped to discover other well-heeled partners to make up some of the difference. Meanwhile, the government indicated that the first phase one auction, expected in July 2015, would be critical to the success of the entire program. It included several blocks in shallower, lower-cost waters close to other successful areas. Mexico's undersecretary for hydrocarbons within SENER, Lourdes Melgar, pointed out that these properties were in a "highly productive oil area," while other fields were more "complicated," including shale and deepwater. Mexico, she said, still had advantages: it was close to "resources, both conventional and unconventional . . . where we have a lot of diversity. You're not talking about a frontier area." Yet clearly, as Luis Miguel Labardini, consultant with Marcos y Asociados, noted, "the Peña Nieto administration put all its eggs in the basket of energy reform. If they mess it up, this administration's doomed."[46]

At the same time, US analysts agreed that Mexico was in a much better situation than many other oil nations, despite the price decline. Carlos Pascual, senior vice-president of IHS Energy Consulting Services and formerly an energy analyst with the US State Department, pointed out that Mexico "is just in a different world" compared with oil nations such as Iraq and Nigeria. At the same time, energy expert Jeremy Martin, at the Institute of the Americas in San Diego, conjectured that it would be very difficult for Mexico to increase production by the promised 500,000 BPD, but still believed that many foreign companies remained as interested investors, at least in the long term, a viewpoint also adhered to by well-known oil analyst David Shields. According to these analysts, the Mexican administration would now have to lower its requirements for bidders to enter the auction process; further, it would be forced to add a wider selection of potential investors, implying the inclusion of some less desirable candidates. Still, the government decided to proceed with the auction. There were opportunities in Mexico, and others were beginning to take interest, though it might take years rather than months. Ali Moshiri, president of Chevron Africa and Latin America Exploration and Production Company, noted that Mexico was at least "a long-term strategy."[47]

By April 2015, forty oil companies had examined the geological information provided to them for the first of the phase one auctions, and in July, more than a dozen were looking at phase two.[48] Shortly thereafter, on 6 May 2015, phase three was announced, and it included twenty-nine onshore areas in five states. Phase one now included fourteen shallow-water exploration blocks, which together amounted to a total of 1,630 square miles in Veracruz, Tabasco, and Campeche. Thirty-one companies, at that point, had filed pre-qualified bids on the contracts. Phase two, now announced for September 30, included nine shallow-water blocks, but the area was relatively small, with only 108 square miles.[49]

Less than two weeks later, Finance Minister Videgaray announced that he was "depetrolizing" Mexico's public finances—largely as a response to the radically reduced oil price. Pemex's contribution to the federal budget revenues in the first quarter 2015 had dropped sharply to 16 per cent of the total, compared to the average 30 per cent for 2014. Nevertheless, Mexican government statistics agency INEGI claimed that the nation's gross domestic product had expanded by 2.5 per cent in that first quarter in spite of the drop in oil prices. Yet the Pemex shift was stunningly steep. Videgaray quickly indicated that "Mexico cannot depend on oil to sustain its public finances," noting that the taxpayer base was increasing and was helping to sustain revenues. The country continued to grow, investment was coming in, and unemployment was dropping, while inflation remained down. Still, the Mexican administration was clearly scampering.

Then suddenly, in June, with the first auction barely a month away, Pemex president Lozoya announced the company's first major oil breakthrough in several years. Located in shallow water off the coasts of Tabasco and Campeche states, the new fields comprised perhaps the largest new finds since the 1976 discoveries of the huge Cantarell field. Lozoya cheerfully estimated that the four new fields would be producing 200,000 BPD of crude oil within sixteen months, and 170 million cubic feet of gas per day in four to five months—an equivalent of 350,000 BPD of oil in no more than two years. José Antonio Escalera, Pemex's director of exploration, was a bit more circumspect, suggesting that it would take three years to reach the fields' full potential; nevertheless, the news overall was highly positive for the government's oil narrative. The blocks for auction, conveniently, were near the locations slated for phase one.[50]

Yet as July 15 arrived, there was almost no interest. Of the thirty-four companies that had initially signed up for pre-qualification, only nine had actually registered to make offers and only two lots received successful bids. These two were submitted together by a consortium comprising US firm Talos Energy, Britain's Premier Oil, and Mexico's Sierra Oil and Gas. While these bids were welcome, the overall dearth was a significant disappointment to the government. Certainly, the continuing glut of oil internationally and the rapid decline in prices contributed substantially to the lack of interest. In addition, however, just before the auction, the world was once again reminded of the widespread presence of corruption and lawlessness within Mexico, and of the government's continuing inability to contain it. On July 11, four days before phase one, Mexico's most notorious drug trafficker, Joaquín "El Chapo" Guzmán Loera, escaped (and apparently, with little difficulty) from maximum-security prison El Altiplano, marking the second time he had escaped from incarceration. While it was unlikely that the story made much difference in the auction, the government was dismayed and embarrassed.

Certainly the auction was partly the result of the cratering of oil prices toward US$50 per barrel, but it was also likely that concerns on regulatory terms were still an issue. Further, no Mexican administration could agree publicly without reasonable terms. The administration claimed that the process was a "solid start" for providing "transparency" in the process. Still, the outcome of the first auction was highly unsatisfactory. Petroleum was not the new answer—not yet, anyway—for Mexico's prosperity.[51]

Given the rough start to the auction process, the potential success of the program remains unclear. Phase two in late September had only five offshore fields, and they were in locations "already discovered." Pablo Medina, of the Wood Mackenzie consultancy of Houston, notes that "the government is doing what it can to create more upside" in order to attract other companies. One tactic was to publish minimums ahead of time, thinking that a bidder that is close may move a bit higher.[52] Fortunately, three of the five blocks were awarded on September 30, though two of them, in the southern section of the Gulf of Mexico, went unclaimed.[53] As phase three moved toward 15 December 2015, the Mexican administration began using different strategies, providing licence contracts that are focused on encouraging its own "upstart Mexican companies."

Meanwhile, the United States and its expanding contribution can be viewed more supportively and collaboratively than in previous decades. US businesses as well as the US government continue to be favourable to Mexican oil; the two countries are just next door, they have been connected by NAFTA for more than twenty years, and they also have multiple reasons to be involved with co-operative economic well-being. Mexico's energy products do not require travelling great distances, and they are geologically accessible.[54] Further, politicians may look more positively at

Mexican economic issues, despite the toxic discussions about narcotics trafficking and immigration. As an example, in early 2015, twenty-one Republican senators suggested that US-Mexico petroleum swaps could work for both countries, despite the many years in which it had been illegal to export US crude. Two of these senators were Ted Cruz of Texas and Marco Rubio of Florida, both candidates for the 2016 Republican presidential nomination.[55] In August of 2015, President Barack Obama made these swaps possible. It may be that Porfirio Díaz's famous refrain—"Poor Mexico: So far from God and so close to the United States"—will lose its negative edge as collaboration between Mexico and the US deepens.

Yet as time has gone by and as energy markets rise, Mexico's auctions have improved. The country has been able to make very reasonable arrangements, and many of them are together in partnerships, in some cases with Pemex itself or with Mexican interests; still, many of these companies are now strong and have resources and technologies that are particularly useful when it comes to developing deepwater crude oil and natural gas. Royal Dutch Shell took nine of the nineteen exploration and exploitation rights, four on its own, four more with Qatar Petroleum International, and one with Pemex. It was indicated that Shell's particular interest was its experience in the Gulf of Mexico. While there was some nervousness at the newly elected leftist Andrés Manuel López Obrador in these auctions, the auctions' success may likely keep these oil resources flowing. As Energy Secretary Pedro Joaquín Coldwell commented confidently to Reuters, "Mexico is no longer a country where a single person makes a decision. . . . These contracts are fully protected."[56]

Although the election of López Obrador signalled a return to the view of energy as a common good that was characteristic of the Mexican Revolution, the new president, despite his earlier opposition to the energy reform, soon pledged not to make any sudden changes. Even the advent of the presidency of Donald Trump, whose hostility toward Mexico led to the renegotiation of NAFTA into the newly styled Canada-United States-Mexico Agreement, did not lead to decreased interest in Mexican oil among US companies. The falling price of oil rather than the personalities involved structured business decisions by industry. By contrast, Venezuela has collapsed politically, taking its petroleum problems with it. Argentina, looking at neoliberal possibilities, gradually privatized its oil industry between 1989 and 1999; by trying to restructure YPF as a private firm, Spanish company Repsol was able to take it over and then began to restructure and disinvest; Argentina had to renationalize in 2015 (see Serrani in this volume). Other Latin American countries are also beginning to use petroleum auctions. Brazil began several international offshore rights auctions underneath its salt flats in 2018 (on Brazil's salt flats, see Gail D. Triner in this volume). Meanwhile, though some old problems in Mexico's petroleum industry—such as pollution, corruption, theft, and inefficiency—are still around, its new players will be exploring and then producing. Pemex itself will pursue new investment strategies, seeking more business-directed means and including partners "to make money." Mexico has moved past article 27, and oil has been taken "outside the Constitution."[57]

NOTES

Robb Corrigan, a London-based communications consultant, served as advisory editor for this chapter. Mr. Corrigan previously had been a business journalist in Mexico City. Throughout the chapter, I have focused on a series of articles by Carlos Navarro of *SourceMex*, in the University of New Mexico's excellent series Latin America Digital Beat (LADB, formerly known as Latin America Data Base), available at https://digitalrepository.unm.edu/sourcemex_pub/.

1   See the complete discussion of the formulation and adoption of article 27 in Linda B. Hall, *Alvaro Obregón: Power and Revolution in Mexico, 1911–1920* (College Station: Texas A&M University Press, 1981), 179–83, and the discussion in Hall, *Oil, Banks, and Politics: The United States and Postrevolutionary Mexico, 1917–1924* (Austin: University of Texas Press, 1995), 3.

2   Hall, *Oil, Banks, and Politics*, 27.

3   Suggestions of Subjects to Be Covered in Proposed Memorandum, United States National Archives 812.6363/1231. This is one of a set of documents organized under this number with the general title "Committee of Oil Executives Documents on Conferences, August–September 1921" submitted by the committee to the State Department. (National Archives hereafter cited as "NA" plus document number.)

4   Minutes of the First Conference, 30 August 1921, Minutes of the Fifth Conference, 3 September 1921, Minutes of Sixth Conference, 3 September 1921, NA 812.6363/1231.

5   Luis Montes de Oca to Obregón, 13 January 1921, Fideicomiso Archivos Plutarco Elías Calles y Fernando Torreblanca 130110201, 27/23 (hereafter cited as "Archivo Calles Torreblanca" plus document number). Although the evidence for this request is uncorroborated by material from other sources, it seems likely that it was authentic. We

know that Fall needed money at this time and that he took bribes of similar amounts for the leasing of the Naval Reserves in Teapot Dome and Elk Hills shortly thereafter from two major US oilmen involved in Mexico. See Burl Noggle, *Teapot Dome: Oil and Politics in the 1920s* (Baton Rouge: Louisiana State University Press, 1962), 16–19. Fall definitely seems to have been in financial difficulty, even haggling over the rate for his hotel room in Washington. See C. V. Safford to Fall, 10 January 1921, 106 (1) b. Albert B. Fall Papers, Huntington Library (hereafter cited as "FA" plus document number).

6   Secretaría de Relaciones Exteriores, "Controversia sostenida entre los gobiernos de México de los Estados Unidos, con motivo de la reanudación de las relaciones diplomáticas," and accompanying documents, Fondo Álvaro Obregón, Serie Relaciones Exteriores para el Reconocimiento del Gobierno, exp. 109, foja 142, Fondo Reservado, Archivo Calles Torreblanca. These papers were among those considered especially sensitive by the Obregón and Calles administrations and were kept in a locked safe in the office of Fernando Torreblanca, private secretary to the two presidents. The safe was opened several years ago in the presence of a number of Mexican scholars and archivists to preserve the integrity of the documents after Torreblanca's death. Unless noted, the discussion that follows is based on the introductory document and the fifteen shorter memoranda included. These are hereafter cited as "Controversia."

7   George Baker of Energia.com and Mexico Energy Intelligence has been consulting government and business in Mexico as to the use of different terms refigured by for petroleum laws, public relations, etc. He also provides a regular byline in *Milenio*. A recent example is his "Filología comparativa," 8 June 2015, http://www.milenio.com/opinion/george-baker/la-energia-de-baker/filologia-comparativa.

8   The certified minutes of the meeting were published in *Proceedings of the United States-Mexican Commission Convened in Mexico City, May 14, 1923* (Washington, DC: Government Printing Office, 1925). A Spanish translation is available in Aarón Saénz, *La política internacional de la Revolución: Estudios y documentos* (Mexico City: Fondo de Cultura Económica, 1961), 374–443.

9   Hall, *Oil, Banks, and Politics*, 149.

10   Summerlin to Hughes, 3 September 1923; Phillips to Summerlin, 4 September 1923, *Papers Relating to the Foreign Relations of the United States, 1923* (Washington, DC: Government Printing Office, 1938), 2:555–67.

11   For example, see José Dolores, "Se acabarán o complicarán los problemas del campo mexicano," in *El Sol de Texas* (Dallas), 12 December 1991. In the article, Dolores complained that Salinas had bought off the "agrarian leaders . . . going against the ideas, sentiments and desires of their own bases."

12   Steven Ranieri, "On Proposals to Privatize Ejido Lands," *SourceMex*, 16 October 1991; Ranieri, "Chamber of Deputies Approves Constitutional Modifications regarding Land Tenure," *SourceMex*, 18 December 1991.

13   Carlos Navarro, "Governing Party, Center-Left Opposition Offer Plans for Energy Reform," *SourceMex*, 28 August 2013.

14   Carlos Navarro, "President Vicente Fox Names Four Corporate Executives to Board of State-Run Oil Company Pemex," *SourceMex*, 21 February 2001.

15 Carlos Navarro, "President Vicente Fox Considers Withdrawing Nomination of Four Corporate Executives to Pemex Board," *SourceMex*, 28 March 2001; "Mexico: President Fox Creates Advisory Committee for Pemex," *BBC News*, 9 May 2001.

16 Carlos Navarro, "President Vicente Fox's Administration under Fire for Secret Concession to U.S. Energy Company to Construct Gas Plant," *SourceMex*, 3 March 2004.

17 Navarro, "President Vicente Fox's Administration under Fire; Navarro, "Chamber of Deputies Votes against Pursuing Constitutional Challenge to Multiple-Services Contracts," *SourceMex*, 21 April 2004; Navarro, "Mexico and Russia Reach Energy-Related Agreements during Visit of President Vladimir Putin to Mexico," *SourceMex*, 16 June 2004; Navarro, "Mexico Joins Mercosur as Associate Member," *SourceMex*, 4 August 2004.

18 Carlos Navarro, "Government Launches Operation to Crack down on Fuel," *SourceMex*, 10 March 2004; Navarro, "Pemex Director Raúl Muñoz Leos Resigns under Pressure," *SourceMex*, 3 November 2004.

19 Carlos Navarro, "Government Fined Six Former Pemex Officials for Diverting Funds to PRI Presidential Race in 2000," *SourceMex*, 18 May 2005.

20 Carlos Navarro, "Congress Overwhelmingly Approves Legislation to Reform State-Run Oil Company Pemex," *SourceMex*, October 29, 2008.

21 Carlos Navarro, "Supreme Court Validates Private Contracts for State-Run Oil Company Pemex," *SourceMex*, 15 December 2010.

22 Carlos Navarro, "President Felipe Calderón, Center-Left Opposition Parties Differ on Energy Policy, State-Run Oil Company Pemex," *SourceMex*, 7 April 2010.

23 Carlos Navarro, "Mexico's Ranking on Transparency International's Corruption Index Worsens in 2010," *SourceMex*, 3 November 2010.

24 Carlos Navarro, "State-Run Oil Company Pemex Awards First Exploration Contracts to British, Mexican Companies," *SourceMex*, 24 August 2011.

25 Carlos Navarro, "Center-Left Candidate Andrés Manuel López Obrador," *SourceMex*, 19 September 2012.

26 Carlos Navarro, "In Dramatic, Low-Risk Move, President Enrique Peña Nieto Orders Arrest of Teachers' Union President Elba Esther Gordillo on Corruption Charges," *SourceMex*, 6 March 2013.

27 Carlos Navarro, "Huge Explosion Rocks Administrative Headquarters," *SourceMex*, 6 February 2013.

28 Lauren Villagran, "Long a State Monopoly, Mexico's Oil Sector Moves to Embrace Outside World," *Christian Science Monitor*, 13 August 2013.

29 Navarro, "Governing Party, Center-Left Opposition."

30 Navarro, "Governing Party, Center-Left Opposition."

31 Carlos Navarro, "Center-Left Parties Pushing for Public Referendum," *SourceMex*, 16 October 2013.

32 "Perfil de Joaquín Hernández Galicia. La Quina," *Excelsior*, 11 November 2013, www.excelsior.com.mx/nacional/2013/11/11/928036.

33 Carlos Navarro, "Center-Left Party Withdraws from Pacto por México," *SourceMex*, 4 December 2013.

34 "Oil and Energy Reform in Mexico: An Interview with George Baker," *Mexidata.info*, 4 November 2013.

35 Carlos Navarro, "Congress Easily Approves Energy Reform Plan," *SourceMex*, 12 December 2013.

36 Carlos Navarro, "Pemex Contractor, Mexico's Largest Bank at Center of Major Financial Scandal," *SourceMex*, 19 March 2014.

37 Carlos Navarro, "New Law Sets Specific Rules for Citizen Consultations," *SourceMex*, 19 March 2014.

38 Carlos Navarro, "Award-Winning Mexican Director Challenges President," *SourceMex*, 7 May 2014; "10 preguntas del ciudadano Alfonso Cuarón al Presidente Enrique Peña Nieto," *La Jornada*, 28 April 2014; "Alfonso Cuarón hace última pregunta de Peña Nieto," *Regeneración*, 5 May 2015.

39 Carlos Navarro, "Congress Approves Secondary Laws to Implement Energy Reforms," *SourceMex*, 6 August 2014.

40 "En dos horas, PRI y Pan aprueban dictámenes de la reforma energética," *La Jornada*, July 16, 2014.

41 "Camacho y Madero celebran 'triunfo del consenso,' " *La Jornada*, 12 August 2014, and "Videgaray: En cinco aõs Pemex tendrá una 'reducción histórica' en su carga fiscal," *La Jornada*, 12 August 201. The Spanish text reads, "reducción histórica . . . debido a que habrá más participantes en la industria invirtiendo y extrayendo hidrocarburos." Ley del Fondo Mexicano del Petróleo para la Estabilización y el Desarrollo, *Diario Oficial de la Federación*, Nueva Ley DOF 11-08-2014, 11 August 2014, http://archivos.diputados.gob.mx/Comisiones_LXIII/Vigilancia_Auditoria/Normas/14.pdf.

42 "Mexico Outlines Plan to Open Oil Fields to Private Companies," *Wall Street Journal*, 13 August 2014.

43 "Mexico's Pemex Adjusts Structure to Compete with Private Companies," *Wall Street Journal*, 20 August 2014.

44 "Mexico's Pemex Looks to Tap U.S. Shale," *Wall Street Journal*, 13 August 2014.

45 Carlos Navarro, "Mexico Announces Budget Cuts in Response to Global Slump," *SourceMex*, 4 February 2015.

46 "Mexico Ramps Up Search for Private Oil Investment," *New York Times*, 14 March 2015.

47 "Mexico Ramps Up Search for Private Oil Investment," *New York Times*, 14 March 2015.

48 "Oil Companies Show Active Interest in Mexican Energy Tracts," *Wall Street Journal*, 1 April 2015.

49 "Energy Industry Investment Expected to Start Flowing into Mexico in Late 2015," *EFE News Service*, 6 May 2015.

50 Jude Weber, "Oil Company Pemex Has Biggest Exploration Success in 5 Years," *Financial Times*, 11 June 2015; Andy Tully, "Could This Trigger a New Oil Boom in Mexico?" *Oilprice.com*, 14 July 2015, https://oilprice.com/Latest-Energy-News/World-News/Could-This-Trigger-A-New-Oil-Boom-In-Mexico.html.

51 Michael Davis, global financial adviser, text message to the author, 16 July 2015; Carlos Navarro, "The First Auction of Oil Fields under New Energy Privatization Scheme Draws Little Interest," *SourceMex*, 22 July 2015.

52 "Mexico Sweetens Oil Auction to Draw Firms Hit by Low Oil Prices," *Wall Street Journal*, 26 August 2015.

53 "Mexico Gets Stronger Demand in Second Oil Auction," *Reuters*, 30 September 2015.

54 Michael Davis, global financial adviser, email to author, 14 June 2015.

55 "Mexico Expects Same Treatment as Canada under NAFTA—Hydrocarbons Official," *BBC Monitoring*, 10 April 2015; Blake Clayton, "The Case for Allowing U.S. Crude Oil Exports," Policy Innovation Memorandum No. 34, Council on Foreign Relations, 8 July 2013; Daniel Fine, "Energy Magazine," *Daily Times* (Farmington, NM), 18 April 2015.

56 Carlos Navarro, "Mexico Holds Successful Auction for Deepwater Reserves," *SourceMex*, 4 February 2018.

57 "Oil and Energy Reform in Mexico: An Interview with George Baker," *Mexidata.info*, 4 November 2013; "Mexico's Pemex Adjusts Structure to Compete with Private Companies," *Wall Street Journal*, 20 August 2014.

The Neoliberal Transformation of Colombia's Energy Sector and Some Implications for Democratization in the Post-conflict Period

Dermot O'Connor and Juan Pablo Bohórquez Montoya

Neoliberal reforms have been implemented across the Americas through new constitutionalist practices of political and economic restructuring designed to open peripheral economies to foreign investment. While neoliberal reforms have been implemented incrementally in various sectors of Colombia's economy since the early 1990s following the adoption of a new constitution,[1] reforms to the energy sector (oil, gas, coal, electricity) came relatively late in comparison to other Latin American countries (see Heidrich's chapter in this volume). And even as some countries such as Argentina, Mexico, and Peru have taken measures to protect energy commodities from market forces by treating them as common goods, Colombia has deepened its commitment to neoliberal restructuring. Since the early 2000s, multinational companies, many headquartered in Canada, are increasingly playing a role in the development of oil and gas extraction and pipeline construction projects in Colombia.[2] Meanwhile Colombian governments have partially privatized the national petroleum company,

Ecopetrol, invited foreign investment in hydroelectricity megaprojects, and cut royalty rates on the extraction of subsoil resources.

The ideological justifications for this investment and development strategy—ostensibly shared by Colombian lawmakers and international allies—is that foreign investment and trade provide solutions to conflict, inequality, and poverty.[3] In theory, by liberalizing the energy sector, the Colombian state, international investors, and even local residents will all benefit from the privatization and expansion of energy production—through enhanced state revenues, profits, and trickle-down benefits in the form of local employment and investment. Neoliberal international governance discourse on energy development promotes the adoption of ethical norms by emphasizing best practices in corporate and social responsibility on the part of multinational corporations.[4] However, such norms are based on free-market ideology that assumes energy resources should be commoditized as market goods. The neoliberal ideology also assumes that corporations will voluntarily act in responsible, ethical, and sustainable ways. Domestically, Colombia's legal codes, and even the Constitution itself, have been reformed in order to promote foreign investment and the commoditization of the energy sector.

Indigenous Peoples, Afro-Colombian communities, artisanal miners, peasant farmers, and residents of rural municipalities are now faced with the social and environmental impacts of large-scale energy resource development fuelled by private and public foreign investment.[5] Mining megaprojects, hydroelectric dams, and extensive pipelines have been implemented by outsiders with the support of national government agencies that may not fully appreciate local or rural concerns.[6] Despite the promise of economic growth that could accompany resource extraction, local economic and social development has been stunted, while energy zones have been plagued by political conflict, violence, and economic inequality.[7] This has occurred despite provisions within Colombia's 1991 Constitution that provide some recognition of minority rights. The commitment to market ideology—involving rent-seeking by the state, power struggles by local elites, and profit-seeking on the part of foreign and domestic firms—has proven more powerful than the constitutional protections for human rights. The development strategy based on foreign-led economic growth in the energy and mining sectors now threatens to infringe upon the rights of subaltern groups and the livelihoods of communities. The post-conflict moment presents opportunities for both peace and democratization of the economy including the energy sector, but without substantial reforms to the neoliberal order and the market-based energy development strategy, these opportunities may be lost.

In this chapter, we examine how new constitutional reforms have been implemented in Colombia to promote extractive resource development. We look at the consequences of these reforms and the ensuing expansion of energy production for Colombian social movements. We also examine the prospects for a more democratic and inclusive approach to energy production in the post-conflict period following the 2016 peace accord between the Colombian government and the FARC (the Revolutionary Armed Forces of Colombia). We begin with a brief conceptual discussion that situates energy policy within the broader political economy. We then describe how the new constitutionalism was used as a means to institute neoliberal reforms in Colombia, particularly in the energy sector, and its accompanying effects on rural peoples, including Indigenous and Afro-Colombian communities. We argue that, despite formal recognition of Indigenous and minority rights, new constitutionalist reforms implemented by the Colombian state have actually functioned to promote foreign-based resource accumulation to the exclusion of local communities through forced displacement, state-led violence, and political marginalization. The contradictory nature of the new constitutionalism has put economic development at odds with democracy. The chapter continues with a brief look at the emergence of popular demands for the democratization of the energy sector from Colombian social movements. We finish by asking if the opportunities opened up by the peace process will lead to more democratic inclusion in the energy sector.

Energy Commodities as Common, Market, or Political Goods

As Pablo Heidrich argues in his chapter in this volume, energy policy must be understood within the broader context of national development strategy. Instead of the one-dimensional axis of states versus markets present in much of the literature on resource nationalism, Heidrich proposes to analyze a state's approach to energy policy along a continuum linking the wider development goals to the relative importance of the energy sector in the overall economy. As such, he proposes that within some states, energy policies reflect a view of "energy" (oil, electricity, gas, coal) as marketable commodities—that is, as market goods. In other cases, energy commodities are viewed as special types of products, and that energy must be developed to service the common good; or, alternatively, the energy sector and energy commodities are viewed as political goods that can support the elaboration of an alternative political and social order (or maintain the power of elites within the status quo). For Heidrich, the transition from a view of energy as a common good (ECG) to the view of energy as a market good (EMG) occurred in Colombia between 2002 and 2005. It was then that the Colombian state cut taxes and royalties to promote investment in its energy sector alongside partial privatization of Ecopetrol, the national oil company, along with state subsidies for the private construction of infrastructure to promote exports such as pipelines, terminals, and ports.

Heidrich's framework is useful in that it situates the energy sector within the broader developmental context of a given Latin American state. In that sense, the typology of energy strategies provides conceptual clarity to better analyze how and why a particular approach to energy policy may have occurred at a given time, in light of both ideological and material factors within the domestic context. Thus, it explains, in theory, how a state could liberalize some sectors where it lacks domestic capital endowments or experience, for example, or where there is strong demand internationally for a commodity. The framework also explains how a state could still buttress its control over another sector—say, electricity or natural gas—where the national utility is better served by retaining monopolies over production or where export markets for the particular commodity are constrained.

It is important to keep in mind, however, as our analysis of reforms in Colombia's energy sector suggests, that external forces including multinational corporations, powerful states, and multilateral organizations impose certain constraints on the range of possibilities in domestic development policy-making, including in the energy sector. These constraints shape how domestic forces—state agencies, private energy firms, and social movements—interact with one another in the propagation, implementation, and contestation of energy policy. This interplay between the domestic and international, public and private, state and civil society has shaped the transformation of energy policy in Colombia. From the approach that characterized the era of import substitution industrialization (ISI) when the development strategy required energy as a common good (or at least a political good that served the interests of the state development status quo), following a series of neoliberal reforms, energy commodities are now viewed as market goods. This has prompted resistance and calls for a renewed focus on the environment and on political, cultural, and social rights. The energy sector has come to the fore in a broader process of political contestation that has coincided with the end of decades of conflict over land and resources. Now that a peace process is formally underway, it remains to be seen whether renewed calls for energy to be put in service of the common good will be submerged within the post-conflict order.

Neoliberalism, the New Constitutionalism, and Colombia's Fractured State

Economic crises and commodity price fluctuations in the 1970s led to a series of multilateral economic arrangements and free trade agreements collectively referred to as "neoliberalism," which served to strengthen North-South economic ties within the western hemisphere. According to David Harvey, the 1970s represented a crisis of over-accumulation of capital by corporations. At the so-called periphery of the world economy, the profitability of capital was at risk if it could not find viable outlets for investment:

> Low corporate tax regimes (set up to attract foreign investment), state-funded infrastructures, easy access to natural resources, a facilitative regulatory environment, a good business climate, all of these elements had to be supplied if the capital surpluses were to be profitably absorbed. If all of this meant that people had to be dispossessed of their assets and their birthrights then so be it. And this is what neoliberalization accomplished. Behind this, institutional

arrangements had to be constructed to facilitate global financial transactions and to guarantee their security. This required the deployment of hegemonic state powers backed by military, political and economic coercive force to secure the international financial regime. US imperial power backed—in collusion with Europe and Japan—the powers of the IMF, the WTO, the World Bank, the International Bank of Settlements and a range of other institutions that would regulate the global system to ensure an ever-expanding terrain of profitable absorption of the ever-increasing quantities of surplus capital produced.[8]

Neoliberalism would have drastic consequences for Colombia's agrarian working classes, peasant farmers, Indigenous Peoples, and Afro-Colombian communities. In the 1980s and '90s, Colombian social movements expressed their demands for land reforms and better wage and working conditions in a context of deepening armed conflict over land and territory and the consolidation of the power of paramilitary groups. The movement would be devastated by the very forces it sought to oppose. Political mobilization through left-wing political parties in the 1980s ended with the slaughter of the Colombian Left: four presidential candidates were assassinated, three thousand party activists were murdered, and tens of thousands of supporters of the Unión Patriótica were displaced, made to disappear, or killed.[9]

In 1991, representatives from various sectors of Colombian society deliberated within a National Constituent Assembly that proposed mechanisms to resolve the prolonged internal conflict. The process led to the passing of the 1991 Constitution, which contained the following elements: consolidation of the capitalist economic system; the democratic organization of society; limited constitutional power for the people; a rights-based social state that limited the capacity for state intervention in the economy; and guarantees of fundamental social, economic, and cultural rights.[10] The consecration of a series of rights and guarantees was ostensibly aimed at the inclusion of Indigenous Peoples, Afro-Colombians, and women in the political system based on the concept of formal equality. While the 1991 Constitution formally recognized citizenship rights for subaltern groups, they were never fully realized in the actual application of the law. During deliberations at the National Constituent Assembly, and already in the formulation of the constitutional norms, *campesino* demands were subsumed into those of other sectors, while the demands of Indigenous and Afro-Colombian communities were treated as separate themes, despite the shared interest in access to land, vulnerability to violence in resource-extraction zones, and the need for inclusion in economic development.

It must be noted that this constitutional model was founded on an implicit assumption that the restructuring of the Colombian economy would unfold according to neoliberal principles. The National Constituent Assembly took place at a time when the Colombian and wider Latin American economies were embroiled in greater political and economic interdependency with developed nations through globalization.[11] The 1991 Constitution formally enshrined the status of the capitalist economy and the rights of property owners. It was thus what Stephen Gill calls a case of "new constitutionalism" whereby neoliberal reforms designed to open the economy up to international integration are institutionalized within the constitutional and legal frameworks of the national state.[12] Indeed, it was not long after the 1991 Constitution was passed that waves of privatization began, a market-based land reform program was proposed, and reforms to enable foreign access to mining and mineral concessions were enacted,[13] in part with assistance from Canadian legal experts and corporate mining interests.[14]

In 2003, after more than fifty years of operations as a state-owned oil producer and refiner—albeit one that relied heavily on partnerships with British, American, and Canadian firms for exploration, transportation, and marketing—Ecopetrol was restructured and re-established as a publicly traded corporation (although the state initially held 100 per cent of its shares). This was done in order to rationalize operations and enhance competitiveness internationally.[15] After restructuring, Ecopetrol doubled production from 399,000 barrels of crude oil per day in 2007 to 755,400 barrels per day in 2014.[16] Following price depressions in the oil sector in recent years, Ecopetrol has focused on sustaining operations, exploring for new deposits, and seeking international investors. In the petroleum industry, foreign direct investment in Colombia went from US$135 million in 1994 to US$5.4 billion in 2012. In the mining sector (including coal), foreign direct investment in 1994 was US$638 million, but it went up to US$3.01 billion by 2009.[17] As the numbers show, new constitutional reforms in Colombia were effectively designed to institute a neoliberal restructuring of state and society while opening the country to foreign investment in mining and energy production.

The implications for Colombian citizens living within resource extraction zones have been profound and violent: large-scale land grabs and megaprojects have entailed the forced displacement of millions of rural people.[18] In addition to violence and human rights violations, displaced persons have lost more than seven million hectares of property.[19] These issues have been studied in the social scientific literature on the causes and conditions of the war in Colombia, the social movements that have participated in the peace process, and the impact of constitutional change on these social movements.[20] This context underlines the inherently violent nature of state-led attempts to promote neoliberal development in Colombia. But it also signals the contradictory nature of constitutional reforms that formally recognize minority rights but fail to prevent the violation of these rights in favour of foreign investment and the appropriation of profits in the national energy sector.

Neoliberal Reforms in Colombia's Energy Sector and Effects on Indigenous Territories

While neoliberal reforms have had wide-reaching implications for Colombian state and society, within the energy sector these reforms have brought foreign mining and energy companies into the traditional territories and domains of Indigenous Peoples, creating potential conflicts between state policy and development priorities, resource development, and minority rights.[21] The terms "rural," "*campesino*," or "Indigenous" as used here refer to particular identity groups or sectors of Colombian society whose constituents collectively identify themselves as distinct in their way of life and culture, and who participate in subsistence or traditional economic activities and depend upon access to energy resources, water, and public lands for production and cultural reproduction. Thirty per cent of Colombia's population (or about sixteen million people) is based in rural areas, many of whom are Indigenous or Afro-Colombian.[22] Afro-Colombians number around eight million, and between 80 and 90 per cent of Afro-Colombians live in rural areas.[23] There are 658,000 Indigenous people in Colombia living on 754 reserves occupying 30 million hectares of land.[24] Of the remaining rural population, many peasants (*campesinos*) are of mixed ethnic ancestry, reflecting Colombia's European, Indigenous, and African heritage.

Collective access to land and control over traditional territories are fundamental for Indigenous and rural communities and the social movements and groups who represent them. As such, so are the laws and policies that regulate ownership and control of subsoil resources and the use, control, and transfer of title for both subsoil and surface access. Article 246 of the 1991 Constitution recognizes the rights of Indigenous Peoples to administrative and jurisdictional control over their traditional territories, and it includes language around the preservation of natural resources (article 330). Permission is granted to extract natural resources only on the condition that extractive activities do not infringe upon or violate the social, cultural, and economic integrity of Indigenous communities. The Colombian state's adherence in 1991 to the International Labour Organization's (ILO) Convention 169 of 1989 regarding the rights of Indigenous and Tribal Peoples appeared to strengthen the position of these groups within Colombian society. The convention established the obligation to prior consultation for any plans to modify, implement, or expedite administrative and legal measures concerning recognized Indigenous Peoples, and likewise, it required consultation prior to the approval of projects, exploratory activity, or mining or energy projects within their territories. As the convention has been implemented in Colombia, the right to participate in prior consultation is legally recognized for Indigenous and Afro-Colombian communities, but the same recognition is not extended to residents of rural communities who do not explicitly self-identify as Indigenous or Afro-Colombian.

Nevertheless, the state and multinational corporations have invoked other constitutional and legal provisions with the intent of implementing mining and energy projects in traditional Indigenous territories. There are a series of articles in the Colombian Constitution, in addition to various legal precedents, that contradict and serve to undermine the rights to consultation. Private property (individual, corporate, and state-owned) is one of the foundations of the Constitution, while collective property (such as Indigenous territories) has secondary importance (article 58). Similarly, property and "other acquired rights" must yield to the public or social interest in cases of resource development, and this social interest refers generally to the plans and development objectives of the Colombian state (articles 80 and 150).

The state is considered in Colombian constitutional law to be the owner of the subsoil resources and non-renewable energy resources (article 332). This power is amplified in Law 685, passed in 2001 and known as the "Mining Code," which stipulates that mineral resources both in the soil and subsoil are the property of the state, and declares that the mining industry is a public utility and in the public interest as per article 80 of the Constitution. While this might appear to give mineral resources the status of common goods, in effect it makes them political goods whereby the state can grant regulatory approval for large-scale, foreign-owned resource extraction over and against the protests or interests of surface occupants, whether these might be landowners, *campesinos*, or Indigenous community occupants. The political utility of these goods for political elites in Colombia depends on their status as market goods, consistent with neoliberal ideology.

The culmination of this series of laws and policies that have undermined the constitutional recognition of Indigenous rights is Presidential Directive No. 10 of 2013, known as "Guide for Prior Consultation." This policy contradicts the provisions of the ILO's Convention 169 by reducing the consultation process to a simple administrative act and authorizing the president to suspend the need for consent (from Afro-Colombian and Indigenous communities). The intent and effect of these legal and administrative measures has been to frame opposition and resistance to mining and energy projects as disputes of a normative nature. The potential confrontation between energy development and Indigenous rights reveals the contradiction between the neoliberal development project institutionalized in Colombia's Constitution and popular demands to preserve and protect alternative ways of life and traditional economic activities.

State Development Planning in Indigenous Territories

In *Prosperidad para todos* (Prosperity for all), the national development plan released by President Juan Manuel Santos during his second term, one of the country's motors of economic growth is mining development and energy expansion.[25] This development strategy calls for the implementation of regulatory reforms to clarify the jurisdiction of various regulatory bodies, the establishment of a national agency to oversee energy and mining, and adherence to the highest technical, social, and environmental standards.[26] However, the emphasis on standards implies that the mining and the energy sector must be consistent with the international legal and institutional order as specified in various free trade agreements signed by the Colombian state and as outlined by the World Trade Organization's Agreements on Dispute Settlement, among others. These norms favour the rights of investors, reduce barriers to capital mobility, and tend to rely on voluntary commitments to standards of corporate and social responsibility. In other words, the energy development plan, while using language implying that energy development will be in the public interest, actually deepens commoditization of Colombian energy resources based on neoliberal ideological principles. Although the Colombian state has signed these agreements and ostensibly backs the neoliberal development model, this does not mean that there is societal consensus around the desirability or adequacy of this model. On the contrary, social and political conflict within Colombia and open opposition to neoliberal reforms have been expressed by social movements, particularly those representing Indigenous Peoples, Afro-Colombians, and small-scale agrarian producers in areas where resource development comes into conflict with traditional Indigenous land use, agricultural production, or wildlife reserves.

The neoliberal model is generated transnationally and appears to be imposed on Colombia from outside; however, neoliberal reforms have been adopted by the national state and applied locally in a context in which this state (or at least its political class) is often at odds over the direction of economic development with its subaltern populations. Since many of these sectors of society rely on access to and control over ancestral territories for their economic, social, and cultural survival, and due to the large-scale requirements of space and resources for energy development, there is a great potential for localized conflict. Indeed, from the perspective of those who feel their way of life and territorial integrity is threatened by resource development, the adoption of neoliberal reforms designed to open up territories for mining and energy projects would appear to be a case of institutionalized accumulation by dispossession.[27]

The National Indigenous Organization of Colombia (Organización Nacional Indígena de Colombia, or ONIC), in a working paper presented to the Agrarian Summit (Cumbre Agraria), reported that in the year 2012 there were 501 mineral titles granted within Indigenous reserves, 2,008 mineral title applications, and at least 419 areas made available for hydrocarbon extraction.[28] According to the ONIC, the government granted mineral titles to 242,317 hectares of land within Indigenous reserves—twenty-seven reserves had 50 per cent of their land under title, and fourteen reserves had all of their land titled for resource development. The result has been "the disintegration and displacement of the communities," all of which has taken place without "consultation or consent of the Indigenous peoples and communities."[29]

It is worth looking in more depth at some examples. In the department of Guajira there is an ongoing dispute between state authorities and the Wayúu de Jamiche community over planned displacement of the community due to the operations of the Cerrejón coal mining company. The activities of this company, according to ONIC, have already caused the destruction and despoilment of natural resources upon which this Atlantic coastal community depends for its subsistence.[30] Traditional Indigenous land use has become impossible in the area as the landscape, once used for cultivation, habitation, and hunting, has been transformed by large-scale strip mining for coal. The mine has caused the forced displacement of the Waayúu and now threatens to destroy their cultural integrity, just as it has destroyed the flora and fauna in their traditional homeland.[31]

A similar situation has occurred for the U'wa as a result of the activities of Oxy (the Occidental Petroleum Company), whose exploratory activities and exploitation of oil and gas wells have been going on within U'wa traditional territory since 1992. The result has been significant destruction of natural resources and the intendant impacts to the community's culture and way of life.[32] The dispute has been taken to the Inter-American

Commission on Human Rights based on the U'wa claims that the norms of free and prior consultation were not followed, in violation of Colombian law and the ILO's Convention 169. Colombia's Constitutional Court sided with the U'wa position and ordered the Colombian state to carry out consultation according to national law and international treaties. Nevertheless, the state's Administrative Tribunal blocked the consultation process, siding with the executive preference to ignore consultation.

As these examples indicate, the way mining and energy projects have been implemented in Colombia implies a grave threat to the cultural, social, and economic integrity of Indigenous Peoples and their territories and violates existing constitutional rights and international treaties and norms. And yet the Colombian state has tended to use its legal and political power to side with energy firms in disputes. Indigenous Peoples, Afro-Colombians, and other rural communities have been obliged to defend themselves and their territories against real and potential infringements of rights through organized resistance. Political actions have included media campaigns in alternative forums, the use of websites, and alliances with international organizations such as Vía Campesina. Direct actions have also been taken; these include protests, action within the national and international legal system, strikes, and even announcements of plans for collective suicides to protest cultural and territorial destruction.[33]

Even though the peace process to end more than fifty years of civil war is now underway, and the formal end to hostilities is likely to hold, international awareness of the ongoing social, cultural, and political conflict over resource development is still necessary. Unsettled issues over territorial rights could threaten the peace process, on the one hand. On the other, the concerns of subaltern communities could be submerged in the push for broader societal consensus around the neoliberal model. It is likely that with a formal end to hostilities, the pattern of development in the minerals and energy sectors will continue and foreign investment will grow.

The Colombian state, by adopting a development model based on externally oriented growth (energy as a market good), has transformed its function from protector of its national territory and guarantor of security to its citizens to that of protector of capital. The result has been the cession of aspects of its national sovereignty, particularly over territorial jurisdiction and resource development, in favour of international norms that empower foreign capital by removing barriers to entry and access to resources, even in places once set aside for traditional Indigenous cultural and economic activities. Although neoliberal development has transformed the state's traditional functions, as Michael Mann points out, the state does not disappear, nor does it become obsolete—rather, it continues to promote the material conditions that underpin the social order but that look to initiate economic growth dependent on global economic integration rather than on the promotion of welfare.[34] The effects of the commoditization of energy are felt most powerfully in regional or local settings, but there is a gap between regulation, profit appropriation, and the experience of negative environmental, social, and cultural effects. As such, resistance to energy-development-related displacement falls outside the institutions and boundaries of formal democracy. In a state that enacts policies that violate the Constitution in accordance with the exigencies of neoliberal capitalism, in part through courting foreign investment in energy to support the established political order, domestic social movements, too, are forced to look outside and beyond the state for allies. These allies include international human rights organizations, international governance institutions, and academics. In other cases, they have included illegal armed groups, insurgents, or even drug traffickers, often to the detriment of local working people.

Part of the strategy to promote ethical approaches to mining within neoliberal thinking is to hold companies accountable to norms of corporate social responsibility (CSR) through measures such as voluntary compliance.[35] This discourse has predominated within international development circles, but its effectiveness is suspect. Writing in 2006, Scott Pearce examined the prospects for CSR on the part of Canadian firms in Colombia and concluded that

> As it is now, Canadian oil investment in Colombia stands a high risk of contributing to human rights violations and fuelling armed conflict. Although some companies have made progress in the area of corporate social responsibility, given the nature of the conflict in Colombia it is difficult, and at times impossible, to pursue oil development with-

out contributing to human rights violations. That contribution occurs at three levels: revenue gained from oil investment is frequently diverted to either the guerrillas or the paramilitaries, and used to buy more arms and thereby escalate the conflict; oil development acts as a catalyst for intensified fighting between rival armed groups—and the rural communities that are the principal casualties in this war over resources are rarely given the chance to decide for themselves whether they approve of oil development in the first place; and foreign oil companies are complicit with a repressive security apparatus that targets communities and individuals considered to be standing in the way of development. Colombia's favourable investment climate—low taxes, low wages, privatization, easy access to land—has been won by silencing voices of dissent through violence and intimidation.[36]

Clearly, during the armed conflict, foreign investment tended to aggravate conflict over territory and resources. However, in the post-conflict moment, there are possibilities for the democratization of energy and resource development. In concrete terms, this would involve more transparent and inclusive approaches to impact assessment and consultation, including opening up spaces for local participation in the development and regulatory process, ensuring respect for community/collective rights, providing access to expertise and information for communities, and committing to local self-determination over the broader process of resource development.[37] In the strongest possible terms, it would also imply that local and national governments and project proponents respect the right of Indigenous Peoples and other local communities to say no to resource development, in line with the principles of the United Nations Declaration on the Rights of Indigenous Peoples.

Democratic approaches to natural resource development include a commitment to "free, prior and informed consent" for projects from local communities, community-based natural resource management, and even co-management of projects between communities and outside proponents.[38] These approaches take seriously the rights, identities, and autonomy of local communities, as well as the potential for resource development that is inclusive, beneficial, and less destructive to the rights, culture, and ways of life of local residents and communities.

So where is the crux of the problem? Neoliberal approaches to CSR rely on the voluntary commitments of foreign firms to follow international norms. In a context where the state itself is lax in its enforcement of regulations around environmental and social protection, or where consultation is not required by law, energy firms have few incentives to participate in community-oriented development or to seek free, prior, and informed consent. Further, if the state is willing to authorize permits over and against local resistance, energy firms have little incentive to respond to the concerns of local people and would therefore be unlikely to halt development due to popular resistance. Voluntary norms of CSR are simply not enough; the national state must assert the rights of its citizens and ensure environmental, social, and cultural protections. In Colombia, the state demonstrated little commitment to democratic inclusion in the energy sector during the armed conflict. Rather, it sided with foreign investors and even paramilitaries to quash opposition. It appears that in the post-conflict order, state support for market-based neoliberal energy development will continue, and we can only hope that the violation of human rights and forced displacement will not.

This is not to say that it is inevitable that foreign investment in energy will aggravate violence and conflict in Colombia. To some degree, international attention on human rights in Colombia, the economic costs of the conflict, and the potential for greater economic development via energy commoditization and resource marketing probably contributed to the peace process in the last few years. This must be said with the caveat that, in some areas, the same focus on Colombian energy resources aggravated the local conditions for conflict in the first place. And these localized conflicts are likely to continue if the energy sector is not democratized. In this sense, the energy sector presents some possibilities and opportunities for more equitable and democratic forms of development. However, considering the marginalization and exclusion of subaltern groups by a state that uses energy commodities and foreign investment to further the political aims of the national elite, these opportunities are fraught with peril. The war might have ended but the neoliberal policies and new constitutional reforms that propagated it, and arguably aggravated it, have not been substantially altered.

The Agrarian Summit: The Response/Proposal

While the armed conflict appears to be over, the social conflict between the Colombian state, subaltern groups, and resource development in the country has not been resolved. As such, the sustainability of the peace process could be threatened. Considering the fractured relationship between state and society, the incursion of multinational firms in Colombia's extractive industries deepens the gap between domestic politics and an increasingly transnational economy, exacerbating existing tensions between the state and marginalized groups. The effects felt by local people within traditional economies and cultural contexts include dislocation, political marginalization, and social, environmental, and productive upheaval.[39] Extractive resource-based development, imposed by outside forces in collusion with a contested domestic regime, has the potential to destroy existing social formations dependent on particular ecosystems and land tenure customs, resulting in the loss of locally situated knowledge and culture.[40]

Colombian rural social movements—Indigenous Peoples, Afro-Colombians, and *campesinos*—have initiated a process of mobilization and an articulation of rights and interests known as the Cumbre-Agraria: Campesina, Étnica y Popular (Agrarian Summit: Peasant, Ethnic, and Popular). The movement has led two national strikes since 2013 and has formulated an organizational mandate and statement of objectives and demands. These are expressed around principles that affirm the autonomy of communities and call for new forms of self-governance to replace neoliberal development policies. This includes more concrete demands to reform existing legislation over territorial planning to empower Indigenous, Afro-Colombian, and *campesino* groups to shape governance and control the direction of energy development.[41]

The Agrarian Summit claims that none of the projects proposed within the territories of its constituent member groups, especially mining and energy projects, have been preceded by a process of prior consultation in any adequate sense.[42] In many cases, no form of consultation with any local community representatives has taken place. Sometimes information sessions are held to announce decisions that have already been made. In this way, the Colombian state regulates the activities of firms within the extractive sector operating in Indigenous territories through administrative actions and without popular consultation or consent, often in violation of norms, laws, and constitutional protections of the rights of local communities and Indigenous Peoples. Far too often the state is complicit in violent actions against local communities to implement large-scale resource-extraction projects.[43]

In the face of this complex and dangerous tendency by the state to exploit power imbalances in the name of economic development and in violation of international norms and conventions, Colombian social movements are formulating public policy alternatives based on more inclusive participatory models of development. In addition, they are calling for the transformation of the decision-making processes in the energy sector based on a commitment to consultation and community engagement, heretofore absent from state practice.[44] In short, the Agrarian Summit demands that energy be viewed as a common good, and one that must be developed only with the informed consent of those who will live with the environmental, social, and cultural consequences of energy production. In this sense, the energy sector has become a contested terrain on which the future of Colombian democracy may be decided.

Through the Agrarian Summit, rural social movements are calling for a moratorium on resource development until the regulatory and consultation process is reformed.[45] A consequence of these demands would be the transformation of the property and territorial management regime with implications for land use, its regulation, and forms of transfer of rights, claims, and title. This would have direct implications for how resource and energy projects are approved, and it might alter the strategic calculus of those looking to invest in Colombian energy.

The political project of the Agrarian Summit is based on the idea that local communities in resource zones have the power and the right to define their own destiny and the future of the territories upon which they depend for their social, cultural, and economic activities. For cultures tied to subsistence from the local landscape and dependent upon the integrity of the soil, air, water, and forest, land cannot be reduced to the status of a commodity.[46] On the contrary, land is the source of life, it nourishes vibrant cultures, and it is the guarantor of a community's future. The legal framework to support Indigenous claims to access and use land suitable for subsistence and traditional production—given the environmentally destructive nature of large-scale extractive projects—is a sine qua non for the survival of subaltern groups. The foundation of agrarian social movements in Colombia is the land itself. Their political project is therefore based on securing formal recognition of land rights in law, but also in practice. Enacting provisions to protect Indigenous, collective, and ancestral rights to land would imply a transformation in how land and property is viewed in Colombia, how laws are enforced, and how alternative modes of living are understood within the liberal capitalist order.

Effective legal enforcement of community rights would require the reorientation of the state's development policy toward the provision of common goods rather than private or individual accumulation. This reorientation could have potentially radical implications for the state and the place of property within the political and legal order.[47] Energy would again be viewed as a component of the common good, but not necessarily via state monopolies over ownership and decision-making. In other words, energy would be a political good destined to promote the democratization of the Colombian state and society. The Agrarian Summit, by disputing the social function of the state and its regulation of property within Colombia, is also calling into question the developmental model of the state within the new constitutional, neoliberal order. At the heart of its demands is a vision of rural space as a foundation for society and culture based on growth, cultivation, and environmental stewardship, which support various forms of life, modes of production, and cultural geographies. This is in stark contrast to a vision of the economy based on state-facilitated, multinational-led extraction and private appropriation of energy commodities, and the intendant environmental, social, and cultural destruction.

Democratic Energy Development?

The armistice is a positive development for the Colombian state, society, and international investors, but underlying tensions over territory, competing land uses, and disputes over the future of the energy sector have not been fully resolved. Considering the fractured state–civil society relationship; the ongoing potential for human rights violations through extra-judicial political actions to promote and facilitate resource extraction; and the absence of the rule of law and enforcement of consultation norms, there is a real danger, despite the promises of the peace process, that the potential for social conflict in Colombia's energy sector will remain. This is especially likely because the formal peace process will probably incite further foreign investment. There is thus a clear moral hazard for multinational corporations looking to invest in Colombia's energy sector, despite, and in some senses because of, the formal peace process. The war is over, but the neoliberal orientation of the new constitutional order has not been fundamentally altered, and it is this order that will continue to draw foreign investors into the territory of Indigenous Peoples, Afro-Colombians, and traditional agricultural producers.

In this context, foreign investors, international human rights advocates, and Colombian social movements have opened some space for dialogue and alternative development initiatives that could have some benefits for local communities. However, without a fundamental modification of the state's approach to consultation, regulation, and approvals, any further democratization of the energy sector will be stunted. Such a fundamental modification would require a shift from the view of energy as a market good toward a view of energy as a common good. However, in contrast to the period of ISI, the common good would not be conceived of as benefiting the state, but rather benefiting society, particularly those sectors that are most vulnerable.

NOTES

1   Jeff Browitt, "Capital Punishment: The Fragmentation of Colombia and the Crisis of the Nation-State," *Third World Quarterly* 22, no. 6 (2001): 1063–78.

2   Todd Gordon and Jeffrey R. Webber, "Imperialism and Resistance: Canadian Mining Companies in Latin America," *Third World Quarterly* 29, no. 1 (2008): 63–87.

3   Scott Pearce, "Tackling Corporate Complicity: Canadian Oil Investment in Colombia," in *Community Rights and Corporate Responsibility: Canadian Mining and Oil Companies in Latin America*, ed. Liisa North, Timothy Clark, and Viviana Patroni, 160–80 (Toronto: Between the Lines, 2006).

4   See, for example, United Nations Global Compact, https://www.unglobalcompact.org/about; Global Mining Standards and Guidelines Group, https://gmggroup.org; International Council on Mining and Metals, https://www.icmm.com.

5   Francisco Ramírez Cuéllar, *The Profits of Extermination: How US Corporate Power is Destroying Colombia*, (Monroe, ME: Common Courage Press, 2005).

6   Dermot O'Connor and Juan Pablo Bohórquez Montoya, "Neoliberal Transformation in Colombia's Goldfields: Development Strategy or Capitalist Imperialism?," *Labour, Capital and Society/Travail, capital et societé* 43, no. 2 (2010): 85–118.

7   Juan Pablo Bohórquez Montoya and Dermot O'Connor, "Indígenas y territorios para los proyectos minero-energéticos en Colombia," *Revista Javeriana—Economía* 151, no. 813 (April 2015): 62–71.

8   David Harvey, *The Limits to Capital* (New York: Verso, 2006), xxv.

9   Jorge Orlando Melo, "The Drug Trade, Politics and the Economy: The Colombian Experience," in *Latin America and the Multinational Drug Trade*, ed. Elizabeth Joyce and Carlos Malamud (New York: St. Martin's Press, 1998), 81.

10 Juan Pablo Bohórquez Montoya, *Concepciones políticas en la Constitución de 1991* (Medellín: Cooimpresos, 2001).

11 See, for example, Olivier Dabène, *La région Amérique Latine: Interdépendance et changement politique* (Paris: Presses de Sciences Po, 1997); James Petras and Henry Veltmeyer, *Social Movements and State Power: Argentina, Brazil, Bolivia, Ecuador* (London: Pluto Press, 2005).

12 Stephen Gill, "Constitutionalizing Inequality and the Clash of Globalizations," *International Studies Review* 4, no. 3 (2002): 247–65; David Schneiderman, "Constitutional Approaches to Privatization: An Inquiry into the Magnitude of Neo-Liberal Constitutionalism," *Law and Contemporary Problems* 63, no. 4 (2000): 83–109.

13 Browitt, "Capital Punishment"; Luis Ernesto Rodríguez, "Are the Characteristics of the New Colombian Mining Code Sufficiently Competitive in Attracting Investment to the Mineral Sector?," *Minerals & Energy* 19, no. 1 (2004): 32–43.

14 Ramírez Cuéllar, *The Profits of Extermination*.

15 Ecopetrol S. A., "Our History," https://www.ecopetrol.com.co/wps/portal/Home/en/Ourcompany/about-us/Our%20History (accessed 2 March 2021).

16 Ecopetrol S. A., "Corporate Strategy," https://www.ecopetrol.com.co/wps/portal/Home/en/Ourcompany/about-us/CorporateStrategy (accessed 2 March 2021).

17 Colombia, Banco de la República, "Inversión extranjera directa en Colombia," http://www.banrep.gov.co/es/inversion-directa (accessed 22 February 2021).

18 From 1985 to 2021, coinciding with the neoliberal period, the Colombian government tallied the total number of victims of forced displacement at 8,101,759. Though violence directed at rural people has declined in the post-conflict period, from 2016 to 2020 there were 920,955 victims of political violence (homicide, forced displacement, threat, etc.). See Unidad para la Atención y Reparación Integral a las Víctimas, "Registro Único

de Víctimas," https://www.unidadvictimas.gov.co/es/registro-unico-de-victimas-ruv/37394 (accessed 2 March 2021).

19 Alejandro Reyes Posada, *Guerreros y campesinos: El despojo de la tierra en Colombia* (Bogotá: Norma, 2009).

20 Mauricio Archila Neira and Mauricio Pardo, eds., *Movimientos sociales, Estado y democracia en Colombia* (Bogotá: Universidad Nacional de Colombia, Instituto Colombiano de Antropología e Historia, 2001); Centro de Investigación y Educación Popular (CINEP), *Sistema de Información General* (Bogotá: Centro de Investigación y Educación Popular, 2003); Mauricio García-Durán, *Movimiento por la paz en Colombia 1978–2003* (Bogotá: UNDP/CINEP/COLCIENCIAS, 2006).

21 Libia Rosario Grueso Castelblanco, *El derecho de las comunidades afrocolombianas a la consulta previa, libre e informada* (Bogotá: Oficina del Alto Comisionado de las Naciones Unidas para los Derechos Humanos Colombia, 2010).

22 Programa de las Naciones Unidas para el Desarrollo (PNUD), *Informe Nacional de Desarrollo Humano 2011. Colombia rural. Razones para la esperanza*, (Bogotá: PNUD, 2011), 56.

23 Fernando Urrea-Giraldo, "La población afrodescendiente en Colombia" (paper presented at the Seminario Internacional Pueblos indígenas y afrodescendientes de América Latina y el Caribe: Relevancia y pertinencia de la información sociodemográfica para políticas y programas, CEPAL, Santiago, 27–29 April 2005), http://www.cepal.org/mujer/noticias/noticias/5/27905/FUrrea.pdf.

24 Rafael Alfonso Montero Ferreira, "Los pueblos indígenas de Colombia y su inmersión en el proceso censal," *Revista de la Información Básica* 1, no. 1 (2006): 70–82.

25 Colombia. Departamento Nacional de Planeación, *Plan Nacional de Desarrollo 2010–2014: Prosperidad para Todos. Más empleo, menos pobreza y más seguridad* (Bogotá: Departamento Nacional de Planeación. 2011), 1:275–96. The same mining and energy development strategy is elaborated in the new national development plan, especially in articles 19, 21, 53, and 173. See Departamento Nacional de Planeación, *Plan Nacional de Desarrollo 2014–2018: Todos por un nuevo país. Paz, equidad y educación (Ley 200 de 2015)* (Bogotá: Departamento Nacional de Planeación. 2015), articles 19, 21, 53, and 173.

26 Departamento Nacional de Planeación, *Plan Nacional de Desarrollo 2010–2014*, 289.

27 David Harvey, "The New Imperialism: Accumulation by Dispossession," *Socialist Register*, no. 40 (2004): 63–87.

28 The Agrarian Summit is the largest and most prominent organization representing rural sectors of the Colombian population to have emerged over the last twenty years. It unites thirteen large social movements representing represent Indigenous Peoples, Afro-Colombians, and *campesinos*. See Organización Nacional Indígena de Colombia (ONIC), "Política minero energética del país" (paper presented to the Cumbre Agraria: Campesina, étnica y popular, en el marco de la negociación del pliego único, exactamente del punto sobre minería, Bogotá, 15–17 March 2014), 2–3.

29 ONIC, "Política minero energética del país," 2–3.

30 ONIC, "ONIC rechaza desalojo a comunidad Wayúu de Jamiche," https://www.elmercuriodigital.net/2014/10/onic-rechaza-el-desalojo-la-comunidad.html (accessed 2 March 2021).

31 Andrés Idárraga Franco, Diego Andrés Muñoz Casallas, and Hildebrando Vélez Galeano, *Conflictos socio-ambientales por la extracción minera en Colombia: Caso de la inversión británica* (Bogotá: CENSAT Agua Viva-Amigos de la Tierra Colombia, 2010), 75.

32 César A. Rodríguez Garavito and Luis Carlos Arenas, "Derechos indígenas, activismo transnacional y movilización legal: La lucha del pueblo U'wa en Colombia," in *El derecho y la globalización desde abajo: Hacia una legalidad cosmopolita*, ed. Boaventura de Sousa Santos and César A. Rodríguez Garavito, trans. Carlos Morales de Setién Ravina, 217–239 (Barcelona: Anthropos/UAM Cuajimalpa, 2007).

33 Idárraga Franco, Muñoz Casallas, and Vélez Galeano, *Conflictos socio-ambientales*; Rodríguez Garavito and Arenas, "Derechos indígenas, activismo transnacional y movilización legal."

34 Michael Mann, "¿Ha terminado la globalización con el imparable ascenso del Estado nacional?," *Zona Abierta*, nos. 92–3 (2000): 177.

35 Viviane Weitzner, *Holding Extractive Companies to Account in Colombia: An Evaluation of CSR Instruments through the Lens of Indigenous and Afro-Descendant Rights* (Ottawa: North-South Institute/Proceso de Comunidades Negras/Resguardo Indígena Cañamomo Lomaprieta, 2012).

36 Pearce, "Tackling Corporate Complicity," 179.

37 Timothy David Clark and Liisa North, "Mining in Latin America: Lessons from the Past, Issues for the Future," in *Community Rights and Corporate Social Responsibility: Canadian Mining Companies in Latin America*, ed. Liisa North, Timothy David Clark, and Viviana Patroni (Toronto: Between the Lines Press, 2006): 13.

38 See, for example, Weitzner, *Holding Extractive Companies to Account in Colombia*.

39 Stephen G. Bunker, "The Poverty of Resource Extraction," in *New Directions in the Sociology of Global Development*, ed. Frederick H. Buttel and Philip McMichael (Amsterdam: Elsevier JAI, 2005), 211–26.

40 James C. Scott, *Seeing Like a State: How Certain Schemes to Improve the Human Condition Have Failed* (New Haven, CT: Yale University Press, 1998).

41 Hernán Camilo Montenegro Lancheros, "Ampliaciones y quiebres del reconocimiento político del campesinado colombiano: Un análisis a la luz de la Cumbre Agraria, Campesina, Étnica y Popular (Cacep)," *Revista Colombiana de Antropología* 52, no. 1 (2016): 169–95.

42 This statement was expressed during an intervention by a spokesperson of the Agrarian Summit at the negotiating table with the Colombian state over royalty rates within the mining and energy sectors at which one of the authors was present. None of the state representatives present at the negotiation contradicted this claim. Meeting held at the Ministerio del Interior, Bogotá, 2 December 2014.

43 O'Connor and Bohórquez Montoya, "Neoliberal Transformation in Colombia's Goldfields."

44 "Abren indagación contra Alcalde de Piedras por consulta minera," *El Tiempo* (Bogotá), 2 April 2014, http://www.eltiempo.com/archivo/documento/CMS-13768315.

45 Cumbre Agraria, *Pliego de exigencias: Mandatos para el buen-vivir, la democracia y la paz* (Bogotá: Cumbre Agraria, 2014).

46 Karl Polanyi identified the tendency in modernity to commoditize land and labour, which are fictitious commodities in that they were not created to be sold and exist independently of their status as commercial objects. See Polanyi, *The Great Transformation: The Political and Economic Origins of Our Time* (Boston: Beacon Press, 2001); Timothy David Clark, "Reclaiming Karl Polanyi, Socialist Intellectual," *Studies in Political Economy* 94, no. 1 (2015): 61–84.

47 C. B. Macpherson, "The Meaning of Property," in *Property, Mainstream and Critical Positions*, ed. C. B. Macpherson (Toronto: University of Toronto Press, 1978), 1–13. In the Colombian context, the Mining Code considers subsoil resources, including oil, natural gas, and minerals, as economic goods. However, this conception is disputed by social movements and environmentalists, who argue that subsoil resources are better thought of within a broader concept of nature that aims to protect the vitality of the soil, forest, and water bodies. See Katherin Andrea Mazabel Pineda and Constanza Flores Ruiz, "Nociones y repercusiones de las políticas públicas relacionadas con la naturaleza en Colombia," *Revista Pluriverso*, no. 7 (2016): 79–93.

List of Contributors

Juan Pablo Bohórquez Montoya is the author of several books and articles on Colombian social movements, political sociology, political philosophy, and transnationalism. He is on the National Committee of the Popular Campesino Association (Colombia) and is director of Willow Springs Strategic Solutions—Colombia.

Michael Camp received his PhD in history from Emory University in 2017 and is the author of *Unnatural Resources: Energy and Environmental Politics in Appalachia after the 1973 Oil Embargo* (2019).

Paul Chastko is a senior instructor in the History Department at the University of Calgary, and the author of *Developing Alberta's Oil Sands, From Karl Clark to Kyoto* (2004) and the forthcoming *Globalization and the World Oil Industry*.

Linda B. Hall is professor emerita of history at the University of New Mexico and the author or co-author of seven books on the history of the Mexican Revolution, the US-Mexican border, and religion, gender, and film in Latin America, including *Oil, Banks, and Politics: The United States and Mexico, 1917–1924* (1995).

Pablo Heidrich is an international political economist specializing in natural resources and development in Latin America and associate professor of global and international studies at Carleton University. He has published several articles and book chapters, and his research has been supported by SSHRC, the IDRC, the Ford Foundation, the Marshall Foundation, and CIDA.

Amelia M. Kiddle is associate professor of history at the University of Calgary and the author or co-editor of three other books, including *Mexico's Relations with Latin America during the Cárdenas Era*. She is completing a SSHRC-supported research project on the roots of resource nationalism in Latin America and the Mexican oil expropriation of 1938.

Daniel Macfarlane is associate professor of environment and sustainability at Western Michigan University and is the author or co-editor of four books, including *Fixing Niagara Falls: Environment, Energy, and Engineers at the World's Most Famous Waterfall* (2020) and *Negotiating a River: Canada, the US, and the Creation of the St. Lawrence Seaway* (2014).

Brian S. McBeth is an affiliate member of the Latin America Centre at Oxford University. He is the author or co-author of thirteen books on the history of Venezuela and other subjects, including *Juan Vicente Gómez and the Oil Companies in Venezuela, 1908–1935* (1983) and *Dictatorship and Politics: Intrigue, Betrayal and Survival in Venezuela, 1908–1935* (2008). His latest book, *La política petrolera venezolana: Una perspectiva histórica, 1922–2005* (Venezuelan oil policy: A historical perspective) was published in Caracas in 2015.

Dermot O'Connor is a PhD candidate in political science at York University who studies conflict over land in Colombia. He is the principal consultant at Oak Road Concepts, where he conducts collaborative research with Indigenous communities on rights and energy development.

Joseph A. Pratt is professor emeritus at the University of Houston and author of *Exxon: Transforming Energy, 1973–2005* (2013) and co-editor of *Energy Capitals: Local Impacts, Global Influence* (2014), as well as ten other books on the history of energy and the city of Houston.

Tyler Priest is associate professor of history and geography at the University of Iowa. He is the author of *The Offshore Imperative: Shell Oil's Search for Petroleum in the Postwar United States* (2007) and the forthcoming *Deepwater Horizons: The Epic Struggle over Offshore Oil in the United States*.

Esteban Serrani received his doctorate in social sciences from the University of Buenos Aires and is a professor at the Universidad Nacional de San Martín. He is a full researcher in the Argentine CONICET (Consejo Nacional de Investigaciones Científicas y Técnicas) and coordinates the CLACSO Working Group on "Energy and Sustainable Development." He is completing an Agencia Nacional de Promoción de la Investigación–supported research project exploring the relationship between energy models and industrial policy in Argentina.

Gail D. Triner is professor emerita of history at Rutgers and the author of *Mining and the State in Brazilian Development* (2015) and *Banking and Economic Development: Brazil, 1889–1930* (2000), in addition to numerous articles and book chapters.

César Yáñez Gallardo received his PhD in history from the Universidad Autónoma de Barcelona and was a full professor at the Universidad de Barcelona before returning to Chile to become full professor at the Universidad de Valparaíso. He is an economic historian and has published numerous articles and book chapters about energy history, in addition to his books *The Economies of Latin America: New Cliometric Data* (co-authored with Albert Casrreras, 2012) and *La renovada historia económica de Chile. Diez tesis* (2021).

Bibliography

ARCHIVES

Brazil
Centro de Pesquisa e Documentação de História Contemporânea do Brasil, Fundação Getúlio Vargas, Rio de Janeiro

Canada
Archives of Ontario, Toronto
    Government of Ontario, 1954–1956
    Hydro-Electric Power Commission of Ontario (HEPCO), SPP Series, 1954–1957
Glenbow Archives, Calgary
    Canadian Petroleum Association (CPA) fonds
    Imperial Oil Limited (IOL) fonds
    Independent Petroleum Association of Canada (IPAC) fonds
    Petroleum Oral History Project

Mexico
Fideicomiso Archivos Plutarco Elías Calles y Fernando Torreblanca, Mexico City

United Kingdom
Bank of London and South America Archives, Commercial Bank of Spanish America Records, University College London Special Collections, London, 1913
National Archives, Kew
    Cabinet Office, 1929
    Foreign Office. General Correspondence
    Ministry of Power, 1938
    Venezuela Embassy and Consular Archives, 1908–1924
Parliamentary Papers, 1914
S. Pearson & Sons Ltd. Archive, 1923

United States

Albert B. Fall Papers, Huntington Library, San Marino, California
DeGolyer Library, Texas Instruments (TI) Records, Southern Methodist University, Dallas
Dolph Briscoe Center for American History, Exxon Oral History Collection, University of Texas at Austin
Dwight D. Eisenhower Library and Archives, Columbia University Oral History Project Transcripts, Abilene, Kansas
Edmund S. Muskie Archives and Special Collections Library, Senate Office and Committee Staff Files, Edmund S. Muskie Papers (MS), Bates College, Lewiston, Maine
Exxon Archive, Exxon Management Committee Records, Irving, Texas
Howard H. Baker Jr. Center for Public Policy, Howard H. Baker Jr. Papers (HBJ), Knoxville, Tennessee
National Archives and Records Administration
    Department of State Central Files (RG 59), College Park, Maryland
    Records of the Department of State Relating to the Internal Affairs of Venezuela, 1908–1924, National Archives at Atlanta
University of Houston Libraries, Oral Histories—Houston History Project, 1996–, Series 7: Energy Development, Houston
University of Tennessee Libraries, Special Collections, Tennessee Valley Authority Reports, 1933–1973, Knoxville

Venezuela

Archivo Histórico del Palacio de Miraflores
    Copiadores, 1908–1924
    Correspondencia Presidencial, 1908–1924
    Correspondencia del Secretario General, 1908–1924
    Varios, 1917–1920
Archivo del Ministerio de Fomento, 1908–1924
Archivo Particular del Dr. Gumersindo Torres, Copiador, 1920
Corte Federal y de Casación, *Memoria*, 1917, 1919–1920, 1924
Ministerio de Relaciones Exteriores, *Memoria*, 1908
Ministerio de Hacienda, *Memoria*, 1917

NEWSPAPERS, DATABASES, AND INTERNET SOURCES

American Oil & Gas Reporter
American Presidency Project, https://www.presidency.ucsb.edu
Associated Press
BBC Monitoring, https://monitoring.bbc.co.uk
BBC News
CanWest News

Christian Science Monitor (Boston)

CODHES (Consultoría para los Derechos Humanos y el Desplazamiento), http://www.codhes.org

Council on Foreign Relations, https://www.cfr.org

Daily Telegraph (London)

Daily Times (Farmington, New Mexico)

Diario Oficial de la Federación (Mexico City)

Ecopetrol, https://www.ecopetrol.com.co

EFE News Service

El Paso Times

El Sol de Texas (Dallas)

El Tiempo (Bogotá)

Energia.com, https://www.energia.com/

Energy Information Administration International Energy Statistics, https://www.eia.gov/beta/international

Energy-pedia News, https://www.energy-pedia.com

Engineering and Technology History Wiki, https://ethw.org

Excelsior (Mexico City)

E&P Magazine, www.epmag.com

Financial Times (London)

Folha de S.Paulo (São Paulo)

Gaceta Oficial (Venezuela)

Global Mining Standards and Guidelines Group, https://gmggroup.org

Globe and Mail (Toronto)

Houston Chronicle

Inflation.eu, https://www.inflation.eu

International Council on Mining and Metals, https://www.icmm.com

La Jornada (Mexico City)

Live Trading News, https://www.livetradingnews.com

Los Angeles Times

Maclean's

Mexidata.info

Milenio (Mexico City)

New York Times

O Estado de São Paulo

Oil and Gas Journal

Oil and Gas Online, https://www.oilandgasonline.com

Oil News (London)

Oilprice.com, https://oilprice.com

Petroleum Economist

Platt's Oilgram Price Service (New York)

PoundSterling Live, https://www.poundsterlinglive.com

Regeneración (Mexico City)

Return to Now, https://returntonow.net

Reuters

Renewable Energy World, https://www.renewableenergyworld.com

Royal Dutch Company, *Annual Report*, 1907–1936

Society of Exploration Geophysicists Wiki, https://wiki.seg.org

SourceMex, Latin America Digital Beat (formerly Latin America Data Base), University of New Mexico, https://digitalrepository.unm.edu/sourcemex_pub/

Shell Trading and Transport Company, *Annual Report*, 1907–1935

Skinner, Walter R., *Oil & Petroleum Manual*, London

Survival International, https://www.survivalinternational.org

Time (magazine)

Times (London)

Toronto Star

UN Comtrade Database, https://comtrade.un.org

United Nations Global Compact, https://www.unglobalcompact.org/about

Valor Econômico (São Paulo)

Wall Street Journal (New York)

Washington Post

Western Profile, https://seg.org/Publications/Journals/Western-Profile

World Bank Open Data, https://data.worldbank.org/

World Oil

SECONDARY AND PRINTED PRIMARY SOURCES

Adria, Marco. *Technology and Nationalism*. Montreal: McGill-Queen's University Press, 2010.

Afonso, José Roberto Rodrigues, and Sérgio Wulff Gobetti. "Rendas de petróleo no Brasil: Alguns aspectos fiscais e federativos." *Revista do BNDES* 15, no. 30 (2008): 231–69.

Alberta Geological Survey. *Geological Atlas of the Western Canada Sedimentary Basin*. Edmonton: Canadian Society of Petroleum Geologists-Alberta Research Council, 1994.

Allen, Robert. *The British Industrial Revolution in Global Perspective*. Cambridge: Cambridge University Press, 2009.

Allitt, Patrick. *A Climate of Crisis: America in the Age of Environmentalism*. New York: Penguin, 2014.

Almeida, Mansueto, Renato Lima de Oliveira, and Ben Ross Schneider. "Política industrial e empresas estatais no Brasil: BNDES e Petrobras." Text for discussion TD2013. Brasília: IPEA, 2014.

Almeida, Paulo Roberto de. "Monteiro Lobato e a emergência da política do petróleo no Brasil." In *Potência Brasil: Gás natural, energia limpa para um futuro sustentável*, edited by Omar L. de Barros Filho and Sylvia Bojunga, 12–33. Porto Alegre, BR: Laser Press, 2008.

Altmeyer, George. "Three Ideas of Nature in Canada, 1893–1914." In *Consuming Canada: Readings in Environmental History*, edited by Chad Gaffield and Pam Gaffield, 96–118. Toronto: Copp Clark, 1995.

Álvarez de la Borda, Joel. *Los orígenes de la industria petrolera en México, 1900–1925*. Mexico City: Archivo Histórico de Petróleos Mexicanos, 2005.

Alveal Contreras, Edelmira del Carmen. *Os desbravadores: A Petrobrás e a construção do Brasil industrial*. Rio de Janeiro: Relume Dumará-ANPOCS, 1993.

American Association of Petroleum Geologists. "Digital Revolutionaries: Technical Advances Reverberated through the Industry." In *AAPG Explorer—A Century*. Tulsa, OK: American Association of Petroleum Geologists, 2000.

Amsden, Alice. "Diffusion of Development: The Late-Industrializing Model and Greater East Asia." *American Economic Review* 81, no. 2 (May 1991): 282–6.

Anastakis, Dimitry. "Multilateralism, Nationalism and Bilateral Free Trade: Competing Visions of Canadian Economic and Trade Policy, 1945–70." In *Creating Postwar Canada: Community, Diversity, and Dissent, 1945–75*, edited by Magda Fahrni and Robert Rutherdale, 137–61. Vancouver: UBC Press, 2008.

Archila Neira, Mauricio, and Mauricio Pardo, eds. *Movimientos sociales, Estado y democracia en Colombia*. Bogotá: Universidad Nacional de Colombia-Instituto Colombiano de Antropología e Historia, 2001.

Armstrong, Christopher, and H. V. Nelles. *Monopoly's Moment: The Organization and Regulation of Canadian Utilities, 1830–1930*. Philadelphia: Temple University Press, 1986.

Atabaki, Elisabetta Bini, and Kaveh Ehsani, eds. *Working for Oil: Comparative Social Histories of Labour in the Global Oil Industry*. New York: Palgrave Macmillan, 2018.

Baer, Werner. *The Brazilian Economy: Growth and Development*. 4th ed. Westport, CT: Praeger, 1995.

Bakke, Gretchen. *The Grid: The Fraying Wires between Americans and Our Energy Future*. New York: Bloomsbury USA, 2016.

Bamberg, James. *British Petroleum and Global Oil, 1950–1975: The Challenge of Nationalism*. Cambridge: Cambridge University Press, 2000.

Barr, John J. "The Impact of Oil on Alberta: Retrospect and Prospect." In *The Making of the Modern West: Western Canada since 1945*, edited by A. W. Rasporich, 97–103. Calgary: University of Calgary Press, 1984.

Barrera, Mariano. "Subexploración y sobreexplotación: La lógica de acumulación del sector hidrocarburífero en Argentina." *Apuntes para el cambio*, no. 2 (March–April 2012): 19–35.

Barrera, Mariano, Ignacio Sabbatella, and Esteban Serrani. *Historia de una privatización: Cómo y por qué se perdió YPF.* Buenos Aires: Capital Intelectual, 2012.

Barton, D. C. "Petroleum Potentialities of Gulf Coast Petroleum Province of Texas and Louisiana." *Bulletin of the American Association of Petroleum Geologists* 14, no. 1 (1930): 1380j.

Beaubouef, Bruce. "Seismic Survey Contractors Hoping for Turnaround." *Offshore* 78, no. 3 (March 2018). https://www.offshore-mag.com/articles/print/volume-78/issue-3/seismic-survey-market-outlook/seismic-survey-contractors-hoping-for-turnaround.html.

Bebbington, Anthony, ed. *Social Conflict, Economic Development and the Extractive Industry: Evidence from South America.* London: Routledge, 2012.

Bebbington, Anthony, and Jeffrey Bury, eds. *Subterranean Struggles: New Dynamics of Mining, Oil, and Gas in Latin America.* Austin: University of Texas Press, 2013.

Beck, Gregory G., and Bruce Littlejohn. *Voices for the Watershed: Environmental Issues in the Great Lakes–St. Lawrence Drainage Basin.* Montreal: McGill-Queen's University Press, 2000.

Bednar, J. Bee. "A Brief History of Seismic Migration." *Geophysics* 70, no. 3 (May–June 2005): 3MJ–20MJ.

Behrends, Andrea, Stephen P. Reyna, and Günther Schlee, eds. *Crude Domination: An Anthropology of Oil.* New York: Berghahn Books, 2011.

Benton, Allyson Lucinda. "Political Institutions, Hydrocarbons Resources and Economic Policy Divergence in Latin America." Paper presented at the annual meeting of the American Political Science Association, Boston, 28–31 August 2008.

Bercovici, Gilberto. *Direito econômico do petróleo e dos recursos minerais.* São Paulo: Editora Quartier Latin do Brasil, 2011.

Berríos, Rubén, Andrae Marak, and Scott Morgenstern. "Explaining Hydrocarbon Nationalization in Latin America: Economics and Political Ideology." *Review of International Political Economy* 18, no. 5 (2010): 673–97.

Bértola, Luis. "Bolivia (Estado Plurinacional de), Chile y Perú desde la Independencia: Una historia de conflictos, transformaciones, inercias y desigualdad." In *Institucionalidad y Desarrollo en América Latina*, edited by Luis Bértola and Pablo Gerchunoff, 221–85. Santiago: CEPAL, 2011.

Betancourt, Rómulo. *Venezuela's Oil.* Translated by Donald Peck. London: Allen & Unwin, 1978.

Binnema, Theodore. "Making Way for Canadian Oil: United States Policy, 1947–1959." *Alberta History* 45, no. 3 (1997): 15–23.

Biro, Andrew. "Half-Empty or Half-Full? Water Politics and the Canadian National Imaginary." In *Eau Canada: The Future of Canada's Water*, edited by Karen Bakker. Vancouver: UBC Press, 2007.

Blades, Bryan W. "Production, Politics, and Pre-salt: Transitioning to a PSC Regime in Brazil." *Texas Journal of Oil, Gas and Energy Law* 7, no. 1 (2011): 31–57.

Bliss, Michael. *Northern Enterprise: Five Centuries of Canadian Business.* Toronto: McClelland & Stewart, 1987.

Bohórquez Montoya, Juan Pablo. *Concepciones políticas en la Constitución de 1991.* Medellín: Cooimpresos, 2001.

Bohórquez Montoya, Juan Pablo, and Dermot O'Connor. "Indígenas y territorios para los proyectos minero-energéticos en Colombia." *Revista Javeriana—Economía* 151, no. 813 (April 2015): 62–71.

———. "Movimientos sociales rurales colombianos: De la resistencia a una cultura política alternativa en un mundo transnacional." *Suma de negocios* 3, no. 1 (2012): 65–87.

Bothwell, Robert, Ian Drummond, and John English. *Canada since 1945.* Rev. ed. Toronto: University of Toronto Press, 1993.

Boué, Juan Carlos. *Venezuela: The Political Economy of Oil.* Oxford: Oxford Institute for Energy Studies, 1993.

Bower, Shannon Stunden. *Wet Prairie: People, Land, and Water in Agricultural Manitoba.* Vancouver: UBC Press, 2011.

Bowser, Sarah. "The Planner's Part." *Canadian Architect* 3, no. 2 (February 1958): 38–40.

Braga, Luciana, and Alexandre S. Szklo. "The Recent Regulatory Changes in Brazilian Petroleum Exploration and Exploitation Activities." *Journal of World Energy Law and Business* 7, no. 2 (2014): 120–39.

Brantly, J. E. *History of Oil Well Drilling.* Houston: Gulf Publishing, 1971.

Brazil. Agência Nacional de Petróleo. *Anuário Estatístico.* Rio de Janeiro: Agência Nacional de Petróleo, various years.

———. "Constituição da República Federativa do Brasil," 5 October 1988. http://pdba.georgetown.edu/Constitutions/Brazil/brazil88.html.

———. Congresso Nacional. "Coleção das Leis e Decretos." Rio de Janeiro/Brasília: Imprensa Nacional, various dates.

———. Instituto Brasileiro de Geografia e Estatística and Conselho Nacional de Estatística. *Anuário estatístico do Brasil.* Brasília: Imprensa Nacional, various years.

———. Ministério das Minas e Energia. "Novo Marco Regulatório: Pré-sal e áreas estratégicas." Rio de Janeiro, 2009.

Breen, David H. *Alberta's Petroleum Industry and the Conservation Board.* Edmonton: University of Alberta Press, 1993.

Bremmer, Ian, and Robert Johnston. "The Rise and Fall of Resource Nationalism." *Survival: Global Politics and Strategy* 51, no. 2 (2009) 149–58.

Bresser-Pereira, Luiz Carlos. "Taxa de câmbio, doença holandesa, e industrialização." Paper presented at Seminário patrocinado por FGV Projetos e pela Escola de Economia de São Paulo da Fundação Getúlio Vargas, São Paulo, March 2010.

British Petroleum. *Statistical Review of World Energy.* London: British Petroleum, various years.

Broitman, Claudio, and Pablo Kreimer. "Knowledge Production, Mobilization and Standardization in Chile's HidroAysén Case." *Minerva* 56, no. 2 (2018): 209–29.

Brossard, Emma. *Petroleum Research and Venezuela's INTEVEP: The Clash of the Giants.* Houston: PennWell Books/INTEVEP, 1993.

Browitt, Jeff. "Capital Punishment: The Fragmentation of Colombia and the Crisis of the Nation-State." *Third World Quarterly* 22, no. 6 (2001): 1063–78.

Brown, David. "Wide Azimuths Combat Salt 'Blur': Resolution Undergoing Revolution." *AAPG Explorer* 29, no. 3 (March 2008): 16–18.

Bulmer-Thomas, Victor. *The Economic History of Latin America since Independence*. 3rd ed. New York: Cambridge University Press, 2014.

Bunker, Stephen G. "The Poverty of Resource Extraction." In *New Directions in the Sociology of Global Development*, edited by Frederick H. Buttel and Philip McMichael, 211–26. Amsterdam: Elsevier JAI, 2005.

Calleja, Gonzalo. "La política energética del gobierno de Alfonsín (II)." *Realidad Económica*, no. 214 (2005): 105–28.

Camp, Michael. *Unnatural Resources: Energy and Environmental Politics in Appalachia after the 1973 Oil Embargo*. Pittsburgh: University of Pittsburgh Press, 2019.

Campbell-Kelly, Martin, and William Aspray. *Computer: A History of the Information Machine*. New York: Basic Books, 1996.

Canada. Bank of Canada, "Selected Historical Interest Rates, 1935–." https://www.bankofcanada.ca/wp-content/uploads/2010/09/selected_historical_v122530.pdf.

———. Department of Energy, Mines and Resources (DEMR). *An Energy Strategy for Canada: Policies for Self-Reliance*. Ottawa: Energy, Mines and Resources Canada, 1976.

———. *National Energy Program 1980*. Ottawa: Energy, Mines and Resources Canada, 1980.

———. *National Energy Program Update 1982*. Ottawa: Energy, Mines and Resources Canada, 1982.

———. Privy Council Office. *Royal Commission on Energy: Second Report*. Ottawa: Privy Council Office, 1959.

———. Statistics Canada. "G227-243 Foreign Direct Investment in Canada All Countries and by Major Areas, By Industry, Selected Year Ends, 1926–1974." https://www.statcan.gc.ca/pub/11-516-x/sectiong/G227_243b-eng.csv.

Canadian Association of Petroleum Producers. *Statistical Handbook for Canada's Upstream Petroleum Industry*. Calgary: CAPP, 2020. https://www.capp.ca/wp-content/uploads/2020/02/Statistical-Handbook-2019-Data_357106.pdf.

———. "Annual Statistical Review." Calgary: CAPP, various years.

Carignan, Richard. "Dynamiques écologiques/Ecosystem Dynamics, Panel: Rivières & Fleuves/Rivers." Paper presented to the Positionner le Québec dans l'histoire environnementale mondiale/Positioning Quebec in Global Environmental History conference, Montreal, 3 September 2005.

Carmignani, Fabrizio. "Development Outcomes, Resource Abundance, and the Transmission through Inequality." *Resource and Energy Economics* 35, no. 3 (2013): 412–28.

Carvalho, Getúlio. *Petrobras: Do monopólio aos contratos de risco*. Rio de Janeiro: Forense-Univeristária, 1977.

Caselli, Francesco, and Guy Michaels. "Do Oil Windfalls Improve Living Standards? Evidence from Brazil." Working paper, London School of Economics, 2012.

Castellani, Ana, and Esteban Serrani. "La persistencia de los ámbitos privilegiados de acumulación en la economía argentina. El caso del mercado de hidrocarburos entre 1977 y 1999." *H-Industri@* 4, no. 2 (January–June 2010): 2–31.

Castonguay, Stephane, and Darin Kinsey. "The Nature of the Liberal Order: State Formation, Conservation, and the Government of Non-humans in Canada." In *Liberalism and Hegemony: Debating the Canadian Liberal Revolution*, edited by Jean-Francois Constant and Michel Ducharme, 221–45. Toronto: University of Toronto Press, 2009.

Centro de Investigación y Educación Popular (CINEP). *Sistema de Información General*. Bogotá: Centro de Investigación y Educación Popular, 2003.

Cepek, Michael. *Life in Oil: Cofán Survival in the Petroleum Fields of Amazonia*. Austin: University of Texas Press, 2018.

Cerda Toro, Hernán. "Evolución de la inversión pública en infraestructuras productivas, 1853–2010." In *Chile y América en su historia económica*, edited by César Yáñez, 179–94. Valparaíso: Asociación Chilena de Historia Económica/Universidad de Valparaíso. 2013

———. "Inversión Pública, infraestructuras y crecimiento económico chileno, 1853–2010." PhD diss., Universidad de Barcelona, 2013.

Chastko, Paul. *Developing Alberta's Oil Sands: From Karl Clark to Kyoto*. Calgary: University of Calgary Press, 2004.

Chile. Biblioteca del Congreso Nacional de Chile. "Informe: Comparación de precios de electricidad en Chile y países de la OCDE y América Latina." 6 November 2017. http://bcn.cl/13vae.

———. Corporación de Fomento de la Producción. *Fomento de la Producción de Energía Eléctrica*. Santiago: Editorial Nascimento, 1939.

———. *Geografía Económica de Chile*. Vol. 3. Santiago: Talleres Gráficos La Nación, 1962.

Christy, Jamie C. "*Somos Petroleros*: Mexican Petroleum Workers' Challenge to the El Águila Oil Company, 1900–1938." PhD diss., University of Houston, 2011.

Cisneros-Lavaller, Alberto. "Latin American Geopolitics vs. Energy Patterns: Ideology, Energy Production Sustainability, and U.S. Security." *Journal of Energy and Development* 32, no. 1 (2007): 23–44.

Claerbout, Jon F. "Coarse Grid Calculations of Waves in Inhomogeneous Media with Application to Delineation of Complicated Seismic Structure." *Geophysics* 35, no. 3 (1970): 407–18.

———. "Toward a Unified Theory of Reflector Mapping." *Geophysics* 36, no. 3 (1971): 467–81.

Clark, Timothy David. "Reclaiming Karl Polanyi, Socialist Intellectual." *Studies in Political Economy* 94, no. 1 (2015): 61–84.

Clark, Timothy David, and Liisa North. "Mining in Latin America: Lessons from the Past, Issues for the Future." In *Community Rights and Corporate Social Responsibility: Canadian Mining Companies in Latin America*, edited by Liisa North, Timothy David Clark, and Viviana Patroni, 1–17. Toronto: Between the Lines Press, 2006.

Clayton, Blake. "The Case for Allowing U.S. Crude Oil Exports." Policy Innovation Memorandum No. 34, Council on Foreign Relations, 8 July 2013.

Coatsworth, John. "Structures, Endowments, and Institutions in the Economic History of Latin America." *Latin American Research Review* 40, no. 3 (2005): 126–44.

Cohn, Julie A. *The Grid: Biography of an American Technology*. Cambridge, MA: MIT Press, 2017.

Colombia. Banco de la República. "Inversión extranjera directa en Colombia." http://www.banrep.gov.co/es/inversion-directa.

———. Departamento Nacional de Planeación. *Plan Nacional de Desarrollo 2010–2014: Prosperidad para Todos. Más empleo, menos pobreza y más seguridad*. Vol. 1. Bogotá: Departamento Nacional de Planeación, 2011.

———. *Plan Nacional de Desarrollo 2014–2018: Todos por un nuevo país. Paz, equidad y educación (Ley 200 de 2015)*. Bogotá: Departamento Nacional de Planeación. 2015.

———. Unidad para la Atención y Reparación Integral a las Víctimas. "Registro Único de Víctimas." https://www.unidadvictimas.gov.co/es/registro-unico-de-victimas-ruv/37394.

Corbo, Vittorio ed. *Growth Opportunities for Chile*. Santiago: Editorial Universitaria, 2014.

Coronil, Fernando. *The Magical State: Nature, Money, and Modernity in Venezuela*. Chicago: University of Chicago Press, 1997.

Costa, Hirdan Katarina de Medeiros, and Edmilson dos Santos. "Institutional Analysis and the 'Resource Curse' in Developing Countries." *Energy Policy*, no. 63 (2013): 788–95.

Cote, Stephen C. *Oil and Nation: A History of Bolivia's Petroleum Sector*. Morgantown: West Virginia University Press, 2016.

Cumbre Agraria. *Pliego de exigencias: Mandatos para el buen-vivir, la democracia y la paz*. Bogotá: Cumbre Agraria, 2014.

Cupertino, Fausto. *Os contratos de risco e a Petrobrás: O petróleo é nosso e o risco deles?* Rio de Janeiro: Civilização Brasileira, 1976.

Dabène, Olivier. *La région Amérique Latine: Interdépendance et changement politique*. Paris: Presses de Science Po, 1997.

Dahm, C. G. and R. J. Graebner. "Field Development with Three-Dimensional Seismic Methods in the Gulf of Thailand—A Case History." *Geophysics* 47, no. 2 (February 1982): 149–76.

Delgado, Elvin. "Spaces of Socio-ecological Distress: Fossil Fuels, Solar Salt, and Fishing Communities in Lake Maracaibo, Venezuela." PhD diss., Syracuse University, 2012.

Deonandan, Kalowatie, and Michael L. Dougherty, eds. *Mining in Latin America: Critical Approaches to the New Extraction*. London: Routledge, 2016.

Desbiens, Caroline. *Power from the North: Territory, Identity, and the Culture of Hydro-electricity in Quebec*. Vancouver: UBC Press, 2014.

Deterding, Sir Henri. *An International Oilman*. London: Ivor Nicholson and Watson, 1934.

Dias, José Luciano de Mattos, and Maria Ana Quaglino. *A questão do petróleo no Brasil: Uma história da Petrobrás*. Rio de Janeiro: CPDOC/SERINST Fundação Getúlio Vargas/Petrobras, 1993.

Di Bella, Gabriel, Lawrence Norton, Joseph Ntamatungiro, Sumiko Ogawa, Issouf Samaké, and Marika Santoro. "Energy Subsidies in Latin America and the Caribbean: Stocktaking and Policy Challenges." IMF Working Paper WP/15/30, International Monetary Fund, Washington, DC, 2015.

Diebold, William, Jr. "Oil Import Quotas and 'Equal Treatment.'" *American Economic Review* 30, no. 3 (1940): 569–73.

Doern, G. Bruce, ed. *How Ottawa Spends: The Liberals, the Opposition, and Federal Priorities, 1983*. Toronto: James Lorimer & Company, 1983.

Doern, G. Bruce, and Glen B. Toner. *The Politics of Energy: The Development and Implementation of the NEP*. Toronto: Methuen, 1985.

Dondurur, Derman. *Acquisition and Processing of Marine Seismic Data*. Amsterdam: Elsevier, 2018.

Drinot, Paulo, and Alan Knight, eds. *The Great Depression in Latin America*. Durham, NC: Duke University Press, 2014.

Dunning, Thad. *Crude Democracy: Natural Resource Wealth and Political Regimes*. New York: Cambridge University Press, 2008.

Earle, Rebecca. *Return of the Native: Indians and Myth-Making in Spanish America, 1810–1930*. Durham, NC: Duke University Press, 2007.

Eayrs, James. *The Art of the Possible: Government and Foreign Policy in Canada*. Toronto: University of Toronto Press, 1961.

Ellsworth, Chris, and Eric Gibbs. *Brazil's Natural Gas Industry: Missed Opportunities on the Road to Liberalizing Markets*. Houston: Baker Institute for Public Policy, Rice University, 2004.

English, John. *Just Watch Me: The Life of Pierre Elliott Trudeau, 1968–2000*. Toronto: Knopf Canada, 2009.

Ernst & Young. *Global Oil and Gas Tax Guide 2014*. London: EY, 2014.

Evans, Paul. *Dependent Development: The Alliance of Multinational, State, and Local Capital in Brazil*. Princeton, NJ: Princeton University Press, 1979.

Evenden, Matthew. *Allied Power: Mobilizing Hydro-Electricity during Canada's Second World War*. Toronto: University of Toronto Press, 2015.

———. *Fish versus Power: An Environmental History of the Fraser River*. Cambridge: Cambridge University Press, 2004.

Farnsworth, Eric. *Energy Security Opportunities in Latin America and the Caribbean*. Washington, DC: Council of the Americas, 2013.

Ferreira, Antônio Luís de Miranda. "Problemas e inconsistências jurídicas de novo marco regulatório: A ótica dos princípios constitucionais da livre iniciativa, da economia de mercado e do direito comercial." In *Petróleo: Reforma e contrarreforma do setor petrolífero brasileiro*, edited by Fabio Giambiagi and Luiz Paulo Vellozo Lucas, 179–99. Rio de Janeiro: Elsevier, 2013.

The Financial Post Survey of Oils, 1949. Montreal: Maclean-Hunter Publishing, 1949.

Finch, David. *Pumped: Everyone's Guide to the Oil Patch.* Calgary: Fifth House, 2008.
Finkel, Alvin. *The Social Credit Phenomenon in Alberta.* Toronto: University of Toronto Press, 1989.
Fishlow, Albert. "Lessons from the Past: Capital Markets during the Nineteenth Century and the Interwar Period." *International Organizations* 39, no. 3 (1985): 381–439.
Folchi Donoso, Mauricio. "La insustentabilidad de la industria del cobre en Chile. Los hornos y los bosques durante el siglo XIX." *Revista Mapocho*, no. 49 (2001): 149–75.
Fort McKay First Nation. *Moose Lake: Home and Refuge.* Online documentary, 20:49. 20 August 2013. https://vimeo.com/72715280.
Foster, Peter. *Other People's Money: The Banks, the Government and Dome.* Toronto: Collins, 1983.
———. *The Sorcerer's Apprentices: Canada's Superbureaucrats and the Energy Mess.* Toronto: Collins, 1982.
Foxley, Alejandro. *La trampa del ingreso medio. El desafío de esta década para América Latina.* Santiago: Cieplan, 2012.
Francis, R. Douglas. *The Technological Imperative in Canada: An Intellectual History.* Vancouver: UBC Press, 2009.
Franko, Patrice. *The Puzzle of Latin American Economic Development.* Lanham, MD: Rowman & Littlefield, 2007.
Freire, William. *Comentários ao Código de Mineração.* Rio de Janeiro: Aide Editora/Comércio de Livros, 1995.
French-Davis, Ricardo, Óscar Muñoz Gomá, José Miguel Benavente, and Gustavo Crespi. "La industrialización chilena durante el proteccionismo (1940–1982)." In *Industrialización y Estado en la América Latina. La leyenda negra de la posguerra*, edited by Enrique Cárdenas, José Antonio Ocampo, and Rosemary Thorp, 159–209. Mexico City: El Trimestre Económico/Fondo de Cultura Económica, 2003.
Frieden, Jeffry A. *Global Capitalism: Its Fall and Rise in the Twentieth Century.* New York: W. W. Norton, 2006.
Froschauer, Karl. *White Gold: Hydroelectric Power in Canada.* Vancouver: UBC Press, 1999.
Fundação Getúlio Vargas, Centro de Pesquisa e Documentação de História Contemporânea do Brasil. "Memória do setor petrolífeiro no Brasil: A história da Petrobras." In *Interviews undertaken for Dias & Quaglino, A questão do petróleo no Brasil: Uma história da Petrobras.* Rio de Janeiro: Fundação Getúlio Vargas, 1987–8. http://cpdoc.fgv.br/acervo/historiaoral/entrevistas.
Gadano, Nicolás, and Federico Sturzenegger. "La privatización de reservas en el sector hidrocarburífero. El caso de Argentina." *Revista de Análisis Económico* 13, no. 1 (June 1998): 75–115.
Gallagher, J. P. *Proposals for a More Prosperous Canada: Excerpts from an Address to the Canadian Society of New York, January 18, 1979.* New York: Dome Petroleum, 1979.
Gama Coutinho, Edna Maria B., Antonio Claret Silva Gomes, Elíada A. S. Teixeira Faria, and Heloísa Helena de Oliveira Fernandes. "O que mudou na indústria

do petróleo?" *Informe Infra-estrutura: Área de projetos de infra-estrutura*, no. 29 (December 1998): 1–7.

García, Fabio, and Pablo Garcés. *La industrialización del petróleo en América Latina y el Caribe*. Quito: Organización Latinoamericana de Energía, 2013.

García-Durán, Mauricio. *Movimiento por la paz en Colombia 1978–2003*. Bogotá: UNDP/CINEP/COLCIENCIAS, 2006.

Garrido Lepe, Martín. "El consumo de carbón en Chile, 1933 a 1960." In *Chile y América en su historia económica*, edited by César Yáñez, 329–452. Valparaíso: Asociación Chilena de Historia Económica/Universidad de Valparaíso, 2013.

Gattinger, Monica. "Canada-United States Energy Relations: From Domestic to North American Energy Policies." In *Policy: From Ideas to Implementation, in Honour of Professor G. Bruce Doern*, edited by Glen Toner, Leslie A. Pal, and Michael J. Prince, 207–31. Montreal: McGill-Queens University Press, 2010.

Gettig, Eric T. "Oil and Revolution in Cuba: Development, Nationalism, and the U.S. Energy Empire, 1902–1961." PhD diss., Georgetown University, 2017.

Gibb, George Sweet, and Evelyn H. Knowlton. *The Resurgent Years, 1911–1927*. Vol. 2 of *History of Standard Oil Company (New Jersey)*. New York: Harper & Brothers, 1956.

Gill, Stephen. "Constitutionalizing Inequality and the Clash of Globalizations." *International Studies Review* 4, no. 3 (2002): 47–65.

Gobetti, Sérgio Wulff. *Federalismo fiscal e petróleo no Brasil e no mundo*. Texto para discussão #1669. Brasília: Instituto de Pesquisa Econômica Aplicada, 2011.

Goodermote, Dean, and Richard B. Mancke. "Nationalizing Oil in the 1970s." *Energy Journal* 4, no. 4 (October 1983): 67–80.

Gordon, Todd, and Jeffrey Webber. "Imperialism and Resistance: Canadian Mining Companies in Latin America." *Third World Quarterly* 29, no. 1 (2008): 63–87.

Gow, Sandy. *Roughnecks, Rock Bits, and Rigs: The Evolution of Oil Well Drilling Technology in Alberta, 1883–1970*. Calgary: University of Calgary Press, 2006.

Graebner, R. J., G. Steel, and C. B. Wason. "Evolution of Seismic Technology into the 1980s, Pt. 1." *Australian Petroleum Exploration Association (APEA) Journal*, no. 20 (1980): 110–20.

Grauer, A. E. D. "The Export of Electricity from Canada." In *Canadian Issues: Essays in Honour of Henry F. Angus*, edited by R. M. Clark, 248–85. Toronto: University of Toronto Press, 1961.

Gray, Earle. *The Great Canadian Oil Patch*. 2nd ed. Toronto: June Warren Publishing, 2005.

Grueso Castelblanco, Libia Rosario. *El derecho de las comunidades afrocolombianas a la consulta previa, libre e informada*. Bogotá: Oficina del Alto Comisionado de las Naciones Unidas para los Derechos Humanos Colombia, 2010.

Haarstad, Håvad, ed. *New Political Spaces in Latin American Natural Resource Governance*. Basingstoke, UK: Palgrave Macmillan, 2012.

Hall, Linda B. *Alvaro Obregón: Power and Revolution in Mexico, 1911–1920*. College Station: Texas A&M Press, 1981.

———. *Oil, Banks, and Politics: The United States and Postrevolutionary Mexico, 1917–1924.* Austin: University of Texas Press, 1995.

Hargrove, Erwin C. *Prisoners of Myth: The Leadership of the Tennessee Valley Authority, 1933–1990.* Princeton, NJ: Princeton University Press, 1994.

Hart, Michael. *A Trading Nation: Canadian Trade Policy from Colonialism to Globalization.* Vancouver: UBC Press, 2003.

Harvey, David. *The Limits to Capital.* New York: Verso, 2006.

———. "The New Imperialism: Accumulation by Dispossession." *Socialist Register*, no. 40 (2004): 63–87.

Haselip, James, and Clive Potter. "Post-neoliberal Electricity Market 'Re-reforms' in Argentina: Diverging from Market Prescriptions?" *Energy Policy* 38, no. 2 (2010): 1168–76.

Hays, Samuel P. *Beauty, Health, and Permanence: Environmental Politics in the United States, 1955–1985.* New York: Cambridge University Press, 1987.

Heasley, Lynne, and Daniel Macfarlane, eds. *Border Flows: A Century of the Canadian-American Water Relationship.* Calgary: University of Calgary Press, 2016.

Herrera Canales, Inés. "Trabajadores y técnicas mineras andinas en las fiebres del oro del mundo en el siglo XIX." *Nuevo Mundo/Mundos Nuevos* (Online, 10 March 2015). https://doi.org/10.4000/nuevomundo.67746.

Hidy, Ralph W., and Muriel Hidy. *Pioneering in Big Business, 1882–1911.* Vol. 1 of *History of Standard Oil Company (New Jersey).* New York: Harper & Brothers, 1955.

Hillmer Nornan, and J. L. Granatstein. *Empire to Umpire: Canada and the World to the 1990s.* Toronto: Copp-Clark Longman, 1994.

Hindery. Derrick. *From Enron to Evo: Pipeline Politics, Global Environmentalism, and Indigenous Rights in Bolivia.* Tucson: University of Arizona Press, 2013.

Hirt, Paul. *The Wired Northwest: The History of Electric Power, 1870s–1970s.* Lawrence: University Press of Kansas, 2012.

Hotelling, Harold. "The Economics of Exhaustible Resources." *Journal of Political Economy* 39, no. 2 (1931): 137–75.

House, J. D. "The Social organization of Multinational Corporations: Canadian Subsidiaries in the Oil Industry." *Canadian Review of Social Anthropology* 14, no. 1 (January 1977): 1–14.

Howarth, Stephen, and Joost Jonker, *Powering the Hydrocarbon Revolution, 1939–1973.* Vol. 2 of *A History of Royal Dutch Shell.* Oxford: Oxford University Press, 2007.

Huber, Matthew T. *Lifeblood: Oil, Freedom, and the Forces of Capital.* Minneapolis: University of Minnesota Press, 2013.

Hughes, Thomas Park. *Networks of Power: Electrification in Western Society, 1880–1930.* Baltimore: Johns Hopkins University Press, 1993.

Idárraga Franco, Andrés, Diego Andrés Muñoz Casallas, and Hildebrando Vélez Galeano. *Conflictos socio-ambientales por la extracción minera en Colombia: Caso de la inversión británica.* Bogotá: CENSAT Agua Viva/Amigos de la Tierra Colombia, 2010.

International Association of Geophysical Contractors. "Industry at a Crossroads: A Message from the Geophysical Industry." *Leading Edge* 22, no. 3 (January 2003): 14–17.

International Energy Agency. *World Energy Outlook*. Paris: IEA, various years.

Jack, Marian. "The Purchase of the British Government's Shares in the British Petroleum Company, 1912–1914." *Past & Present*, no. 39 (April 1968): 139–69.

Jackson, John N., with John Burtniak and Gregory P. Stein. *The Mighty Niagara. One River—Two Frontiers*. Amherst, NY: Prometheus Books, 2003.

Jacobs, Meg. *Panic at the Pump: The Energy Crisis and the Transformation of American Politics in the 1970s*. New York: Hill and Wang, 2016.

Jones, Christopher F. *Routes of Power: Energy and Modern America*. Cambridge, MA: Harvard University Press, 2014.

Jordan, Dale. "Evolution of Alberta's Petroleum and Natural Gas Land Regulations." *Journal of Canadian Petroleum Technology* 20, no. 2 (1981): 101–3.

Karl, Terry Lynn. *The Paradox of Plenty: Oil Booms and Petro-States*. Berkeley: University of California Press, 1997.

Kenny, James L., and Andrew G. Secord. "Engineering Modernity: Hydroelectric Development in New Brunswick, 1945–1970." *Acadiensis* 39, no. 1 (Winter/Spring 2010): 3–26.

Kerr, Aubrey. *Leduc*. Altona, AB: Friesen Printers, 1991.

———. *Redwater*. Winnipeg: Kromar Printing, 1994.

Klotz, J. A. "Geophysical Exploration Methods." *Journal of Petroleum Technology* 4, no. 6 (June 1952): 20–1.

Knight, Oliver. "Oil: Canada's New Wealth." *Business History Review* 30, no. 3 (1956): 297–328.

Kobrin, Stephen. "Foreign Enterprise and Forced Divestment in LDCs." *International Organization* 34, no. 1 (1980): 65–88.

Kohler, Larry. "Canadian/American Oil Diplomacy: The Adjustment of Conflicting National Oil Policies, 1955–1973." PhD diss., Johns Hopkins University, 1983.

Kozulj, Roberto. *Balance de la privatización de la industria petrolera en Argentina y su impacto sobre las inversiones y la competencia en los mercados minoristas*. Santiago: CEPAL, 2002.

———.*The Quest for Energy Security in Argentina*. Winnipeg: International Institute for Sustainable Development, 2010.

Kozulj, Roberto, and Víctor Bravo. *La política de desregulación petrolera argentina. Antecedentes e impactos*. Buenos Aires: Centro Editor de América Latina, 1993.

Larson, Henrietta M., Evelyn H. Knowlton, and Charles S. Popple. *New Horizons, 1927–1950*. Vol. 3 of *History of Standard Oil Company (New Jersey)*. New York: Harper and Row, 1971.

Larson, Henrietta M., and Kenneth Wiggins Porter. *History of Humble Oil & Refining Company: A Study in Industrial Growth*. New York: Harper, 1959.

Lawyer, L. C., Charles C. Bates and Robert B. Rice. *Geophysics in the Affairs of Mankind: A Personalized History of Exploration Geophysics*. Tulsa, OK: Society of Exploration Geophysicists, 2001.

Lazzarini, Sérgio G., and Aldo Musacchio. *Reinventing State Capitalism: Leviathan in Business, Brazil and Beyond*. Cambridge, MA: Harvard University Press, 2014.

Leopoldi, Maria Antonieta P. "O difícil caminho do meio: Estado, burguesia e industrialização no segundo governo Vargas (1951–1954)." In *Vargas e a crise dos anos 50*, edited by Angela de Castro Gomes, 161–203. Rio de Janeiro: Relume Dumaná, 1994.

Lieuwen, Edwin. *Petroleum in Venezuela: A History*. Berkeley: University of California Press, 1954.

Lima, Paulo César Ribeiro. *Pré-Sal: O novo marco legal e a capitalização da Petrobras*. Rio de Janeiro: Synergia Editora, 2011.

Lloyd-Jones, Chester. "Oil in the Caribbean and Elsewhere." *North American Review* 202, no. 719 (October 1915): 536–43.

Loo, Tina. "High Modernism, Conflict, and the Nature of Change in Canada." *Canadian Historical Review* 97, no. 1 (Spring 2016): 34–58.

———. "People in the Way: Modernity, Environment, and Society on the Arrow Lakes," *BC Studies* 142–3 (Summer/Autumn 2004): 169–71.

Loo, Tina, and Meg Stanley. "An Environmental History of Progress: Damming the Peace and Columbia Rivers." *Canadian Historical Review* 92, no. 3 (September 2011): 399–427.

"Looking Ahead in Marine and Land Geophysics—A Conversation with Woody Nestvold and Ian Jack." *Leading Edge* 14, no. 10 (October 1995): 1061–7.

Lora, Eduardo. "Structural Reforms in Latin America: What Has Been Reformed and How to Measure It." Working Paper No. 466, Inter-American Development Bank, Washington, DC, 2001.

Luby, Brittany. "From Milk-Medicine to Public (Re)Education Programs: An Examination of Anishinabek Mothers' Responses to Hydro-Electric Flooding in the Treaty #3 District, 1900–1975." *Canadian Bulletin of Medical History* 32, no. 2 (2015): 363–89.

Luong, Pauline Jones, and Erika Weinthal. *Oil Is Not a Curse: Ownership Structure and Institutions in Soviet Successor States*. New York: Cambridge University Press, 2010.

MacEachen, Alan. "The Budget." Ottawa: Department of Finance, 28 June 1982. http://publications.gc.ca/collections/collection_2016/fin/F1-23-3-1982-eng.pdf.

MacFadyen, Alan, and G. Campbell Watkins. *Petropolitics: Petroleum Development, Markets and Regulations, Alberta as an Illustrative History*. Calgary: University of Calgary Press, 2014.

MacFadyen, Joshua. "Hewers of Wood: A History of Wood Energy in Canada." In *Powering Up Canada: The History of Power, Fuel, and Energy from 1600*, edited by R. W. Sandwell, 129–61. Montreal: McGill-Queen's University Press, 2016.

Macfarlane, Daniel. "Dam the Consequences: Hydropolitics, Nationalism, and the Niagara–St. Lawrence Projects." In *Border Flows: A Century of the Canadian-*

American Water Relationship, edited by Lynne Heasley and Daniel Macfarlane, 123–50. Calgary: University of Calgary Press, 2016.

———. *Fixing Niagara Falls: Environment, Energy, and Engineers at the World's Most Famous Waterfall*. Vancouver: UBC Press, 2020.

———. "Natural Security: Canada-US Environmental Diplomacy." In *Undiplomatic History: The New Study of Canada and the World*, edited by Asa McKercher and Philip Van Huizen, 107–36. Montreal: McGill-Queen's University Press, 2019.

———. *Negotiating a River: Canada, the US, and the Creation of the St. Lawrence Seaway*. Vancouver: UBC Press, 2014.

Macfarlane, Daniel, and Peter Kitay. "Hydraulic Imperialism: Hydro-electric Development and Treaty 9 in the Abitibi Region." *American Review of Canadian Studies* 46, no. 3 (2016): 380–97.

Macfarlane, Daniel, and Andrew Watson. "Hydro Democracy: Water Power and Political Power in Ontario," *Scientia Canadensis* 40, no. 1 (2018): 1–18.

Macpherson, C. B. "The Meaning of Property." In *Property, Mainstream and Critical Positions*, edited by C. B. Macpherson, 1–13. Toronto: University of Toronto Press, 1978.

Maia, Fernanda Fernandes, Denise Cunha Tavares Terra, and Ludmila Gonçalves da Matta. "O nova sistema de partilha dos royalties do petróleo: Avaliando o debate na mídia." *Petróleo Royalties & Região* 12, no. 45 (2014): 4–7.

Malm, Andreas. *Fossil Capital: The Rise of Steam Power and the Roots of Global Warming*. New York: Verso, 2016.

Mann, Charles C., and Mark L. Plummer. *Noah's Choice: The Future of Endangered Species*. New York: Alfred A. Knopf, 1995.

Mann, Michael. "¿Ha terminado la globalización con el imparable ascenso del Estado nacional?" *Zona Abierta*, nos. 92–3 (2000): 175–212.

Manore, Jean. "Rivers as Text: From Pre-modern to Post-modern Understandings of Development, Technology and the Environment in Canada and Abroad." In *A History of Water*. Vol. 3, *The World of Water*, edited by Terje Tvedt and Eva Jakobsson, 229–53. London: I. B. Tauris, 2006.

Mares, David. *The Geopolitics of Natural Gas: Political Economy of Shale Gas in Argentina*. Houston: Baker Institute for Public Policy, Rice University, 2013.

———. *Oil Policy Reform in Resource Nationalist States: Lessons from Mexico*. Houston: Baker Institute for Public Policy, Rice University, 2011.

———. *Resource Nationalism and Energy Security in Latin America*. Houston: Baker Institute for Public Policy, Rice University, 2010.

———. "Sector energético latinoamericano: Integración a todo gas." *Contrapunto* (Mexico City) (April–June 2006): 90–6.

Marinho, Ilmar Penna, Jr. *Petróleo: Política e poder—um novo choque do petróleo?* Rio de Janeiro: José Olympio Editora, 1989.

Martin-Nielsen, Janet. "South over the Wires: Hydroelectricity Exports from Canada, 1900–1925." *Water History* 1, no. 2 (2009): 109–29.

Matus, Mario. *Crecimiento sin desarrollo. Precios y salarios reales durante el Ciclo Salitrero en Chile (1880-1930)*. Santiago: Editorial Universitaria, 2012.

Mau, Mark, and Henry Edmundson. *Groundbreakers: The Story of Oilfield Technology and the People Who Made It Happen*. Peterborough, UK: Fast-Print Publishing, 2015.

Mayne, W. Harry. *50 Years of Geophysical Ideas*. Tulsa, OK: SEG, 1989.

Mayorga-Alba, Eleodoro. "Revisiting Energy Policies in Latin America and Africa: A Redefinition of the Private and Public Sector Roles." *Energy Policy* 20, no. 10 (1992): 995–1004.

Mazabel Pineda, Katherin Andrea, and Constanza Flores Ruiz. "Nociones y repercusiones de las políticas públicas relacionadas con la naturaleza en Colombia." *Revista Pluriverso*, no. 7 (2016): 79–93.

McBeth, Brian S. *British Oil Policy, 1919–1939*. London: Frank Cass & Co., 1985.

———. *Dictatorship & Politics: Intrigue, Betrayal, and Survival in Venezuela, 1908–1935*. Notre Dame, IN: University of Notre Dame Press, 2008.

———. *Juan Vicente Gómez and the Oil Companies in Venezuela, 1908–1935*. Cambridge: Cambridge University Press, 1983.

McDougall, John N. *Fuels and the National Policy*. Toronto: Butterworths, 1982.

McGreevy, Patrick. *Imagining Niagara: The Meaning and Making of Niagara Falls*. Amherst: University of Massachusetts Press, 1994.

———. *The Wall of Mirrors: Nationalism and Perceptions of the Border at Niagara Falls*. Orono, ME: Canadian-American Center, University of Maine, 1991.

McKay, Ian. "The Liberal Order Framework: A Prospectus for a Reconnaissance of Canadian History." *Canadian Historical Review* 81, no. 4 (2000): 617–45.

McMahon, Robert J., William F. Sanford, and Sherrill B. Wells, eds. *Foreign Relations of the United States, 1955–1957*. Vol. 10, *Foreign Aid and Economic Defense Policy*. Washington, DC: US Government Printing Office, 1989.

McNally, Robert. *Crude Volatility: The History and Future of Boom-Bust Oil Prices*. New York: Columbia University Press, 2017.

McNeish, John-Andrew, Axel Borchgrevnik, and Owen Logan, eds. *Contested Powers: The Politics of Energy and Development in Latin America*. London: Zed Books, 2015.

McRae, Robert N. "A Survey of Canadian Energy Policy, 1974–1983." *Energy Journal* 6, no. 4 (1985): 49–64.

Melgarejo Moreno, Joaquín, Mª Immaculada López Ortiz, and Borja Montaño Sanz. "From Privatisation to Nationalisation: Repsol-YPF, 1999–2012." *Utilities Policy*, no. 26 (2013): 45–55.

Meller, Patricio. *Un siglo de economía política chilena (1890–1990)*. Santiago: Editorial Andrés Bello, 1996.

Melo, Jorge Orlando. "The Drug Trade, Politics and the Economy: The Colombian Experience." In *Latin America and the Multinational Drug Trade*, edited by Elizabeth Joyce and Carlos Malamud, 63–96. New York: St. Martin's Press, 1998.

Miranda, Maria Augusta Tibiriçá. *O petróleo é nosso: A luta contra o "entreguismo," pelo monopólio estatal, 1947–1953, 1953–1981*. Petrópolis, BR: Vozes, 1983.

Mitchell, Timothy. *Carbon Democracy: Political Power in the Age of Oil.* New York: Verso, 2011.

Molburg, J. C., J. A. Kavicky, and K. C. Picel. *The Design, Construction, and Operation of Long-Distance High Voltage Electricity Transmission Technologies.* Lemont, IL: Argonne National Laboratory, 2007.

Monaldi, Fernando. *Is Resource Nationalism Fading in Latin America? The Case of the Oil Industry.* Houston: Baker Institute for Public Policy, Rice University, 2014.

Montamat, Daniel. *La energía argentina. Otra víctima del desarrollo ausente.* Buenos Aires: Editorial El Ateneo, 2005.

Montenegro Lancheros, Hernán Camilo. "Ampliaciones y quiebres del reconocimiento político del campesinado colombiano: Un análisis a la luz de la Cumbre Agraria, Campesina, Étnica y Popular (Cacep)." *Revista Colombiana de Antropología* 52, no. 1 (2016): 169–95.

Montero Ferreira, Rafael Alfonso. "Los pueblos indígenas de Colombia y su inmersión en el proceso censal." *Revista de la Información Básica* 1, no. 1 (2006): 70–82.

Morales, Isidro. *The Twilight of Mexico's State Oil Monopolism: Policy, Economic and Political Trends in Mexico's Natural Gas Industry.* Houston: Baker Institute for Public Policy, Rice University, 2013.

Moran, Theodore. *Multinational Corporations: The Political Economy of Foreign Direct Investment.* New York: Lexington Books, 1985.

Murchison, Kenneth M. *The Snail Darter Case: TVA versus the Endangered Species Act.* Lawrence: University Press of Kansas, 2007.

Murton, James. *Creating a Modern Countryside: Liberalism and Land Resettlement in British Columbia.* Vancouver: UBC Press, 2007.

Nash, Gerald D. *United States Oil Policy, 1890–1964: Business and Government in Twentieth-Century America.* Pittsburgh: University of Pittsburgh Press, 1968.

National Inquiry into Missing and Murdered Indigenous Women and Girls. *A Legal Analysis of Genocide: Supplementary Report of the National Inquiry into Missing and Murdered Indigenous Women and Girls.* Ottawa: National Inquiry into Missing and Murdered Indigenous Women and Girls, 2019. https://www.mmiwg-ffada.ca/wp-content/uploads/2019/06/Supplementary-Report_Genocide.pdf.

———. *Reclaiming Power and Place: The Final Report of the National Inquiry into Missing and Murdered Indigenous Women and Girls.* Ottawa: National Inquiry into Missing and Murdered Indigenous Women and Girls, 2019. https://www.mmiwg-ffada.ca/final-report.

Nelles, H. V. *The Politics of Development: Forests, Mines and Hydro-Electric Power in Ontario, 1849–1941.* 2nd ed. Montreal: McGill-Queen's University Press, 2005.

Nelson, Kerry, Michael DeJesus, Alex Chakhmakhchev, and Melissa Manning. "Deepwater Operators Look to New Frontiers." *Offshore* 73, no. 5 (May 2013). https://www.offshore-mag.com/articles/print/volume-73/issue-5/international-report/deepwater-operators-look-to-new-frontiers.html.

Nemeth, Tammy Lynn. "Canada-U.S. Oil and Gas Relations 1958 to 1974." PhD diss., University of British Columbia, 2007.

———. "Pat Carney and the Dismantling of the National Energy Program." MA thesis, University of Alberta, 1997.

Ngoasong, Michael Zisuh. "How International Oil and Gas Companies Respond to Local Content Policies in Petroleum-Producing Developing Countries: A Narrative Enquiry." *Energy Policy*, no. 73 (2014): 471–9.

Nickle, Carl. "Western Canada's Oil and Gas: Part of Canada's Progress, and North America's Security." Address to Society of Petroleum Engineers Annual Meeting, San Francisco, 16 February 1959. In Paul Chastko's possession.

Noggle, Burl. *Teapot Dome: Oil and Politics in the 1920s*. Baton Rouge: Louisiana State University Press, 1962.

Norrie, Kenneth H. "A Regional Economic Overview of the West since 1945." In *The Making of the Modern West: Western Canada since 1945*, edited by A. W. Rasporich, 63–78. Calgary: University of Calgary Press, 1984.

Norrie, Kenneth, Douglas Owram, and J. C. Herbert Emery. *A History of the Canadian Economy*. 4th ed. Toronto: Nelson, 2008.

Nye, David E. *American Technological Sublime*. Cambridge, MA: MIT Press, 1996.

———. *Electrifying America: Social Meanings of a New Technology, 1880–1940*. New ed. Cambridge, MA: MIT Press, 1992.

O'Connor, Dermot, and Juan Pablo Bohórquez Montoya. "Neoliberal Transformation in Colombia's Goldfields: Development Strategy or Capitalist Imperialism?" *Labour, Capital and Society/Travail, capital et societé* 43, no. 2 (2010): 85–118.

Oddone da Costa, Décio Fabrício, Renato Sanches Rodrigues, and Álvaro Felippe Negrão. "The Evolution of Deepwater Drilling in Brazil." Paper Presented at the Society of Petroleum Engineers Latin American Petroleum Engineering Conference, Rio de Janeiro, October 14–19, 1990.

O'Keefe, Hsu Yuet Heung. *A crise do petróleo e a economia brasileira*. São Paulo: Instituto de Pesquisas Econômicas, 1984.

Oliveira, Adilson de. *Energy Security in South America: The Role of Brazil*. Winnipeg: International Institute for Sustainable Development, 2010.

Olsson, Tore C. *Agrarian Crossings: Reformers and the Remaking of the US and Mexican Countryside*. Princeton, NJ: Princeton University Press, 2017.

Organización Nacional Indígena de Colombia. "Política minero energética del país." Paper presented at the Cumbre Agraria: Campesina, étnica y popular, en el marco de la negociación del pliego único, exactamente del punto sobre minería, Bogotá, March 2014.

Ortega Martínez, Luis. *Chile en ruta al capitalismo. Cambio, euforia y depresión 1850–1880*. Santiago: DIBAM-LOM/Centro de Investigaciones Diego Barros Arana, 2006.

Owen, Edgar Wesley. *Trek of the Oil Finders: A History of Exploration for Petroleum*. Tulsa, OK: American Association of Petroleum Geologists, 1975.

Owram, Doug. "1951: Oil's Magic Wand." In *Alberta Formed: Alberta Transformed*. Vol. 2, edited by Michael Payne, Donald Wetherell, and Catherine Cavanaugh, 567–86. Calgary: University of Calgary Press, 2006.

Palermo, Hernán. *Cadenas de oro negro en el esplendor y ocaso de YPF*. Buenos Aires: Antropofagia, 2012.

Para, Francisco. *Oil Politics: A Modern History of Petroleum*. London: I. B. Taurus, 2003.

Paz Antolín, María José, and Juan Manuel Ramírez Cendrero. "How Important Are National Companies for Oil and Gas Sector Performance? Lessons from the Bolivia and Brazil Case Studies." *Energy Policy*, no. 61 (2013): 707–16.

Paz, José. "Oil and Development in Brazil: Between an Extractive and an Industrialization Strategy." *Energy Policy*, no. 73 (2014): 501–11.

Pearce, Scott. "Tackling Corporate Complicity: Canadian Oil Investment in Colombia." In *Community Rights and Corporate Social Responsibility: Canadian Mining Companies in Latin America*, edited by Liisa North, Timothy David Clark, and Viviana Patroni, 160–80. Toronto: Between the Lines, 2006.

Perlgut, Mark. *Electricity across the Border: The U.S.-Canadian Experience*. New York: C. D. Howe Research Institute, 1978.

Perron, Dominique. " 'On est Hydro-Québecois': Consommateur, producteur ou citoyen? Analyse de la nationalisation symbolique d'Hydro-Québec." *Globe: Revue internationale d'études québécoises* 6, no. 2 (2003): 73–97.

Petersen, Shannon. *Acting for Endangered Species: The Statutory Ark*. Lawrence: University Press of Kansas, 2002.

Petras, James, and Henry Veltmeyer. *Social Movements and State Power: Argentina, Brazil, Bolivia, Ecuador*. London: Pluto Press, 2005.

Petrobras. "Relatório Anual/Annual Report." Rio de Janeiro: Petrobras, various years. http://www.investidorpetrobras.com.br.

Phillips, Sarah T. *This Land, This Nation: Conservation, Rural America, and the New Deal*. New York: Cambridge University Press, 2007.

Pinheiro, Armando Castelar, and Fabio Giambiagi. "The Macroeconomic Background and Institutional Framework of Brazilian Privatization." Paper presented at the conference Privatization in Brazil: The Case of Public Utilities, Rio de Janeiro, April 1999.

Pinheiro, Ricardo Pinto. *Abastecimento nacional de combustíveis no ambiente de flexibilização do monopólio de petróleo*. Rio de Janeiro: Ministério de Minas e Energia, 1996.

Pinho, Cláudio A. *Pré-sal: História, doutrina e comentários às leis*. Belo Horizonte: Editora Legal, 2010.

Pires, Adriano, and Rafael Schechtman. "Os resultados da reforma: uma estratégia vencedora." In *Petróleo: Reforma e contrarreforma do setor petrolífero brasileiro*, edited by Fabio Giambiagi and Luiz Paulo Velloso Lucas, 81–103. Rio de Janeiro: Elsevier, 2013.

Pires, Paulo Valois. *A evolução do monopólio estatal do petróleo*. Rio de Janeiro: Editora Lumen Juris, 2000.

Pirtle, Caleb III. *Engineering the World: Stories from the First 75 Years of Texas Instruments*. Dallas: Southern Methodist University Press, 2005.

Plater, Zygmunt J. B. *The Snail Darter and the Dam: How Pork-Barrel Politics Endangered a Little Fish and Killed a River.* New Haven, CT: Yale University Press, 2013.

Platt, Harold L. *The Electric City: Energy and the Growth of the Chicago Area, 1880–1930.* Chicago: University of Chicago Press, 1991.

Plourde, André. "The Changing Nature of National and Continental Energy Markets." In *Canadian Energy Policy and the Struggle for Sustainable Development,* edited by G. Bruce Doern, 51–82. Toronto: University of Toronto Press, 2005.

Polanyi, Karl. *The Great Transformation: The Political and Economic Origins of Our Time.* Boston: Beacon Press, 2001.

Pollock, David, and Grant Manuge. "The Mulroney Doctrine." *International Perspectives* (January/February 1985): 5–8.

Pomeranz, Kenneth. *The Great Divergence: Europe, China, and the Making of the Modern World Economy.* Princeton, NJ: Princeton University Press, 2000.

Pratt, Joseph A. "Exxon and the Control of Oil." *Journal of American History* 99, no. 1 (2012): 145–54.

Pratt, Joseph A., with William E. Hale. *Exxon: Transforming Energy, 1973–2005.* Austin: Dolph Briscoe Center for American History/University of Texas Press, 2013.

Priest, Tyler. "Extraction Not Creation: The History of Offshore Petroleum in the Gulf of Mexico." *Enterprise & Society* 8, no 2 (June 2007): 227–67.

———. "Hubbert's Peak: The Great Debate Over the End of Oil." *Historical Studies in the Natural Sciences* 44, no. 1 (February 2014): 37–79.

———. *The Offshore Imperative: Shell Oil's Search for Petroleum in Postwar America.* College Station: Texas A&M University Press, 2007.

———. "Petrobras in the History of Offshore Oil." In *New Order and Progress: Development and Democracy in Brazil,* edited by Ben Ross Schneider, 53–77. New York: Oxford University Press, 2016.

Pritchard, Sara B. *Confluence: The Nature of Technology and the Remaking of the Rhône.* Cambridge, MA: Harvard University Press, 2011.

Pritchard, Sara B., and Thomas Zeller, "The Nature of Industrialization." In *The Illusory Boundary: Environment and Technology in History,* edited by Stephen H. Cutcliffe and Martin Reuss, 69–100. Charlottesville: University of Virginia Press, 2010.

Proceedings of the United States-Mexican Commission Convened in Mexico City, May 14, 1923. Washington, DC: Government Printing Office, 1925.

Proffitt, Jack M. "A History of Innovation in Marine Seismic Data Acquisition." *Geophysics: The Leading Edge of Exploration* 10, no. 3 (March 1991): 24–30.

Programa de las Naciones Unidas para el Desarrollo. *Informe Nacional de Desarrollo Humano 2011. Colombia rural. Razones para la esperanza.* Bogotá: PNUD, 2011.

Proubasta, Delores. "Henry Salvatori." *Geophysics: The Leading Edge of Exploration* 2, no. 8 (August 1983): 14–22.

Public Papers of the Presidents of the United States: Jimmy Carter: 1979. Washington, DC: Government Printing Office, 1979.

Quintas, Humberto, and Luiz Cezar P. Quintans. *A história do petróleo no Brasil e no mundo.* Rio de Janeiro: IBP/Freitas Bastos Editora, 2009.

Quintans, Luiz Cezar P. *Contratos de petróleo: Concessão e partilha—propostas e leis para o pré-sal*. Rio de Janeiro: Benício Biz/IBP, 2011.

———. *Direito do petróleo: Conteúdo local—a evolução do modelo de contrato e o conteúdo local nas atividades de E&P no Brasil*. Rio de Janeiro: IBP/Freitas Bastos Editora, 2011.

Raibmon, Paige. *Authentic Indians: Episodes of Encounter from the Late-Nineteenth-Century Northwest Coast*. Durham, NC: Duke University Press, 2005.

Ramírez Cuéllar, Francisco. *The Profits of Extermination: How US Corporate Power Is Destroying Colombia*. Monroe, ME: Common Courage Press, 2005.

Randall, Laura. *The Political Economy of Brazilian Oil*. Westport, CT: Praeger, 1993.

Randall, Stephen J. *United States Foreign Oil Policy since World War I: For Profits and Security*. Montreal: McGill-Queen's University Press, 2005.

Reyes Posada, Alejandro. *Guerreros y campesinos: El despojo de la tierra en Colombia*. Bogotá: Norma, 2009.

Reynolds, F. and Robert H. Ray. "Binary-Gain Recording and Processing." *AAPG Bulletin* 51, no. 5 (May 1967): 814.

Riordan, Michael, and Lillian Hoddeson. *Crystal Fire: The Birth of the Information Age*. New York: W. W. Norton, 1997.

Robinson, Enders A. "Geophysical Exploration: Past and Future." *Leading Edge* 25, no. 1 (January 2006): 96–99.

———. "The MIT Geophysical Analysis Group (GAG) from Inception to 1954." *Geophysics* 70, no. 4 (July–August 2005): 7JA–30JA.

Rodríguez Weber, Javier. *Desarrollo y desigualdad en Chile (1850–2009). Historia de su economía política*. Santiago: Centro de Investigaciones Barros Arana/DIBAM, 2017.

———. "La economía política de la desigualdad del ingreso en Chile, 1850–2009." PhD diss., Universidad de la República (Uruguay), 2014.

———. "De Manuel Montt a Michelle Bachelet. 160 años de distribución del ingreso en Chile." In *Chile y América en su historia económica*, edited by César Yáñez, 455–73. Valparaíso: Asociación Chilena de Historia Económica/Universidad de Valparaíso, 2013.

Rodríguez, José Santiago. *Informes ante el Tribunal de Primera Instancia en lo Civil del Distrito Federal en representación de la compañía inglesa 'The Venezuelan Oil Concessions Limited' en el juicio promovido contra ella y contra el señor Antonio Aranguren por el señor Lorenzo Mercado y sentencia recaída en el asunto*. Caracas: Lit. y Tip. del Comercio, 1916.

———. *Informes leídos ante la Corte Superior del Distrito Federal en representación de la compañía inglesa 'The Venezuelan Oil Concessions Ltd.' en el juicio seguido contra ellos y contra el señor Antonio Aranguren por el señor Lorenzo Mercado y sentencia recaída en el asunto*. Caracas: Lit y Tip, del Comercio, 1917.

Rodríguez, Luis Ernesto. "Are the Characteristics of the New Colombian Mining Code Sufficiently Competitive in Attracting Investment to the Mineral Sector?" *Minerals & Energy* 19, no. 1 (2004): 32–43.

Rodríguez Garavito, César A., and Luis Carlos Arenas. "Derechos indígenas, activismo transnacional y movilización legal: La lucha del pueblo U'wa en Colombia." In *El derecho y la globalización desde abajo: Hacia una legalidad cosmopolita*, edited by Boaventura de Sousa Santos and César A. Rodríguez Garavito; translated by Carlos Morales de Setién Ravina, 217–39. Barcelona: Anthropos/UAM Cuajimalpa, 2007.

Rodriguez, Karyna, Neil Hodgson, and Richie Miller. "Hydrocarbon Prospectivity in Brazil." *GeoExpro* 15, no. 3 (2018). https://www.geoexpro.com/articles/2018/08/hydrocarbon-prospectivity-in-brazil.

Ross, Michael L. *The Oil Curse: How Petroleum Wealth Shapes the Development of Nations*. Princeton, NJ: Princeton University Press, 2012

Rubio, María del Mar, César Yáñez, Mauricio Folchi, and Albert Carreras. "Energy as an Indicator of Modernization in Latin America, 1890–1925." *Economic History Review* 63, no. 3 (2010): 769–804.

Ruiz Caro, Ariela. *La seguridad energética de América Latina y el Caribe en el contexto mundial*. Santiago: CEPAL, 2007.

Runte, Alfred. "Beyond the Spectacular: The Niagara Falls Preservation Campaign." *New York Historical Society Quarterly*, no. 57 (January 1973): 30–50.

Sabbatella, Ignacio. "La política petrolera de la posconvertibilidad: De la herencia neoliberal a la expropiación de YPF." *Argumentos*, no. 14 (January–June 2012): 149–80.

Sabbatella, Ignacio, and Esteban Serrani. "A 20 años de la privatización de YPF. Balance y perspectivas." *Voces en el Fénix* 2, no. 10 (July–December 2011): 7–15.

Sachs, Jeffrey D., and Andrew M. Warner. "Natural Resource Abundance and Economic Growth." NBER Working Paper No. 5398, National Bureau of Economic Research, Cambridge, MA, December 1995.

Sáenz, Aarón. *La política internacional de la Revolución: Estudios y documentos*. Mexico City: Fondo de Cultura Económica, 1961.

Salazar-Carrillo, Jorge, and Bernadette West. *Oil and Development in Venezuela during the 20th Century*. Westport, CT: Praeger, 2004.

Sampson, Anthony. *The Seven Sisters: The Great Oil Companies and the World They Shaped*. New York: Viking Press, 1975.

Sandwell, R. W. *Canada's Rural Majority: Households, Environments, and Economies, 1870–1940*. Toronto: University of Toronto Press, 2016.

———. "Mapping Fuel Use in Canada: Exploring the Social History of Canadians' Great Fuel Transformation." In *Historical GIS in Canada*, edited by Jennifer Bonnell and Marcel Fortin, 239–70. Calgary: University of Calgary Press, 2014.

———. "Pedagogies of the Unimpressed: Re-educating Ontario Women for the Modern Energy Regime, 1900–1940." *Ontario History* 107, no. 1 (Spring 2015): 36–59.

———. "People, Place and Power: Rural Electrification in Canada, 1890–1950." In *Transforming the Countryside: The Electrification of Rural Britain*, edited by Paul Brassley, Jeremy Burchardt, and Karen Sayer, 178–204. New York: Routledge, 2017.

———, ed. *Powering Up Canada: The History of Power, Fuel, and Energy from 1600*. Montreal: McGill-Queen's University Press, 2016.

Santiago, Myrna I. *The Ecology of Oil: Environment, Labor, and the Mexican Revolution, 1900–1938*. New York: Cambridge University Press, 2006.

Sarbu, Bianca. *Ownership and Control of Oil: Explaining Policy Choices across Producing Countries*. London: Routledge, 2014.

Sawyer, Suzana. *Crude Chronicles: Indigenous Politics, Multinational Oil, and Neoliberalism in Ecuador*. Durham, NC: Duke University Press, 2004.

Scaff, Fernando Facury. "Impasses regulatórios do pré-sal e o plano de negócios da Petrobras." *Petróleo Royalties & Região* 12, no. 46 (2014): 6–7.

Schneider, William A. "3-D Seismic: A Historical Note." *Leading Edge* 17, no. 3 (March 1998): 375–80.

Schneiderman, David. "Constitutional Approaches to Privatization: An Inquiry into the Magnitude of Neo-liberal Constitutionalism." *Law and Contemporary Problems* 63, no. 4 (2000): 83–109.

Schurr, Sam H., and Bruce C. Netchert. *Energy in the American Economy, 1850–1922*. Baltimore: John Hopkins University Press, 1960.

Scott, James C. *Seeing Like a State: How Certain Schemes to Improve the Human Condition Have Failed*. New Haven, CT: Yale University Press, 1998.

"Seismic Technology: Evolution of a Vital Tool for Reservoir Engineers." *Journal of Petroleum Technology* 51, no. 2 (February 1999): 22–8.

Serrani, Esteban. "América Latina y su política petrolera frente a las últimas tendencias internacionales. Perspectivas regionales a partir del análisis de Brasil y Argentina." *Foro Internacional* 53, no. 1 (January–March 2013): 182–213.

———. "Estado, empresarios y acumulación de privilegio. Análisis de la industria petrolera argentina, 1988–2008." PhD diss., Universidad de Buenos Aires, 2012.

Shever, Elana. *Resources for Reform: Oil and Neoliberalism in Argentina*. Stanford, CA: Stanford University Press, 2012.

Shrivastava, Meenal, and Lorna Stefanick, eds. *Alberta Oil and the Decline of Democracy in Canada*. Edmonton: Athabasca University Press, 2015.

Shrock, Robert R. *A Cooperative Plan in Geophysical Education: The GSI Student Cooperative Plan, the First Fifteen Summers, 1951–1965*. Dallas: Geophysical Service, 1966.

Sickles, Robin C., Patrik Hultberg, Fernando Orozco Ruiz, and Joya Mukerjie. *Convergence, Regulatory Distortions, Deregulatory Dynamics and Growth Experiences of the Latin American and Brazilian Economies*. Houston: Baker Institute for Public Policy, Rice University, 2004.

Singh, Jewellord Tolentino Nem. "Towards Post-neoliberal Resource Politics? The International Political Economy of Oil and Copper in Brazil and Chile." *New Political Economy* 19, no. 3 (2014): 329–58.

Smil, Vaclav. *Creating the Twentieth Century: Technical Innovations of 1876–1914 and Their Lasting Impact*. New York: Oxford University Press, 2005.

———. *Energías. Una guía ilustrada de la biósfera y la civilización*. Translated by Ignacio Zúñiga. Barcelona: Crítica, 2001.

———. *Energy at the Crossroads: Global Perspectives and Uncertainties*. Cambridge, MA: MIT Press. 2003.

———. *Energy in Nature and Society. General Energetics of Complex Systems*. Cambridge, MA: MIT Press. 2008.

———. *Energy in World History*. Boulder, CA: Westview Press, 1994.

———. *Energy Transitions: Global and National Perspectives*. 2nd ed. Santa Barbara, CA: Praeger, 2017.

Smith, Benjamin B. *Hard Times in the Lands of Plenty: Oil Politics in Iran and Indonesia*. Ithaca, NY: Cornell University Press, 2007.

Smith, Mark. "The Seismic Digital Revolution." Unpublished manuscript provided by Smith to Tyler Priest.

Smith, Peter Seaborn. *Oil and Politics in Modern Brazil*. Toronto: MacMillan, 1976.

———. "Petrobrás: The Politicizing of a State Company, 1953–1964." *Business History Review* 46, no. 2 (1972): 183–201.

Smith, Sherry, and Brian Frehner, eds. *Indians and Energy: Exploitation and Opportunity in the American Southwest*. Santa Fe, NM: School for Advanced Research Press, 2010.

Solberg, Carl E. *Oil and Nationalism in Argentina*. Stanford, CA: Stanford University Press, 1979.

Solnick, Steven Lee. *Stealing the State: Control and Collapse in Soviet Institutions*. Cambridge, MA: Harvard University Press, 1998.

Souza, Amaury de, and Carlos Pereira. "A flexibilização do monopólio do petróleo no contexto das reformas dos anos 1990." In *Petróleo: Reforma e contrarreforma do setor petrolífero brasileiro*, edited by Fabio Giambiagi and Luiz Paulo Vellozo Lucas, 39–54. Rio de Janeiro: Elsevier, 2013.

Sproule-Jones, Mark, Carolyn Johns, and B. Timothy Heinmiller, eds., *Canadian Water Politics: Conflicts and Institutions*. Montreal: McGill-Queen's University Press, 2008.

Stairs, Denis. "Architects or Engineers? The Conservatives and Foreign Policy." In *Diplomatic Departures: The Conservative Era in Canadian Foreign Policy, 1984–1993*, edited by Nelson Michaud and Kim Richard Nossal, 25–42. Vancouver: UBC Press, 2001.

Stevens, Paul. "National Oil Companies and International Oil Companies in the Middle East: Under the Shadow of Government and the Resource Nationalism Cycle." *Journal of World Energy Law and Business* 1, no. 1 (2008): 5–30.

Stevens, Paul, and Evelyn Dietsche. "Resource Curse: An Analysis of Causes, Experiences and Possible Ways Forward." *Energy Policy* 36, no. 1 (2008): 56–65.

Stokes, Peter. "St. Lawrence, a Criticism." *Canadian Architect* 3, no. 2 (February 1958): 43–8.

Strand, Ginger. *Inventing Niagara: Beauty, Power, and Lies*. Toronto: Simon & Schuster, 2008.

Stuven, Ana María. *La seducción de un orden. Las elites y la construcción de Chile en las polémicas culturales y políticas del siglo XIX*. Santiago: Ediciones de la Universidad Católica de Chile, 2000.

Sweet, George Elliott. *The History of Geophysical Prospecting*. Los Angeles: Science Press, 1966.

Távora, Juarez. "O Código de Minas e o desenvolvimento da mineração no Brasil." *Geologia e Metallurgia*, no. 14 (1956): 156–67.

Taylor, Graham. "From Branch Operation to Integrated Subsidiary: The Reorganization of Imperial Oil under Walter Teagle, 1911–1917." *Business History* 34, no. 3 (1992): 49–67.

Thompson, John Herd, and Stephen J. Randall. *Canada and the United States: Ambivalent Allies*. 4th ed. Montreal: McGill-Queen's University Press, 2008.

Thorp, Rosemary. *Progress, Poverty and Exclusion: An Economic History of Latin America*. Washington, DC: Inter-American Development Bank, 1998.

Tinker Salas, Miguel. *The Enduring Legacy: Oil, Culture, and Society in Venezuela*. Durham, NC: Duke University Press, 2009.

Tissot, Richard. "Latin America's Energy Future." Discussion Paper IDB-DP-252, Inter-American Development Bank, Washington, DC, 2012.

Toner, Glen, Leslie A. Pal, and Michael J. Prince, eds. *Policy: From Ideas to Implementation, in Honour of Professor G. Bruce Doern*. Montreal: McGill-Queen's University Press, 2010.

Trebat, Thomas J. *Brazil's State-Owned Enterprises: A Case Study of the State as Entrepreneur*. Cambridge: Cambridge University Press, 1983.

Trim, Henry. "Planning for the Future: The Conserver Society and Canadian Sustainability." *The Canadian Historical Review* 96, no. 3 (September 2015): 375–404.

Triner, Gail D. "From Regulatory State to Entrepreneurial State? Brazilian Political Economy in the Wake of Privatization." Conference paper, XVIII World Economic History Congress, Cambridge, MA, 1 August 2018.

———. *Mining and the State in Brazilian Development*. London: Pickering and Chatto, 2011.

———. "Regulatory Regimes for Petroleum Production in Brazil." In *The Political Economy of Resource Regulation: An International and Comparative History, 1850–2015*, edited by Andreas R. D. Sanders, Pål Thonstad Sandvik, and Espen Storli. Vancouver: UBC Press, forthcoming.

Truth and Reconciliation Commission of Canada. *Honouring the Truth, Reconciling for the Future: Summary of the Final Report of the Truth and Reconciliation Commission of Canada*. Winnipeg: Truth and Reconciliation Commission of Canada, 2015. http://www.trc.ca/assets/pdf/Honouring_the_Truth_Reconciling_for_the_Future_July_23_2015.pdf.

Unger, Richard W., and John Thistle. *Energy Consumption in Canada in the 19th and 20th Centuries: A Statistical Outline, Series on Energy Consumption*. Naples: Consiglio Nazionale delle Richerche, Istituto di Studi sulle Società del Mediterraneo, 2013.

United Nations Statistical Office. *International Trade Statistics Yearbook.* New York: United Nations, various years.

United States. Congressional Research Service. "Cross-Border Energy Trade in North America: Present and Potential." EveryCRSReport.com, 30 January 2017. https://www.everycrsreport.com/reports/R44747.html#_Toc473645486.

———. Department of the Interior. Bureau of Ocean Energy Management. Gulf of Mexico OCS Region. Office of Resource Evaluation. *Deepwater Gulf of Mexico December 31, 2014.* OCS Report BOEM 2016-057, New Orleans, August 2016.

———. Department of the Interior. Minerals Management Service. *History of the Offshore Oil and Gas Industry in Southern Louisiana.* 6 Vols. OCS Study MMS 2008-042, New Orleans, September 2008. https://www.boem.gov/espis.

———. House of Representatives. "Production Costs of Crude Petroleum and of Refined Petroleum Products." House Document No. 195, 72 Cong. 1 Sess., Washington, DC, 1932.

———. Tennessee Valley Authority. *Environmental Statement: Tellico Project.* Chattanooga, TN: TVA Office of Health and Environmental Science, 1972.

Urrea-Giraldo, Fernando. "La población afrodescendiente en Colombia." Paper presented at the Seminario Internacional. Pueblos indígenas y afrodescendientes de América Latina y el Caribe: Relevancia y pertinencia de la información sociodemográfica para políticas y programas, CEPAL, Santiago, 2005. http://www.cepal.org/mujer/noticias/noticias/5/27905/FUrrea.pdf.

Vargas, Getúlio. "Discurso em Leopoldina, Minas, 24 Outubro 1939." In *A política nacionalista do petróleo no Brasil,* 54–5. Rio de Janeiro: Tempo Brasileiro, 1964.

Vellozo Lucas, Luiz Paulo. "A derrota de um modelo de sucesso." In *Petróleo: Reforma e contrarreforma do setor petrolífero brasileiro,* edited by Fabio Giambiagi and Luiz Paulo Vellozo Lucas, 125–52. Rio de Janeiro: Elsevier, 2013.

Venezuela. *Recopilación de leyes y decretos de Venezuela.* Vol. 36. Caracas: Imprenta Bolívar, 1913.

———. *Recopilación de leyes y decretos de Venezuela.* Vol. 38. Caracas: Imprenta Bolívar, 1915.

———. Distrito Federal, Juzgado de la Primera Instancia en lo Civil. *Juicio seguido por Lorenzo Mercado contra Antonio Aranguren y la Compañía Venezuelan Oil Concessions Limited. Informes de los Doctores L. Herrera Mendoza y F. Arroyo Parejo en Primera y Segundas Instancias.* Caracas: Empresa El Cojo, 1916.

———. Ministerio de Minas e Hidrocarburos. *Petróleo y otros datos estadísticos, 1964.* Caracas: Central de Evaluaciones, 1964.

Verma, Rajni K. *Offshore Seismic Exploration: Data Acquisition, Processing, Interpretation.* Houston: Gulf Publishing, 1986.

Vernon, Raymond. *Sovereignty at Bay: The Multinational Spread of U.S. Enterprises.* New York: Basic Books, 1971.

Vietor, Richard H. K. *Energy Policy in America since 1945: A Study of Business-Government Relations.* Cambridge: Cambridge University Press, 1987.

Vitz, Matthew. " 'To Save the Forests': Power, Narrative, and Environment in Mexico City's Cooking Fuel Transition." *Mexican Studies/Estudios Mexicanos* 31, no. 1 (Winter 2015): 125–55.

Wade, Robert. *El mercado dirigido: A teoría económica y la función del gobierno en la industrialización del este de Asia.* Translated by Mónica Utrilla de Neira. Mexico City: Fondo de Cultura Económica, 1999.

Wall, Bennett H. *Growth in a Changing Environment: A History of Standard Oil Company (New Jersey), Exxon Corporation, 1950–1975.* New York: McGraw-Hill, 1988.

Walton, G. G. "Three-Dimensional Seismic Method." *Geophysics* 37, no. 3 (June 1972): 417–30.

Ward, Halina. "Resource Nationalism and Sustainable Development: A Primer and Key Issues." Working paper, International Institute for Environment and Development, London, 2009.

Waterhouse, Benjamin C. *Lobbying America: The Politics of Business from Nixon to NAFTA.* Princeton, NJ: Princeton University Press, 2014.

Weintraub, Sidney, ed. *Energy Cooperation in the Western Hemisphere: Benefits and Impediments.* Washington, DC: Center for Strategic and International Studies, 2007.

Weitzner, Viviane. *Holding Extractive Companies to Account in Colombia: An Evaluation of CSR Instruments through the Lens of Indigenous and Afro-Descendant Rights.* Ottawa: North-South Institute/Proceso de Comunidades Negras/Resguardo Indígena Cañamomo Lomaprieta, 2012.

Weyland, Kurt. "Neopopulism and Neoliberalism in Latin America: Unexpected Affinities." *Studies in Comparative International Development* 31, no. 3 (1996): 3–31.

Wheeler, William Bruce, and Michael McDonald. *TVA and the Tellico Dam, 1936–1979: A Bureaucratic Crisis in Post-industrial America.* Knoxville: University of Tennessee Press, 1986.

White, Richard. *The Middle Ground: Indians, Empires, and Republics in the Great Lakes Region, 1650–1815.* 20th anniv. ed. New York: Cambridge University Press, 2010.

Whitham, W. B. "Les investissements américains et les origines de l'industrie pétrolière canadiennne." *Actualité économique* 44, no. 4 (January/March 1969): 689–710.

Wilentz, Sean. *The Age of Reagan: A History, 1974–2008.* New York: HarperCollins, 2008.

Wilson, Jeffrey. "Resource Powers? Minerals, Energy and the Rise of the BRICS." *Third World Quarterly* 36, no. 2 (2015): 223–39.

———. "Understanding Resource Nationalism: Economic Dynamics and Political Institutions." *Contemporary Politics* 21, no. 4 (2015): 399–416.

Williams, Peggy. "Deep Water Delivers." *Oil & Gas Investor* 26, no. 5 (May 2006): 32.

Williamson, Jeffrey G. *Trade and Poverty: When the Third World Fell Behind.* Cambridge, MA: MIT Press, 2011.

World Bank. *World Development Report 1987.* New York: World Bank/Oxford University Press, 1987.

Worster, Donald. "Wild, Tame, and Free: Comparing Canadian and U.S. Views of Nature." In *Parallel Destinies: Canadian American Relations West of the Rockies*, edited by John M. Findlay and Kenneth S. Coates, 246–75. Montreal: McGill-Queen's Press, 2002.

Wrigley, Edward A. *Continuity, Chance and Change: The Character of the Industrial Revolution in England*. New York: Cambridge University Press, 1988.

———. *Energy and the English Industrial Revolution*. Cambridge: Cambridge University Press, 2010.

———. *The Path to Sustained Growth: England's Transition from an Organic Economy to an Industrial Revolution*. Cambridge: Cambridge University Press, 2016.

Yáñez, César. "Economic Modernization in Adverse Institutional Environments: The Cases of Cuba and Chile." In *The Economies of Latin America: New Cliometric Data*, edited by César Yáñez and Albert Carreras, 105–17. London: Pickering and Chatto, 2012.

———. "El tercer ciclo del carbón en Chile de 1973 a 2013: Del climaterio al rejuvenecimiento." *América Latina en la historia económica* 24, no. 3 (September–December 2017): 224–58.

Yáñez, César, and Albert Carreras, eds. *The Economies of Latin America: New Cliometric Data*. London: Pickering and Chatto, 2012.

Yáñez, César, and Martín Garrido Lepe. "El consumo de carbón en Chile entre 1933–1960. Transición energética y cambio estructural." *Revista Uruguaya de Historia Económica* 5, no. 8 (2015): 76–95.

Yáñez, César, and José Jofré. "Modernización económica y consumo energético en Chile, 1844–1930." *Historia 396* 1, no. 1 (2011): 127–56.

Yáñez, César, María del Mar Rubio, José Jofré, and Albert Carreras. "El consumo aparente de carbón mineral en América Latina, 1841–2000. Una historia de progreso y frustración." *Revista de Historia Industrial* 53, no. 21 (2013): 25–77.

Yáñez, Juan Carlos. *La intervención social en Chile, 1907–1932*. Santiago: RIL Editores, 2008.

Yergin, Daniel. *The Prize: The Epic Quest for Oil, Money and Power*. New York: Simon & Schuster, 1992.

Young, Kevin A. *Blood of the Earth: Resource Nationalism, Revolution, and Empire in Bolivia*. Austin: University of Texas Press, 2017.

———. "From Open Door to Nationalization: Oil and Development Visions in Bolivia, 1952–1969." *Hispanic American Historical Review* 97, no. 1 (2017): 95–129.

YPF. *Memoria de YPF 1993*. Buenos Aires: Library of the Ministry of Economy, 1994.

Zeiler, Thomas W. "Opening Doors in the World Economy." In *Global Interdependence: The World after 1945*, edited by Akira Iriye, 203–361. Cambridge, MA: Belknap Press of Harvard University, 2014.

Index

A

Acción Democrática (AD) (Venezuela), 104, 108–110. *See also* Pérez, Carlos Andrés
Afro-Colombians, 324–325, 328–329, 331–333, 335, 339, 342
Agência Nacional de Petróleo (ANP) (Brazil), 258, 264
Agrarian Summit (Cumbre-Agraria), 334, 339–341
ALBA (Alianza Bolivariana para los Pueblos de Nuestra América), 3
Alberta Energy Company, 226
Alfonsín, Raúl, 275, 276
Alliance for Progress, 9
Aluminum Company of America (ALCOA), 126, 140
asphalt mining, 84, 88

B

Beaufort Sea oil field, 227, 230
Betancourt, Rómulo, 105, 108. *See also* Acción Democrática
Boeing Corporation, 154, 160
Bolsonaro, Jair, 3, 7
Boundary Waters Treaty, (1909) 127, 131. *See also* International Joint Commission
Bretton Woods system, 214, 224
British Controlled Oilfields Ltd. (BCO), 71, 80, 82
British-American Oil, 218
Bucareli agreements, 299–301

C

Calderón, Felipe, 303, 305
campesinos, 329–332, 339. *See also* ejidos
Canada Oil and Gas Lands Administration. *See* National Energy Program
Canada-US Free Trade Agreement (CUFTA), 212, 234. *See also* Canada-USA-Mexico Agreement; North American Free Trade Agreement

Canada-USA-Mexico Agreement (CUSMA), 316. *See also* Canada-US Free Trade Agreement; North American Free Trade Agreement
Canadian Association of Petroleum Producers (CAPP), 218, 228
Canadian Ownership Account. *See* National Energy Program
Cárdenas, Cuauhtémoc, 306, 308
Cárdenas, Lázaro, 9, 296, 301, 306
Cardoso, Fernando Henrique, 36–37
Carib Syndicate Ltd. (CS), 78, 80, 83
Caribbean Petroleum Company (CPC), 70–71, 76–77, 84–90
Carranza, Venustiano, 296–297
Carter, Jimmy, 152, 161, 163–164, 169, 174
Castro, Cipriano, 74
Chávez, Hugo, 2, 17, 101, 115–119
Chevron, 6, 35, 197, 214, 275, 303, 313. *See also* Texaco
climate change, 2–3. *See also* environmental impact
coal: in Brazil 245; in Canada 125, 127, 129–130, 133, 143; in Chile 8, 43–47, 51–53, 55–62; in Colombia 323, 326, 330, 334; in US 152, 158, 171
Cold War, 9, 119, 124, 133, 156
Colon Development Company (CDC), 70, 78–84, 87, 90
Conoco Inc., 118, 231. *See also* Phillips Petroleum Co.
Constitution of 1917 (Mexico), 3, 296–297, 299, 301–302, 317
Constitution of 1988 (Brazil), 252–253, 255, 263, 265
Constitution of 1991 (Colombia), 323, 324, 328–329, 331–332, 336
corporate social responsibility (CSR), 119, 324, 333, 336–338
Creole Petroleum Corp., 101, 105–112

381

D

Democratic Party (US), 162–163
deregulation of energy industry, 22, 23, 32, 36, 144, 174–175, 233, 274, 276–277, 286, 289
Díaz, Porfirio, 296, 309, 315
Dickey Dam, 9, 12, 151, 153–154, 164–172, 175
direct hydrocarbon indicators (DHI), 194, 201
Dome Petroleum, 220–221, 227–228, 231–233
Dormer, Cecil, 78–84
Duhalde, Eduardo, 33; 280
Dutch disease. *See* resource curse

E

Ecopetrol (Empresa Colombiana de Petróleos), 324, 326, 329
Eisenhower, Dwight, 137, 156, 221, 223
ejidos, 302, 309. *See also* campesinos
embargo, oil, 151, 154–155, 164–165, 175, 211, 223, 225–226, 246, 252. *See also* Middle East, conflict; OPEC
Endangered Species Act (1973), 152, 154–155, 160–164, 168–169, 173, 175. *See also* environmental impact; Environmental Protection Agency
ENARSA (Energía Argentina S.A.), 34, 282
energy as common good (ECG), 11–12, 24, 26–38, 124, 280, 316, 323, 326–327, 332, 340–342
energy as market good (EMG), 11, 25–26, 28, 30, 32–34, 38, 175, 276, 280, 324, 326–327, 332, 335, 342
energy as political good (EPG), 11,18, 22–24, 28–32, 38, 124, 280, 325–327, 332, 341
environmental impact: climate change 2, 3; in Argentina 3; in Brazil 254, 256; in Canada 12, 130, 139–144, 235; in Colombia 324, 327, 333, 336, 338–341; in Mexico 298, 307, 309–310; in Venezuela 7; in US 9, 12, 140–144, 151–175, 180. *See also* Endangered Species Act; Environmental Protection Agency
Environmental Protection Agency (EPA), 162
Esso. *See* Exxon
expropriation of oil producers: in Argentina, 273–274, 287–289; in Mexico, 10, 100, 105, 296, 301. *See also* deregulation; nationalization; privatization
Exxon: in Argentina 275; in Canada 212; in Guyana 203; in US 196; in Venezuela, 12, 69, 71, 79–80, 89, 99, 101–113, 114–119. *See also* Mobil; Imperial Oil

F

FARC (Revolutionary Armed Forces of Colombia), 325
Fernández de Kirchner, Cristina, 34, 280
firewood, 7, 47, 50–54, 61–62, 129, 133
First World War, 46, 53, 55–56, 69, 76, 127, 181
foreign direct investment (FDI), 23, 25, 32, 36, 213, 221, 329–330
Foreign Investment Review Agency (FIRA), 225, 230, 234
Fox, Vicente, 303, 305
Frondizi, Arturo, 274–275
Furbish lousewort, 151, 154, 168–169, 173

G

Gallagher, Jack, 220, 227–228, 233
General Agreement on Tariffs and Trade (GATT), 215, 223
General Asphalt Company (GAC), 70, 80, 86–88
Geophysical Analysis Group (GAG), 189–190
Geophysical Research Corporation (GRC), 182, 186
Geophysical Service Inc. (GSI), 182–183, 186, 188, 190–193, 196–197, 200, 204. *See also* Texas Instruments
Gil Borges, Esteban, 78–79, 81–82, 86
Global Positioning System (GPS), 199
Gómez, Juan Vicente, 67–68, 73, 75–90, 102–104–106, 295
Gómez, Juancho, 73, 75, 80, 82, 84–85, 88, 90
Great Depression, 10, 55–57, 62, 68, 211
Gulf Oil, 69, 111, 295

H

Halliburton, 197–198, 200
Hydro-Electric Power Commission of Ontario (HEPCO). *See* Ontario Hydro
Hydroelectricity, 7, 35, 129; in Argentina 34; in Brazil 35–36; in Chile 8–9, 43, 47, 55, 58–62; in Canada 5–6, 8–9, 12, 123–144; in Colombia 324; in Mexico 128; in Brazil 130; in US 9, 12, 125, 127–133, 141–144, 151–158, 164, 169–170, 172

I

IBM, 191, 193
Imperial Oil (Canada), 211, 212, 214–216, 218. *See also* Exxon
imperialism, 125, 130, 144, 328

import substitution industrialization (ISI), 8, 10, 22, 32, 35, 246, 251–252, 258, 274, 327, 342. *See also* resource nationalism

Indigenous peoples: Cofán 6; consent for resource development, 2, 7, 130, 332–335, 337, 340–341; Colombian, 324–325, 328–342; Fort McKay First Nation (Cree, Dene, and Métis), 7; Hunkpapa Lakota, 6; Motilone, 71; Sihasapa Lakota, 6; Yanktonai Dakota, 7. *See also* ONIC; United Nations Declaration on the Rights of Indigenous Peoples

Instituto Brasileiro de Petróleo, 260

International Bank of Settlements, 328

International Joint Commission, 123, 127, 134. *See also* Boundary Waters Treaty

International Labour Organization, 7, 331–332, 335

International Monetary Fund (IMF), 214, 328

K

Kirchner, Néstor, 33, 280, 285

L

Lagoven. *See* Creole Petroleum Corp.
Lake St. Lawrence, 137–140
Leduc oil strike, 216–217
Liberal Party (Canada), 126, 132, 234
Lincoln School Dam, 170, 172
López Obrador, Andrés Manuel, 1, 304–306, 308, 316. *See also* Morena
Lost Villages, 139–140
Lougheed, Peter, 225, 231
Lula da Silva, Luiz Inácio, 3, 36–37

M

Mackenzie King, William Lyon, 127, 217
Maduro, Nicolás, 2–3
Malthusian trap. *See* resource curse
Manning, Ernest, 217, 219, 223
Maraven. *See* Shell Oil in Venezuela
McColl-Frontenac Oil Co. *See* Texaco
McGoodwin, Preston, 79, 82–83, 85–86, 90
Menem, Carlos, 32, 277, 279
Meneven. *See* Gulf Oil
Middle East: oil producers, 35, 69, 109, 114, 152, 211, 220, 224; conflict, 60, 164, 170, 221–222, 228. *See also* embargo, oil; OPEC
Ministry of Mines and Energy (Brazil), 37
Mobil, 115–116, 192, 194, 197. *See also* Exxon

Morales, Evo, 5, 7, 17
Morena (Movimiento Regeneración Nacional) (Mexico), 306–308, 310. *See also* López Obrador, Andrés Manuel
Moreno, Lenín, 3
Mosquera, Bernardino, 76, 85
Mulroney, Brian, 233
Muskie, Edmund, 164, 169–170

N

National Development Bank (Brazil) (BNDES), 259, 261, 263–264
National Energy Board (NEB) (Canada), 223–225
National Energy Fund (Argentina), 276
National Energy Program (NEP) (Canada), 212, 228–234
National Oil Policy (NOP) (Canada), 223–224
nationalization of energy, 29, 211; in Argentina, 11, 273–274; in Bolivia, 5; in Brazil, 216; in Canada, 9; 228, 232–233; in Venezuela, 101, 106, 108–115, 119, 152, 216, 226. *See also* deregulation; expropriation; privatization
natural gas: in Argentina, 284, 288; in Bolivia, 5; in Brazil, 253; in Canada, 211, 213–216, 230, 234; in Chile, 43, 55, 60, 62; in Colombia, 326; in Mexico, 303–306, 310, 316; in Venezuela, 100, 110
New Deal, 9, 155
New Democratic Party (Alberta), 3
Niagara Falls: as scenery, 124–125, 127, 134, 136, 142; hydroelectric projects, 123–126, 131–132, 134, 140–142, 144
Nixon, Richard, 152, 224–226
North American Free Trade Agreement (NAFTA), 11, 296, 302, 315–316. *See also* Canada-US Free Trade Agreement; Canada-USA-Mexico Agreement
North Venezuelan Petroleum Company (NVPC), 82

O

Obama, Barack, 7, 310
Obregón, Álvaro, 297–299, 301
Occidental Petroleum, 334
ONIC (Organización Nacional Indigena de Colombia), 334. *See also* Indigenous peoples: Colombia
Ontario Hydro (formerly HEPCO), 9, 126–127, 131, 134, 139–140

OPEC (Organization of the Petroleum Exporting Countries), 101, 108, 114, 118, 225, 231–232. *See also* embargo, oil; Middle East
Operation Car Wash, 3, 8
Orinoco basin oil fields, 100, 114–115, 117–118

P

Partido de Acción Nacional (PAN) (Mexico), 303, 305, 307–310
Partido de la Revolución Democrática (PRD) (Mexico), 304–310
Partido Revolucionario Institucional (PRI) (Mexico), 303, 305, 307–310
PDVSA (Petróleos de Venezuela), 101, 111, 113, 115–117, 226, 230
Pemex (Petróleos Mexicanos), 11, 230, 301, 303–317; corruption, 304–305, 308–309; reforms, 307–311
Peña Nieto, Enrique, 3, 305–306, 308–310, 313
Pequiven, 116
Pérez, Carlos Andrés, 109–111, 114–116. *See also* Acción Democrática
Perón, Juan, 274; Peronism 274, 280
Petrobras (Petróleo Brasileiro S.A.), 3, 5, 7–8, 11, 35–37, 101, 195, 202, 245–254, 258–264, 276, 284, 304, 311; Campos Basin oil fields, 35, 195, 252, 256; corruption, 260–261; pre-salt deposits, 3, 11, 202, 243, 249, 254–255, 259–260, 263–265, 317; Santos basin, 37, 202, 204
Petro-Canada, 4, 226, 230–231, 234
Petroleum Administration for Defense (PAD), 220
Petroleum Gas and Revenue Tax (PGRT). *See* National Energy Program
Petroleum Incentives Payments (PIP). *See* National Energy Program
Phillips Petroleum Co., 197. *See also* Conoco Inc.
pipelines, 3, 20, 25, 27, 30, 33, 70, 217, 220, 253, 259–260, 323–326; Dakota Access, 7; in Colombia, 323; Interprovincial, 219, 223; Keystone XL, 126; Trans-Andean, 284; Trans Mountain, 219, 221–223
Power Authority of the State of New York (PASNY), 131, 134, 136, 140
Pré-Sal Petróleo S.A. (PPSA), 258, 264
privatization of energy industry, 30, 33, 144, 233–234, 252–253, 261, 273–279, 286, 289, 301, 324, 326, 329, 337. *See also* deregulation; expropriation; nationalization
profit-sharing, 101, 254–255, 258, 264
Progressive Conservative Party: Alberta, 3; Canada, 223, 228, 233
protectionism, 221, 224–225, 243

R

rail transport, 51, 53, 61, 132, 139, 175, 217, 312
Reagan, Ronald, 170–172, 175, 233
regulation of energy industry, 4, 11, 13, 19–20–23, 25–29, 34, 36; in Brazil, 260, 264; in Canada, 126, 218, 228, 230, 233; in Colombia, 336–342; in Mexico, 298; in US, 154, 162–164, 171, 174–175, 180; in Venezuela, 74, 76
rents and rent-seeking, 3, 11, 19–20, 26–32, 38, 130, 225, 244–245, 254–255, 264, 281, 298, 324. *See also* royalties; taxes and duties
Repsol, 34–35, 274, 279, 283–285, 287–289, 317
Republican Party (US), 169, 221, 316
resource curse, 2, 8, 51, 53, 100, 129, 243–244
resource nationalism, 3, 5, 8, 12, 17–24, 29, 31, 37, 124, 179; in Brazil, 245–246; in Canada, 124, 143–144, 224; in Colombia, 325; in Mexico, 296; in Venezuela, 99, 108–110, 114, 116–117. *See also* import substitution industrialization
Roosevelt, Franklin, 9, 131–132, 155
Rousseff, Dilma, 3, 37
royalties, 5, 19, 25–31, 103–105, 115–117, 221, 254–258, 264, 277, 297–298, 326. *See also* rents and rent-seeking; taxes and duties

S

Salinas de Gortari, Carlos, 302, 306
Santos, Juan Manuel, 333
Schlumberger, 197–198, 200, 204
Second World War, 10, 55, 70, 106, 108, 119, 132–134, 183, 190, 211, 213
seismology, 181, 218; refraction, 181, 183–184; digital analysis, 188–195; three-dimensional, 195–201; AVO analysis, 201–202; FWI, 202
Shell Oil (Royal Dutch/Shell Group): in Argentina, 275; in Canada, 215; in Mexico, 71, 316; in US, 71, 194, 199; in Venezuela, 67–74, 78–79, 82, 86–87, 89–90, 111, 295
snail darter, 154, 161, 163–164, 173
Social Credit Party (Alberta), 217–218

384 Index

St. Laurent, Louis, 132–133, 217
St. Lawrence Seaway and Power Project, 123–124, 126, 131–133, 136–144; displacement by, 137–142
Standard Oil of California. *See* Chevron
Standard Oil of New Jersey. *See* Exxon; Imperial Oil
steam power, 43–45, 51, 53, 56, 61, 158,
subsalt oil deposits, 201–202
subsidies, 156; to industry, 20, 25–30, 33–35, 227–228, 277, 326; to state, 110
Sun Oil Co. (Sunoco), 80
Syncrude, 227

taxes and duties, 10, 19–38; in Argentina, 277, 281–282, 286; in Canada, 127–128, 212, 215, 220–221, 224–234; in Colombia, 326–327, 337; in Mexico 297–301, 310; in Venezuela, 77–84, 89, 103–107, 112–117. *See also* rents and rent-seeking; royalties
Tellico Dam, 151, 153–155, 157–164, 168, 172–173, 175
Tennessee Valley Authority (TVA), 9, 154–161, 165, 172
Texaco, 6, 192, 197, 212, 303. *See also* Chevron
Texas Instruments (TI), 190–192; TIAC, 192. *See also* Geophysical Service Inc.
Torres, Gumersindo, 77–79, 81–83
Trudeau, Pierre Elliott, 212, 225, 227–228, 231, 233–234

U

United Nations Declaration on the Rights of Indigenous Peoples (UNDRIP), 337. *See also* Indigenous peoples
US Army Corps of Engineers, 134, 151, 154, 164, 166–169, 172
US Fish and Wildlife Service, 161–162

V

Vargas, Getúlio, 245
VEB Company, 84–90
Venezuelan Oil Concessions Ltd. (VOC), 71, 74–76, 80, 82–84
Vía Campesina, 335
Villegas Pulido, Guillermo Tell, 79, 82, 84

W

Wartime Oils Ltd., 213
Western Canadian Petroleum Association. *See* Canadian Association of Petroleum Producers
Western Canadian Sedimentary Basin (WCSB), 211, 216, 221, 225–227
Western Geophysical Company, 183, 186–187, 193, 200, 204
World Bank, 214, 328
WTO (World Trade Organization), 328, 333

Y

YPF (Yacimientos Petrolíferos Fiscales), 3, 5, 33–35, 273–289, 317; Comodoro Rivadavia oil fields, 274; Vaca Muerta oil field, 3. *See also* Kirchner, Nestor; Repsol

www.ingramcontent.com/pod-product-compliance
Lightning Source LLC
Chambersburg PA
CBHW040745020526
44114CB00049B/2920